Lecture Notes in Computer Science

Lecture Notes in Artificial Intelligence 16265

Founding Editor

Jörg Siekmann

The series Lecture Notes in Artificial Intelligence (LNAI) was established in 1988 as a topical subseries of LNCS devoted to artificial intelligence.

The series publishes state-of-the-art research results at a high level. As with the LNCS mother series, the mission of the series is to serve the international R & D community by providing an invaluable service, mainly focused on the publication of conference and workshop proceedings and postproceedings.

Lourdes Martínez-Villaseñor ·
Roberto A. Vázquez · Gilberto Ochoa-Ruiz ·
Martín Montes Rivera ·
Saúl Zapotecas-Martínez ·
María Lucía Barrón-Estrada ·
Efrén Mezura-Montes · Arturo Gomez Chavez
Editors

Advances in Computational Intelligence

MICAI 2025 International Workshops

HIS 2025, CIAPP 2025, WILE 2025, CHARAL 2025
ECSI 2025 Workshops, Guanajuato, Mexico, November 3–7, 2025
Proceedings, Part II

Editors
Lourdes Martínez-Villaseñor
Universidad Panamericana
Ciudad de México, Mexico

Gilberto Ochoa-Ruiz
Instituto Tecnológico y de Estudios Superiores de Monterrey
Zapopan, Mexico

Saúl Zapotecas-Martínez
Instituto Nacional de Astrofísica, Óptica y Electrónica
San Andrés Cholula, Mexico

Efrén Mezura-Montes
University of Veracruz. Xalapa
Mexico, Mexico

Roberto A. Vázquez
Universidad La Salle México
Ciudad de México, Mexico

Martín Montes Rivera
Universidad Politécnica de Aguascalientes
Aguascalientes, Mexico

María Lucía Barrón-Estrada
TecNM-Instituto Tecnológico de Culiacán
Culiacán, Mexico

Arturo Gomez Chavez
Constructor University Bremen
Bremen, Germany

ISSN 0302-9743 ISSN 1611-3349 (electronic)
Lecture Notes in Artificial Intelligence
ISBN 978-3-032-17932-6 ISBN 978-3-032-17933-3 (eBook)
https://doi.org/10.1007/978-3-032-17933-3

LNCS Sublibrary: SL7 – Artificial Intelligence

This Springer imprint is published by the registered company Springer Nature Switzerland AG
The registered company address is: Gewerbestrasse 11, 6330 Cham, Switzerland

Preface

The Mexican International Conference on Artificial Intelligence (MICAI) is a yearly international conference series that has been organized by the Mexican Society for Artificial Intelligence (SMIA) since 2000. MICAI is an important international artificial intelligence (AI) forum and the main event in the academic life of the growing AI community in the country.

This year, MICAI 2025 was organized by the Mexican Society for Artificial Intelligence (SMIA, Sociedad Mexicana de Inteligencia Artificial) in collaboration with the Centro de Investigaciones en Matemáticas (CIMAT) and the Universidad de Guanajuato (UG).

The MICAI series website is www.MICAI.org. The website of the Mexican Society for Artificial Intelligence, SMIA, is www.SMIA.mx. Contact options and additional information can be found on these websites.

The conference, as is traditional, showcased a wide variety of research fields and topics. Moreover, the conference included cutting-edge keynote lectures, as well as detailed paper presentations and comprehensive hands-on tutorials. Furthermore, thought-provoking panels and niche workshops provided a rich and exciting experience that aimed to cater to a wide audience.

Moreover, we continued the legacy of announcing the José Negrete Award, the SMIA Best Thesis in Artificial Intelligence Contest's results. This year, the historic and culturally rich city of Guanajuato was our chosen destination.

MICAI conferences publish high-quality papers in all areas of AI and its applications. The proceedings of the previous MICAI events have been published by Springer in its Lecture Notes in Artificial Intelligence (LNAI) series (volumes: 1793, 2313, 2972, 3789, 4293, 4827, 5317, 5845, 6437, 6438, 7094, 7095, 7629, 7630, 8265, 8266, 8856, 8857, 9413, 9414, 10061, 10062, 10632, 10633, 11288, 11289, 11835, 12468, 12469, 13067, 13068, 13612, 13613, 14502, 14391, 14392, 15246, 15247, 15464, and 15465). Since its foundation in 2000, the conference has grown in popularity and improved in quality.

Five workshops were held jointly with the conference. The proceedings of the MICAI 2025 workshops are published in two volumes. The first volume contains 33 papers from the 18th Workshop of Hybrid Intelligent Systems (HIS 2025) and the 1st Workshop on Evolutionary Computation and Swarm Intelligence (ECSI 2025). The second volume contains 26 papers from the 18th Workshop on Intelligent Learning Environments (WILE 2025), the 7th Workshop on New Trends in Computational Intelligence and Applications (CIAPP 2025), and the 1st Workshop on Challenges in Holistic AI for Real-world Applications and Learning Systems (CHARAL 2025).

These volumes will be of interest for researchers in all fields of artificial intelligence, students specializing in related topics, and the general public interested in recent developments in AI.

The MICAI workshops received for evaluation 85 submissions. From these submissions, 59 papers were selected for publication in these volumes after a double-blind peer-reviewing process and three reviews per submission. It was carried out by the Program Committee of the workshops. The acceptance rate was 69%.

HIS 2025

Hybrid Intelligent Systems (HIS) offers a compelling solution to complex challenges in various application domains, including biology, medicine, logistics, management, engineering, technology, social sciences, and humanities. The XVIII Workshop of Hybrid Intelligent Systems (HIS 2025) featured relevant research on HIS and their capabilities for managing complex processes.

HIS 2025 was hosted by the Mexican Society of Artificial Intelligence (SMIA), nested within the Mexican International Conference on Artificial Intelligence (MICAI 2025). This year, the workshop featured a selection of research articles managed with the CMT platform. All articles underwent rigorous double-blind peer review, with an acceptance rate of 72.5%, covering topics such as Machine Learning, Fuzzy Systems, Reasoning, Intelligent Control, Computer Vision, Optimization, and Expert Systems.

HIS 2025 presented the latest advancements in the field through three tracks: the first featured articles with completed research, the second consisted of posters showcasing proposals and prototypes for future research, and the third addressed life support on Mars, where recently graduated students proposed uses of artificial intelligence applied to survival on Mars. The workshop's primary objective is to present expert model systems applied to specific research topics.

We sincerely thank Arturo Hernández Aguirre from the Department of Computer Science at CIMAT Guanajuato, Mexico, our keynote speaker, for his valuable contribution to our event with the presentation "HIS 2025 he Evolutionary Algorithms: Past, Present, and Future." HIS 2025 was enriched by his extensive experience and remarkable achievements in the field. We greatly appreciate his presence and the insight he shared with our audience.

We would also like to thank SMIA and the MICAI organizers for their continued collaboration in developing this prestigious event. It was our honor to contribute to the MICAI event with research in Hybrid Intelligent Systems.

ECSI 2025

The first workshop on Evolutionary Computation and Swarm Intelligence (ECSI) explored two pivotal areas of Artificial Intelligence: Evolutionary Computation and Swarm Intelligence, both of which are crucial for solving optimization problems. Evolutionary Computation mimics natural selection and genetics through populations of candidate solutions that evolve via selection, crossover, and mutation, exemplified by Genetic Algorithms (GA) and Evolution Strategies (ES). In contrast, Swarm Intelligence, inspired by natural collective behaviors such as ant colonies and bird flocks, leads to algorithms like Particle Swarm Optimization (PSO) and Ant Colony Optimization (ACO), utilizing simple interactions among individual agents. Both methodologies find extensive applications in optimization, machine learning, and robotics, enabling the discovery of innovative solutions to complex challenges. Participants gain a comprehensive understanding of these techniques, their principles, and practical implementations. The workshop explores the dynamic field of Evolutionary Computation and Swarm Intelligence, focusing on their theoretical foundations, recent algorithmic advancements, and practical applications.

The workshop covered various topics and activities, focusing on examining the latest advancements in Evolutionary Computation and Swarm Intelligence. The program featured:

1. Technical Sessions: Oral presentations and discussions highlighted recent findings in Evolutionary Computation and Swarm Intelligence. These presentations were based on the full accepted papers.
2. Poster Sessions: Opportunities for participants to present their research in a more informal setting, encouraging feedback and collaboration.

WILE 2025

Artificial Intelligence (AI) continues to yield a profound and sustained influence across multiple domains of human activity. AI possesses the transformative potential to revolutionize education by enabling more personalized instruction, adaptive learning experiences, and improved academic outcomes. Over the past decades, diverse educational systems and tools have been developed to support these goals. Among them, Intelligent Tutoring Systems (ITSs) and Intelligent Learning Environments (ILEs) represent key milestones in the evolution of technology-enhanced learning.

ILEs integrate a combination of established and emerging AI technologies. Traditional methods include artificial neural networks, Bayesian networks, and fuzzy logic, which provide a foundation for decision-making and personalization. More recent advances involve the incorporation of affective computing, Generative AI, and extended reality systems with immersion detection aimed at enhancing the quality and effectiveness of learning experiences.

Generative AI stands out as one of the most disruptive and promising developments in recent years. In education, these systems can generate personalized learning materials, adapt content to students' cognitive levels, simulate human tutors, and provide formative feedback in real time. Their integration into ILEs opens new opportunities for adaptive instruction, automatic assessment, and interactive dialogue systems that can accompany students throughout the learning process.

The Workshop on Intelligent Learning Environments (WILE) is convened to foster the advancement of innovative applications, methodologies, and technologies that enhance education. This workshop presents new ideas, research, and technology developed to assist students in their learning process and employees in training, employing diverse educational methodologies and artificial intelligence techniques. This workshop aims to convene active researchers and students in Intelligent Learning Environments to present and discuss innovative theoretical work and original applications, exchange ideas, establish collaborative links, review significant recent achievements, and deliberate on the implications of results for the broader field of AI. Our goal for WILE 2025 was to give researchers a platform to showcase their work while also investigating new approaches to integrate AI techniques in the creation of educational systems.

This edition includes 11 double blind peer-reviewed research papers selected from WILE 2025, covering various dimensions of intelligent learning environments. Each paper underwent two or three independent evaluations by members of the Technical Committee. The editorial board carefully considered criteria such as relevance, originality, clarity, and scientific contribution in the final selection process.

We would like to express our sincere gratitude to all participants who contributed to the success of WILE 2025. We acknowledge the collaboration of members of RedICA (Thematic Network in Applied Computational Intelligence) and the Mexican Society for Artificial Intelligence (SMIA). As in previous years, MICAI 2025 served as an outstanding host for this event, providing an ideal setting for the exchange of ideas and the advancement of research in intelligent learning environments.

CIAPP 2025

The 7th Workshop on New Trends in Computational Intelligence and Applications (CIAPP 2025) aimed to bring together researchers, students, and end users to explore the latest advances in computational intelligence. This year's workshop focused on evolutionary algorithms, Bayesian learning, computer vision, quantum circuits, and their applications in various fields, including nutrition, robotics, speech recognition, and green AI. Participants had the opportunity to share their findings, engage in discussions, and start collaborations, fostering a vibrant community dedicated to pushing the boundaries of computational intelligence.

We thank the Mexican Society for Artificial Intelligence (SMIA) for organizing the 24th Mexican International Conference on Artificial Intelligence (MICAI 2025). Their dedication and hard work created a platform for researchers and students to share knowledge, foster collaboration, and advance the field of artificial intelligence.

We also extend our most sincere thanks and recognition to the Centro de Investigación en Matemáticas (CIMAT) and the Universidad de Guanajuato (UG) for their outstanding support and their exceptional organization as a local committee of MICAI 2025. Their commitment to organizing this event created an environment that was both attractive and conducive to collaboration and knowledge sharing. Thank you for your invaluable contributions to the success of CIAPP 2025.

CHARAL 2025

The 1st Workshop on Challenges in Holistic AI for Real-world Applications and Learning Systems (CHARAL) took place on November 4, 2025, during the Mexican International Conference on Artificial Intelligence (MICAI) in Guanajuato, Mexico. The event provided a unique forum for researchers, practitioners, and policymakers to explore how artificial intelligence can move beyond controlled environments toward robust, explainable, and trustworthy systems capable of operating in complex, real-world conditions.

The workshop opened with a short introduction, followed by a full day of invited keynote talks from leading experts across academia, government, and industry. Topics included uncertainty in vision-language models, data-centric AI for safe perception, deep generative modeling for human motion prediction, AI for medical imaging and healthcare, and efficient training of large language models. These sessions provided a multidisciplinary perspective on the technological and operational barriers to reliable AI deployment.

Complementing the keynotes, the workshop featured a curated selection of spotlight and lightning talks drawn from peer-reviewed papers from international researchers. These contributions showcased both theoretical advances and empirical studies on AI robustness, perception, and adaptation, emphasizing reproducibility and real-world performance.

A central highlight of CHARAL 2025 was the panel discussion co-organized with Young AI Leaders (YAIL CDMX), titled "AI in the Wild: From Scholar/Lab Models to Living Systems." This interactive 60-minute session examined how the new generation of AI practitioners perceives the balance between academia, industry, and civic engagement; how AI success can be measured beyond accuracy, drawing from YAIL's AI Impact Scorecard initiative; and what sustainable research-to-deployment pipelines might look like for emerging economies such as Mexico. The discussion encouraged reflection on whether current development pathways are fast and inclusive enough to ensure independence and long-term resilience.

The workshop concluded with a synthesis and open-floor discussion connecting insights from all sessions. By combining keynotes, short talks, and an inter-generational panel, CHARAL 2025 aimed to cultivate collaboration across disciplines and generations. It sought to transform AI research into practice: building systems that are not only intelligent but also resilient, responsible, and socially grounded within real-world environments.

We want to thank all the people involved in the organization of this conference: the authors of the papers published in these two volumes –it is their research work that gives value to the proceedings– and the organizers for their work. We thank the reviewers for their great effort spent on reviewing the submissions and the Program and Organizing Committee members.

A special acknowledgment to the local committee led by Alejandro Rosales Pérez and Adrian Pastor López Monroy, whose meticulous coordination was instrumental in realizing MICAI 2025 in Guanajuato, Mexico. Our acknowledgments extend to Rafael Herrera Guzmán (Director General, CIMAT), and to Óscar Susano Dalmau Cedeño (Coordinador de Ciencias de la Computación, CIMAT). We are also indebted to the following authorities at Universidad de Guanajuato: Héctor Fabián Gutiérez Rangel (Director de la División de Ciencias Económico Administrativas), Martin Picón Núñez (Rector de Campus Guanajuato, Universidad de Guanajuato), and Claudia Susana Gómez López (Rectora General) for their invaluable assistance in securing the university facilities to complement the facilities of CIMAT.

In addition, the success of this conference and the breadth of its program are a testament to the collaborative efforts of our organizing and local committees and sponsors.

The entire submission, reviewing, and selection process, as well as the preparation of the proceedings, was supported by Microsoft's Conference Management Toolkit (https://cmt3.research.microsoft.com/). Last but not least, we are grateful to Springer for their patience and help in the preparation of these volumes.

In conclusion, MICAI 2025 was more than just a conference. It was a confluence of minds, a testament to the indefatigable spirit of the AI community, and a beacon for the future of Artificial Intelligence. As you navigate through these proceedings, may you find inspiration, knowledge, and connections that propel you forward in your journey.

November 2025

Lourdes Martínez-Villaseñor
Roberto A. Vázquez
Gilberto Ochoa-Ruiz
Martín Montes Rivera
Saúl Zapotecas-Martínez
María Lucía Barrón-Estrada
Efrén Mezura-Montes
Arturo Gomez Chavez

Organization

Conference Committee

General Chair

Lourdes Martínez-Villaseñor	Universidad Panamericana, Mexico

Program Chairs

Gilberto Ochoa-Ruiz	Tecnológico de Monterrey, Mexico
Roberto A. Vazquez	Universidad La Salle México, Mexico

Workshop Chair

Iris Mendez	Universidad Autónoma de Ciudad Juárez, Mexico

Tutorials Chair

David Pinto	Benemérita Universidad Autónoma de Puebla, Mexico

Doctoral Consortium Chairs

Miguel González Mendoza	Tecnológico de Monterrey, Mexico
Néstor Valasco Bermeo	Experient, USA
Gustavo Arroyo Figueroa	Instituto Nacional de Electricidad y Energías Limpias, Mexico

Keynote Talks Chair

Hugo Jair Escalante	Instituto Nacional de Astrofísica, Óptica y Electrónica, Mexico

Publication Chair

Hiram Ponce	Universidad Panamericana, Mexico

Publicity Chairs

Bella Martinez	Instituto Politécnico Nacional, Mexico
Claudia Gonzalez	Instituto Tecnológico de Tijuana, Mexico

Communication and Design Chairs

Iván Olvera	Grupo Software de Alta Calidad, Mexico
Omar Saldivar	Barbarous, Mexico
Luis Gerardo Téllez	Barbarous, Mexico

Grant Chair

Leobardo Morales	IBM, Mexico

Local Organizing Committee

Local Chairs

Alejandro Rosales Pérez	Centro de Investigación en Matemáticas (CIMAT), Mexico
Adrian Pastor López Monroy	Centro de Investigación en Matemáticas (CIMAT), Mexico

Logistics Chairs

Jorge Alberto Soria Alcaraz	Universidad de Guanajuato, Mexico
Marco Aurelio Sotelo Figueroa	Universidad de Guanajuato, Mexico

Program Committee

Abel García Nájera	Universidad Autónoma Metropolitana Unidad Cuajimalpa, Mexico
Alberto Gonzalez-Sanchez	Instituto Mexicano de Tecnología del Agua, Mexico
Alberto Ochoa-Zezzatti	Universidad Autónoma de Ciudad Juárez, Mexico
Aldo Márquez-Grajales	Universidad Veracruzana, Mexico
Alexander V Bozhenyuk	Southern Federal University, Russia
Ana Laura Lezama-Sánchez	SECIHTI, BUAP, Mexico

Esmeralda Arreola Marin — TecNM campus Cd. Hidalgo, Mexico
Fernando Gudino — National Autonomous University of Mexico, Mexico
Fevrier Valdez — Tijuana Institute of Technology/TecNM, Mexico
Francisco Lopez-Tiro — Tecnológico de Monterrey, Mexico
Gabriel González-Serna — TecNM/CENIDET, Mexico
Garibaldi Pineda Garcia — Applied AGI, UK
Genoveva Vargas-Solar — Grenoble Alpes University, CNRS, France
Gilberto Ochoa-Ruiz — Tecnológico de Monterrey, Mexico
Gildardo Sanchez-Ante — Tecnológico de Monterrey, Mexico
Grissel Rodríguez Roldán — Instituto Artek, Mexico
Guadalupe Carmona Arroyo — Universidad Veracruzana, Mexico
Guillermo Santamaría-Bonfil — BBVA México, Mexico
Gustavo Arroyo — Instituto Nacional de Electricidad y Energías Limpias, Mexico
Haimei Wen — University of Texas at Dallas, USA
Hiram Calvo — Center for Computing Research - Instituto Politécnico Nacional, Mexico
Hiram Ponce — Universidad Panamericana, Mexico
Hugo Jair Escalante — Instituto Nacional de Astrofísica, Óptica y Electrónica, Mexico
Humberto Sossa — CIC-Instituto Politécnico Nacional, Mexico
Iris Iddaly Méndez-Gurrola — Universidad Autónoma de Ciudad Juárez, Mexico
Ismael Osuna-Galán — Universidad Autónoma del Estado de Quintana Roo, Mexico
Israel Tabarez — Universidad Autónoma del Estado de México, Mexico
Jaime Cerda — Universidad Michoacana de San Nicolás de Hidalgo, Mexico
Jerusa Marchi — Federal University of Santa Catarina, Brazil
Jesús García-Ramírez — UPIIT-Instituto Politécnico Nacional, Mexico
Jesús-Adolfo Mejía-de-Dios — Universidad Autónoma de Coahuila, Mexico
Jiale Li — University of Auckland, New Zealand
Jiechen Zhao — University of Toronto, Canada
Joanna Alvarado Uribe — Tecnológico de Monterrey, Mexico
Jonathan Rojas-Simón — Autonomous University of the State of Mexico, Mexico
Jose D. Alanis — Universidad Tecnológica de Puebla, Mexico
Jose Sosa — University of Luxembourg, Luxembourg
Jose Alberto Hernandez-Aguilar — Universidad Autónoma del Estado de Morelos, Mexico
José Carlos Ortiz-Bayliss — Tecnológico de Monterrey, Mexico
José Luis M Reyes — Universidad Veracruzana, Mexico

José Luis Vilchis Medina	ENSTA Bretagne, France
Jose-Federico Ramirez-Cruz	TecNM - Instituto Tecnológico de Apizaco, Mexico
Juan Martínez-Miranda	CICESE-Unidad Académica Tepic, Mexico
Juan Villegas-Cortez	Universidad Autónoma Metropolitana - Azcapotzalco, Mexico
Juan Carlos Olivares Rojas	Tecnológico Nacional de México/Instituto Tecnológico de Morelia, Mexico
Juana Isabel Méndez	Tecnológico de Monterrey, Mexico
Juan-Carlos Gonzalez-Islas	Universidad Autónoma del Estado de Hidalgo, Mexico
Julio Santisteban	Universidad Católica San Pablo, Peru
Karina Mariela Figueroa Mora	Universidad Michoacana de San Nicolás de Hidalgo, Mexico
Leticia Flores Pulido	Universidad Autónoma de Tlaxcala, Mexico
Li Yu	Zhejiang University, China
Lourdes Martinez-Villaseñor	Universidad Panamericana, Mexico
Luis M. Torres-Treviño	Universidad Autónoma de Nuevo León, Mexico
Mansoor Ali	Tecnológico de Monterrey, Mexico
Maria de la Concepción Pérez de Celis Herrero	Benemérita Universidad Autónoma de Puebla, Mexico
Maria Lucia Barrón Estrada	TecNM-Instituto Tecnológico de Culiacán, Mexico
Mario Anzures-García	Benemérita Universidad Autónoma de Puebla, Mexico
Masaki Murata	Tottori University, Japan
Miguel Gonzalez-Mendoza	Tecnológico de Monterrey, Mexico
Miguel Sanchez Brito	Instituto Politécnico Nacional, Mexico
Mohd. Saif Wajid	BBD University, India
Nancy Pérez-Castro	Universidad del Papaloapan, Mexico
Nestor Velasco Bermeo	Experient, USA
Nidiyare Hevia Montiel	Universidad Nacional Autónoma de México, Mexico
Noé-Alejandro Castro-Sánchez	TecNM-CENIDET, Mexico
Obdulia Pichardo-Lagunas	Instituto Politécnico Nacional, Mexico
Omar Velazquez Lopez	Universidad Nacional Autónoma de México, Mexico
Pagon Gatchalee	Chiang Mai University, Thailand
Pengfei Hu	Stevens Institute of Technology, USA
Qi Chang	Accenture, USA
Quanchao Lu	Georgia Tech, USA
Rafael Batres	Tecnológico de Monterrey, Mexico
Rafael Guzman-Cabrera	Universidad de Guanajuato, Mexico

Rafael Rivera-Lopez	Tecnológico Nacional de México/Instituto Tecnológico de Veracruz, Mexico
Ramon F. Brena	Instituto Tecnológico de Sonora, Mexico
Ramón Zatarain Cabada	Tec Culiacán, Mexico
Rashi Dhenia	Hitachi, USA
Raúl Monroy Borja	Tecnológico de Monterrey, Mexico
Ricardo Espinosa	Universidad Panamericana, Mexico
Ricardo Landa	Cinvestav, Mexico
Roberto Antonio Vazquez	Universidad La Salle México, Mexico
Rocio O. Ochoa-Montiel	Universidad Autónoma de Tlaxcala, Mexico
Rosa M. Ortega-Mendoza	Universidad Autónoma del Estado de Hidalgo, Mexico
Sabino Miranda	Universidad Autónoma de la Ciudad de México, Mexico
Salvador M Hinojosa	Tecnológico de Monterrey, Mexico
Samuel Efren Viñas Alvarez	Tecnológico Nacional de México campus Zitácuaro, Mexico
Sandra Leticia Juárez-Osorio	Centro de Investigación y Estudios Avanzados del Politécnico Nacional, Mexico
Sheng Gao	University of Pennsylvania, USA
Shuo Li	Carnegie Mellon University, USA
Sofia N. Galicia Haro	SNI, Mexico
Stephen A. Sunday	Ohio University, USA
Tania A. Ramirez-delReal	CONACyT-CentroGeo, Mexico
Vadim Borisov	Branch of National Research University "Moscow Power Engineering Institute" in Smolensk, Russia
Valery Solovyev	Kazan Federal University, Russia
Vicente Garcia Jimenez	Universidad Autónoma de Ciudad Juárez, Mexico
Victor Lomas-Barrie	IIMAS-UNAM, Mexico
Víctor J. Ruiz	TecNM/CENIDET, Mexico
Yasmín Hernández	Centro Nacional de Investigación y Desarrollo Tecnológico, Mexico
Yaxk'in U. Kan Coronado	Universidad La Salle México, Mexico
Yubo Wang	Meta Platforms, inc, USA
Yucheng Zhou	University of Macau, China

Workshops Organization

HIS 2025

General Chairs

Martín Montes Rivera	Universidad Politécnica de Aguascalientes, Mexico
Carlos Alberto Ochoa Zezzatti	Universidad Autónoma de Ciudad Juárez, Mexico
José Alberto Hernández Aguilar	Universidad Autónoma del Estado de Morelos, Mexico
Julio César Ponce Gallegos	Universidad Autónoma de Aguascalientes, Mexico
Daniela Paola López Betancur	Universidad Autónoma de Zacatecas, Mexico
Carlos Alejandro Guerrero Méndez	Universidad Autónoma de Zacatecas, Mexico
Lourdes Margain Fuentes	Universidad Internacional de Innovación, Mexico

Program Committee

Edgar Gonzalo Cossio Franco	Instituto de Información Estadística y Geográfica de Jalisco, México
Humberto Velasco Arellano	Universidad Politécnica de Aguascalientes, México
Daniela Paola López Betancourt	Universidad Politécnica de Aguascalientes, México
Carlos Alejandro Guerrero Méndez	Universidad Autónoma de Zacatecas, México
Humberto Muñoz Bautista	Universidad Tecnológica Metropolitana de Aguascalientes, México
Miguel Ángel Ortiz Esparza	Universidad Autónoma de Aguascalientes, México
Himer Avila George	Universidad de Guadalajara, México
Alejandro Padilla Díaz	Universidad Autónoma de Aguascalientes, México
Carlos Alberto Lara Alvarez	CIMAT Zacatecas, México
Roberto Antonio Contreras Masse	Instituto Tecnológico Ciudad Juárez, México
Irma Yazmín Hernández Báez	Universidad Politécnica del Estado de Morelos, México

ECSI 2025

General Chairs

Saúl Zapotecas-Martínez	Instituto Nacional de Astrofísica, Óptica y Electrónica, Mexico
Alejandro Rosales-Pérez	Centro de Investigación en Matemáticas, Mexico

Program Committee

Alberto Ochoa-Zezzatti	Universidad Autónoma de Ciudad Juárez, Mexico
Jesús G. Falcón-Cardona	Centro de Investigación Científica y de Educación Superior de Ensenada, Mexico
José-Antonio Fuentes-Tomás	Universidad Veracruzana, Mexico
Miguel A. Jiménez-Domínguez	Instituto Nacional de Astrofísica, Óptica y Electrónica, Mexico
Néstor García-Rojas	Instituto Nacional de Astrofísica, Óptica y Electrónica, Mexico
Luis Rosas-Ordaz	Instituto Nacional de Astrofísica, Óptica y Electrónica, Mexico
Adriana Menchaca-Méndez	Escuela Nacional de Estudios Superiores Unidad Morelia UNAM, Mexico

WILE 2025

General Chairs

María Lucía Barrón Estrada	TecNM-Instituto Tecnológico de Culiacán, México
Ramón Zatarain Cabada	TecNM-Instituto Tecnológico de Culiacán, México
Carlos A. Reyes García	Instituto Nacional de Astrofísica, Óptica y Electróni, México
Yasmín Hernández Pérez	TecNM-Cenidet, México
Karina M. Figueroa Mora	Universidad Michoacana de San Nicolás de Hidalgo, Mexico

Program Committee

Ramón Zatarain Cabada	Instituto Tecnológico de Culiacán, Mexico
María Lucía Barrón Estrada	Instituto Tecnológico de Culiacán, Mexico
Yasmín Hernández Pérez	Cenidet, Mexico
Carlos A. Reyes García	Instituto Nacional de Astrofísica, Óptica y Electrónica, Mexico
Karina Mariela Figueroa Mora	Universidad Michoacana de San Nicolás de Hidalgo, Mexico

Giner Alor Hernández	Instituto Tecnológico de Orizaba, Mexico
Miguel Pérez Ramírez	Mexico
Jaime Muñoz Arteaga	Universidad Autónoma de Aguascalientes, Mexico
Rafael Morales Gamboa	Universidad de Guadalajara, Mexico
Guillermo Santamaría Bonfil	BBVA México, Mexico
Carlos Alberto Lara Álvarez	CIMAT Zacatecas, Mexico
Hugo Arnoldo Mitre Hernández	CIMAT Zacatecas, Mexico
María Elena Chávez Echeagaray	Arizona State University, USA
Javier González	Arizona State University, USA
María Blanca Ibáñez Espiga	Universidad Carlos III de Madrid, Spain
Alicia Martínez Rebollar	Cenidet, Mexico
María Lucila Morales Rodríguez	Instituto Tecnológico de Cd. Madero, Mexico
Héctor Rodríguez Rangel	Instituto Tecnológico de Culiacán, Mexico
Julieta Noguez Monroy	Mexico
Samuel González López	Instituto Tecnológico de Nogales, Mexico
Raúl Oramas Bustillos	Universidad Autónoma de Occidente, Mexico
Francisco González Hernández	Instituto Tecnológico de Culiacán, Mexico
José Mario Ríos Félix	Instituto Tecnológico de Culiacán, Mexico
Luis Alberto Morales Rosales	Universidad Michoacana de San Nicolás de Hidalgo, Mexico

CIAPP 2025

General Chairs

Rocío Erandi Barrientos Martínez	Universidad Veracruzana, Mexico
Marcela Quiroz Castellanos	Universidad Veracruzana, Mexico
Efrén Mezura Montes	Universidad Veracruzana, Mexico
Héctor Gabriel Acosta Mesa	Universidad Veracruzana, Mexico

Program Committee

Ángel J. Sánchez García	Universidad Veracruzana, Mexico
Carlos Alberto Fernández y Fernández	Universidad Tecnológica de la Mixteca, Mexico
Carlos Alberto López Herrera	Universidad Veracruzana, Mexico
Carmen Mezura-Godoy	Universidad Veracruzana, Mexico
Daniel Molina Pérez	Instituto Politécnico Nacional, Mexico
David Herrera Sánchez	Universidad Veracruzana, Mexico
Edgard Benítez Guerrero	Universidad Veracruzana, Mexico
Guadalupe Carmona Arroyo	Universidad Veracruzana, Mexico
Jesús Adolfo Mejía de Dios	Universidad Autónoma de Coahuila, Mexico

Jesús Arnulfo Barradas Palmeros	Universidad Veracruzana, Mexico
José Luis Llaguno Roque	Universidad Veracruzana, Mexico
Rogelio Portillo Vélez	Universidad Veracruzana, Mexico
Sonia L. Mestizo-Gutiérrez	Universidad Veracruzana, Mexico

CHARAL 2025

General Chairs

Arturo Gomez Chavez	Constructor University, Germany
Emmanuel Ovalle-Magallanes	Universidad La Salle Bajío, Mexico
José Martínez Carranza	Instituto Nacional de Astrofísica, Óptica y Electrónica, Mexico

Program Committee

Ana Laura Lezama-Sánchez	SECIHTI, Mexico
Babak Rokh	University of Zanjan, Iran
Diego Uribe	Instituto Tecnólogico de La Laguna, Mexico
Grissel Rodríguez Roldán	Instituto Artek, Mexico
Jaime Cerda	Universidad Michoacana de San Nicolás de Hidalgo, Mexico
Juan Carlos Olivares Rojas	Instituto Tecnológico de Morelia, Mexico
Leticia Flores Pulido	Universidad Autónoma de Tlaxcala, Mexico
Marco Escobar	Universidad La Salle Bajío, Mexico
Mario Anzures-García	Benemérita Universidad Autónoma de Puebla, Mexico
Omar Velazquez Lopez	Universidad Nacional Autónoma de México, Mexico
Rocio Ochoa-Montiel	Universidad Autónoma de Tlaxcala, Mexico
Francesco Maurelli	Constructor University, Germany

Contents

WILE 2025

Generation of STEAM-Based Games with Augmented Reality

Valeria Contreras-Zaragoza(✉), Giner Alor-Hernández, Humberto Marín-Vega, Maritza Bustos-López, Mónica Ruiz-Martínez, and Norma Leticia Hernández-Chaparro

Division of Resarch and Postgraduate Studies, Tecnológico Nacional de México/ I. T. de Orizaba, Orizaba, México
{m24010201,giner.ah,humberto.mv,maritza.bl,monica.rm, D02010021}@orizaba.tecnm.mx

1 Introduction

The STEAM approach integrates Science, Technology, Engineering, Art, and Mathematics to develop essential 21st-century competencies such as critical thinking, creativity, and collaboration through active methodologies and project-based learning. [1].

A bibliometric study [2] indicates that the United States and Spain account for 60% of STEAM publications worldwide, while in Mexico, with 1.2 million teachers in elementary education, according to National Institute of Statistics, Geography and Informatics (INEGI) [3]. Only approximately 5,000 educators in Mexico were trained through the STEAM Movement program in 2020, highlighting challenges in teacher training concerning international academic production [4].

Current pedagogical methods, which focus on repetition and memorization, fail to foster essential competencies for educational development, such as innovation, analytical thinking, and collaborative work—skills that are fundamental in the STEAM field. While more dynamic methodologies exist, the absence of engaging pedagogical resources limits their potential.

In this context, AR emerges as a promising alternative, capable of transforming teaching by offering interactive and immersive environments that enhance students' understanding and engagement with learning content.

To address this problem, we propose a generator of STEAM-based games with AR for elementary education. The generator simplifies the process of designing and developing innovative educational resources, making them more attractive and accessible to both students and teachers.

The paper consists of five main sections: Sect. 2 presents the State-of-the-Art, which analyzes a set of related works; Sect. 3 presents the development process of the generator and describes the general architecture; Sect. 4 presents a case study as a proof-of-concept; and finally, Sect. 5 details the conclusions and future work.

L. Martínez-Villaseñor et al. (Eds.): MICAI 2025, LNAI 16265, pp. 3–11, 2026.
https://doi.org/10.1007/978-3-032-17933-3_1

2 State-of-the-Art

In this section, a set of related works that have developed projects using the STEAM approach is presented.

Juškevičienė et al. [5] developed a STEAM strategy with physical computing to teach Computational Thinking (CT) to inexperienced students. The results showed significant improvements in 14 CT skills and served as a practical guide for teachers in elementary education. In a similar line, Ananda et al. [6] highlighted the importance of Computational Thinking (CT) for solving complex problems. Using online platforms, 41 tenth-grade students improved their computational skills (decomposition, algorithms, data, abstraction) while linking chemistry with real situations. For their part, Zhu et al. [7] applied a STEAM approach in IT courses through a "Smart Agricultural Greenhouse System", fostering hands-on and collaborative learning. Results showed increased student engagement (76.7%), improved problem-solving (49.1%), and better interdisciplinary connections (72.1%). Montés et al. [8] used STEAM in the EXPLORIA project to motivate students in physics and engineering. Through practical challenges, they improved their understanding of concepts such as gravity and Newton's laws (91–100% effectiveness). The method increased interest in STEM and proved effective for applied learning.

Complementarily, Chacon & Estela [9] introduced STEAM workshops in civil engineering programs, combining digital fabrication and programming. Students successfully developed a Tangible Learning System (TLS), acquiring key competencies in 3D modeling and data analysis within the given time frame. In the context of practical applications, Pristianti et al. [10] addressed rainfall unpredictability in Indonesia by developing a STEAM-based rainfall warning system using the ADDIE model. The prototype was effective, with sensitive sensors, and improved environmental awareness in students. Breda et al. [11] detected high dropout rates in Calculus I among university students, so they applied STEAM and PBL methodologies. The results showed lower academic failure, better perception of mathematics, and greater preference for collaborative learning. Lee et al. [12] integrated a generative AI (Stable Diffusion) in STEAM art education to enhance creativity and critical thinking. The approach reduced gender gaps, increasing interest in AI (especially in males). Likewise, Eitah & Abueita [13] demonstrated that the STEAM approach significantly improves creative thinking (fluency, flexibility, and originality) and academic performance in students, outperforming traditional methods through interdisciplinary approaches, collaborative projects, and hands-on curricula. In this same line, Perales & Aróstegui [14] highlighted that the integration of the arts into STEM (making it STEAM) fosters creativity, problem-solving, and holistic learning. This holistic approach combined technical training with an ethical and social perspective, promoting a more humanistic and democratic education. Finally, Tran et al. [15] evaluated the impact of STEAM on scientific creativity through hands-on projects with children. Both groups improved in fluency, flexibility, and originality, with no gender differences, demonstrating the effectiveness of the approach. Montés et al. [16] proposed two methodologies: Forward (identifying connections between subjects) and Retrospective (starting from a specific topic), fostering creativity and innovation. The strategy succeeded in reducing redundancies, confirmed high STEAM integrability (86%), and highlighted the need for teacher training. Saimon et al. [17] addressed teachers' difficulties in designing transdisciplinary STEAM problems in low-resource contexts. They proposed a six-phase model using real-world crises (COVID-19, famines) as teaching resources. The model facilitated sustainable transdisciplinary STEAM education and promoted action-oriented learning for addressing local challenges. Jatnkoon et al. [18] identified limitations in traditional STEAM education for online environments. They developed a comprehensive model integrating STEAM, microlearning, and AR within MOOCs. Expert evaluation ($n = 10$) showed exceptional results ($mean = 4.72$, $SD = 0.46$), demonstrating effectiveness for transdisciplinary integration in digital settings. On the other hand, McGuinness [19] criticized traditional STEAM methods for prioritizing memorization over interpersonal skills. They developed a self-assessment tool for teachers and improved students' test performance, with students also perceiving gains in their social skills. Anisimova et al. [20] analyzed the gap in teacher and student readiness for STEAM education. Through surveys, the study revealed that 67% of teachers felt prepared compared to 15% of students, and that students' readiness for project activities increased with each year of study. Abdulwahid et al. [21] developed two predictive models in Iraq, one traditional academic performance system and another based on STEAM skills, both achieving 99% accuracy and 10^{-5} errors in academic prediction.

The aforementioned studies show that the STEAM approach improves learning from multiple perspectives: it develops computational and digital competencies, strengthens understanding of concepts in engineering and applied sciences, improves mathematical reasoning, enhances creativity and critical thinking through arts integration, establishes innovative pedagogical methodologies, evidences teacher training needs, and provides effective tools to evaluate and predict academic performance. However, its implementation requires automated tools that facilitate the development of intuitive educational applications, reducing technical barriers for teachers and promoting its widespread adoption.

3 Development Process for Automated Generation of STEAM-Based Games

The general architecture (Fig. 1) presents four interconnected layers that facilitate the automated generation of STEAM-based games with AR.

The general architecture comprises four interconnected layers that work together to facilitate the automated generation of STEAM-based games with AR capabilities. Each layer has specific responsibilities and functions within the overall system:

Presentation Layer: In this layer, a Web interface developed with Angular is presented, where educators and developers configure STEAM categories, select activities, and customize parameters to generate STEAM-based games with AR.

Integration Layer: This layer acts as an intermediary between the Web interface and the system services through two main specialized modules. The Activity Configuration Module receives and processes the requests coming from the Web interface, validating the selected parameters (STEAM categories, educational levels, interactivity types) and verifying the compatibility between components. It transforms the configurations into comprehensible data structures for the services layer, ensuring the pedagogical coherence

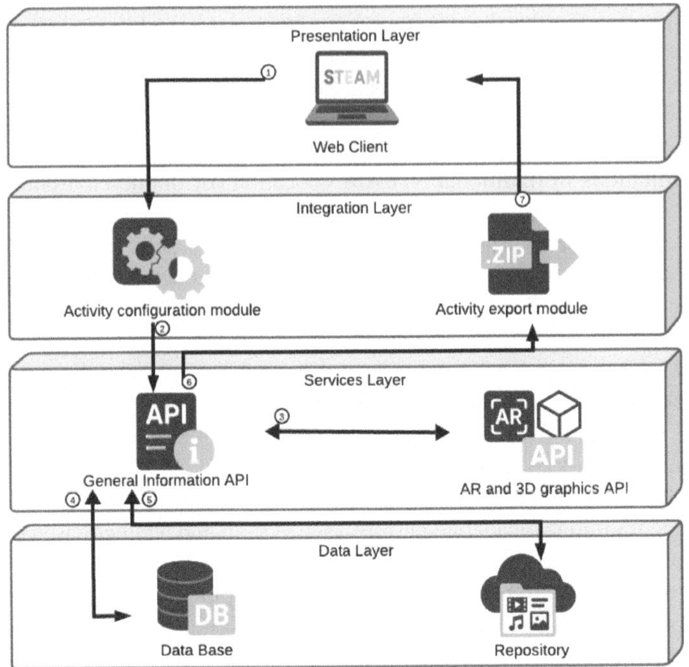

Fig. 1. General architecture for the generation process of STEAM-based games

of the activities. In other hand, the Activity Export Module manages the packaging and distribution of the generated applications, collecting all the necessary resources (HTML files, JavaScript, AR.js and Three.js libraries, multimedia content), organizing them in appropriate directory structures, and compressing them into ZIP files with documentation and installation instructions to facilitate their implementation in different educational environments.

Services Layer: This layer contains business logic through a General Information API that processes requests and coordinates the generation of applications. It integrates AR.js and Three.js technologies with educational content, applies the STEAM approach, and coordinates the creation of immersive experiences customized according to the established educational objectives. The General Information API manages the business rules and orchestrates the generation flow, while the AR and 3D graphics API uses AR.js to implement browser-based augmented reality functionalities with marker recognition, and Three.js as a 3D rendering engine to create interactive objects and visual effects.

Data Layer: This layer manages the persistence of information through a MySQL database and a resource repository. The database stores configurations, activity parameters, and system metadata, while the repository contains multimedia resources, templates, and educational content required for application generation. The repository functions as a centralized warehouse that includes 3D models, textures, AR markers, multimedia files, and STEAM templates, allowing efficient access to reusable content for customizing educational experiences across different devices and platforms.

The generator workflow is described as follows: The process starts when the user configures the STEAM categories and educational parameters through the Web interface (1), which sends the request to the Integration Layer (2), where the Activity Configuration Module validates and processes the selected parameters (3). Subsequently, the request is sent to the Services Layer (4), where the General Information API coordinates the business logic and communicates with the AR and 3D Graphics API to integrate AR.js and Three.js technologies (5). The system queries the Data Layer to obtain multimedia resources, templates, and configurations stored in the MySQL database and repository (6). Finally, the process returns to the Integration Layer, where the Activity Export Module packages all the generated components in a ZIP file ready for implementation (7), thus completing the generation of the augmented reality educational games based on the STEAM approach.

4 Case Study: Generation of a STEAM-Based Game of Block Programming for Identifying Even and Odd Numbers

The objective of the generator is to enable a user without application development knowledge to generate a STEAM-based game for learning. In this case, it is focused on the area of mathematics, specifically the identification of even and odd numbers, because mathematics constitutes one of the main foundations of the STEAM approach and represents one of the areas with the greatest difficulty of comprehension in elementary education [22].

The generator currently has 15 games available, distributed evenly with three games for each of the five STEAM areas (Science, Technology, Engineering, Arts, Mathematics). This structure allows for comprehensive coverage of the STEAM educational approach, ensuring that users can develop diversified learning experiences adapted to different pedagogical needs.

In the generator, users can select the different STEAM areas that their application will focus on. Based on the selected area, the generator presents a series of available skills from which the user can choose to implement in their application. Depending on the user's skill selection, the generator presents a set of STEAM-based games that can be developed (Fig. 2).

The generator can develop several STEAM-based games; this case study is focused specifically on block-based programming. Block-based programming is a visual programming paradigm that allows users to create programs by assembling graphical blocks that represent code elements such as commands, functions, and control structures [20]. The main elements for generating block-based programming games can be observed in Fig. 3, which shows the taskbar that serves the user to add elements to the game. The block commands consist of components that the user can add to the game, with available options including logic, loops, lists, variables, functions, and text. These elements are designed to allow users to progressively build the STEAM-based games depending on the topic being addressed.

Figure 4 shows the result of generating a block-based programming game focused on identifying even and odd numbers, a 6th-grade arithmetic topic that challenges students.

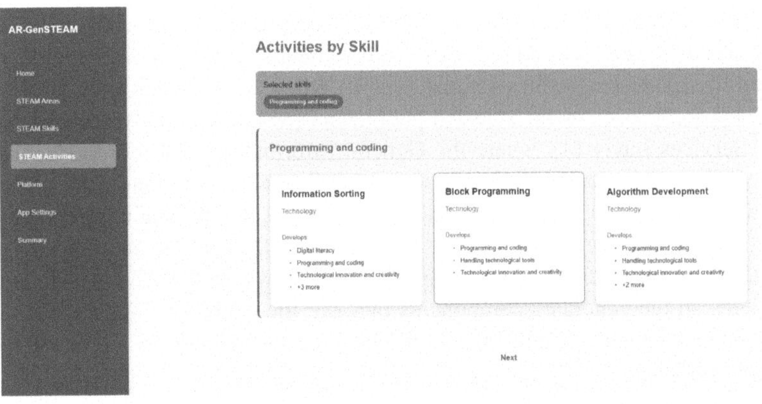

Fig. 2. Activity Selection for STEAM-based games

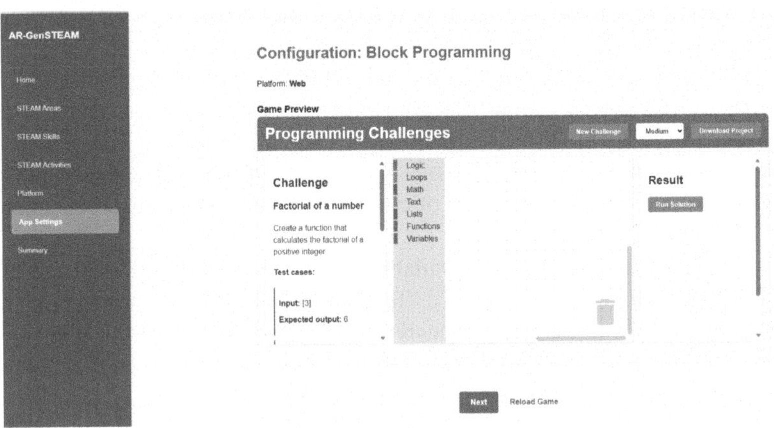

Fig. 3. Web Interface for generating STEAM-based games using a block-based programming paradigm.

The objective is to develop mathematical modeling and logical thinking skills, covering STEAM areas of mathematics, engineering, and technology.

The game generator analyzes game actions and allows users to select which interactions will include augmented content. The system supports the addition of video, text, images, and multimedia combinations to enhance the educational experience.

According to Fig. 5 demonstrates the block-based programming game with AR functionality in action. Upon clicking the execute button and successful validation of the solution, a modal window appears displaying the message "Excellent! Your solution is correct" along with the question "Is 5 even or odd?" Most notably, the application activates the camera to show augmented reality content that visually represents the mathematical concept being learned. The AR overlay displays a graphical representation of the even number concept directly on the camera view, showing visual elements that reinforce the student's understanding. This integration of AR provides immediate visual

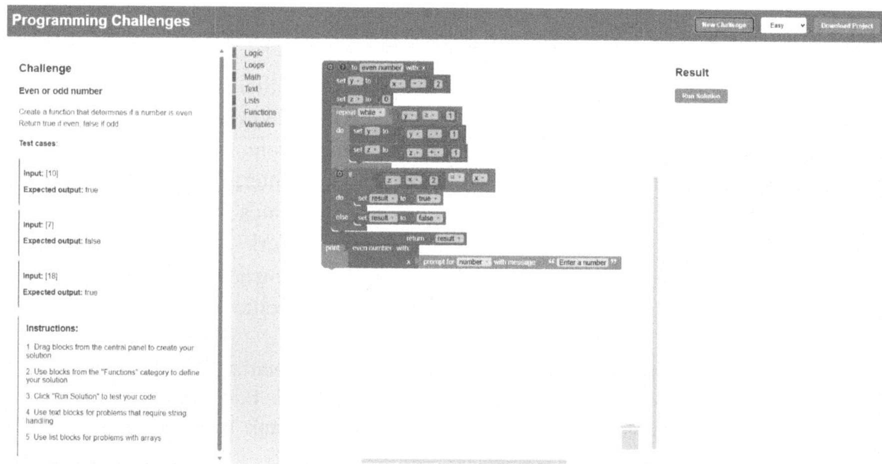

Fig. 4. STEAM block-based programming game

feedback to students, reinforcing their learning achievement in identifying even and odd numbers through an immersive, block-based programming approach that bridges abstract mathematical concepts with concrete visual representations.

Fig. 5. STEAM block-based programming game with AR.

This case study shows the system's effectiveness in the games generation process for identifying even and odd numbers, showing how mathematics, engineering, and technology can be combined in a playful and visual experience that promotes the development of logical and structured thinking.

5 Conclusions

Games generators are fundamental tools in the digital age that democratize software development by allowing users without specialized technical knowledge to create functional applications, eliminating technological barriers and accelerating innovation in various sectors, especially in education, where the demand for interactive digital resources is growing. We have proposed a games generator that integrates the STEAM approach with AR technologies for elementary education. As future work, we have considered to increase the repository of educational templates and developing advanced customization features to be adapted to different educational levels and specific pedagogical contexts.

Acknowledgments. This research work was sponsored by the Secretariat of Science, Humanities, Technology, and Innovation (SECIHTI) and the Secretariat of Public Education (SEP) of Mexico through the PRODEP program. Additionally, we would like to thank Tecnológico Nacional de México (TecNM) for its support of this project.

References

1. Amanova, A.K., Butabayeva, L.A., Abayeva, G.A., Umirbekova, A.N., Abildina, S.K., Makhmetova, A.A.: A systematic review of the implementation of STEAM education in schools. Eurasia Journal of Mathematics, Science and Technology Education **21**(1), em2568–em2568 (2025). https://doi.org/10.29333/ejmste/15894
2. Tapullima-Mori, C., Pizzán-Tomanguillo, S.L., del P. Pizzán-Tomanguillo, N., Gómez Sangama, L.R., Vázquez Sánchez, M., Iñipe Cachay, M.: A bibliometric review of the STEAM approach in university education 2010–2022. Digital Journal of Research in University Teaching **18**(1), e1790 (2023). https://doi.org/10.19083/ridu.2024.1790
3. STATISTICS ABOUT TEACHERS' DAY (MAY 15). Accessed 14 Feb 2025. http://www.diputados.gob.mx/LeyesBiblio/pdf/LGE_300919.pdf
4. Annual Report 2020 STEAM Movement, Accessed 14 Feb 2025. https://www.movimientostem.org/wp-content/uploads/2021/03/Informe-anual-2020_Movimiento-STEAM.pdf
5. Juškevičienė, A., Stupurienė, G., Jevsikova, T.: Computational thinking development through physical computing activities in STEAM education. Comput. Appl. Eng. Educ. **29**(1), 175–190 (2021). https://doi.org/10.1002/cae.22365
6. Ananda, L.R., Rahmawati, Y., Khairi, F., Irwanto: Developing the Computational Thinking Skills of Chemistry Students by Integrating Design Thinking with STEAM-PjBL. AIP Conf Proc **2982**(1) (2024). https://doi.org/10.1063/5.0183005
7. Zhu, M., Guo, B., Liu, X., Chen, X.: On the STEAM Concept-Based Design Instructional Case for Junior High Students in Information Technology Courses (2024)
8. Montés, N., Aloy, P., Ferrer, T., Romero, P.D., Barquero, S., Carbonell, A.M.: EXPLORIA, STEAM education at university level as a new way to teach engineering mechanics in an integrated learning process. Applied Sciences (Switzerland) **12**(10) (2022). https://doi.org/10.3390/app12105105
9. Chacon, R., Estela, M.R.: Designing maths-based STEAM activities for civil engineering curricula. Proceedings - Frontiers in Education Conference, FIE, vol. 2020-October, pp. 1–5 (2020). https://doi.org/10.1109/FIE44824.2020.9273989
10. Pristianti, M.C., Hariyono, E., Wulandari, D.: Studies in Learning and Teaching Studies in Learning and Teaching Development of STEAM-Based Rain Alarm Prototype Article Info ABSTRACT **3**(2), 156–167 (2022). https://doi.org/10.46627/silet

11. Breda, A., Neves, A., Dos Santos, J., Lavicza, Z.: Utilising a STEAM-based approach to support calculus students' positive attitudes towards mathematics and enhance their learning outcomes. Open Education Studies **5**(1) (2023). https://doi.org/10.1515/edu-2022-0210
12. Lee, U., et al.: Prompt Aloud!: Incorporating image-generative AI into STEAM class with learning analytics using prompt data. Educ Inf Technol (Dordr) **29**(8), 9575–9605 (2024). https://doi.org/10.1007/s10639-023-12150-4
13. Eitah, R., Abueita, J.: The effectiveness of a STEAM-based learning approach in creative thinking among eighth-grade students in Jordan. International Journal for Research in Education **47**(3), 172–202 (2023). https://doi.org/10.36771/ijre.47.3.23-pp172-202
14. Perales, F.J., Aróstegui, J.L.: The STEAM approach: Implementation and educational, social and economic consequences. Arts Education Policy Review **125**(2), 59–67 (2024). https://doi.org/10.1080/10632913.2021.1974997
15. Tran, N.H., Huang, C.F., Hsiao, K.H., Lin, K.L., Hung, J.F.: Investigation on the influences of STEAM-based curriculum on scientific creativity of elementary school students. Front Educ (Lausanne) **6** (2021). https://doi.org/10.3389/feduc.2021.694516
16. Montés, N., et al.: A novel methodology to develop STEAM projects according to national curricula. Educ Sci (Basel) **13**(2) (2023). https://doi.org/10.3390/educsci13020169
17. Saimon, M., Lavicza, Z., Houghton, T., Mtenzi, F., Carranza, P.: A model for utilising crises-related issues to facilitate transdisciplinary outdoor STEAM education for sustainability in integrated mathematics, language arts and technology classrooms. Discover (2025). https://doi.org/10.1007/s44217-025-00405-w
18. Jatnkoon, T., Jantakun, K., Jantakun, T., Pasmala, R.: STEAM micro-learning model based on massive open online courses with augmented reality technology to enhance creativity and innovation. High. Educ. Stud. **15**(2), 321 (2025). https://doi.org/10.5539/hes.v15n2p321
19. Mcguinness, O.: Open Research Online Investigating the Assessment of Soft Skills Development within STEAM based learning EMA-E822
20. Anisimova, T.I., Sabirova, F.M., Shatunova, O.V.: Formation of design and research competencies in future teachers in the framework of STEAM education. Int. J. Emerg. Technol. Learn. **15**(2), 204–217 (2020). https://doi.org/10.3991/ijet.v15i02.11537
21. Abdulwahid, N.O., Fakhfakh, S., Amous, I.: Simulating and predicting students' academic performance using a new approach based on STEAM education. J. Univ. Comput. Sci. **28**(12), 1252–1281 (2022). https://doi.org/10.3897/JUCS.86340
22. Tang, M., Wijaya, T.T., Li, X., Cao, Y., Yu, Q.: Exploring the determinants of mathematics teachers' willingness to implement STEAM education using structural equation modeling. Sci Rep **15**(1) (2025). https://doi.org/10.1038/s41598-025-90772-z

Training Students as AI Ambassadors: Explaining Artificial Intelligence Through Case-Based Learning

Paloma Suárez-Brito(✉)

14420 Mexico City, Mexico
suarez.paloma@outlook.com

1 Introduction

The societal impact of Artificial Intelligence (AI) today is multifaceted. AI has become a pivotal tool across various sectors, influencing fields such as healthcare, business, education, and social media. In healthcare, AI enhances diagnostic precision and personalizes treatment plans, although it also raises ethical and societal implications that need careful consideration, particularly concerning vulnerable populations [1]. In business, AI drives transformation by automating tasks and enabling innovations like self-driving cars, although it also poses challenges, such as privacy concerns and potential job displacement [2].

Social media platforms employ AI for personalized content and real-time analysis, which improves user experience but also introduces risks like algorithmic bias and misinformation [3]. The emergence of hybrid collective intelligence, which integrates both human and AI agents, is seen as a potential way to tackle challenges that arise at the collective, systemic level [4].

Regarding AI literacy and public understanding, several challenges persist. The public's understanding of AI—what it is, how it functions, and its impacts—remains limited. This gap in AI literacy is an issue due to the rapid deployment and reliance on AI technologies across multiple facets of daily life. Challenges include ensuring equitable access to AI education, addressing ethical concerns about data privacy, and overcoming technical barriers [5, 6]. Furthermore, many educators lack sufficient AI training, which hinders their ability to integrate AI technologies into educational settings effectively [7].

Students and professionals can play a crucial role in bridging the knowledge gaps between technical experts and the public. By acting as intermediaries, they can enhance public understanding and build trust in AI technologies. They can facilitate informed discussions, demystify AI applications, and promote ethical AI practices. Furthermore, they can advocate for AI literacy, pushing for educational reforms that incorporate a better understanding of AI into curricula, thus preparing future generations to engage with AI technologies more critically and effectively [8, 9].

1.1 Context

AI literacy has become a key educational goal as artificial intelligence (AI) increasingly permeates society. Prior research identifies four main themes in promoting AI

L. Martínez-Villaseñor et al. (Eds.): MICAI 2025, LNAI 16265, pp. 12–20, 2026.
https://doi.org/10.1007/978-3-032-17933-3_2

literacy. First, learners require a foundational understanding of AI technologies—its capabilities, limitations, and societal impacts—as well as ethical and social considerations [10]. Second, educational programs should integrate skills and critical thinking across awareness, usage, evaluation, and ethics [11, 12]. Third, AI literacy should be embedded in curricula through project-based, collaborative, and game-based learning approaches to engage diverse students [13]. Fourth, competency-based frameworks can guide curriculum design and support learners in developing AI-related skills [14, 15]. The UNESCO AI Competency Framework for Students [16] further emphasizes cognitive, socio-emotional, and behavioral competencies, aligning AI education with the broader goals of sustainable development and global collaboration.

Related Work. Building upon these foundations, recent initiatives have positioned AI literacy as a core element of digital competence and lifelong learning in higher education. The increasing presence of generative AI tools has prompted international organizations to propose frameworks guiding educators toward ethical and critical AI use. At the global level, UNESCO [17] introduced the AI Competency Framework for Teachers, defining AI literacy as awareness of AI systems, their implications, and their pedagogical integration. Similarly, the European Commission and OECD [18] proposed the AI Lit Framework, which highlights four domains—awareness, critical understanding, creative use, and social responsibility—emphasizing not only technical but also behavioral and ethical engagement.

Recent research has also sought to operationalize AI literacy through psychometric models. Carolus and colleagues [19] developed the Meta AI Literacy Scale (MAILS) to assess meta-competencies and self-regulation, Li and colleagues [20] proposed the A-Factor model, conceptualizing AI literacy as encompassing reasoning, interpretation, and ethical discernment. Despite these advances, most training programs remain exploratory and rarely address the integration of generative AI into higher education contexts. Existing approaches tend to emphasize technical proficiency over ethical reflection and contextual adaptation. The present proposal responds to this gap by integrating observable indicators of AI competence into a self-administered, digital toolkit for higher education professionals. Aligned with UNESCO and OECD frameworks, it promotes ethical awareness, responsible tool adoption, and continuous professional development through sustained self-assessment.

1.2 Objectives

The primary goal of this workshop is to prepare participants to become effective AI Ambassadors, capable of communicating core Artificial Intelligence (AI) concepts to non-specialized audiences. By the end of the program, participants are expected to achieve the following objectives:

1. Understand the basic concepts and applications of AI. Participants gain foundational knowledge through a tailored online mini course covering AI definitions, real-world applications, and ethical considerations.
2. Analyze real-world AI case studies. Using a case-based learning (CBL) approach, participants explore authentic AI scenarios in sectors such as education, healthcare, entertainment, and the workplace.

3. Translate technical concepts into accessible explanations. This objective addresses the soft skills necessary for effective science communication.
4. Practice structured communication techniques. Through debate activities participants develop confidence and clarity in explaining AI concepts, improving their ability to engage audiences and respond to questions or misconceptions.
5. Produce tangible outputs for outreach. As a result of the workshop, participants create Infographic cheat sheets, that serve as reusable resources for future educational or community outreach activities.

2 Methodology

The methodology of this work combines case-based learning (CBL) with a design-thinking-informed instructional design. The approach was chosen to foster active engagement, critical thinking, and practical application of Artificial Intelligence (AI) concepts. The case-based learning approach enhances cognitive engagement, encourages metacognitive knowledge, and improves resource management among students. In AI education, case-based learning can involve examining ethical dilemmas, practical AI applications, and challenges of integrating AI into various domains [21, 22]. Real-world cases reflecting AI concerns, such as ethical dilemmas, data privacy issues, and the balance between AI use and human agency, are crucial for fostering AI literacy. These scenarios help students understand the implications of AI technologies and the importance of ethical considerations, ensuring they are prepared to navigate the complexities of AI-driven environments responsibly [23, 24].

Design thinking informs the creation of workshops and mini courses by emphasizing a user-centered approach that includes ideation, prototyping, and testing. This approach fosters creativity and innovation, ensuring that the instructional design aligns with the participants' needs and learning habits [13]. Iterative steps such as constant feedback gathering, prototype testing, and iterative design revisions are commonly used to adapt instructional designs to better fit participant needs, providing a more tailored educational experience [16].

2.1 Instructional Design Process

The development of the generative AI mini course followed a structured design-thinking approach across five phases:

- Phase 1 Empathize: Previous literature revealed that learners often perceive generative AI as complex, with gaps in foundational knowledge, practical applications, and ethical understanding [25, 26].
- Phase 2 Define: Clear learning objectives were established: (1) understanding generative AI fundamentals and history, (2) exploring real-world applications via case studies, and (3) critically reflecting on ethical and societal implications. Success criteria focused on learners' ability to explain concepts, analyze cases, and discuss ethical issues confidently.
- Phase 3 Ideate: Instructional strategies were designed to promote conceptual understanding and active engagement. Topic 1 used visual timelines on AI evolution; Topic 2 featured real-world case studies with embedded quizzes; Topic 3 incorporated ethical dilemma scenarios, debates, and reflection exercises. Additional activities included collaborative discussions and debates.
- Phase 4 Prototype: Pilot modules were developed using the Mini course Generator platform, structured around three core topics: (1) Introduction to Generative AI, (2) Applications of Generative AI, and (3) Ethical and Societal Considerations. Each module incorporated interactive activities designed to reinforce key concepts, including quizzes, simulations, and scenario-based exercises. Small formative assessments were embedded throughout to monitor comprehension and provide immediate feedback.
- Phase 5 Test: Pilot sessions with representative learners collected feedback using a combination of a structured checklist, satisfaction ratings on a star scale, and qualitative evaluations through interviews and observations. Iterative refinements improved clarity, relevance, and engagement, such as simplifying technical explanations, adding contextual examples, enhancing ethical scenarios, and introducing micro-quizzes. After two cycles, the minicourse achieved high learner motivation and met the established objectives.

Figure 1 illustrates the structured process used in the AI minicourse, highlighting the five main phases: Diagnostic, Design, Implementation, Evaluation, and Continuous Development. Each phase includes specific activities and objectives that guide learners and professionals through a comprehensive, ethical, and reflective engagement with AI.

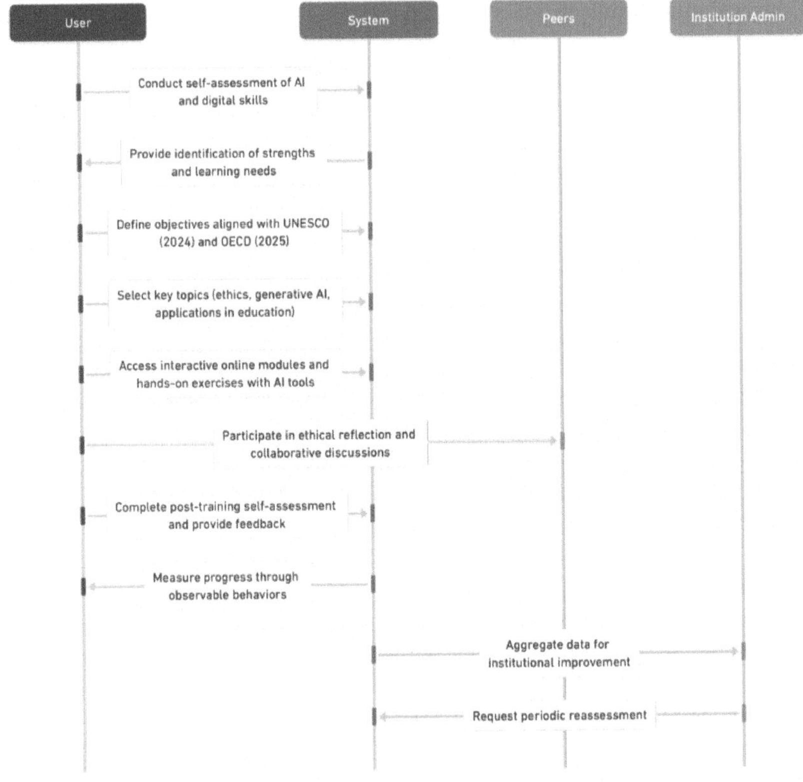

Fig. 1. Design process for the AI minicourse.

2.2 Participants

The workshop was attended by 10 university students and early-career professionals between 20 and 35 years of age, representing diverse academic backgrounds in the social sciences, education, engineering, and health-related fields. This age range reflects a population in transition from advanced undergraduate studies to professional practice, a stage in which the development of both technical and transversal skills becomes particularly relevant. Participants were selected based on their interest in artificial intelligence (AI) and their motivation to enhance their communication skills, ensuring a heterogeneous group that fostered interdisciplinary dialogue and peer learning.

2.3 Minicourse Content

The content of the course is presented below, organized to reflect the integration of theoretical foundations, case-based analysis, and communicative practice. This structure highlights the progression from core AI concepts to applied activities, demonstrating how participants engaged with both the technical and the soft skills required to act as effective AI Ambassadors.

Topic 1: What Is AI and How Is It Used Today? Overview: Understand the true meaning of artificial intelligence, explore its history, and learn how generative AI works. Content: Definition of Intelligence, AI, and Generative AI; Explanation of Generative Models and Contrast with Discriminative Models; Historical Timeline; Applications of Generative AI.

Topic 2: Should We Be Worried? Fears Around AI. Overview: Explore the impact of AI on society, including fairness, job security, and control. Content: Creativity and Reality in AI; Bias, Knowledge, and Perceptions; Impact on Society and Economy; Power, Control, and Future Risks.

Topic 3: Safe and Responsible AI Use: Ethics & Good Practices Around AI. Overview: Practical guidelines for using AI responsibly and securely. Content: Ethics and Smart Habits for Using AI; Key Facts Everyone Should Know About Using Generative AI; Safe and Responsible AI Use: Tips for Ethical and Secure Interaction; Future Implications.

Once the mini course was ready, it was implemented on the Mini course Generator platform for participants to complete the three core topics at their own pace, including interactive activities and small formative assessments. A single face-to-face session complemented the online mini course by engaging participants in the analysis of real-world AI case studies.

3 Results

Quantitative outcomes from the Mini course Generator platform showed that 91% of registered learners actively engaged with the content, 100% completed all three modules, and the average success score across formative assessments was 87%, indicating strong comprehension of core concepts. Complementing these metrics, qualitative feedback collected through surveys and facilitator observation highlighted the quality, relevance, and clarity of explanations and examples, as well as the ease of understanding and usefulness of interactive activities. Participants consistently reported that the content was clear, engaging, and practical, with interactive exercises being particularly effective in reinforcing conceptual understanding. These combined results demonstrate that the workshop effectively achieved its learning objectives and provided an accessible and engaging introduction to generative AI.

For instance, one participant noted: "Working through the ethical scenarios on deepfakes made me realize the potential risks for privacy and misinformation. I now feel more aware of the responsibilities involved in using and explaining AI responsibly". This feedback reinforces the quantitative results and shows that the workshop successfully promoted both conceptual understanding and practical communication skills. Figure 2 presents a summary of participant feedback, combining quantitative indicators of satisfaction with qualitative insights on pedagogical design, engagement, and impact.

Fig. 2. Analysis of participant feedback on the course "AI for the Rest of Us".

4 Applications

The workshop and accompanying mini course represent the main contribution of this work, providing a structured, scalable approach to train participants as AI Ambassadors. By completing the three online modules and participating in the face-to-face session with case-based learning and debate activities, participants were able to achieve all established objectives. They gained a foundational understanding of AI concepts and applications, successfully analyzed real-world case studies to identify opportunities, risks, and societal implications, practiced translating technical concepts into accessible explanations, engaged in structured communication exercises, and produced tangible outputs in the form of Infographic Cheat Sheets for educational and community outreach.

The outputs generated during the workshop can be leveraged by professors, researchers, and educational institutions to support teaching, outreach, and public engagement. The course design allows for adaptation across diverse audiences and contexts, including undergraduate and graduate students, professional learners, or members of the broader community. Interactive activities, authentic case studies, and structured communication exercises make the course a reusable and practical tool for enhancing AI literacy, promoting ethical awareness, and fostering the development of soft skills necessary for effective science communication.

5 Conclusion

The workshop successfully fulfilled its objectives, demonstrating that participants can understand and explain AI concepts, analyze real-world applications, and communicate these effectively to non-specialized audiences. Quantitative results indicated strong engagement, full completion of modules, and high success scores in formative assessments, while qualitative feedback highlighted the clarity, relevance, and practical utility of content and activities. Participants also reflected on ethical implications, particularly regarding deepfakes, privacy, and responsible AI use, showing the program's effectiveness in developing both technical knowledge and ethical awareness.

Limitations of the work include the reliance on a single face-to-face session and the focus on participants with prior interest in AI, which may affect generalizability. Lessons learned emphasize the importance of iterative design, relevant examples, and structured communication exercises in fostering AI literacy. Future directions include expanding in-person interactions, longitudinal follow-up to assess retention and community impact, and adapting the course for broader professional and international audiences. Overall, this workshop provides a practical, scalable, and reproducible model for AI education, enabling participants to act as informed AI Ambassadors and promoting responsible engagement with artificial intelligence in diverse contexts.

Overall, the results of this work align with previous literature emphasizing the transformative impact of Artificial Intelligence (AI) across sectors such as healthcare, business, and education, confirming that AI offers both opportunities and ethical challenges, including privacy risks and societal implications. Some authors [4], suggest that hybrid collective intelligence can help address systemic challenges, a perspective supported by participants' reflections on AI applications. Our findings also corroborate prior studies highlighting persistent gaps in AI literacy and the need for educator training, as reported by previous literature [5–7]. Moreover, in line with previous work [8, 9] the results indicate that training students and professionals as AI Ambassadors enhances public understanding, fosters ethical awareness, and strengthens communication of complex AI concepts.

Acknowledgments. This work was carried out independently. No external assistance, funding or institutional collaboration was involved in the development of this research.

Disclosure of Interests. The author declares that there are no conflicts of interest.

References

1. Goisauf, M., Cano Abadia, M.: Ethics of AI in radiology: a review of ethical and societal implications. Front Big Data **5**, 850383 (2022)
2. Kumar, S., Talukder, M.B., Kaiser, F.: Artificial intelligence in business. In: Advances in Human Resources Management and Organizational Development. IGI Global, pp. 81–97 (2024)
3. Mohamed, E.A.S., Osman, M.E., Mohamed, B.A.: The impact of artificial intelligence on social media content. J Soc Sci **20**, 12–16 (2024)
4. Peeters, M.M.M., van Diggelen, J., van den Bosch, K., et al.: Hybrid collective intelligence in a human–AI society. AI Soc. **36**, 217–238 (2021)
5. Familoni, B.T., Onyebuchi, N.C.: Advancements and challenges in Ai integration for technical literacy: a systematic review. Eng Sci Technol j **5**, 1415–1430 (2024)
6. Ng, D.T.K., Leung, J.K.L., Chu, K.W.S., Qiao, M.S.: AI literacy: Definition, teaching, evaluation and ethical issues. Proc Assoc Inf Sci Technol **58**, 504–509 (2021)
7. Vashishth, T.K., Sharma, V., Sharma, K.K., Kumar, B.: Enhancing literacy education in higher institutions with AI opportunities and challenges. In: Advances in Educational Technologies and Instructional Design. IGI Global, pp, 198–215 (2024)
8. Ibrahim, A.B.: Assessing the knowledge and perception of artificial intelligence for teaching and research among lecturers in the faculties of arts in Nigeria. Journal of Global Research in Education and Social Science **18**, 25–33 (2024)

9. Love, A.S., Niu, C., Labay-Marquez, J.: Artificial Intelligence in public health education: navigating ethical challenges and empowering the next generation of professionals. Health Promot Pract 15248399251320988 (2025)
10. Varadarajan, M.N.: Educational program for AI literacy. In: Advances in Library and Information Science. IGI Global, pp. 134–154 (2024)
11. Ma, S., Chen, Z.: The development and validation of the artificial intelligence literacy scale for Chinese college students (AILS-CCS). IEEE Access **12**, 146419–146429 (2024)
12. Mansoor, H.M.H., Bawazir, A., Alsabri, M.A., et al.: Artificial intelligence literacy among university students—a comparative transnational survey. Front Commun **9** (2024)
13. Yim, I.H.Y., Su, J.: Artificial intelligence (AI) learning tools in K-12 education: a scoping review. J Comput Educ (2024)
14. Annapureddy, R., Fornaroli, A., Gatica-Perez, D.: Generative ai literacy: twelve defining competencies. Digit Gov Res Pract **6**, 1–21 (2025)
15. Faruqe, F., Watkins, R., Medsker, L.: Competency model approach to AI Literacy: research-based path from initial framework to model. Advances in Artificial Intelligence and Machine Learning **02**, 580–587 (2022)
16. Yue, M., Jong, M.S.-Y., Dai, Y., Lau, W.W.-F.: Students as AI literate designers: a pedagogical framework for learning and teaching AI literacy in elementary education. J Res Technol Educ, pp. 1–22 (2025)
17. AI competency framework for teachers. UNESCO (2024)
18. OECD: Proceedings of the 2024 16th International Conference on Education Technology and Computers. Association for Computing Machinery (2024)
19. Carolus, A.: Measuring meta-competencies in AI literacy: Development and validation of the Meta AI Literacy Scale (MAILS). Comput Human Behav **152** (2023)
20. Li, Y., Deng, L., Chen, W.: The a-factor model: conceptualizing ai literacy for university students. Int J Artif Intell Educ., pp. 412–431 (2025)
21. Wang, K., Cui, W., Yuan, X.: Artificial intelligence in higher education: the impact of need satisfaction on artificial intelligence literacy mediated by self-regulated learning strategies. Behav Sci (Basel) **15**, 165 (2025)
22. Wang, X., Liu, Q., Pang, H., et al.: What matters in AI-supported learning: a study of human-AI interactions in language learning using cluster analysis and epistemic network analysis. Comput Educ **194**, 104703. https://doi.org/10.1016/j.compedu.2022.104703 (2023)
23. Michalak, R., Ellixson, D.: Fostering ethical AI integration in first-year writing: a case study on human-tool collaboration in artificial intelligence literacy. J. Libr. Adm. **65**, 361–377 (2025)
24. Rudolph, J., Mohamed Ismail, F.M., Popenici, S.: Higher education's generative Artificial Intelligence paradox: The meaning of chatbot mania. J Univ Teach Learn Pract **21** (2024)
25. Rusandi, M.A., Ahman, Saripah, I., et al.: No worries with ChatGPT: building bridges between artificial intelligence and education with critical thinking soft skills. J Public Health (Oxf) **45**, e602–e603 (2023)
26. Gupta, S., Kaur, S., Gupta, M., Singh, T.: AI empowered academia: a fuzzy prioritization framework for academic challenges. J Int Educ Bus (2024)

Ask First, Test on Demand: A Deference-Gated Socratic Agent Design

J. Carlos Urteaga-Reyesvera(✉) and Rodrigo Cadena Martínez

Universidad Americana de Europa, 77500 Cancón, Mexico
carlos.urteaga@globant.com, rodrigo.cadena@aulagrupo.es
https://unade.edu.mx/

Abstract. Large Language Models (LLMs) are increasingly embedded in everyday study practices, assisting with content generation, explanations, and exam preparation. LLMs are now deeply embedded in classroom instruction, facilitating content generation and explanations. However, the traditional LLM model is prone to exposing the model's internal chain-of-thought. In this paper, a Socratic Agent is presented as auditable tutoring model that foregrounds the learner's reasoning rather than exposing its internal chain of thought. An evaluation plan is outlined across numeric and unit-conversion tasks, diagram reading, rubric-graded responses, and conceptual probes; outcome measures cover learning and retention, metacognitive coverage, trace quality, deference compliance, and cost/latency. Limitations, ablations, and a practical path from design to evidence are also detailed.

Keywords: Socratic Agent · Large Language Models · AI Agents

1 Introduction

Large Language Models (LLMs) are now deeply embedded in everyday study practices, assisting with content generation, explanations, and exam preparation [2,11]. While such access can enhance productivity, it also raises pedagogical concerns about intellectual dependency, reduced cognitive effort, and diminished retention—patterns long theorized in the cognitive offloading literature [13,18]. Recent experimental evidence adds atenttion: a study from the MIT Media Lab reports that students composing essays with an LLM exhibited lower neural engagement and reduced originality compared with search-only and unaided conditions, with some effects persisting even after AI assistance was removed [8]. Although preliminary, these findings align with the broader literature on cognitive offloading.

At the same time, LLMs are increasingly being integrated into formal instruction by educational institutions. Across regions, from China to the United States, policies that promote responsible use while emphasizing that students should remain the primary agents of their learning are being developed by universities [5,15]. Tools such as Khanmigo [6] and Claude for Education [1] attempt to

L. Martínez-Villaseñor et al. (Eds.): MICAI 2025, LNAI 16265, pp. 21–29, 2026.
https://doi.org/10.1007/978-3-032-17933-3_3

scaffold learning through interaction rather than through direct answer delivery. However, these systems are largely built on general-purpose LLMs that are optimized for efficiency and answer completeness rather than for the cultivation of student reasoning and reflective learning. A different design focus is motivated by this gap, auditable tutors in which general-purpose LLMs are wrapped and interaction is reoptimized to elicit and structure the learner's reasoning.

Emphasis is shifted from answer delivery to learner side reasoning by the design stance. Rather than revealing a model's chain of thought, the learner's reasoning is externalized and a framework with an accompanying evaluation for LLM use is provided. Building on problem decomposition prompting [12,19], assumptions are elicited, steps are structured, criteria are set, and counterexamples are tested by disciplined questions, practices linked to deeper learning and transfer [3,4,9].

A deference-gated tutoring pattern for auditable LLMs centers disciplined dialogue, externalized learner reasoning, and a minimal control loop *Elicit*→ *Structure*→ *Test*→ *Summarize* with $s_t \in \{\text{EXPLORE}, \text{VERIFY}\}$. Answer tokens are withheld until readiness criteria are satisfied under VERIFY, and progress is made auditable via two learner-facing artifacts: the Learner Reasoning Trace (LRT) and a metacognitive ledger. The design is instantiated in an auditable agent with tool discipline ("ask first, test on demand") and an executable controller featuring logit-bias gating, readiness signals, and runtime instrumentation; subsequent sections detail baselines, ablations, and metrics to evaluate deference-gate compliance, answer-leakage rate, tool-discipline adherence, metacognitive coverage, and delayed retention.

2 Related Work

AI in education draws on pedagogy, cognitive science, and machine learning. Constructivist accounts emphasize inquiry, reflection, and active meaning-making; Socratic pedagogy operationalizes these aims through guided questioning that elicits assumptions and repairs inconsistencies, cultivating metacognitive control. Metacognition concerns monitoring what is known, what is uncertain, and which strategies to try next; learners who plan, track, and adapt generally achieve better transfer and more durable understanding. Complementing these perspectives, the self-explanation effect shows that articulating intermediate rationales—why a step follows, which alternative was rejected, how a representation changes—deepens comprehension beyond exposure to worked solutions alone [3,4,9,10,17].

Building on these traditions, an *elicitation-first* design for AI tutors prompts learners to externalize partial models, structure their reasoning, and test hypotheses before conclusions are delivered. Questions target mental models rather than mere answers; summaries re-present the learner's claims and uncertainties; and feedback links strategy choices to observed outcomes—operationalizing Socratic aims and leveraging self-explanation as the mechanism by which explicit reasoning drives learning and transfer [3,10]. Intelligent Tutoring Systems (ITS) show that structured feedback can approach human tutoring [16], and learning analytics enables adaptive use of process data [7]; yet most LLM-based tutors (e.g., Khanmigo, Claude for Education) adapt general-purpose models optimized for answer completeness rather than for eliciting learners' reasoning [1,6].

Prompting strategies such as Chain of Thought, Self-Ask, Tree of Thoughts, and ReAct structure intermediate steps, branch the search, or interleave actions with tool calls to improve the model's own inference [12,19–21]. These traces—whether linear, branched, or action-annotated—optimize solution quality and sometimes transparency, but they are model-centric artifacts: they neither elicit nor represent the learner's evolving concepts, uncertainties, or strategy choices. Even when tool traces are logged (as in ReAct), the record describes what the model did, not what the student believes, doubts, or plans to try next. As a result, such methods can make the assistant more capable without making the learner more metacognitively engaged.

Work labeled "Socratic" in the modeling literature likewise targets robustness and modularity of model reasoning rather than pedagogy. For example, Zeng et al.'s Socratic decomposition coordinates specialized models to critique or refine each other's outputs, improving reliability through inter-model dialogue [22]. The "questioning" here is instrumental—it helps the system reason better—but it is not designed to surface, structure, or assess a human learner's reasoning state. By contrast, classroom-oriented tutoring approaches seek to scaffold the student's process, yet most LLM-based tutors still default to answer-forward behavior and do not maintain an explicit, external record of the learner's assumptions, hypotheses, and criteria.

Our Socratic agent addresses this gap by shifting the unit of optimization from the model's internal chain to the learner's externalized reasoning. Instead of exposing the model's intermediate thoughts, it elicits the student's; in place of using tools to solve the task outright, it uses tools only to test the student's hypotheses; and rather than relying on transient dialogue memory, it maintains auditable artifacts—the Learner Reasoning Trace and a metacognitive ledger—that track claims, uncertainties, strategies, and evidence over time. In short, prior prompting and "Socratic" modeling improve how the system thinks; our approach is designed to improve how the learner thinks, and to make that learning process visible and accountable.

3 Socratic Agent Design

The agent is designed to elicit and structure the learner's reasoning while withholding conclusions until a deference gate is met. Control follows a finite-state loop with stance $s_t \in \{\text{EXPLORE}, \text{VERIFY}\}$, a readiness score $R_t \in [0, 1]$, and decoding control that down-weights early tokens in $\mathcal{V}_{\text{answer}}$ by a logit bias γ. Finalization occurs only when $R_t \geq \tau$ and $s_t = \text{VERIFY}$. Figure 1 summarizes the process flow: *User Input* enters above the controller; *Tutor Output* is conditioned by the gate; and the left arc denotes progression from turn t to $t+1$. The deference predicate masks answer tokens if and only if $(s_t = \text{EXPLORE}) \vee (R_t < \tau)$.

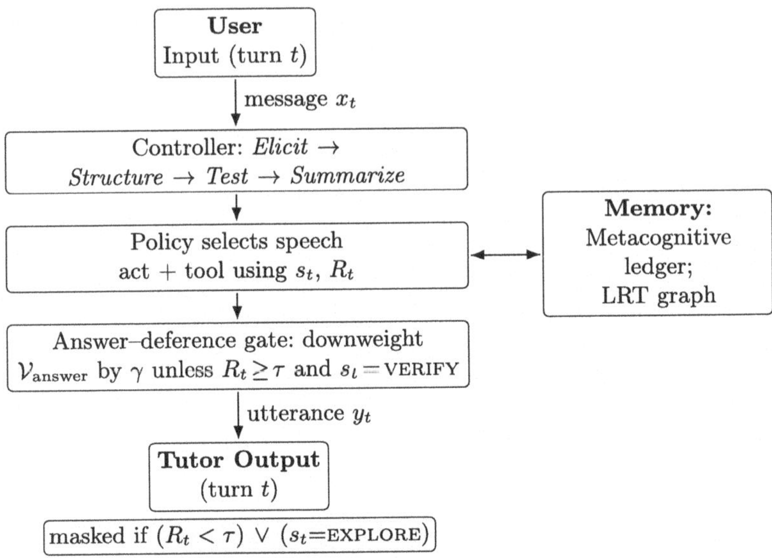

Fig. 1. Agent stack with policy control, answer–deference gate, and conversation loop. The user message x_t enters the controller; the gate conditions the emitted utterance y_t (masked unless $R_t \geq \tau$ and $s_t = \text{VERIFY}$). The left loop indicates turn progression from Tutor Output to the next User Input.

The controller's action set is restricted to an auditable family of speech acts—*ask*, *clarify*, *probe*, *challenge*, *summarize*, and *verify*—to keep behavior legible and policy-driven. *Ask* elicits goals, assumptions, or next steps; *clarify* resolves ambiguity; *probe* requests evidence or criteria; *challenge* surfaces counterexamples or boundary conditions; *summarize* synchronizes the Learner Reasoning Trace (LRT) and the metacognitive ledger; and *verify* checks the learner's stated criteria via minimal tool use. Table 1 maps each act to an intent, a prompt sketch, and its expected impact on R_t.

Two external artifacts anchor the policy and make progress auditable. The LRT is a typed graph with nodes {*claim*, *step*, *evidence*, *counterexample*} and edges {*supports*, *refutes*, *depends_on*}. The metacognitive ledger is a keyed record {*goal*, *assumptions*, *plan*, *criteria*, *confidence*, *open_questions*} updated every two to three turns. Both are visible to the learner and feed features into the readiness function R_t. Table 2 summarizes contents, cadence, privacy, and policy use.

The controller algorithm below implements the process in Fig. 1. At each turn, policy selects a speech act conditioned on (s_t, R_t); if evidence is required, a curated tool is invoked strictly to test the learner's current hypothesis. The emitted utterance is masked by the answer–deference gate whenever $R_t < \tau$ or

Table 1. Speech acts, intents, and updates.

Act	Intent	Prompt sketch	LRT write	$\mathbf{R_t}$ effect
ASK	Surface goals or assumptions	*"What is your goal? What do you assume?"*	`add` {claim/step}	↑ if no empty
CLARIFY	Repair ambiguity	*"When you say X, do you mean Y?"*	—	↑ if ambiguity resolved
PROBE	Elicit evidence/criteria	*"What evidence or criterion would show X?"*	`add` {evidence}	↑ on criteria coverage
CHALLENGE	Counter example/boundary	*"Where would this fail?"*	`add` {counter example}	↑ on stress tests
SUMMARIZE	Reflect state	*"Here is your current plan and evidence..."*	sync LRT/ledger	↑ on consistency
VERIFY	Check stated criteria	run minimal test; report finding	`add` {findings}	↑ if criteria satisfied

s_t = EXPLORE, and termination checks rely on completeness and stability signals derived from the LRT and ledger.

```
while not done:
  s_t, R_t <- controller_state(LRT, ledger, dialogue)
  if (s_t == EXPLORE) or (R_t < tau):
      a <- choose({ASK, CLARIFY, PROBE, CHALLENGE})
  else:
      a <- choose({SUMMARIZE, VERIFY})
  if a in {PROBE, CHALLENGE} and evidence_required(a):
      tool <- select_curated_tool(LRT, ledger)    # test-only
      obs  <- tool(test(hypothesis_from(learner)))
      write(LRT, obs); update(ledger, obs)
  utter(a, next_question_or_summary,
        mask=(R_t < tau or s_t == EXPLORE))  # deference gate
  done <- termination_check(LRT, ledger, dialogue)
```

Table 2. Memory taxonomy, cadence, and policy use.

Store	Contents	Cadence	Privacy	Policy use
LEDGER	goal, assumptions, plan, criteria, confidence, open_questions	every 2–3 turns	visible to learner	readiness features
LRT	claim, step, evidence, counterexample; edges	on each act	visible to learner	readiness + verification

4 Agent Implementation

The agent is implemented as an auditable stack using a Python runtime and a lightweight web layer. For question conditioned lookups, top-k passages are served by a FastAPI retriever; inference with *Qwen2.5-7B-Instruct*; and curated tool calls limited to hypothesis testing are provided by a compact RAG with SMOLagent module [14]. Traces of utterances, controller state, tool calls, and gate decisions are logged to files, which enables direct reconstruction of tables and excerpts.

Control adheres to the finite-state loop introduced in the previous section and Fig. 1. The controller wires a speech-act policy (ASK, CLARIFY, PROBE, CHALLENGE, SUMMARIZE, VERIFY) to an answer-deference gate that down-weights tokens in $\mathcal{V}_{\text{answer}}$ through logit bias γ. Table 3 summarizes runtime signals collected under this policy. The readiness $R_t \in [0, 1]$ and the position $s_t \in \{\text{EXPLORE}, \text{VERIFY}\}$ are calculated from the Learner Reasoning Trace (LRT), the metacognitive ledger, recent dialogue turns, and retrieval features; decoding of $\mathcal{V}_{\text{answer}}$ is allowed only when $R_t \geq \tau$ under VERIFY.

Runtime signals (linked to design constraints). Four metrics are computed directly from logs:

- **Deference compliance**—fraction of turns where $\mathcal{V}_{\text{answer}}$ remains suppressed while $(s_t = \text{EXPLORE}) \vee (R_t < \tau)$.
- **Tool discipline**—fraction of tool calls issued under $s_t = \text{VERIFY}$ to test a learner hypothesis.
- **Leakage**—proportion of answer tokens emitted while the deference predicate is not satisfied.
- **Success**—task-specific correctness at finalization.

Illustrative interaction snippets. The traces below show ask-first, test-on-demand behavior: elicitation under EXPLORE, deferred answers until the gate opens, and tools used solely to test the learner's hypothesis.

Numeric r=3 (True).

Table 3. Executable runs on two numeric checks and a RAG mini-lesson. Higher is better for Deference, Tool, Success; lower is better for Turns and Leakage.

Scenario	Deference↑	Tool↑	Success↑	Turns↓	Final R	Leakage↓	Quiz
Numeric r=3 (True)	1.00	1.00	✓	4	0.55	0.00	–
Numeric r=4 (False)	1.00	1.00	✓	4	0.80	0.00	–
RAG mini-lesson	1.00	1.00	✓	4	0.80	0.00	1

Note. "Final R" records the readiness at the *last non-answer turn*. Finalization is permitted only when $R_t \geq \tau$ and s_t = VERIFY. "Quiz" flags a brief check-for-understanding at the end of VERIFY.

ELICIT (ASK/EXPLORE) Can you explain how you arrived at the area being 28?
REVIEW (SUMMARIZE/VERIFY) Why is plugging r=3 into $A = \pi r^2$ a convincing criterion for the area?

RAG mini-lesson.

ELICIT (ASK/EXPLORE) Before I look things up: what do you already know and what do you most want to understand (e.g., *why it reduces hallucinations*, *how to wire it in code*)
RETRIEVE (VERIFY) Here are relevant snippets. Read them, then draft your explanation. (Top passages retrieved for the stated question.)
REVIEW+QUIZ (SUMMARIZE) Quick check: in one sentence, how does RAG reduce hallucinations?

5 Conclusion

Socratic agent is engineered to foster learning by shifting optimization from answer delivery to the learner's reasoning processes. The core mechanism is an answer deference gate by which solution tokens are withheld until readiness criteria are met, giving a principled lever to align behavior with pedagogical intent; when coupled with disciplined dialogue (*Elicit*→ *Structure*→ *Test*→ *Summarize*), explicit stance control (EXPLORE/VERIFY), and learner facing artifacts (Learner Reasoning Trace and metacognitive ledger), agency, metacognitive coverage, and auditable progress are promoted.

Operational guarantees are enabled by the gate: premature answer leakage is reduced, tool use is constrained to hypothesis testing ("ask first, test on demand"), and runtime signals (deference compliance, tool discipline, leakage, task success) are exposed so that the system is falsifiable, tunable, and governable; compatibility with small, auditable models and light retrieval allows deployment under modest compute and privacy constraints, and reproducible evidence together with a route from prototype to classroom study is provided by the artifacts and controller traces.

6 Future Work

Future research should investigate SLM deployments that preserve the proposed behavioral guarantees. Key directions include: calibrating the answer–deference mechanism by sweeping the readiness threshold τ and logit down-weighting γ to map the leakage–efficiency frontier; reducing latency and energy via quantization, speculative or partial decoding, and retrieval caching; testing retrieval robustness under constrained contexts (compressed passages, top-k tuning, stale or noisy sources); and extending tasks to figure reading and rubric-graded short answers, with outcomes measured by immediate accuracy, one-week retention, and near/far transfer. In parallel, scope and governance can be operationalized through Agent Cards documenting memory structures, tool policies, readiness metrics, and deference-compliance logs.

References

1. Anthropic: Introducing claude for education (2025). Available at https://www.anthropic.com/news/introducing-claude-for-education
2. Bommasani, R., Hudson, D.A., Adeli, E., et al.: On the opportunities and risks of foundation models. arXiv preprint arXiv:2108.07258 (2021)
3. Chi, M.T.H., Bassok, M., Lewis, M.W., Reimann, P., Glaser, R.: Self-explanations: How students study and use examples in learning to solve problems. Cogn. Sci. **13**(2), 145–182 (1989). https://doi.org/10.1207/s15516709cog1302_1
4. Flavell, J.H.: Metacognition and cognitive monitoring: A new area of cognitive-developmental inquiry. Am. Psychol. **34**(10), 906–911 (1979). https://doi.org/10.1037/0003-066X.34.10.906
5. Global Times Staff Reporters: Multiple chinese universities standardize the use of ai for academic writing. https://www.globaltimes.cn/page/202405/1312210.shtml (2024). Accessed 14 Aug 2025
6. Khan Academy: Khanmigo. https://www.khanmigo.ai/ (2023). AI-powered tutor and teaching assistant introduced on March 14, 2023; based on GPT-4, challenges students to discover answers themselves and supports educators with instructional tools
7. Koedinger, K.R., D'Mello, S., McLaughlin, E.A., Pardos, Z.A., Rosé, C.P.: Data mining and education. Wiley Interdisc. Rev. Cog. Sci. **6**(4), 333–353 (2015)
8. Kosmyna, N., et al.: Your brain on chatgpt: Accumulation of cognitive debt when using an ai assistant for essay writing task. arXiv preprint arXiv:2506.08872 (2025)
9. Kuhn, D.: Metacognitive development. Curr. Dir. Psychol. Sci. **8**(5), 178–181 (1999). https://doi.org/10.1111/1467-8721.00042
10. Lipman, M.: Thinking in education. Cambridge university press (2003)
11. OpenAI: Introducing chatgpt study mode (2025). Retrieved 14 Aug 2025 from https://openai.com/index/chatgpt-study-mode/
12. Press, O., Zhang, M., Min, S., Schmidt, L., Smith, N.A., Lewis, M.: Measuring and narrowing the compositionality gap in language models. arXiv preprint arXiv:2210.03350 (2022)
13. Risko, E.F., Gilbert, S.J.: Cognitive offloading. Trends Cogn. Sci. **20**(9), 676–688 (2016)

14. Roucher, A., del Moral, A.V., Wolf, T., von Werra, L., Kaunismäki, E.: 'smolagents': a smol library to build great agentic systems. https://github.com/huggingface/smolagents (2025)
15. U.S. Department of Education: U.s. department of education issues guidance on artificial intelligence use in schools, proposes additional supplemental priority. https://www.ed.gov/about/news/press-release/us-department-of-education-issues-guidance-artificial-intelligence-use-schools-proposes-additional-supplemental-priority (2025). Accessed 15 Aug 2025
16. VanLehn, K.: The relative effectiveness of human tutoring, intelligent tutoring systems, and other tutoring systems. Edu. Psychol. **46**(4), 197–221 (2011)
17. Vygotsky, L.S.: Mind in society: The development of higher psychological processes, vol. 86. Harvard university press (1978)
18. Ward, A.F.: Supernormal: how the internet is changing our memories and our minds. Psychol. Inq. **24**(4), 341–348 (2013)
19. Wei, J., Wang, X., Schuurmans, D., Bosma, M., Xia, F., Chi, E., Le, Q.V., Zhou, D., et al.: Chain-of-thought prompting elicits reasoning in large language models. Adv. Neural. Inf. Process. Syst. **35**, 24824–24837 (2022)
20. Yao, S., et al.: Tree of thoughts: Deliberate problem solving with large language models. Adv. Neural. Inf. Process. Syst. **36**, 11809–11822 (2023)
21. Yao, S., et al.: React: Synergizing reasoning and acting in language models. In: International Conference on Learning Representations (ICLR) (2023)
22. Zeng, A., Fried, D., Rohlfing, A., Yang, J., Tan, J., et al.: Socratic models: Composing zero-shot multimodal reasoning with language. arXiv preprint arXiv:2204.00598 (2022). https://arxiv.org/abs/2204.00598

An Argument Mining Tool for Spanish Academic Texts

Joel David González-Barros[1], Jesús Miguel García-Gorrostieta[2](✉), Aurelio López-López[3], and Samuel González-López[4]

[1] Universidad Tecnológica De Bolívar, Cartagena de Indias, Colombia
joegonzalez@utb.edu.co
[2] Universidad de la Sierra, Sonora, México
jgarcia@unisierra.edu.mx
[3] Instituto Nacional de Astrofísica, Óptica y Electrónica, Puebla, México
allopez@inaoep.mx
[4] Tecnológico Nacional de México Campus Nogales, Sonora, México
samuel.gl@nogales.tecnm.mx

Abstract. This paper presents the development of a functional tool for the automatic detection and analysis of argumentative structures in Spanish academic texts. The system integrates a Conditional Random Fields (CRF) model trained on the CATyPI corpus, which consists of annotated thesis excerpts labeled with BIO tags for argumentative components. The model achieved a macro F1-score of 0.5896 and an accuracy of 0.657 using a context window size of three tokens, proving effective for identifying premises and conclusions. The system also incorporates a REST API developed with FastAPI and a user interface that visualizes the tagged text and offers real-time suggestions. These suggestions are generated by the ChatGPT 3.5 Turbo model based on the CRF model's output to support academic writing improvement. The interface highlights argumentative elements and provides feedback that helps users refine their texts. Evaluation of the tool shows that it performs well in real use cases, although it still faces challenges with ambiguous or implicit argumentative structures. The project is publicly available through a GitHub repository and an interactive demo hosted on Hugging Face Spaces. This work demonstrates the feasibility of combining machine learning models with large language models to support argumentation in educational contexts, particularly for Spanish-speaking users.

Keywords: Argumentative Structure Detection · Spanish Academic Text · Conditional Random Fields (CRF) · Educational Technology · BIO Tagging

1 Introduction

The ability to argue clearly, coherently, and with sound reasoning is a fundamental skill in the academic and professional development of university students.

L. Martínez-Villaseñor et al. (Eds.): MICAI 2025, LNAI 16265, pp. 30–40, 2026.
https://doi.org/10.1007/978-3-032-17933-3_4

Written argumentation, in particular, enables students to support ideas, evaluate opposing viewpoints, and construct critical discourse in the context of scientific research. Despite its importance, several studies have shown that university students frequently struggle to produce well-structured argumentative texts, facing challenges in organizing claims, integrating evidence, and articulating counterarguments, which ultimately affects the quality of their writing and overall academic performance [11]. This situation underscores the need for pedagogical and technological approaches that can assist students in developing stronger argumentative skills. In this context, advances in language technologies and natural language processing (NLP) have opened new opportunities to support learning processes through automated analysis and feedback tools.

This paper presents the development of a computational tool designed to identify argumentative structures in academic texts written in Spanish. The tool employs machine learning and NLP techniques to assist students in improving their argumentative writing by providing targeted feedback on the quality and structure of arguments. It integrates a CRF-based classification model trained on an annotated corpus, an API that connects this model to a generative language model for producing context-aware suggestions, and a user interface that visualizes the annotated texts along with the generated recommendations.

The structure of this article is organized as follows. Section 2 reviews the theoretical background and related work in argument mining and academic writing support. Section 3 describes the dataset and annotation schema used for model training. Section 4 outlines the methodology, including feature extraction and model training. Section 5 describes the system architecture. Section 6 presents the evaluation results and a discussion of the challenges encountered. Finally, Sect. 7 offers conclusions and suggests future directions to enhance the pedagogical and technical capabilities of the system.

2 Related Work

Argument mining has gained increasing attention in recent years, particularly in the context of academic writing and education [11]. Early research focused on identifying argumentative components in persuasive essays, where frameworks such as Toulmin's model were frequently used to annotate corpora and structure analysis [9]. Supervised learning approaches, relying on annotated datasets, have dominated the field, enabling the automatic detection of claims, premises, and their relationships [2]. Resources such as CATyPI have played a crucial role in advancing argument mining for Spanish-language academic texts [4].

Various machine learning and NLP techniques have been applied to argument mining tasks. Conditional Random Fields (CRF) were among the first models successfully used to classify argumentative components in text sequences [5]. These models employed lexical, syntactic, and positional features to detect components (i.e., premises and conclusions). Later approaches integrated CRF with BiLSTM networks and attention mechanisms to capture richer contextual dependencies in academic discourse [10]. In parallel, the introduction of transformer-based architectures such as BERT and specialized variants such as SciBERT and RoBERTa enabled the generation of deep contextual representations, significantly enhancing classification efficacy in argumentative structure detection [1,3]. Studies have shown that combining transformers with CRF layers results in improved sequence-labeling capabilities, particularly in complex texts [7].

Despite these advances, most models and corpora have focused on English texts. In the Spanish-speaking academic context, resources such as the CATyPI corpus [4], which includes annotated Spanish academic texts, have facilitated the application of argument mining techniques to this language. Furthermore, the availability of Spanish-pretrained models such as BETO and MarIA has allowed researchers to adapt cutting-edge techniques to Spanish with promising results. However, challenges remain, including the scarcity of annotated data and the need for domain-specific adaptations to fully support educational writing tools in Spanish-language contexts. These limitations motivate the development of domain-adapted tools that combine linguistic analysis with automated feedback generation, as proposed in this work.

3 Corpus

The dataset used for this study is the CATyPI corpus (Argumentative Corpus of Theses and Research Proposals), developed by Garcia-Gorrostieta and Lopez-Lopez [4]. This corpus consists of 444 argumentative sections extracted from 468 academic theses (bachelor's, master's, and doctoral levels) in the field of Information Technologies. The selected sections include problem statements, justifications, and conclusions—portions of the documents recognized as particularly rich in argumentative content.

Each token in the corpus is manually annotated using the BIO scheme, which classifies tokens as Beginning-Premise (B-P), Inside-Premise (I-P), Beginning-Conclusion (B-C), Inside-Conclusion (I-C), or Outside (O). This fine-grained annotation supports supervised sequence labeling tasks, allowing precise training and evaluation of argument mining models.

The Corpus was refined by [8] and organized into 10 cross-validation folds, each consisting of a training and a test file in a 90/10 split. This configuration allowed for generalizable performance evaluations while preserving sentence-level context and label continuity.

Each fold in the corpus is stored as a plain .txt file, where every line represents a token-label pair. The format consists of the word (token) followed by a single space and its corresponding BIO label (e.g., B-P, I-C, O). This simple structure facilitates sequential reading and processing of the data for training sequence labeling models. Sentences are separated by empty lines, allowing the system to correctly identify sentence boundaries during preprocessing. Figure 1 presents an example of this organization.

The annotated corpus contains a total of 108,436 tokens, distributed across five BIO tags as shown in Table 1. Specifically, 38,797 tokens are labeled as argumentative components, with 1,615 and 37,182 tokens corresponding to the beginning (`B-P`) and continuation (`I-P`) of premises, and 984 and 19,666 tokens

```
Los B-P
ingenieros I-P
también I-P
saben I-P
que I-P
deben I-P
trabajar I-P
con I-P
restricciones I-P
financieras I-P
y I-P
organizacionales I-P
```

Fig. 1. Sample from the annotated corpus with BIO tagging.

corresponding to the beginning (B-C) and continuation (I-C) of conclusions. The remaining 48,989 tokens are labeled as O, representing non-argumentative content. Finally, in the original corpus described in [4], a total of 4,989 segments of premise, conclusion, or none types were obtained, and the agreement reached for the annotation of argumentative components was 0.461, i.e., a 'moderate' level [6]. In this work, a depurated subset of the corpus is used in BIO format.

Table 1. Distribution of tokens per BIO tag in the corpus.

Label	Token count
B-P	1,615
I-P	37,182
B-C	984
I-C	19,666
O	48,989
Total	108,436

4 Detecting Argumentation

The experiments were conducted using Google Colaboratory (Colab), which offers cloud-based notebooks with GPU support, collaborative tools, and integration with Google Drive. Each sentence was coded as a list of tuples containing: (1) the token, (2) its POS tag provided by spaCy, and (3) its BIO label.

Feature extraction played a central role in preparing the input for the CRF classifier. For each token, a structured set of attributes was compiled to capture different linguistic dimensions. **Syntactic features** included the part-of-speech (POS) tag of the token and its immediate neighbors (e.g., *"argument"* → NOUN), along with common morphological elements such as prefixes (*"pre-"* in *"premise"*) and suffixes (*"-sion"* in *"conclusion"*). **Lexical features** encompassed the token in lowercase form (*"Argument"* → *"argument"*), capitalization indicators (*"University"* begins with a capital letter), digit checks (*"2023"* is numeric), and lemmatized forms (*"running"* → *"run"*). **Structural features** captured sentence boundaries, using BOS (beginning of sentence) and EOS (end of sentence) markers, as well as punctuation indicators (*";"* or *"."*). Finally, **sentiment analysis** at the sentence level was incorporated using the *sentiment_analysis_spanish* library, giving polarity scores that could highlight subtle evaluative cues (e.g., a conclusion sentence with a positive score of +0.15). In Fig. 2, a fragment of the token-level feature dictionary is presented, illustrating the set of extracted attributes for each token in the corpus. Context windows were used to include features from neighboring tokens, enhancing the model's ability to capture transitions between argument components.

```
{'bias': 1.0,
 'token.lower()': 'primera',
 'token.upper()': 'PRIMERA',
 'word[-3:]': 'era',
 'word[-2:]': 'ra',
 'word[-1:]': 'a',
 'word[:2]': 'pr',
 'word[:3]': 'pri',
 'word.isupper()': False,
 'word.islower()': True,
 'word.istitle()': False,
 'word.isdigit()': False,
 'word.isalpha()': True,
 'word.isalnum()': True,
 'word.length': 7,
 'word.has_hyphen': False,
 'word.has_apostrophe': False,
 'postag': 'ADJ',
 'postag[:2]': 'AD',
 'sentiment': np.float64(0.48709576716385694),
 '-1:token.lower()': 'la',
 '-1:word[-3:]': 'La',
 '-1:word[-2:]': 'La',
```

Fig. 2. features sample.

The CRF model was implemented using the sklearn-crfsuite library, which supports feature-rich training and customizable regularization. During training, a ten-fold cross-validation setup was used to ensure generalizability. For each fold, a distinct CRF model was trained with the following optimal hyperparameters: the L-BFGS optimization algorithm, C1 regularization coefficient (c1=1.25182077), C2 regularization coefficient (c2=0.01650852), and a maximum of 300 iterations. These C1 and C2 values were *adopted* from [8], who obtained them using `RandomizedSearchCV` over the `sklearn` ecosystem. Given that this study employed the same corpus and highly similar linguistic feature representations as the cited work, adopting those hyperparameters was considered appropriate to preserve methodological consistency and facilitate comparison of results.

5 System Architecture

The proposed system integrates a FastAPI backend for argumentative processing and a lightweight web interface for user interaction.

5.1 Backend API

The argumentation detection process, illustrated in Fig. 3, is encapsulated within a modular RESTful API built with FastAPI. The backend loads the CRF model weights and the feature configuration at startup and exposes two HTTPS endpoints: /**predict** and /**recommend**. The /**predict** route receives raw text from the web frontend and executes the internal pipeline *spaCy* → *features* → *CRF* → *BIO* → *JSON*. Concretely, the input is tokenized and POS-tagged with spaCy; a feature extractor computes syntactic, lexical, structural, and sentence-level sentiment attributes; and a preloaded Conditional Random Fields (CRF) model assigns a BIO label to each token (begin/inside of premise or conclusion, or outside). The response returns a structured JSON object with tokens and predicted labels.

In parallel, the /**recommend** endpoint takes the tokens plus BIO tags (either from the client or produced by `/predict`) and queries an LLM (GPT-3.5-turbo) to generate real-time, role-aware writing suggestions. The suggestions are returned as JSON and the frontend renders them alongside the highlighted argumentative components (e.g., reinforcing a weak conclusion or clarifying a vague premise).

5.2 Frontend Interface

The frontend is a lightweight HTML-based interface, enhanced with CSS and JavaScript, that allows users to interact with the system via a web browser. It is composed of two primary sections:

- **Text editor panel:** A formatted text area where users can write or paste argumentative content. Basic formatting tools (bold, italic, lists) are provided to enhance usability.
- **Suggestions panel:** Located adjacent to the editor, this section displays improvement suggestions returned by the LLM, linked directly to the identified premises and conclusions.

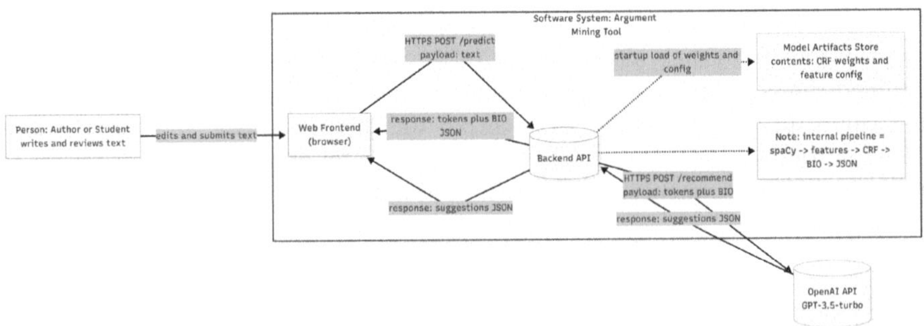

Fig. 3. System architecture.

Upon clicking the **Analyze** button, the system sends the user's text to the /**predict** route of the backend API. The response is parsed, and argument components are visually highlighted: conclusions are marked in orange, and premises in blue. Then, the /**recommend** route is triggered to generate detailed suggestions, which are rendered in the suggestions panel.

The complete source code of the system, encompassing both the API backend and the web interface, is publicly available on GitHub[1].

Furthermore, an interactive demonstration implemented with Gradio is hosted on Hugging Face Spaces[2] , enabling users to experiment with the classifier directly in a web environment. Figure 4 presents an example of the interface.

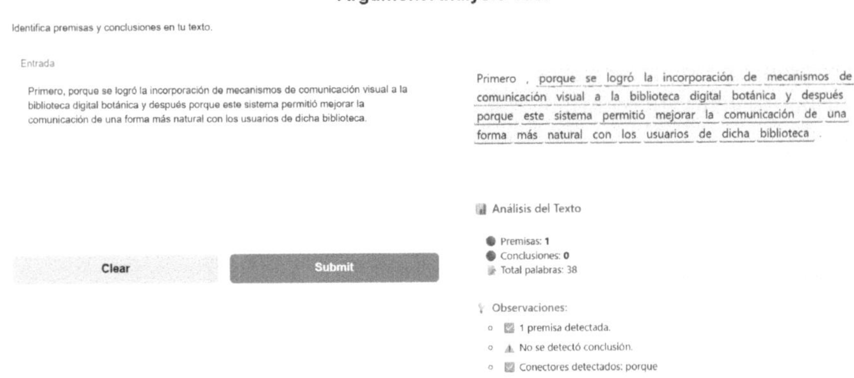

Fig. 4. Demonstrative interface using Gradio.

[1] https://github.com/JoelGonzalez08/Analizador-de-Argumentos-Delfin.
[2] https://huggingface.co/spaces/JoelGonzalez08/Detector-Argumentos-CRF.

6 Results

The CRF-based argument mining model was quantitatively evaluated using 10-fold cross-validation on the CATyPI corpus. The evaluation included experimentation with context window sizes from 1 to 4. The results showed that the average F1-scores obtained were 0.5630 for a context window of size 1, 0.5796 for size 2, 0.5896 for size 3, and 0.5844 for size 4. The best performance was obtained with a context window size of 3, which achieved a macro-averaged F1-score of **0.5896** and a token-level accuracy of **0.657**. These metrics indicate that the model is moderately effective at identifying argumentative structures within Spanish academic texts.

The Table 2 highlights that the model from fold 7 with a window size of 3 performs best in recognizing continuation tokens of premises (`I-P`) and non-argumentative content (`O`). In contrast, it has more difficulty identifying the beginning of conclusions (`B-C`), likely due to the imbalanced distribution of tags and the complexity of linguistic structures that signal conclusions.

Table 2. Token-level performance metrics.

Label	Precision	Recall/Sensitivity	F1-score
B-P	0.602	0.490	0.540
I-P	0.658	0.600	0.628
B-C	0.500	0.426	0.460
I-C	0.509	0.519	0.514
O	0.708	0.752	0.730

For the testing stage, the tool was evaluated with various texts from the corpus. In many cases, the CRF model correctly labeled complete sequences of premises and conclusions, validating the effectiveness of the features used and the selected window. However, errors also occurred, such as the omission of argumentative labels in obvious fragments or the inversion of premises and conclusions. This suggests the need to incorporate deeper features (such as contextual embeddings) or more robust models (such as BiLSTM-CRF or transformers).

As for the tool developed, we were able to implement a functional application that integrates the CRF model through an API in FastAPI and a GPT-3.5 large language model for generating suggestions. The user can enter text in a web editor, obtain the classification of arguments through text coloring (blue for premises, orange for conclusions), and view the suggestions generated by the large language model in a side panel, as shown in Fig. 5.

One of the most notable features was the automatic generation of recommendations based on the argumentative labels detected. However, this feature also faced significant limitations. The quality and specificity of the suggestions depended directly on the CRF model; if it mislabeled a segment, the large language model generated inappropriate recommendations. However, GPT-3.5, in

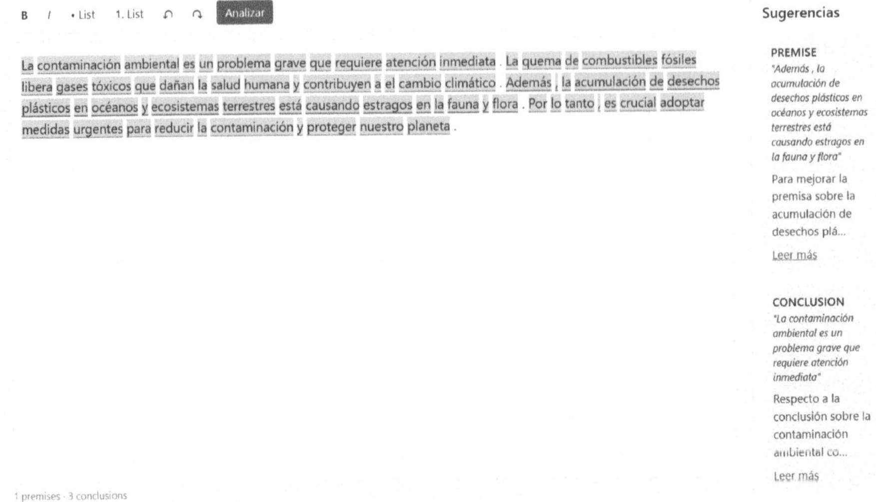

Fig. 5. Example of API usage.

some cases, generated vague or irrelevant responses, focusing on aspects such as the lack of examples or overall clarity, rather than on the argumentative structure itself.

The prompt designed for the suggestion generation model was the following:

> *Eres un asistente experto en argumentación académica. A continuación verás una lista de premisas y conclusiones extraídas de un texto. Para cada elemento, genera exactamente una sugerencia clara y práctica que ayude a mejorar esa premisa o conclusión. Premisas: [...]. Conclusiones: [...]. Ahora, genera las sugerencias solicitadas.*

Challenges were also encountered in adjusting the prompt to ensure that the language model focused its suggestions on improving argumentative quality. In addition, technical limitations were encountered, such as token consumption management, OpenAI API cost control, and latency between requests. However, these difficulties open up new lines of work to improve communication between models and more efficient designs.

7 Conclusion

This work presents a computational tool designed to support argumentative writing in Spanish academic contexts through the identification and analysis of argument structures. By integrating a Conditional Random Fields (CRF) classifier with a feature-rich preprocessing pipeline and a web-based interface, the system enables users to visualize argumentative components such as premises and conclusions directly within their text.

The training of the CRF model on the CATyPI corpus, annotated under the BIO scheme, yielded promising results. The model achieved a macro F1-score of 0.5896 and a token-level accuracy of 0.657, particularly excelling in the classification of non-argumentative segments and internal premise tokens. These results demonstrate the feasibility of employing sequence labeling models for the automatic detection of argumentative units in Spanish texts, while also highlighting areas of improvement, particularly in recognizing conclusion boundaries and implicit arguments.

The user interface further enhances the educational potential of the system by providing visual feedback and AI-powered suggestions for improving argumentative clarity. However, some recommendations generated by the language model were overly generic, indicating the need for fine-tuning to improve alignment with argument-specific roles.

Overall, this system establishes a functional and adaptable prototype for assisting students in improving their academic writing. Future research will focus on including transformer-based architectures for deeper contextual understanding, expanding the annotated corpus to cover additional domains, and conducting formal usability studies to measure impact. The integration of NLP technologies in educational environments represents a significant step toward fostering critical thinking and improving the quality of written academic discourse.

Acknowledgement. Authors were partially supported by SNII-Secihti.

References

1. Binder, T., Nanni, F., Hätty, A.: Argumentation mining in scientific publications: A hybrid approach using scibert and crf. In Proceedings of the 2023 Conference of the North American Chapter of the Association for Computational Linguistics (NAACL) (2023)
2. Cabrio, E., Villata, S.: Five years of argument mining: a data-driven analysis. Artif. Intell. **261**, 25–54 (2018)
3. Devlin, J., Chang, M.-W., Lee, K., Toutanova, K.: Bert: Pre-training of deep bidirectional transformers for language understanding. In Proceedings of NAACL-HLT, pp. 4171–4186, (2019)
4. García-Gorrostieta, J.M., López-López, A., Rico-Sulayes, A., Carrillo, M.: Argument corpus development and argument component classification: A study in academic spanish. Digital Sch. Humanit. **36**(2), 287–306 (2021)
5. Lafferty, J., McCallum, A., Pereira, F.: Conditional random fields: probabilistic models for segmenting and labeling sequence data. In: Proceedings of the 18th International Conference on Machine Learning, pages 282–289 (2001)
6. Landis JRKoch, G.: The measurement of observer agreement for categorical data. Biometrics, **33**(1), 159174 (1977)
7. Patel, H.: Survey of machine learning techniques for argument mining in educational texts. J. Comput. Linguist. Appl. **16**(1), 55–78 (2024)
8. Ramirez-Rangel, P.E.: Extracción de componentes argumentativos en textos académicos utilizando procesamiento del lenguaje natural. Universidad de Guanajuato, Guanajuato, Noviembre, Tesis de licenciatura (2022)

9. Stab, C., Gurevych, I.: Parsing argumentation structures in persuasive essays. Comput. Linguist. **43**(3), 619–659 (2017)
10. Yang, J., Zheng, M., Liu, Y.: Fusion weighted features and bilstm-attention model for argument mining of efl writing. Frontiers Psychol. **14**(2023) (2023)
11. Zhao, X., Stab, C., Gurevych, I.: Automated evaluation for student argumentative writing: A survey. arXiv preprint arXiv:2205.04083, (2022)

ASTRA: A Web Scraping Tool Devoted to Academic Content Retrieval and Text Complexity Analysis

Jonathan Rojas-Simón[1](✉), Yulia Ledeneva[1], Verónica Neri-Mendoza[1,2], René A. García-Hernández[1], Abner A. Gil-García[1], and Angel Barón-García[1]

[1] Autonomous University of the State of Mexico, Instituto Literario No. 100, 50000 Toluca, State of Mexico, Mexico
{jrojass,ynledeneva,reagarciah}@uaemex.mx,
{vnerim001,agilg003,abarong001}@alumno.uaemex.mx
[2] Secretariat of Science, Humanities, Technology and Innovation, No. 1582, Insurgentes Sur Avenue, Credito Constructor, Benito Juarez, Mexico City, Mexico

Abstract. Online academic content has become a key area of research for text analysis and the development of recommender systems. However, while existing tools typically offer content scraping or text complexity assessment, few integrate both within a unified framework. This paper introduces ASTRA (Academic Scraper for Text and Reading Analysis), a system that automates the collection of scholarly texts and evaluates their linguistic and readability features. ASTRA combines web scraping with Natural Language Processing (NLP) techniques to extract metadata, preprocess text, and compute lexical diversity and readability indexes. Unlike other tools, ASTRA generates text complexity information that supports the development of educational technology, academic writing evaluation, and large-scale corpus studies. Preliminary experiments show that ASTRA effectively retrieves relevant academic material while producing reliable complexity assessments. In general, ASTRA represents a practical resource for researchers and educators seeking to bridge automated data collection with advanced text analysis.

Keywords: ASTRA · Web Scraping · Academic Content · Text Complexity Analysis

1 Introduction

Nowadays, digital learning environments have become an essential resource to disseminate education and knowledge on a global scale. Some of them include Massive Open Online Courses (MOOCs) [2], Learning Management Systems (LMS) [3], Collaborative Knowledge Platforms (CKP) [10], or online discussion forums that support skill and knowledge development. However, the academic content provided in them has been a valuable resource in creating Educational Recommender Systems (ERS) that can capture learners' needs and interests [7].

L. Martínez-Villaseñor et al. (Eds.): MICAI 2025, LNAI 16265, pp. 41–49, 2026.
https://doi.org/10.1007/978-3-032-17933-3_5

One of the most significant challenges in creating these systems has been designing and developing high-quality datasets. Without well-structured and contextually grounded datasets, even the most advanced systems and approaches can be rendered or biased [4]. Regarding this, previous studies highlight the need to take into account methodological factors when constructing datasets for ERS [16]. In particular, web scraping is crucial for large-scale data collection.

Within web scraping techniques, methods, and commercial tools, key stages include *fetching*, *extraction*, and *transformation* [11], which involve applying regular expressions, *HTML parsing*, *XPath*, *DOM*, and *embedded browser-based* scraping, as well as Python libraries such as *BeautifulSoup*[1] and *lxml*[2] Although their use has been linked to copyright issues or server overload, they are also helpful for monitoring market trends, collecting up-to-date news/social media content, analyzing user-generated content (*e.g.*, reviews and Q&A websites), and building corpora for Natural Language Processing (NLP) tasks. Despite its richness, the scholarly literature indexed in Google Scholar has not been fully leveraged by NLP tools that analyze text complexity. Integrating this content with student-generated information could support the development of ERS.

In this paper, we propose ASTRA, a web scraping tool that extracts metadata from scholarly documents and applies NLP tools for text analysis. This analysis involves calculating text complexity based on word diversity/inflection, sentence length, readability, and word/sentence entropy. It aims to associate this information with student-generated content and measure the complexity of academic documents. The paper is organized as follows: Sect. 2 summarizes and describes state-of-the-art methods and commercial tools for web scraping. Section 3 presents a general description of ASTRA and its modules. Section 4 shows the experiments and the results obtained from ASTRA in academic documents. Finally, Sect. 5 presents the conclusions and future directions of this research.

2 Related Works

According to [16], one of the key factors in constructing datasets for ERS is collecting information from the Internet through web scrapers. Their use has been addressed for several tasks aimed at extracting and structuring relevant textual data for subsequent analysis and interpretation. In this section, we briefly describe how web scrapers have been used in academic settings and the commercial web scraping tools relevant to this field.

2.1 State-of-the-Art Web Scrapers

In the context of MOOCs, dropout rates have been studied using data obtained through web scraping. For instance, the authors in [12] collected student reviews

[1] BeautifulSoup Python package website: https://pypi.org/project/BeautifulSoup/.

[2] Lxml Python package website: https://pypi.org/project/lxml/.

from five Coursera courses related to data science and programming by employing custom HTML parsing scripts and the BeautifulSoup library. The extracted data included review date, textual content, and star rating, which were later analyzed using sentiment analysis and topic modeling to investigate dropout behavior. Similarly, in [1], an ERS was proposed based on a multi-criteria recommendation approach, relying on a dataset built from 145 Udemy courses. Reviews and ratings were collected through web scraping to support the system's evaluation.

In addition to MOOCs, web scraping has also been applied to extract information on Learning Management Systems (LMS). In particular, in [8], a real-time web scraping system was developed to analyze the clickstream of course materials in Moodle. The information provided by this system enabled the analysis of the learner's behavior and performance during a class.

On the other hand, recent studies have highlighted the role of web scraping in supporting academic planning and course management in higher education. In particular, when information is spread across university platforms and is not accessible through public APIs, web scraping methods provide an alternative for collecting and centralizing data [14]. After comparing APIs, RSS (Really Simple Syndication), and web scraping, it was concluded that web scraping through BeautifulSoup represents the most viable alternative. Moreover, web scraping has been applied to extract and organize large volumes of job-related information, enabling institutions to detect patterns in course offerings, specialization areas, and labor market skill demands [18].

Regarding employability studies for job market analysis, web scraping tools have been applied. For example, a comparison and evaluation of 11 scraping tools was performed in [6] to examine university employability in Mexico using data from INEGI, ANUIES, and OLA institutions. Their findings revealed gender gaps and regional inequalities, although some tools faced challenges due to variability in web structures, compatibility issues, and pop-ups. In another study [13], an NLP-based web scraping approach was applied to extract and analyze 3,824 computer science job postings from Indeed.com across five cities in the United States ranked highly for tech talent, identifying current trends in the job market for computer science students.

Beyond research applications, web scraping has also been incorporated into statistics and data science curricula. In the work done in [9], it was demonstrated how web scraping fosters students' programming skills, critical thinking, and ethical awareness. However, these implementations have not yet explored the analysis of textual data to assess text complexity, which could provide valuable insights for linking web-scraped content to ERS.

2.2 Web Scraping Commercial Tools

Unlike Python-based libraries, commercial web scraping tools offer a more accessible alternative for users without programming expertise. They are designed to simplify the data extraction process, but they also present limitations in terms of flexibility and scalability. Below, we describe some of the most popular web scraping commercial tools.

- **Octoparse:** It is a no-code web scraping platform that enables users to extract structured data from websites through intuitive interfaces. It offers features such as task scheduling, cloud-based extraction, and prebuilt templates, making it suitable for non-programming users.
- **ParseHub:** It is a graphical tool for building scraping projects that supports data extraction from dynamic websites using JavaScript and AJAX. Its flexibility enables the creation of complex workflows, making it accessible to both beginners and advanced users.
- **WebHarvy:** Unlike previous tools, WebHarvy is a visual tool that detects patterns in web pages to extract images, text, and URLs with minimal configuration. It is suitable to use in repetitive tasks and small- to medium-scale projects, but its scalability is limited compared to custom-coded scrapers.

In general, while tools such as Octoparse, ParseHub, and WebHarvy provide user interfaces, they generally lack the flexibility, scalability, and customization capabilities, making them more suitable for small- to medium-scale projects. However, it is necessary to develop applications to extract and analyze scholarly literature from Google Scholar for ERS. Moreover, state-of-the-art web scrapers indicate that in education, these tools have primarily focused on: (i) course analysis and reviews, (ii) assessment of student competencies, and (iii) job placement studies. In this context, we hypothesize that web scraping could further support academic content personalization by analyzing the complexity of the text and adapting the materials to students' reading and comprehension levels.

3 ASTRA: Academic Scraper for Text Reading Analysis

As mentioned in previous sections, specialized and commercial web scraping tools have supported MOOCs and LMS in employability analysis and competency assessment. However, scholarly content from academic sources remains underexplored for ERS development. To address this gap, we present ASTRA[3] a framework whose components are illustrated in Fig. 1 and described below.

Manual Metadata Collection: Before web scraping, it is necessary to create a list of documents to extract. For this, we suggest that a team of users is tasked with compiling titles of academic documents, keywords, and the year of publication to ensure a specific extraction and search of metadata.

Scholarly web scraping: After metadata collection, we used the Scholarly Python library to perform the web scraping process [5]. This component enables the extraction of various metadata from academic documents indexed in Google Scholar, including titles, abstracts, keywords, and download links, without requiring manual searches. Finally, full documents are extracted (if available).

[3] ASTRA GitLab repository: https://gitlab.com/complexity-indexes/ASTRA/,.

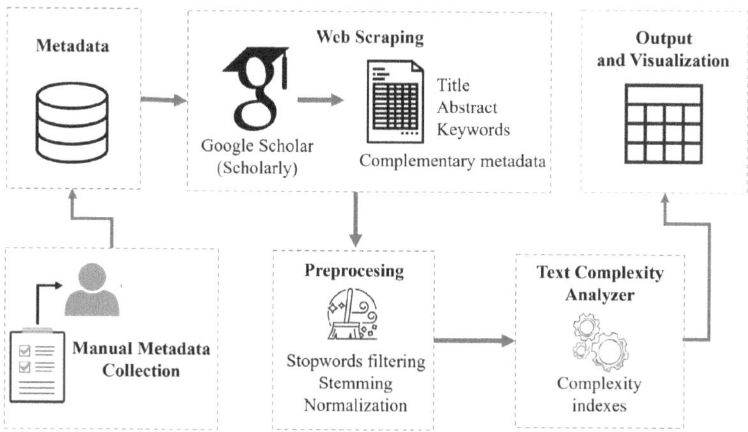

Fig. 1. ASTRA's components and stages.

Preprocessing: Both abstracts and academic documents require NLP preprocessing, which includes text normalization, stopwords removal, and stemming to reduce words to their stems. These steps enable a suitable document preparation to calculate text complexity.

Text Complexity Analyzer: Preprocessed documents are then input into an assembly of seven components that calculate their complexity, whose purpose is to assess the text's difficulty (on a scale from 0 to 1 [15]) and thus adapt the reading material to the reader's level, facilitating comprehension and learning. These indices consider quantitative and qualitative factors, which are described as follows:

- **Type-Token Ratio (TTR).** The TTR index is used to assess the linguistic diversity of a text. In general, this index measures the quantity of different words that appear in the text.
- **Ratio of Stopwords (RSW).** In NLP, stopwords (*e.g.*, the, of, is, are) often contribute little semantic value and may introduce noise. Therefore, the RSW index measures the overall presence of these terms within a document.
- **Ratio of Inflected Words (RIW).** Many languages exhibit word inflection; in English, for instance, "organize" becomes *organizing* or *organization*. This feature reflects lexical complexity, and the RIW index measures the proportion of inflected words in a document.
- **Automated Readability Index (ARI).** The ARI estimates the readability level of a text by considering the average word and sentence length.
- **Average Characters per Word (ACW).** The ACW index calculates the average word length in one or more documents.
- **Word Entropy (H_w).** Entropy is a measure that reflects the average uncertainty of a random variable. In this case, it applies to using the probability of words in a document to estimate its entropy.

- **Sentence Entropy (H_s).** Also known as *sentence length uniformity*, this index is computed like word entropy but uses the probabilities of words per sentence to estimate the average uncertainty in sentence length.

Output and Visualization: Finally, a complexity visualization and statistical details were provided for each document to support the retrieval processes.

4 Experiments and Results

To evaluate ASTRA's performance, we employed reference lists compiled by 51 software engineering students aged 20–27, of whom 78.4% identified as men and 21.6% as women. Their task was to collect academic metadata (*e.g.*, titles, keywords, and publication years) for subsequent web scraping and complexity index computation. The resulting lists covered topics across three technological areas: Artificial Intelligence (AI), Pattern Recognition (PR), and Software Engineering Models and Methods (SEMMs). We have selected these areas since they represent core domains in computer science and engineering education, frequently addressed in academic coursework and research. However, ASTRA is not limited to them and can analyze documents from other areas.

After applying the scholarly web scraping process, 50 academic documents were obtained for each subject, such as articles, theses, and lab reports, from which their metadata and abstracts were extracted. With this information, complexity indices were calculated for each abstract and full document, and the results are presented in Table 1. Moreover, the minimum, maximum, mean, and standard deviation (Std) values for each subject are included in the comparison.

Table 1. Text complexity results across different subjects.

Subject	Feature	TTR	RSW	RIW	ARI	ACW	H_w	H_s
AI	Min	0.7700	0.0000	0.0714	0.9986	0.4690	0.9703	0.0000
	Max	1.0000	0.0800	0.2500	1.0000	0.6592	0.9928	0.9997
	Mean	0.9130	0.0054	0.1370	0.9996	0.5493	0.9783	0.0303
	Std	0.0762	0.0096	0.0614	0.0002	0.0541	0.0069	0.1582
PR	Min	0.6969	0.0000	0.0333	0.7710	0.4068	0.9444	0.0000
	Max	1.0000	0.0652	0.3529	1.0000	0.6944	1.0000	0.9927
	Mean	0.8559	0.0017	0.1644	0.9844	0.5649	0.9864	0.0573
	Std	0.0714	0.0095	0.0713	0.0531	0.0628	0.0613	0.2273
SEMMs	Min	0.7977	0.0000	0.7600	0.7288	0.4567	0.9638	0.0000
	Max	0.9756	0.0400	1.0000	1.0000	0.6620	0.9925	0.9929
	Mean	0.8848	0.0024	0.8660	0.9940	0.5588	0.9777	0.0588
	Std	0.0548	0.0081	0.0607	0.0391	0.0659	0.0077	0.2283

According to the results shown in Table 1, complexity values vary according to the materials given across all subjects. In particular, we observe that all subjects show high lexical diversity (TTR mean > 0.85) and readability (ARI mean ≈ 1.0), with AI and SEMM showing high word entropy ($H_w \approx 0.978$) but low sentence entropy ($H_s < 0.06$), indicating diverse vocabulary within relatively uniform sentence structures. PR texts demonstrate slightly lower lexical diversity and higher variability in sentence complexity (H_s Std = 0.2273). SEMMs documents have a high proportion of domain-specific words (RIW mean = 0.8660), reflecting its technical nature. Overall, these results suggest that while all subjects contain complex and information-rich texts, differences in vocabulary specialization and sentence structure may influence readability and comprehension.

5 Conclusions and Future Works

In this paper, we introduce ASTRA, a software component designed to integrate large-scale retrieval of scholarly abstracts and academic documents with advanced text complexity indexes. The main contributions can be summarized as follows:

- Automated Data Acquisition: ASTRA incorporates a web scraping module that can query and extract metadata and abstracts from Google Scholar, allowing researchers to build domain-specific corpora without requiring manual collection or relying on specialized or commercial web scraper tools.
- Complexity Assessment Framework: ASTRA computes a wide range of linguistic and readability indices, including surface features, lexical diversity, and syntactic complexity. This allows for a multifaceted evaluation of abstracts and text documents.
- Cross-Disciplinary Applicability: By supporting the automated comparison of abstracts across domains, ASTRA provides insights into disciplinary variations in academic writing styles, readability, and accessibility.

Several directions remain open to extend the scope and impact of ASTRA, including multilingual expansion. The current implementation focuses primarily on abstracts and documents in both Spanish and English. As future work, we seek to incorporate multilingual processing capabilities, enabling comparative analyses in diverse linguistic contexts. Beyond surface-level and syntactic complexity, ASTRA could be extended with semantic similarity measures, discourse cohesion indices, and embedding-based representations to provide a deeper characterization of academic texts.

On the other hand, a systematic validation of ASTRA's complexity scores against expert judgments and educational benchmarks would strengthen its reliability for pedagogical applications (especially for ERS). Regarding scalability and API development, future work will include creating an open API and enhancing the handling of large-scale datasets to facilitate broader adoption by the research community. Finally, the integration of ASTRA into digital learning environments, writing support systems, and educational dashboards represents a promising avenue to translate research results into practical applications.

References

1. Alghamdi, A., Nilashi, M., Abumalloh, R.A., Ahmadi, H., Alrizq, M., Alyami, S.: Analysis of social data for accuracy improvement of collaborative filtering in MOOCs using text mining and deep learning techniques. Discov. Comput. **28**(1), 1–21 (2025)
2. Baturay, M.H.: An overview of the world of MOOCs. Procedia. Soc. Behav. Sci. **174**, 427–433 (2015)
3. Bradley, V.M.: Learning Management System (LMS) use with online instruction. Int. J. Technol. Edu. **4**(1), 68–92 (2021)
4. Chen, J., Dong, H., Wang, X., Feng, F., Wang, M., He, X.: Bias and debias in recommender system: A survey and future directions. ACM Trans. Inf. Sys. **41**(3), 1–39 (2023)
5. Cholewiak, S., Ipeirotis, P., Silva, V., Kannawadi, A.: scholarly (1.5.0). Zenodo. (2021). https://doi.org/10.5281/zenodo.5764802
6. Cocón, F., et al.: Web scraping: Uso de plataformas de extracción de datos aplicadas a un sitio web sobre profesiones en México. Revista Ibérica Sistemas e Tecnol. Inf. **52**, 61–73 (2023)
7. Da Silva, F.L., Slodkowski, B.K., Da Silva, K.K.A., Cazella, S.C.: A systematic literature review on educational recommender systems for teaching and learning: research trends, limitations and opportunities. Educ. Inf. Technol. **28**(3), 3289–3328 (2023)
8. Dobashi, K.: Real-Time Web Scraping for Analyzing Moodle Course Material Clickstream. In: 2021 19th International Conference on Information Technology Based Higher Education and Training (ITHET) pp. 1–10 (2021)
9. Dogucu, M., Çetinkaya-Rundel, M.: Web scraping in the statistics and data science curriculum: Challenges and opportunities. J. Statist. Data Sci. Edu. **29**(1), 112–122 (2021)
10. Haasz, G., Baracskai, Z.: Collaborative Knowledge Platform: when the learning route provides data for the Knowledge-based System. Knowl. Manag. Res. Pract. **20**(6), 925–934 (2022)
11. Khder, M.A.: Web scraping or web crawling: State of art, techniques, approaches and application. Int. J. Adv. Soft Comput. Its Appl., **13**(3) (2021)
12. Knöös, J., & Rääf, S.A.: Sentiment Analysis of MOOC learner reviews: What motivates learners to complete a course? (2021)
13. Lunn, S., Zhu, J., Ross, M.: Utilizing web scraping and natural language processing to better inform pedagogical practice. In: 2020 IEEE Frontiers in Education Conference (FIE). pp. 1–9 (2020). https://doi.org/10.1109/FIE44824.2020.9274270
14. Rivero, J., et al.: Web scraping para la centralización de cursos de extensión en universidades públicas argentinas. In: XXX Congreso Argentino de Ciencias de la Computación (CACIC). (2024)
15. Rojas-Simón, J., Ledeneva, Y., García-Hernández, R.A.: Selection of Content Measures for Evaluation of Text Summaries Using Genetic Algorithms. Computación y Sistemas **28**(4), 2261–2278 (2024)
16. Rojas-Simón, J., Ledeneva, Y., Neri-Mendoza, V., García-Hernández, R.A., Gil-García, A.A., García-Baron, A.: Dataset Construction for Personalized Academic Recommendations: Methodology and challenges. In: 1st Conference on CSNLP. Mexico City, Mexico. pp. 1–12 (2025)
17. Romero, C., Ventura, S.: Educational data mining and learning analytics: an updated survey. WIREs Data Min. Knowl. Discov. **10**(3), 1–21 (2020)

18. Norcross, J.S., Schuessler, J.H., Jones, D.G.: Web scraping to inform curriculum decisions. J. Higher Edu. Theo. Pract., **20**(10), pp. 100–112 (2020). https://doi.org/10.33423/jhetp.v20i10.3655

Validation of Short Answers for Open Questions from the FairytaleQA-Sp Corpus

Margarita Aviña-Corral(✉), Delia Irazú Hernández-Farías, Aurelio López-López, Manuel Montes-y-Gómez, and Luis Villaseñor-Pineda

Coordinación de Ciencias Computacionales, Instituto Nacional de Astrofísica, Óptica y Electrónica (INAOE), Luis Enrique Erro No. 1, Tonantzintla, Puebla C.P. 72840, Mexico
{mavina,dirazuhf,allopez,mmontesg,villasen}@inaoep.mx
https://www.inaoep.mx/

Abstract. Short-response grading is a central issue in reading comprehension evaluation. In this regard, this work first introduces an enriched dataset with both human-written and artificial intelligence–generated responses, and then compares transformer-based models, similarity metrics, and large language models for automatic validation of open-ended responses. The fine-tuned RoBERTa binary classifier achieved competitive performance, but DeepSeek-V3 outperformed all models, including ChatGPT-4o. A Sentence Transformer model trained with contrastive learning showed limitations in detecting incorrect answers. We discuss the strengths and weaknesses of each approach and propose hybrid models that are better aligned with pedagogical goals.

Keywords: automatic validation · open-ended responses · contrastive learning · binary classification · FairytaleQA-sp

1 Introduction

The expansion of online learning platforms, accelerated by the pandemic, has increased the demand for automatic tools to analyze and evaluate open-ended responses. Although such responses enable richer expression and foster cognitive skills, their automatic analysis remains difficult due to linguistic variability, whereas manual review is costly, biased, and not scalable.

Several approaches have been proposed for the automatic evaluation of open-ended responses, ranging from knowledge-based systems using ontologies [1], to predictive models that infer response quality [2], and more recently to semantic approaches based on Transformer architectures [3,4].

The objective of this work is to compare traditional, similarity-based, and neural approaches to short-answer validation in Spanish. By examining their respective strengths and limitations, it provides the foundation for future hybrid frameworks that integrate their complementary capabilities. It also introduces an enriched dataset with both human-written and artificial intelligence–generated

L. Martínez-Villaseñor et al. (Eds.): MICAI 2025, LNAI 16265, pp. 50–60, 2026.
https://doi.org/10.1007/978-3-032-17933-3_6

responses, which increases lexical variability and enables a more rigorous evaluation. The value of the study lies in linking technical effectiveness with the pedagogical goals of reading comprehension, thus guiding research toward more effective and educationally relevant models.

This paper is organized as follows. Section 2 describes the dataset used and its extension. The applied methodology and experimental design are included in Sect. 3. The main results are detailed in Sect. 4, and the conclusion is presented in Sect. 5, along with ideas for future work.

2 Dataset and Contrastive Example Generation

2.1 The FairytaleQA-Sp Corpus

The FairytaleQA-sp [5] dataset, originally developed in English [6] by education experts and subsequently automatically translated into Spanish using DeepL, is publicly available on the HuggingFace platform [7]. It contains children's stories and some related annotated questions that assess multiple dimensions of reading comprehension.

In the Spanish version, the corpus contains 278 stories and 10,580 question–answer pairs. Table 1 presents some general statistics of the dataset, while Table 2 shows a sample instance from the corpus.

Table 1. Split of the FairytaleQA-sp dataset (translated into Spanish)

Data type	Training	Validation	Test	Total
Stories	232	23	23	278
Question–answer pairs	8548	1025	1007	10 580

Table 2. Example instance from the FairytaleQA-sp dataset

Question	<Quién era la vieja Mujer Sapo? *(Who was the old Toad Woman?)*
Gold answer	Una ladrona de niños. *(A child thief.)*
Story passage (excerpt)	Salieron al bosque y, al caer la tarde, ... Ella le dijo que era su verdadera madre y que ***la vieja Mujer Sapo, ladrona de niños y bruja,*** se lo había robado..." *(They went out into the forest and, as evening fell, ... She told him that she was his real mother and that* ***the old Toad Woman, a child thief and witch,*** *had stolen him...)*

Contrastive Example Generation for Training. Contrastive examples were generated using the DeepSeek-V3 Application Programming Interface (API) to build the training dataset. Table 3 shows representative responses for a single corpus instance. The generated variants were divided in two categories: *correct responses*, consisting of paraphrases of the reference answer and reformulations with alternative syntactic structures; and *incorrect responses*, which either contradicted the reference answer or were contextually plausible but incorrect. For each instance, five responses of each subtype were produced, resulting in ten correct and ten incorrect responses. Overall, the models were trained with 85,480 correct pairs and an equal number of incorrect pairs.

Table 3. Examples of generated responses by category for the training set, corresponding to the reference answer "Una ladrona de niños. *(A child thief.)*" shown in Table 2

Correct - Paraphrase	Correct - Different Structure
1. - Una secuestradora de pequeños. *(A kidnapper of little ones.)*	1. - La anciana Mujer Sapo era una bruja que robaba niños para quedárselos. (*The old Toad Woman was a witch who stole children to keep them.*)
...	...
5. - Una delincuente que sustraía menores. *(A criminal who abducted minors.)*	5. - Su verdadera naturaleza era la de una usurpadora que se llevaba a los niños para criarlos como suyos. *(Her true nature was that of an usurper who took the children to raise them as her own.)*
Incorrect - Contradictory	**Incorrect – Contextually Plausible**
1. - La benefactora del pueblo que cuidaba a los huérfanos. *(The benefactor of the village who cared for the orphans.)*	1. - La anciana que cuidaba del joven desde su infancia. *(The old woman who had cared for the young man since his childhood.)*
...	...
5. - La verdadera madre del joven, que lo crió desde pequeño. *(The young man's real mother, who raised him since he was little.)*	5. - La encargada de distribuir la comida entre los habitantes del bosque. *(The person in charge of distributing the food among the forest dwellers.)*

2.2 Evaluation Dataset

The objective is to test the models with real and challenging responses, in order to verify whether they are capable of learning patterns from the diversity of correct and incorrect answers that can be transferred to more realistic data. Although the `FairytaleQA-sp` corpus includes a predefined training split, as well as test and validation partitions, these only contain pairs of questions and model answers, but not a variety of correct and incorrect responses. For this reason, the evaluation set was collected separately. The evaluation set consisted of 390 unique responses from students of primary and secondary education level, collected using Google Forms and associated with nine stories from the `FairyTaleQA-sp` corpus. After removing duplicate responses to the same question, two raters annotated the majority of responses as *Correct*, resolving any disagreements through consensus. However, some methods tended to classify most responses as correct, revealing a limited capacity to discriminate between answers.

Table 4. Examples of additional responses used to expand the test set

Correct variant (Human-written)	Incorrect variant (AI-augmented with ChatGPT-4o)
Question: <Qué vio el viejo monje budista cuando había recorrido unos kilómetros? *(What did the old Buddhist monk see after he had walked a few kilometers?)* **Gold answer:** A una muchacha vestida con un abrigo rojo, descalza y con el pelo alborotado, que corría tan deprisa como el viento. *(A young woman dressed in a red coat, barefoot and with disheveled hair, who was running as fast as the wind.)* **Human-written:** Una mujer vestida de rojo que corría con gran rapidez, como el viento. *(A woman dressed in red who was running very fast, like the wind.)*	**Question:** <Qué construyó el gallo? *(What did the rooster build?)* **Gold answer:** Un hermoso carruaje con cuatro ruedas rojas. *(A beautiful carriage with four red wheels.)* **AI-augmented:** Un nido adornado con plumas de colores brillantes. *(A nest decorated with brightly colored feathers.)*

Table 5. Distribution of the expanded test set

Source	Count	%	Description
Students	390	34.57	Collected from primary and secondary level students.
Additional correct	134	11.88	Manually written to add lexical and structural variation.
Generated incorrect	604	53.55	Generated by `ChatGPT-4o`.
Total	**1128**	**100**	

To address this limitation, we expanded the dataset by adding: (1) manually written correct responses that employed alternative syntactic structures and vocabulary; and (2) incorrect responses automatically generated using `ChatGPT-4o`, designed to remain grammatically coherent while being inconsistent with the expected answer and narrative. This augmentation gave more challenging examples, enabling a more rigorous evaluation of model generalization (see Table 4).

Table 5 summarizes the overall dataset distribution, while Tables 6 and 7 present the proportions of Correct and Incorrect responses across both ***Human-written*** and ***AI-augmented*** subsets.

Table 6. Distribution of classes in the Human-written set

Class	Count	%
Correct	406	77.48
Incorrect	118	22.52
Total	**524**	**100**

Table 7. Distribution of classes in the AI-augmented set

Class	Count	%
Correct	406	35.99
Incorrect	722	64.01
Total	**1128**	**100**

3 Methodology and Experimental Design

The study compares two main approaches for response evaluation: a contrastive learning model and a binary classifier, both trained on the corpus augmented with generated contrastive responses. To benchmark their performance, the study also includes several baseline methods with lexical and semantic similarity metrics, textual entailment models, and LLMs without fine-tuning.

All methods were evaluated on a common test set using standard metrics: accuracy, precision, recall, and F1 score. The evaluation considered both human-written and AI-augmented subsets, allowing for a robust assessment across different levels of response complexity. This design also allowed the analysis of model efficacy under conditions of class imbalance, ensuring a more comprehensive evaluation of each method's generalization capabilities.

3.1 Contrastive Learning

Response validation is formulated as a comparison task, where the model learns to minimize the distance between representations of responses from the same category and maximize the distance between those from different categories. For each instance, triplets are constructed in the form of (*anchor, positive, negative*): the *anchor* is the gold answer, the *positive* a valid variant, and the *negative* an incorrect response. To enhance variability and improve training robustness, all combinations of positive and negative samples for each anchor are generated.

Each component is encoded using a pretrained multilingual Sentence Transformer [8,9], which is kept *frozen* during training. The resulting *mean-pooled* sentence embeddings are passed through a lightweight projection layer, which is trained to map them into a shared comparison space suitable for contrastive learning.

The model is then trained using contrastive learning with a margin-based *triplet loss* [10], minimizing the *anchor positive* distance while maximizing the *anchor negative* one. Thus, correct responses cluster around the *anchor*, while incorrect ones are pushed farther in the representation space.

3.2 Binary Classification

A RoBERTa-based model [11] was fine-tuned for binary classification of open-ended responses. The input is a pair of texts (the reference answer and a candidate response, correct or incorrect) processed jointly to obtain a global representation, which feeds a binary classification layer. Training optimized both encoder and classifier with *CrossEntropy* loss, penalizing high-confidence errors. The model outputs a binary label indicating whether the candidate matches the reference.

3.3 Baseline and Reference Methods

As a complementary reference, pretrained metrics and models that measure coherence and semantic similarity without additional training were evaluated, including n-gram-based metrics (BLEU [12], ROUGE [13]), inference-based methods [14], and large language models (LLMs). BLEU was computed as BLEU-4 with equal weights for 1–4 g precisions (0.25 each), capturing surface-level n-gram precision but disregarding synonyms and deeper semantics. ROUGE was reported in its ROUGE-1, ROUGE-2, and ROUGE-L variants, emphasizing recall over unigram, bigram, and subsequence matches.

Inference-based methods, implemented through XLM-RoBERTa, a natural language inference (NLI) model, allow for deeper validation through logical reasoning, particularly by assessing entailment or contradiction between the answer to be evaluated and the reference answer. On the other hand, LLMs such as DeepSeek and GPT evaluate responses within a full semantic context, offering adaptability at the cost of reduced transparency. Both were prompted in a *zero-shot* setting, using only the reference answer and the candidate response, and instructed to act as expert evaluators, returning a label *("Correct" or "Incorrect")* with a brief explanation. DeepSeek was accessed through its API with a low temperature (0.3) for consistency, while GPT was used via the web interface, which required setting a decision threshold; tests with 0.7 and 0.4 showed that the latter produced better results and is reported here.

4 Results

To evaluate efficacy, all approaches were tested on the same set. Adding the passage or question as extra context consistently reduced performance, so models were ultimately trained only with the reference answer and contrastive examples. For approaches that do not output a discrete label, such as lexical or semantic similarity metrics, empirical thresholds were defined to determine the validity of the answers.

Figure 1 presents the validation results for both test sets (***Human-written*** and ***AI-augmented***), comparing the models against reference metrics and techniques. DeepSeek-V3 achieved the highest F1-score (0.90), followed by the Binary Classifier based on RoBERTa and, in third place, a hybrid model that combines inference with semantic similarity, demonstrating that integrating different approaches can enhance robustness. The contrastive learning model with a threshold of 0.6 ranked fourth; however, when evaluated with a null threshold, its performance dropped to ninth out of eleven positions, highlighting how threshold selection can significantly influence the results.

RoBERTa-based binary classifier showed competitive performance, achieving a more balanced prediction of the *"Correct"* and *"Incorrect"* classes across both test sets. Conversely, the contrastive learning model tended to predict the *"Correct"* class, likely due to the difficulty of distinguishing semantically similar terms (e.g., *"Cat"* vs. *"duck"*) that are not interchangeable in the context of answers.

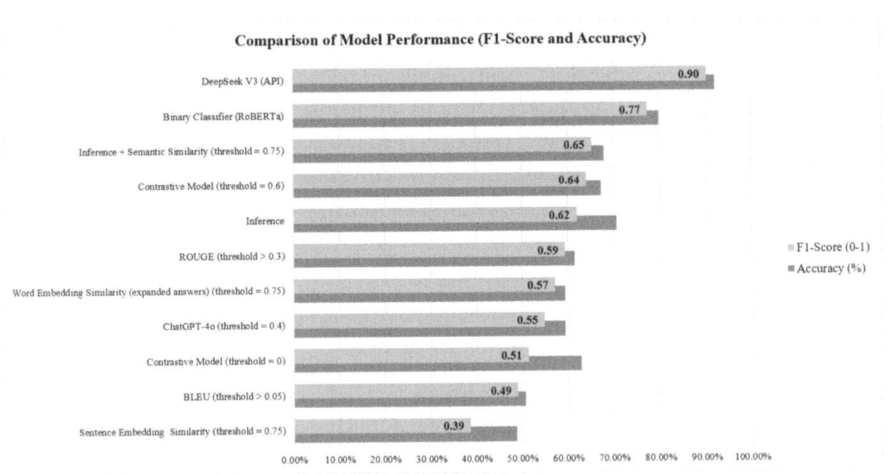

Fig. 1. Average F1-score and accuracy across the two test sets.

On the *Human-written* set, the binary classifier reached 75% accuracy and 0.77 macro F1, though with bias toward the *"Incorrect"* class and challenges in identifying short or ambiguous correct answers. On the *AI-augmented* set—more balanced and diverse—performance improved to 84.66% accuracy, with a better trade-off between precision and recall, although this gain may have been influenced by the relative ease of detecting artificially generated incorrect responses.

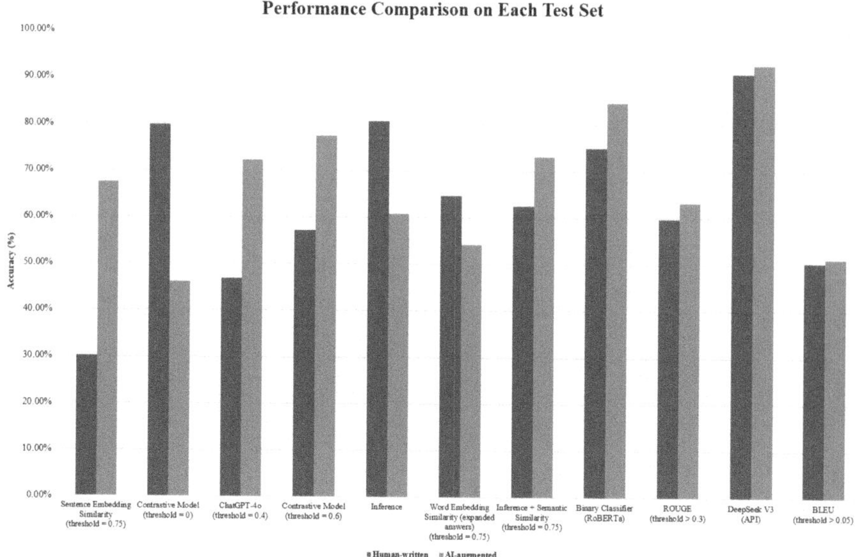

Fig. 2. Efficacy of the evaluated methods across both test sets.

The original test set, dominated by *"Correct"* responses, was expanded with manually written correct answers and AI-generated incorrect ones. This introduced greater lexical and semantic variability, allowing a more rigorous evaluation of the models' ability to discriminate and generalize across the *Human-written* and *AI-augmented* scenarios. Figure 2 shows a comparison of the efficacy of different methods on both test sets. Models with higher variability between the two sets are those based on Sentence Transformer, such as cosine similarity without adjustment and fine-tuning with contrastive training. In contrast, traditional metrics such as **BLEU**, **ROUGE**, and the **DeepSeek-V3** model produced more consistent results across both subsets.

Figure 3 shows the efficacy of the models when predicting the *"Correct"* and *"Incorrect"* classes. The contrastive model with a null threshold tends to overestimate correct answers, while the method based on **cosine similarity** with Sentence Transformer exhibits the opposite behavior, indicating that fine-tuning modified the semantic distribution in a not always favorable way. This outcome may be due to both the lexical similarity between answers and the training method, and it was also influenced by the **similarity threshold** defined in the results table.

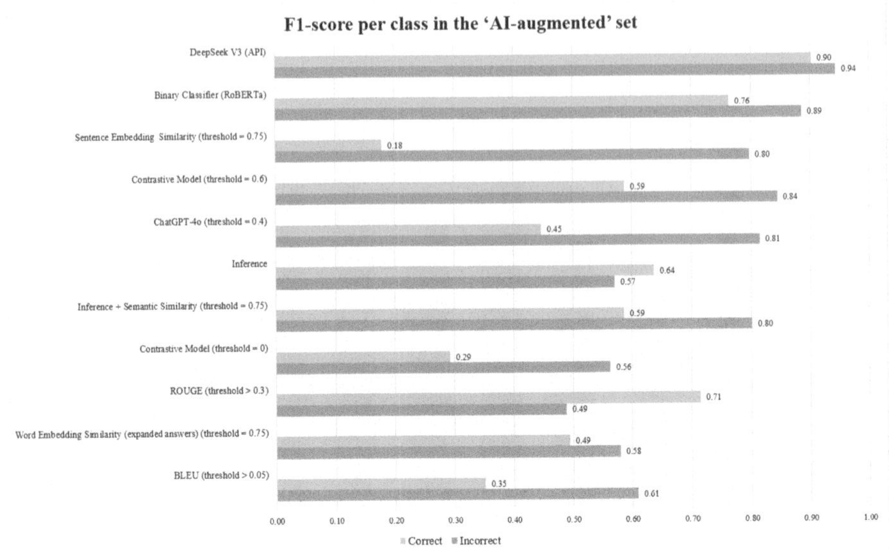

Fig. 3. F1-score for predicting each class in the *AI-augmented* test set.

5 Conclusions and Future Work

In this work, we compared different approaches for the automatic validation of open-ended answers in Spanish. Two methods based on transformer models fine-tuned with training data were evaluated: a supervised binary classifier based on RoBERTa and a contrastive model trained with *TripletMarginLoss* using a Sentence Transformer. The former showed consistent overall performance but struggled to recognize correct answers expressed with diverse phrasing. The latter demonstrated greater semantic flexibility, though with a tendency to over-classify answers as correct.

This analysis suggests that the contrastive learning approach, while promising due to its capacity for generalization and reusability of representations, requires finer adjustments to prevent over-classification of the correct class in real educational environments.

As future work, we propose the following: a) combine both approaches to build a more robust system, leveraging the strengths of each while overcoming their limitations; b) incorporate features that enhance class discrimination and interpretability; c) expand the dataset with higher linguistic variability and manual annotations; d) evaluate generalization in different levels of education and types of school tasks.

These results open new possibilities for the development of more flexible automatic evaluation tools tailored to the Spanish language, which are particularly valuable in educational settings where specialized resources remain scarce.

Acknowledgements. The first author gratefully acknowledges the support provided by a scholarship from the Secretaría de Innovación, Ciencia y Tecnología (Secihti), under Currículum Vitae Único (CVU) No. 1199450, which made this research possible. The authors also wish to thank the Instituto Nacional de Astrofísica, Óptica y Electrónica (INAOE) for fostering an excellent academic environment and for its institutional support throughout this work. Partial support from the Sistema Nacional de Investigadoras e Investigadores (SNII) is also acknowledged, as well as the valuable feedback and collaboration of the Computational Sciences Coordination team during the experimental analysis and manuscript review stages.

References

1. Arbaaeen, A., Omar, N., Omar, N., Albared, M.: An ontology-based approach for short answer assessment. Indonesian J. Elect.Eng. Comput. Sci. **24**(1), 120–127 (2021)
2. Jamil, N., Saeed, M., Qamar, U.: Deep learning-based predictive model for automatic short answer grading. Expert Syst. Appl. **226**, 120230 (2023)
3. Vaswani, A., Shazeer, N., Parmar, N., et al.: Attention is all you need. In: Advances in Neural Information Processing Systems (NeurIPS), vol. 30 (2017)
4. Nassiri, A., Frasson, C.: A transformer-based approach for short answer grading. In: International Conference on Artificial Intelligence in Education, pp. 165–170. Springer, Cham (2022)
5. Leite, B., Osório, T.F., Cardoso, H.L.: FairytaleQA Translated: Enabling Educational Question and Answer Generation in Less-Resourced Languages. In: Ferreira Mello, R., et al. (eds.) Technology Enhanced Learning for Inclusive and Equitable Quality Education, pp. 222–236. Springer, Cham (2024)
6. Xu, Y., et al.: Fantastic Questions and Where to Find Them: FairytaleQA – An Authentic Dataset for Narrative Comprehension. In: Proceedings of the 60th Annual Meeting of the Association for Computational Linguistics (ACL), pp. 447–460. Dublin (2022). https://aclanthology.org/2022.acl-long.34
7. Leite, B.: FairytaleQA Translated Spanish Dataset. HuggingFace Datasets. Available at: https://huggingface.co/datasets/benjleite/FairytaleQA-translated-spanish (2024)
8. Devlin, J., Chang, M.-W., Lee, K., Toutanova, K.: BERT: Pre-training of deep bidirectional transformers for language understanding. In: Proceedings of the 2019 Conference of the North American Chapter of the Association for Computational Linguistics (NAACL), pp. 4171–4186 (2019)
9. Reimers, N., Gurevych, I.: Sentence-BERT: Sentence embeddings using Siamese BERT-networks. In: Proceedings of the 2019 Conference on Empirical Methods in Natural Language Processing (EMNLP), pp. 3982–3992 (2019)
10. Hadsell, R., Chopra, S., LeCun, Y.: Dimensionality reduction by learning an invariant mapping. In: 2006 IEEE Computer Society Conference on Computer Vision and Pattern Recognition (CVPR), vol. 2, pp. 1735–1742. IEEE (2006)
11. Liu, Y., Ott, M., Goyal, N., et al.: RoBERTa: A robustly optimized BERT pretraining approach. *arXiv preprint* arXiv:1907.11692 (2019)
12. Papineni, K., Roukos, S., Ward, T., Zhu, W.-J.: BLEU: a method for automatic evaluation of machine translation. In: Proceedings of the 40th Annual Meeting of the Association for Computational Linguistics (ACL), pp. 311–318 (2002)

13. Lin, C.-Y.: ROUGE: A package for automatic evaluation of summaries. In: Text Summarization Branches Out: Proceedings of the ACL-04 Workshop, vol. 8, pp. 74–81 (2004)
14. Menli, D., Garcia-Sancho, C., Peñas, A.: Combining entailment and text similarity for open response assessment. In: Proceedings of the 18th Workshop on Innovative Use of NLP for Building Educational Applications (BEA 2023), pp. 263–273 (2023)

Assessing Writing Progress in Engineering Students Through Lexical Richness and Argumentation Approach

Chantal Mendivil Navarro[1], Samuel González-López[1](✉), Jesús Miguel García-Gorrostieta[2], Aurelio López-López[4], Francisca Cecilia Encinas Orozco[3], and Jesús Raul Cruz Rentería[1]

[1] Tecnológico Nacional de México, Campus Nogales, Nogales, Mexico
samuelgonzalezlopez@gmail.com
[2] Universidad de la Sierra, Sonora, Mexico
[3] Universidad de Sonora, Sonora, Mexico
[4] Instituto Nacional de Astrofísica, Óptica y Electrónica, Puebla, Mexico

Abstract. Academic writing remains a significant challenge for many university students, especially in engineering programs, where technical mastery often takes priority over communicative skills. Consequently, students frequently struggle to organize ideas, construct coherent arguments, and employ formal language appropriately. This study evaluates engineering students' writing progress across two key dimensions: lexical richness and argumentative structure. Analyzing 69 documents from one semester, it applies Natural Language Processing (NLP) techniques to measure lexical variety, density, and sophistication, and uses a Conditional Random Fields (CRF)-based sequence-labeling model to identify premises and conclusions. Plagiarism checks and AI-generated text detection ensured authenticity. Results show notable improvements in vocabulary and argumentative clarity in some groups, with variations linked to pedagogical methods and the growing influence of generative AI. Overall, the study highlights the potential of NLP tools to provide a comprehensive assessment of academic writing in engineering education.

Keywords: Academic Writing · Engineering Education · Lexical Richness · Argumentation · Natural Language Processing (NLP)

1 Introduction

Academic writing presents a continuous challenge for university students, particularly in engineering programs, where technical knowledge often takes precedence over communicative competencies. The study [1] highlights that difficulties in organizing ideas, constructing clear arguments, and employing formal language are common obstacles that diminish the quality of written texts. Therefore, it is necessary to systematically examine both vocabulary use and the argumentative structure in student work.

L. Martínez-Villaseñor et al. (Eds.): MICAI 2025, LNAI 16265, pp. 61–69, 2026.
https://doi.org/10.1007/978-3-032-17933-3_7

The literature indicates that lexical variety, density, and sophistication are useful indicators for identifying improvements in research drafts [2]. However, [3] notes that higher lexical richness does not necessarily ensure better argumentative quality, while [4] emphasizes that academic genre significantly influences lexical patterns in texts.

Regarding argumentation, [5] highlights the importance of teaching specific strategies to develop sound reasoning. Complementarily, [6] demonstrates that Natural Language Processing (NLP) techniques can automatically identify premises and conclusions. Additionally, [7] develops an automatic assessment system for argumentation in final project reports, integrated into Moodle via the LTI standard, which identifies argumentative paragraphs, estimates the level of argumentation, and provides feedback on key sections.

This study analyzes the evolution of writing and argumentation in students over a semester, based on 69 documents from three courses—Research Workshop, Research Workshop II, and Project Formulation—comparing initial and final submissions to assess progress in lexical richness and argument construction, while considering the potential impact of emerging digital tools. Finally, Turnitin and isgen.ai were employed to detect plagiarism and potentially AI-generated content, ensuring that the analysis reflected students' authentic work [8].

2 Methodology

Students' writing and argumentative skills were systematically analyzed by quantifying lexical richness with RetmeePro, detecting argumentative structures using a CRF model, and assessing plagiarism and AI-generated content through Turnitin and isgen.ai, with a comparative examination of initial and final submissions to determine the progression of these competencies over the semester.

2.1 Dataset

In this study, a total of 69 documents produced by students from three academic groups corresponding to the aforementioned courses were collected during the JanuaryJune 2025 semester. These specific courses were selected because they provide the most evident opportunities for students to practice their writing and argumentation skills. For writing, the analysis focused on the lexical richness of the texts, considering the variety, sophistication, and density of the vocabulary used. With respect to argumentation, the construction of arguments was evaluated by observing the number of premises and conclusions present in the assignments. The texts were produced by students of industrial engineering, mechanical engineering and electronic engineering, thereby ensuring a diverse and representative sample from different areas within engineering education.

Group A was organized into six teams, leading to the development of six preliminary documents and six final documents.

For Group S, it should be acknowledged that, due to specific limitations, access to the remaining seven documents was not possible. Consequently, these materials were excluded from the final analysis.

Table 1. Data collection

Section	Group A	Group R	Group S
Subject	Research workshop II	Project formulation	Research workshop
Field of study	Mechatronics Eng.	Mechatronics Eng. Electronic Eng.	Industrial Eng.
No. of students	18	22	10
No. of preliminary projects	6	22	10
No. of final projects	6	22	3

2.2 Lexical Richness

After compiling the documents from the three groups, the analysis examined the sections on hypotheses, justification, objectives, problem statement, research questions, methodology, and conclusion. The evaluation was carried out with the RetmeePro[1] application, which applies three metrics: lexical variety, lexical density, and lexical sophistication. These measures capture the lexical richness of the vocabulary used in the texts.

Lexical variety refers to the breadth of vocabulary used, reflecting the author's ability to employ different terms appropriately. Lexical density indicates the proportion of meaningful words relative to the total text, highlighting both the accuracy and the informational richness of the content. Lexical sophistication, in turn, evaluates the use of more complex or less frequent words compared to the most common words in Spanish, based on the standards established by the Royal Spanish Academy.

The analysis covered both initial and final documents, allowing calculation of the percentages for each indicator.

2.3 Argumentation

For the extraction of argumentative components (e.g., premises and conclusions) from Spanish academic texts, we employed the sequence labeling model proposed by [6], based on a Conditional Random Fields (CRF) framework. The model utilizes the IOB tagging scheme to classify each token as the beginning (B) or inside (I) of a premise or conclusion, or outside (O) any component. This approach allows the CRF to effectively capture contextual dependencies between tokens, offering a significant advantage over models that treat words in isolation. To maximize predictive accuracy, the model integrates a comprehensive set of handcrafted linguistic features. These include lexical lemmatization, syntactic (part-of-speech tags), and morphological descriptors. The feature set is further enriched with dependency relations, named entity recognition (NER) tags, sentiment values, and structural indicators such as token position. Lowercasing, suffix analysis, and capitalization patterns are also incorporated. Most

[1] https://retmeepro.turet.com.mx/.

features were extracted using the Stanza library, and the model was implemented in sklearn-crfsuite, optimized with the L-BFGS algorithm. Hyperparameter tuning was performed on regularization parameters and a context window size of 4. The model achieved a macro F1-score of 0.5828 and an accuracy of 0.6455. These results demonstrate the strong performance of traditional, feature-rich CRF models in scenarios with limited annotated data. For Argumentation, only the sections containing the most text and which should contain arguments and premises were used: conclusion, justification, and problem statement.

2.4 Plagiarism Detection and Use of AI Tools

To analyze the 69 documents, we utilized tools to assess originality and authorship. Turnitin[2] was employed to measure similarity and detect potential plagiarism, while isgen.ai[3] estimated the proportion of AI-generated content. Certain sections exhibited high similarity or AI-generated text, indicating diminished originality. The combined use of both tools allowed for more accurate interpretation, ensuring that the analysis of lexical richness and argumentation genuinely reflected students' skills.

2.5 Statistical Comparative Analysis

This study employed a descriptive-comparative approach to examine the evolution of lexical richness and argumentation in students' written work across different engineering programs, focusing on the beginning and end of the semester. Group differences (A, R, and S) were analyzed using box plots, while potential external factors, such as the use of digital tools and large language models (LLMs), were also considered.

3 Discussions and Results

This section reports the comparative outcomes for the evaluated dimensions—Lexical Richness, Argumentation, Plagiarism Detection, and AI-generated Text Detection—across the student groups.

Lexical Richness. Table 2 shows the results for each section of the students' documents. For instance, in the Hypothesis section, Group A scored 62% in lexical richness at the beginning of the semester and 74% at the end. In some sections the value is 0%, which indicates that no text was written in that part at either the beginning or the end. Overall, the highest lexical richness is found in the Hypothesis and Conclusions sections, both reaching values above 70% by the end of the semester.

[2] https://www.turnitin.com.mx.

[3] https://isgen.ai/es.

Table 2. Lexical Richness per Section

Section	Group A	Group R	Group S
Hypothesis	62% 74%	69% 68%	75% 75%
Justification	57.95% 71.79%	68.74% 66.44%	47.27% 37.92%
Objective	50.01% 47.40%	71.57% 71.46%	70.05% 66.67%
Problem statement	11.16% 60.97%	67% 67.12%	49% 70%
Research questions	0% 44.61%	0% 0%	0% 0%
Methodology	12.01% 71.29%	0% 0%	25.65% 55.99%
Conclusion	35.90% 71.06%	0% 70.24%	23.73% 0%

Figure 1 shows a comparative boxplot of Lexical Richness for three student groups (A, R, and S), with results from the Beginning and End of the semester. The vertical axis gives percentage values of performance, and the horizontal axis separates the groups. From the figure, we can note the following:

- In Group A, the median increased by more than 15%, while variability narrowed toward the end of the semester. Together, these changes suggest a consistent improvement in lexical richness. This may be related to stronger teaching practices, although the influence of digital tools and LLMs as writing supports cannot be ruled out.
- In Group R, the values remain fairly stable from Beginning to End, with only a small rise in the median (about 2%). This suggests consistent performance but little overall progress. The limited change may be linked to the disciplinary orientation of the program, or perhaps to a less intensive use of LLMs compared to other groups.
- In Group S, the median rises by about 10%, but the wider dispersion shows that progress was uneven across students. This variation may be linked to differences in student and teacher profiles, as well as to the unequal use of tools such as LLMs to support writing.

Although all groups come from engineering programs, factors such as pedagogy (teacher and methodology), disciplinary differences, and the emerging use of generative AI tools likely shaped the evolution of lexical richness. In this study, we examine lexical richness and argumentative development in relation to the use of AI tools.

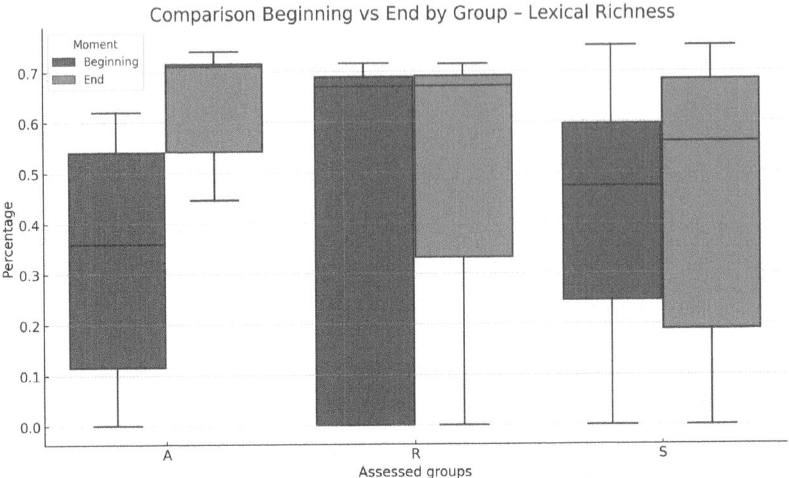

Fig. 1. Lexical Richness results by groups: A, R, S

Argumentation. Table 3 provides an analysis of the argumentative structure in the academic papers of three groups of engineering students (A, R, and S). Three sections were evaluated—Justification, Problem Statement, and Conclusion—considering both premises and conclusions. Each cell reports two values: the first refers to the initial submissions, and the second to the final versions. The group A shows steady and balanced progress in incorporating premises and conclusions in all sections, demonstrating sustained improvement in argumentation skills. The Group R begins with an appropriate use of premises, but shows a significant decline in the generation of conclusions, indicating a certain imbalance in their arguments. Finally, the Group S demonstrates limited ability in developing arguments, particularly in the Conclusion section, where no argumentative development is observed.

Figure 2 presents a boxplot of the distribution of premises and conclusions in the argumentative texts produced by engineering students. This comparison highlights meaningful distinctions in students' argumentative performance across groups. The variation in medians and interquartile ranges indicates that the groups did not progress uniformly, which may stem from differences in academic preparation and instructional focus. Most groups show an upward shift in their End distributions compared to the Beginning, suggesting that students produced more premises and conclusions as the semester advanced. Such improvement likely reflects the cumulative effect of sustained writing practice and targeted pedagogical interventions. However, the wide interquartile ranges and several outliers point to considerable within-group variability: while some students developed higher argumentative density and structure, others demonstrated limited progress. These findings suggest that instructional methods may benefit certain learners more effectively than others, underscoring the need for differentiated support in argumentation-based writing. The heterogeneous distributions across

Table 3. Argumentation

Section	Grupo A	Grupo R	Grupo S
Justification (Premise)	9 38	85 100	23 30
Justification (Conclusion)	4 14	53 30	3 14
Problem statement (Premise)	10 28	82 92	19 27
Problem statement (Conclusion)	3 6	34 30	6 21
Conclusion (Premise)	13 32	35 116	0 0
Conclusion (Conclusion)	3 11	25 44	0 0

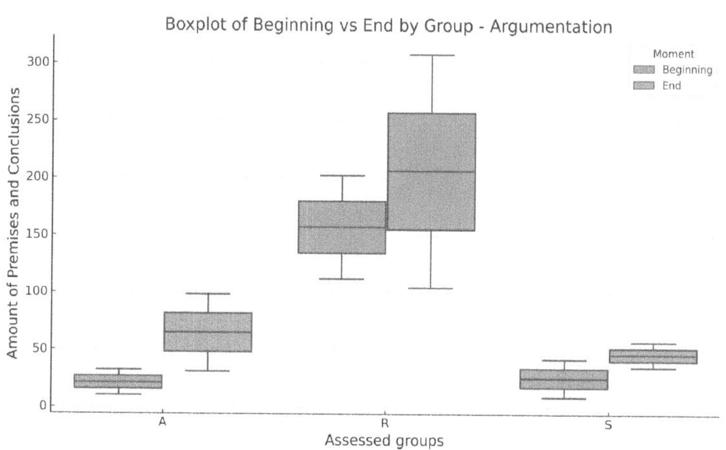

Fig. 2. Argumentation results by groups: A, R, S

groups highlight the influence of the instructional context and external factors, including the use of digital tools and large language models (LLMs), which could differentially impact student performance.

AI Generative Text and Plagiarism. Fig. 3 presents the values for Generative AI and Plagiarism across groups A, R, and S, distinguishing between the Beginning and End phases. The following section outlines the results and discusses potential explanations.

In Group A, AI use increased markedly (from 0.35 to 0.64), while plagiarism declined (from 0.37 to 0.21), suggesting that greater reliance on AI tools may have reduced traditional plagiarism. In Group R, AI use slightly decreased (from

0.33 to 0.29), whereas plagiarism almost doubled (from 0.21 to 0.44), showing an inverse pattern compared to Group A. In Group S, AI use dropped from 0.62 to 0.43, with plagiarism remaining stable (0.34 to 0.37). However, the limited number of submissions in this group restricts the reliability of the comparison. Overall, the results point to a possible link between AI adoption and students' approaches to academic integrity.

Finally, in group S, Generative AI use dropped from 0.62 at the Beginning to 0.43 at the End, pointing to lower reliance on these tools later in the semester. Plagiarism, however, stayed almost the same (0.34 to 0.37). It is worth noting that only three students turned in a final paper, so these figures should be read with caution.

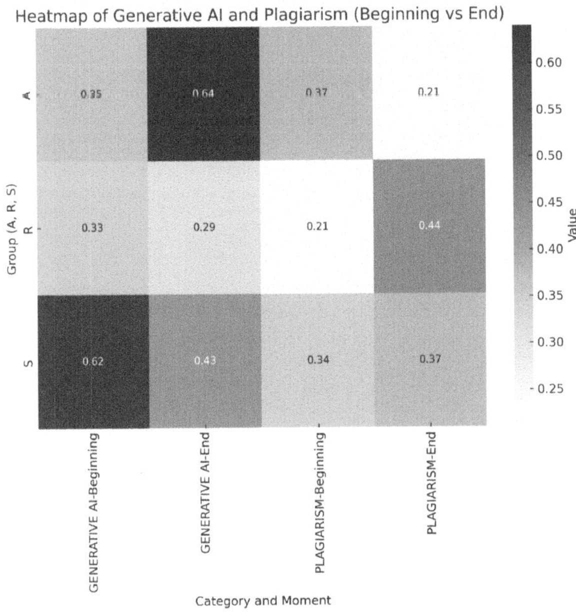

Fig. 3. Heatmap of Plagiarism and Generative AI

4 Conclusion

This study demonstrates that assessing the progress of engineering students' academic writing can be effectively approached through a combined analysis of lexical richness and argumentative structure, supported by Natural Language Processing (NLP) tools. The findings reveal significant improvements in vocabulary diversity and sophistication, as well as a gradual development in the ability to construct coherent and well-founded arguments, particularly in groups where pedagogical strategies encouraged continuous writing practice.

However, observed differences between groups underscore the influence of contextual factors, such as instructional methodology, specific disciplinary focus, and the emerging use of generative artificial intelligence tools.

The application of sequence modeling based on Conditional Random Fields (CRF) and lexical richness metrics enabled an objective and detailed assessment of written competence progress. Similarly, the integration of plagiarism detection and AI-generated content systems contributed to ensuring the authenticity of the analyzed corpus, thereby strengthening the validity of the results.

Collectively, the findings reaffirm the value of NLP technologies as complementary assessment instruments in engineering education, providing precise and comparable indicators of communicative skill development. Furthermore, they highlight the necessity of promoting academic literacy that balances technical mastery with the ability to argue and communicate ideas effectively, particularly in an educational context where the ethical and critical use of artificial intelligence constitutes an emerging challenge.

Acknowledgements. The author expresses sincere appreciation to the Tecnológico de México/ Campus Nogales for its valuable support and commitment to the development of this research project. The institution's academic environment and resources provided the foundation for achieving the objectives of this study.

References

1. Almarwani, Manal. (2020). Academic Writing: Challenges and Potential Solutions. Arab World English Journal. 6. 114-121. 10.24093/awej/call6.8. https://doi.org/10.24093/awej/call6.8
2. González-López, S., López-López, A.: Lexical analysis of student research drafts in computing. Comput. Appl. Eng. Educ., **23**, 638–644 (2015). https://doi.org/10.1002/cae.21638
3. Valdés-León, G.: Habilidades argumentativas y riqueza léxica en un curso de educación superior. Cogency, **13** (2021). https://doi.org/10.32995/cogency.v13i1.371
4. Heng, R., Pu, L., Liu, X.: The effects of genre on the lexical richness of argumentative and expository writing by Chinese EFL learners. Front. Psychol. **13**, 1082228 (2023). https://doi.org/10.3389/fpsyg.2022.1082228
5. Yáñez, R., Valdés-León, G.: Araya, Enseñanza de la argumentación escrita en estudiantes de ingeniería: Una experiencia de alfabetización académica. RECUS Revista Electrónica Cooperación Universidad Sociedad (2020). ISSN 2528-8075. 5. 13-23. https://doi.org/10.33936/recus.v5i2.2407
6. Garcia-Gorrostieta J.M., López-López, A., González-López, S., López-Monroy, A.P.: Improved argumentative paragraphs detection in academic theses supported with unit segmentation. J. Intell. Fuzzy Sys. **42**(5), 4481–4491. (2022). https://doi.org/10.3233/JIFS-219237
7. García-Gorrostieta J.M., López-López, A., González-López, S.: Automatic argument assessment of final project reports of computer engineering students. Comput. Appl. Eng. Educ. **26**, 1217–1226 (2018). https://doi.org/10.1002/cae.21996
8. Kim, J., Yu, S., Detrick, R. et al.: Exploring students' perspectives on Generative AI-assisted academic writing. Educ. Inf. Technol. **30**, 1265–1300 (2025). https://doi.org/10.1007/s10639-024-12878-7

Counting of Students in Educational Environments Using Pretrained Convolutional Neural Networks

Lizeth Meza Alegría[1], Jose Alberto Hernandez-Aguilar[1](✉), María Yasmín Hernández Pérez[2], Pedro Moreno Bernal[1], Outmane Oubram[3], Víctor Pacheco-Valencia[4], and Julio Cesar Ponce Gallegos[5]

[1] Facultad de Contaduría, Administración e Informática - UAEMor, Cuernavaca, Mexico
jose.hernandez@uaem.mx
[2] Centro Nacional de Investigación y Desarrollo Tecnológico - CENIDET, Cuernavaca, Mexico
[3] Facultad de Ciencias Química e Ingeniería - UAEMor, Cuernavaca, Mexico
[4] Centro de Investigación en Ingeniería y Ciencias Aplicadas - UAEMor, Cuernavaca, Mexico
[5] Universidad Autónoma de Aguascalientes, Cuernavaca, Mexico

Abstract. This research presents a model for detecting and counting students in educational environments. To achieve this, computer vision and computational neural networks (CNN) were used to analyze the "Classroom Monitoring Dataset." Data cleaning and image normalization were performed with a 640×640 resolution. An annotation process was performed using Roboflow. Different pretrained CNN models were tested using YOLOv8 to verify the accuracy of student identification and counting. The database was divided into 80% for training, 10% for testing, and 10% for evaluation. The goal was to develop a robust, efficient system that accurately counts students in a classroom in real time. This system was able to adapt to a variety of environmental and occlusion conditions, as well as classroom diversity, and provide reliable attendance metrics for use in educational strategies.

Keywords: Student counting · CNNs · YOLO

1 Introduction

Artificial Intelligence is a discipline in computer science that uses algorithms to solve specific problems (e.g., automating repetitive tasks, advanced data analysis, and improved customer service). The advantage of artificial intelligence is that it doesn't require programming a specific algorithm for every scenario, as it can be trained (Machine Learning) or learn on its own (Deep Learning). Variants of each exist, but they can be defined this way in a general sense [1].

L. Martínez-Villaseñor et al. (Eds.): MICAI 2025, LNAI 16265, pp. 70–81, 2026.
https://doi.org/10.1007/978-3-032-17933-3_8

Among the branches of artificial intelligence is Computer Vision. This field offers several benefits, including the ability to process images using strategic algorithms that achieve specific purposes. Some of the most widely used computer vision techniques include image classification, object detection, and object tracking [1].

Object detection is a highly useful tool that can accomplish various tasks and is the foundation for many others, for example, instance segmentation and image captioning [2].

Face detection is also part of computer vision. This technology is used, for example, in cameras to improve focus and to perform more relevant searches for people in images [3].

Although distinguishing an object in an image is a trivial task for a sighted human, the same is not true for a computer; for each object to be detected, different aspects and various models or approaches must be considered. This research is focused on head detection, which serves as the basis for people counting.

People counting is essential for assessing the duration of people's stay in a location, the frequency with which they enter or exit, identifying days with high or low foot traffic, and providing information on traffic patterns. All this data, in turn, gives us information about human behavior [4].

The proposed work focuses on implementing an algorithm that uses pretrained convolutional neural networks (CNNs) to identify and count students in classrooms from video camera images. The justification for this research lies in three key areas: resource management, security, and attendance analysis. Accurate identification and counting of students will facilitate the optimal planning and allocation of educational resources, enable the implementation of adequate security measures by monitoring space occupancy, and eventually allow for the automation of the attendance-taking process, reducing the administrative burden and increasing accuracy. It is worth noting that there are few works reported in the literature in which a presented model performs student counting in real-world environments and in real-time.

The main objective of this research is to implement a student counting algorithm in educational settings using pretrained convolutional neural networks to generate accurate occupancy statistics and support educational management.

The central hypothesis of this research is H1. The number of students in a classroom can be efficiently detected and counted using CNNs trained on video camera images. And the null hypothesis can be formulated as follows: H0. The number of students in a classroom cannot be efficiently detected and counted using CNNs trained on video camera images.

The contribution of this research work is an optimized approach for detecting students in images of real-world educational settings by identifying their heads. This approach utilizes the nano and large versions of the YOLOv8 models and explores the impact of preprocessing on performance through an exhaustive evaluation of the architectures.

The paper is organized as follows. In the **Introduction**, the context is presented, which will be part of this research work, discussing the detection and counting of students using artificial intelligence models. In the **Related Work** section, relevant research on person detection using computer vision techniques is explored, highlighting machine learning and deep learning, among others. This section also discusses YOLOv8, a pre-trained deep learning model. Subsequently, in the **Methodology** section, the image labeling process, the preprocessing techniques, and the hyperparameters used during model training are described, along with the configurations and evaluation metrics. Next, in the **Results and Discussion** section, the findings from evaluating different configurations of the YOLOv8 model are presented, analyzing the performance of each configuration and the impact of preprocessing techniques on detection accuracy. Finally, in **Conclusions and Future Work**, the main contributions of the research are summarized, and possible improvements and future applications are proposed to optimize and expand the model for automated monitoring systems in educational environments.

2 Related Work

People detection in indoor environments has been an active area of research, with various approaches and techniques developed to improve accuracy and efficiency. The underlying theory prioritizes improving the network's ability to correctly extract features, fine-tune details, and adapt to environmental dynamics.

Figure 1 shows the basic operation of a CNN to detect students. The input consists of images of students from educational facilities (e.g., classrooms, computer labs, other closed settings). These input layers are preprocessed (resized, rotated, normalized) and analyzed in the hidden layers (using convolutions to identify parts). These parts allow the identification of objects (students, chairs, windows), and finally, the class student is filtered from other classes.

In an educational context, there are reports of works that focus on detecting student behavior in the classroom. Han et al. propose combining two approaches, WAD-YOLOv8, and suggest the CA-C2f and 2DPE-MHA modules, along with dynamic sampling (Dysample), to enrich the receptive field, capture long-distance dependencies, and focus on relevant details, improving the detection of multiscale and occluded targets [6]. Similarly, Cao et al. present YOLO-AMM, which integrates an Adaptive Efficient Feature Fusion (AEFF) module to improve detail capture and a Multidimensional Feature Flow Network (MFFN) along with a Multiscale Detection and Fusion Head (MSPF-Head) to optimize feature correlation and multiscale adaptivity [5].

For person detection in complex interiors, Xu and Fu developed the CIHD-YOLO approach, a variant of YOLOv8s (small). This proposal combines Spatial Pyramid Pooling with Efficient Partial Self-Attention (SPPEPSA) to capture global dependencies and features at various scales. It even introduces the GSEAM and GSCConv modules into the neck network to mitigate the effects of variable lighting and reduce feature redundancy, improving feature extraction in low-light conditions [7]. These state-of-the-art studies share the use of YOLO, a tool known for its efficiency and detection capabilities, particularly YOLOv8, which is widely used for people detection and counting tasks.

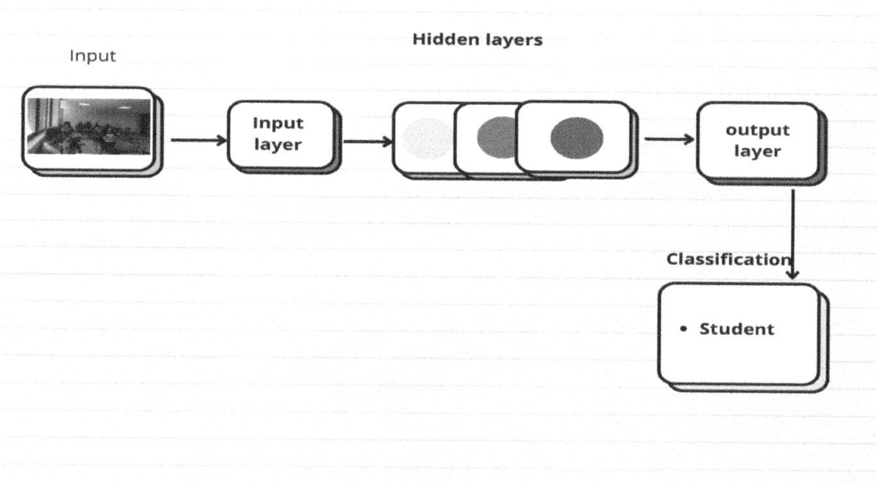

Fig. 1. Generalized operation of a CNN

Table 1. Recent related work

Author and year	Title	Database	Technique	Results
Cao, Y., et al. 2025	YOLO-AMM: Real time Classroom Behavior Detection	POCO	YOLO-AMM (AEFF, MFFN, MSPF-Head)	mAP@0.5 +3.1%, mAP@0.5:0.95 +4.0%, FPS +12.9 vs YOLOv8m. CMeets real-time requirements.
Xu, Y., Fu, Y. 2024	CIHD-YOLO: Complex Indoor Human Detection	HCIE (propio)	CIHD-YOLOv8	mAP +2.67 vs YOLOv8s. Reduced FLOPs. Improved low-light and small-scale performance.
Han, L., et al. 2025	WAD-YOLOv8: Classroom Student Behavior Detection	SCB, SCB2, SCB-S, SCB-U	WAD-YOLOv8	mAP@0.5 +2.2% to +18.7%, mAP@0.5:0.95 +2.3% to +14.8% vs current methods. Keeps real-time inference.
Che, Jin, Xu. 2020	A classroom student counting system based on improved context-based face detector	surveillance camera images	FEM and sysmen based on improved context	P=89.47% R=88.35% F1=88.91%
Hernandez-Aguilar, J.A. et al., 2023	A new approach for counting and identification of students' sentiments in online virtual environments using convolutional neural networks	Images obtained from online virtual classrooms	YOLOv3 and Deep face	P=96.7% AP=96.7%

The Table 1 shows the recent related work for this research, organized by author, title, database, employed technique, and main results.

3 Methodology

The proposed methodology for this research work consists of six stages (see Fig. 2), these stages are: 1) Data collection, 2) Preprocessing, 3) Setup of libraries and frameworks, 4) Model Training, 5) Model Testing, and 6) Metrics evaluation. These stages are explained below:

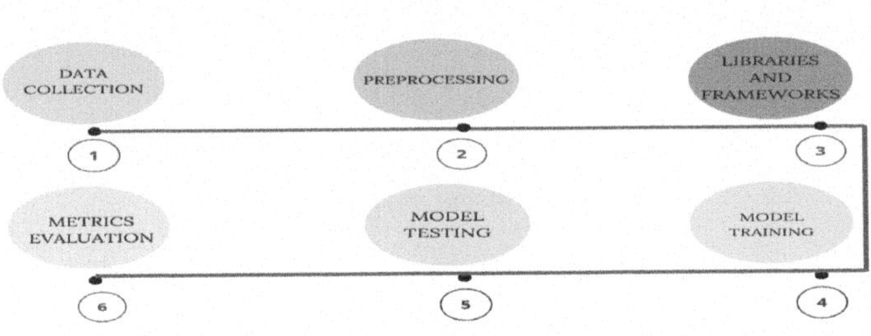

Fig. 2. Proposed methodology

Data Collection. A search was conducted for a freely available image database that met the requirements of containing color images in educational settings and with a variety of occupations and angles, to test the initial versions of the student counting model subsequently. The database used was the "Classroom Monitoring Dataset" [10], obtained from the following website: https://www.kaggle.com. This dataset comprises 4,342 images and four videos, divided into two parts, A and B. Part A contains images extracted from a security camera video located at the top of a classroom. The images have different dimensions. On the other hand, part B includes images of different educational environments, mostly closed spaces such as classrooms or auditoriums, also in various angles, occupancy and lighting, which makes it more suitable to assign it to the training of the models since a variety in lighting, angles, occlusions and all the environments already mentioned is sought, which will help us so that the model can be trained with different scenarios. In Fig. 3 are shown some images of Part A (left side) and Part B (right side) of the Classroom Monitoring Dataset.

Secondly, the **Preprocessing** was carried out. This step is essential because it reduces the model's processing costs. For this, the images were resized to

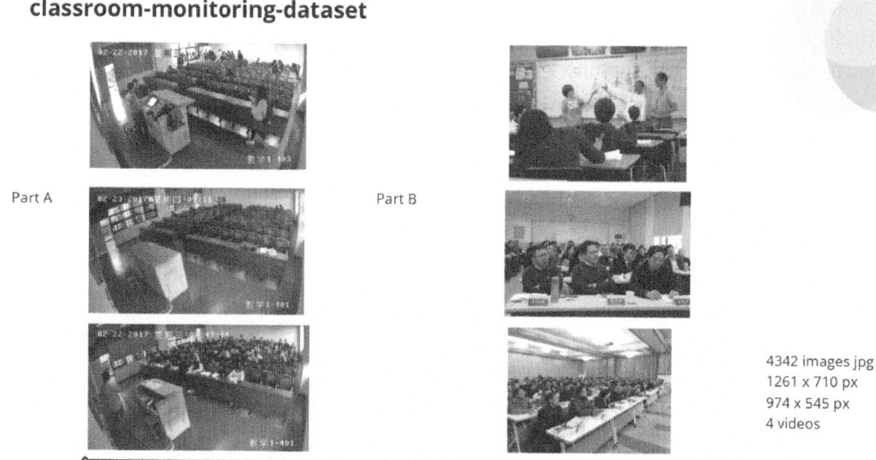

Fig. 3. Dataset description of Classroom-monitoring-dataset [10]

a single size of 640×640 and converted to grayscale. This way, the images will have a single channel instead of three, as is the case with color images. Later, the process continued with the assignment of labels to the images during annotation. The labels delimit the head of each detected student. Of the total images in the database, 950 from Part B were used for labeling. Additionally, 60 more images were added, collected from classrooms at the Faculty of Accounting, Administration, and Computer Science at UAEM, with the students' informed

Fig. 4. Labeling processing on the Roboflow platform

consent. This action was carried out to enrich the database with images from educational settings. The augmentation technique was then applied, which allows for increasing the number of images. The entire process yielded a database of 2,500 images. To train the models, the labeled dataset was split into 80% for training, 10% for validation, and 10% for testing.

Figure 4 shows the image labeling in Roboflow as part of the preprocessing stage, where the bounding boxes located on the head of each target are assigned. Figure 5 shows the tools available in this same platform for resizing, augmenting, and grayscaling the dataset.

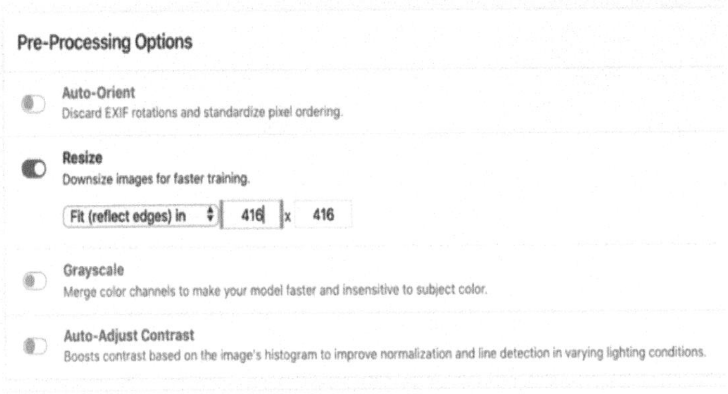

Fig. 5. Preprocessing tools in Roboflow

In the third step, the **Libraries and frameworks** were identified. In this research project, the Roboflow library was used for labeling, preprocessing, and image augmentation. YOLOv8 has been used as a framework for its image detection efficiency.

Before training the models, the hardware was configured. A laptop with the following specifications was purchased: 16GB of RAM, an Nvidia GeForce RTX 4060 graphics card, and an Intel Core i7 processor. The Ubuntu operating system, derived from the Linux distribution, was installed for practical purposes, along with the necessary drivers and software.

After completing the YOLOv8 installation, **Training the model** was carried out using transfer learning to analyze the preprocessed dataset, with the proposed data splits; the large and nano models were trained with 10, 30, 50, and 100 epochs, the following hyperparameters were used: imgsz=640, optimizer="Adam", batch=16.

For the large model, it was trained for 100 epochs, and the batch size was reduced to 4 due to hardware memory limitations.

Model testing began in real-life classroom situations at the Faculty of Accounting, Administration, and Computer Science.

Evaluation metrics in the training stage. According to [5–7], the following metrics were used to evaluate the models:

- Mean Average Precision (mAP) (see Eq. 1)
  and
- F1 score (see Eq. 5).

$$MAP = \frac{\sum_{q=1}^{Q} AveP(q)}{Q} \tag{1}$$

where Q is the number of queries in the set and AveP(q) is the average Precision (AP) (see Eq. 2) for a given query [13].

$$AP = \sum_{n} (R_n - R_{n-1}) Pn \tag{2}$$

where Pn and Rn are the Precision and Recall at the nth threshold [12].

$$Precision = TP/(TP + FP) \tag{3}$$

Precision (see Eq. 3) answers the question: Of all the cases the model said were positive, how many were positive?

$$Recall = TP/(TP + FN) \tag{4}$$

Recall answers the question: What proportion of true positives were correctly identified? In the Eq. 4, TP and FN are True Positives and False Negatives [10].

$$F1 = \frac{2 * TP}{2 * TP + FP + FN} \tag{5}$$

FP is the number of False Positives. F1 (see Eq. 5) is calculated by default as 0.0 when there are no true positives, false negatives, or false positives [11].

4 Results and Discussion

As a result of the training carried out with all the epochs mentioned in the methodology, a comparative table of results obtained for YOLOv8n and YOLOv8l was built, see Table 2:

As shown in Table 2, the YOLOv8l Model achieved the best metrics, particularly mAP50 and Precision, during training with 100 epochs. Similarly, the nano version of the model, also trained for 100 epochs, yielded the best metrics. Due to hardware limitations, the large model was the largest supported by the available resources, with training times of 10, 30, 50, and 100 epochs for each model version.

In Fig. 6 are shown some of the tests carried out in: (a) the auditorium, (b) a classroom near windows, (c) a classroom front view, and (d) a computer lab. As previously mentioned, all of these are closed educational settings with their

Table 2. Performance of YOLOv8 models with different training epochs

Model	Epochs	mAP50	mAP50-95	Precision	Recall	F1 Score
YOLOv8n	10	0.88983	0.52775	0.85825	0.83545	0.846697
YOLOv8n	30	0.90663	0.55572	0.87796	0.85508	0.866369
YOLOv8n	50	0.91308	0.55929	0.88935	0.86649	0.877771
YOLOv8n	100	0.91132	0.56191	0.89248	0.86218	0.877068
YOLOv8l	10	0.90357	0.54427	0.87180	0.83238	0.851634
YOLOv8l	30	0.91347	0.56910	0.89787	0.85912	0.878068
YOLOv8l	50	0.91805	0.57689	0.90096	0.87067	0.885556
YOLOv8l	**100**	**0.92179**	**0.57412**	**0.90237**	**0.88124**	**0.891680**

(a) Auditorium [15]

(b) Classroom near windows

(c) Classroom front view

(d) Computer lab

Fig. 6. Testing in real environments

respective detection challenges, including lighting conditions, occlusion from chairs and computers, and crowd density.

In these four tests, was verified that the YOLOv8 large model, trained with 100 epochs using appropriately preprocessed images, performs successfully in a variety of environments: in the auditorium, detecting people of different sizes, positions and in large numbers; in the computer lab with low lighting conditions and occlusions with computers and students; and finally in the classroom, for the

Table 3. Testing of model YOLOv8 large on 100 epochs to count persons

Image	Ground Truth	Predictions	TP	FP	FN	Precision	Recall	F1.Score
auditorium 1	158	128	99	29	59	0.77	0.62	0.69
auditorium 2	151	143	138	5	13	0.96	0.91	0.93
auditorium 3	6	6	0	0	0	1.00	1.00	1.00
auditorium 4	4	5	4	1	0	0.80	1.00	0.88
auditorium 5	39	42	39	3	0	0.92	1.00	0.96
auditorium 6	39	42	36	7	4	0.83	0.89	0.86
auditorium 7	20	20	14	6	6	0.70	0.70	0.70
laboratory 1	16	15	15	0	0	1.00	0.93	0.96
laboratory 2	12	11	11	0	1	1.00	0.91	0.95
laboratory 3	14	15	14	1	0	0.93	1.00	0.96
laboratory 4	16	15	15	0	1	1.00	0.93	0.96
laboratory 5	10	11	9	2	1	0.81	0.90	0.85
laboratory 6	12	12	12	0	0	1.00	1.00	1.00
laboratory 7	16	16	16	0	0	1.00	1.00	1.00
laboratory 8	10	9	8	1	2	0.88	0.80	0.84
laboratory 9	16	16	16	0	0	1.00	1.00	1.00
laboratory 10	13	13	13	0	0	1.00	1.00	1.00
classroom 1	10	11	10	1	0	0.90	1.00	0.95
classroom 2	14	14	14	0	0	1.00	1.00	1.00
classroom 3	14	14	14	0	0	1.00	1.00	1.00
classroom 4	12	12	11	1	1	0.91	0.91	0.91
classroom 5	11	11	10	1	1	0.90	0.90	0.90
classroom 6	11	11	10	1	1	0.90	0.90	0.90
classroom 7	8	8	8	0	0	1.00	1.00	1.00
classroom 8	8	7	6	1	2	0.85	0.75	0.80
classroom 9	6	6	6	0	0	1.00	1.00	1.00
classroom 10	6	6	6	0	0	1.00	1.00	1.00
classroom 11	6	6	6	0	0	1.00	1.00	1.00
classroom 12	6	6	6	0	0	1.00	1.00	1.00
classroom 13	6	6	6	0	0	1.00	1.00	1.00

last two experiments near windows and from front view, successfully detecting all students present. It is essential to note that double detections of a single object, or false detections, were almost nonexistent despite setting a confidence level of 0.2.

Table 3 shows the highly effective performance of the YOLOv8 Large model with 100 epochs of training for person counting in educational settings. The model demonstrates exceptional capability and precision, particularly in structured environments such as classrooms and laboratories. Across numerous test images—for example, classroom 2.jpg, classroom 13.jpg, laboratory6.jpg, and laboratory 10.jpg—the model consistently achieved flawless F1-scores of 1.0000. This perfect score indicates that the number of true positives matched the ground truth exactly, resulting in ideal precision and recall with zero detection errors. This level of accuracy was maintained even in selected images from other categories, such as auditorium 3.jpg, demonstrating the model's reliability and robustness in correctly identifying all target objects.

5 Conclusions and Future Work

The effectiveness of convolutional neural networks, specifically the YOLOv8 model, in detecting and counting students in educational environments was confirmed. Therefore, the hypothesis H1 is valid and was subsequently verified by testing the YOLOv8 models in their nano and large versions. However, challenges remain, such as measuring accuracy across varying conditions (e.g., lighting, occlusion, and occupancy), and optimizing model resource use for rapid response.

As future work on this research, it is planned to leverage the advantages of student detection as a first stage to develop algorithms that classify students' mood and attention states to provide educational content tailored to these states, and to integrate them into an Intelligent Learning Environment (ILE).

References

1. Alonso, R.: AI, Machine Learning, and Deep Learning: What's the Difference? HardZone., https://hardzone.es/tutoriales/rendimiento/diferencias-ia-deep-machine-learning/ (2023)
2. Sandoval, C.: Let's talk about object detection. LISA Insurtech.https://lisainsurtech.com/hablemos-de-la-deteccion-de-objetos/ (2023)
3. Briega, R.E.L.: (s. f.-b). Computer Vision - IAAR online book.https://iaarbook.github.io/vision-por-computadora/ (2018)
4. Getin. The importance of scientific people counters in the era of omnichannel commerce - Getin. https://getin.mx/blog/contador-cientifico-personas-en-comercio-omnicanal/ (2023)
5. Cao, Y., Cao, Q., Qian, C., Chen, D.: YOLO-AMM: a real-time classroom behavior detection algorithm based on multi-dimensional feature optimization. Sensors **25**(4), 1142 (2025)

6. Han, L., Ma, X., Dai, M., Bai, L.: A WAD-YOLOv8-based method for classroom student behavior detection. Sci. Rep. **15**, 9655 (2025)
7. Xu, Y., Fu, Y.: Complex indoor human detection with you only look once: an improved network designed for human detection in complex indoor scenes. Appl. Sci. **14**(22), 10713 (2024)
8. Singh, U., Gupta, P., Shukla, M.: Activity detection and counting people using Mask-RCNN with bidirectional ConvLSTM. J. Intell. Fuzzy Sys. (2022). https://doi.org/10.3233/jifs-220503
9. Classroom Monitoring Dataset. https://www.kaggle.com/datasets/lunarwhite/classroom-monitoring-dataset
10. Raschka, S. Mirjalili, V.: Python machine learning: Machine learning and deep learning with Python, scikit-learn, and TensorFlow 2, Packt Publishing Ltd (2019)
11. Scikit-learn. f1-score. (s.f.) scikit-learn.org/stable/modules/generated/sklearn.metrics.f1_score.html
12. Scikit-learn. average_precision_score. (s.f.-b) scikitlearn.org/stable/modules/generated/sklearn.metrics.average-precision-score.html
13. Tan, R.J.: Mean Average Precision (MAP) explained. Built In. (2024, 18 julio).https://builtin.com/articles/mean-average-precision
14. Jocher, G., Chaurasia, A., and Qiu, J.: Ultralytics YOLO (Version 8.0.0) (Computer software).https://github.com/ultralytics/ultralytics (2023)
15. FCaeI. FCAeI official webpage.https://www.facebook.com/FCAeI (2024)

An Intelligent Learning Environment for Mathematics: SmartMathAI with Generative AI and Problem-Based Learning

Julio César Mendívil-Casanova[1], María-Lucia Barrón-Estrada[1](✉), Ramon Zatarain-Cabada[1], and Aldo Uriarte-Portillo[1,2]

[1] TecNM-Instituto Tecnológico de Culiacán, Culiacán, Sin CP 80210, México
{julio.mc,lucia.be,ramon.zc,aldo.up}@culiacan.tecnm.mx, aldouriarte@ccs.edu.mx

[2] Coordinación General Para El Fomento a La Investigación Científica E Innovación, del Estado de Sinaloa (CONFIE), Culiacán, Sin CP 80050, México

1 Introduction

In Mexico, elementary and middle school students are struggling to learn several topics in STEM. Although this has been a longstanding issue, it has recently worsened. The report of the 2023 PISA test, conducted by the Organization for Economic Cooperation and Development (OECD), shows that Mexico's average results in 2022 declined compared to 2018 in mathematics and science confirming that learning advances observed during the 2003–2009 period were lost, and average scores went back to levels like those observed in 2003 or 2006. On the other hand, only 34% of students achieved at least level 2 proficiency in mathematics, significantly less than the average of 69% for OECD countries. This indicates that most Mexican students are unable to represent simple situations without direct instructions [1].

Looking forward to improving learning in mathematics and science, the Mexican government has made changes to the educational system, proposing a new pedagogical model called New Mexican School (Nueva Escuela Mexicana), which promotes the use of several methodologies, one of which is problem-based learning (PBL) [2]. This approach places the student at the center of the learning process, giving them the responsibility of constructing their own knowledge through problem solving [3].

Problem-Based Learning (PBL) is a method that has gained popularity in recent years due to its benefits in education. Its approach looks to foster the development of cognitive, metacognitive, and social skills through the resolution of real problems.

PBL requires the presence of a tutor to guide the student, providing clues and suggestions without directly giving them the answer. This tutor is key to ensuring that the student does not feel lost in the learning process. However, the need for personalized feedback becomes a significant limitation in classrooms with many students, as a single teacher cannot provide individualized attention to each student.

On the other hand, Artificial Intelligence (AI) is a discipline of computer science that aims to enable computers and systems to simulate human intelligence, as well as the ability to perform tasks and solve problems. AI can be defined as "the study of agents that

L. Martínez-Villaseñor et al. (Eds.): MICAI 2025, LNAI 16265, pp. 82–94, 2026.
https://doi.org/10.1007/978-3-032-17933-3_9

receive perceptions from the environment and perform actions" [4] to maximize their chances of success. This definition highlights the ability of machines to mimic human cognitive functions through algorithms.

The use of AI can be a solution to the need for a tutor to guide the student. Technologies such as Large Language Models (LLM), which are AI systems capable of processing and generating natural language in an advanced way, have proven to be effective in tasks such as answering questions, generating detailed explanations, and providing adaptive assistance.

In 2017, Transformer models were introduced in [5], allowing selective focus on distinct parts of the text input, resulting in the models processing the sequence in parallel, improving efficiency and the ability to capture complex contextual relationships in the text. The Transformer model revolutionized natural language processing by eliminating recurrent networks and proposing an architecture based solely on attention mechanisms. This innovation changed the way models are trained and led to the creation of LLM by large companies, among the most popular of which are BERT, GPT, LLaMa, Mistral, Gemini, and others.

In 2018, the GPT model, developed by OpenAI [6], was introduced with the advantage of being trained with unsupervised training and fine-tuned for specific tasks; more recently GPT-4 released in 2023, improved comprehension and logical reasoning, expanding its domain to different languages and specialized tasks. Also in 2023, Meta introduced the first version of Llama (Large Language Model Meta AI), an open-source language model that includes several versions. These models were trained using only public data, proving that models could be trained to achieve great results without the need for test data. In 2023, Llama 2 appeared, developed in collaboration with Microsoft, and was also released in an accessible manner, allowing academic research and private industry to experiment with high-performance models, removing barriers that previously only large companies could overcome [7].

The use of artificial intelligence (AI) in education has the potential to become a powerful tool for facilitating access, equity, and quality in learning. Easy access to this technology has the capacity to reduce barriers to knowledge and improve current teaching methods.

Artificial intelligence chatbots are applications or interfaces that can hold human-like conversations through natural language processing. They leverage LLM to generate text responses and can answer questions, provide guidance, resolve doubts, and execute specific tasks, among other things.

SmartMathAI was designed as an educational application that implements a problem-based learning methodology, using an AI-based virtual tutor to guide students as a teacher would. This application focuses on middle school (7th and 8th grade) mathematics topics based on the current official educational program in Mexico.

2 Related Works

The work of Ad-Abril [8] explored how students used ChatGPT as a virtual tutor to assist in answering questions, for preparing for exams, and to improve writing. The results of 68 undergraduate students found it especially helpful for exam prep and easy access highlighting the potential of LLM to address the limitations of the intelligent tutoring systems and a personalized approach to assist students' learning. The findings suggest ChatGPT can make online learning more personalized and supportive, though it still needs better context and feedback.

El Hajji, et al. [9] explore how virtual reality can enhance education by using intelligent tutoring systems with AI-powered such as the LLaMA LLM model, to generate text and a dynamic dialogue. The learning tool supports adaptive dialogue and multimodal interaction through gestures, gaze, and feedback, with speech synchronized to character animations. Results showed that VR-based tutoring can boost and enhance learner engagement, though slight delays in speech processing highlight the need for further technical improvements.

In [10] authors show how LLM can support deaf and hard-of-hearing learners by adapting to their cultural and communication needs. 16 learners take part and interact with ChatGPT and AI tutors designed with varying levels of DHH education experience. Tutors with cultural knowledge were seen as more human-like and trustworthy, highlighting the value of context-awareness. Participants expressed the need for transparency about each tutor's background and for multimodal support, such as sign language integration, to make systems more inclusive.

Molina et. al [11] explored how LLM tutors can support Non-Native English-Speaking (NNES) students in an accelerated computing course. While NNES students signed up at similar rates as native speakers, they used the system less often but asked more multilingual questions, mixing English keywords with their native languages. Both groups valued the tutor's accessibility and conversational style, with NNES students especially appreciating that they didn't need perfect English to engage. Findings suggest LLM tutors can help bridge language barriers and make computing education more inclusive.

Finally, Markel et. al [12] introduce GPTEACH, a chat-based tool where novice teachers practice with AI-simulated students. In this work, participants valued the safe environment to refine their responses, adapt to different student needs, and build confidence without real-world pressure. Participants using GPTeach gave it higher recommendation scores than those using the dialogue-based baseline, suggesting that tools like GPTeach could play a key role in making teacher training more engaging and scalable.

3 The Learning Tool

Based on the definition of the problem, the need to innovate in the learning method was identified by adopting technology as a support when implementing PBL through a virtual tutor that provides a personalized guide to students. It was decided to create a software tool that provides help to students through artificial intelligence, to help students gain a deeper understanding of the subject and develop critical thinking.

To ensure 24/7 availability, it was decided to develop an educational web application that seeks to support students in learning mathematics, specifically the Pythagorean theorem. The tool was designed to guide students through the learning process in a personalized way. The software architecture is described below.

3.1 Software Architecture

SmartMathAI implements the client-server model using a layered architecture. This approach allows the system to be organized into a presentation layer, business layer, and data layer, distributing these across the client and server components. Figure 1 shows the software architecture of SmartMathAI.

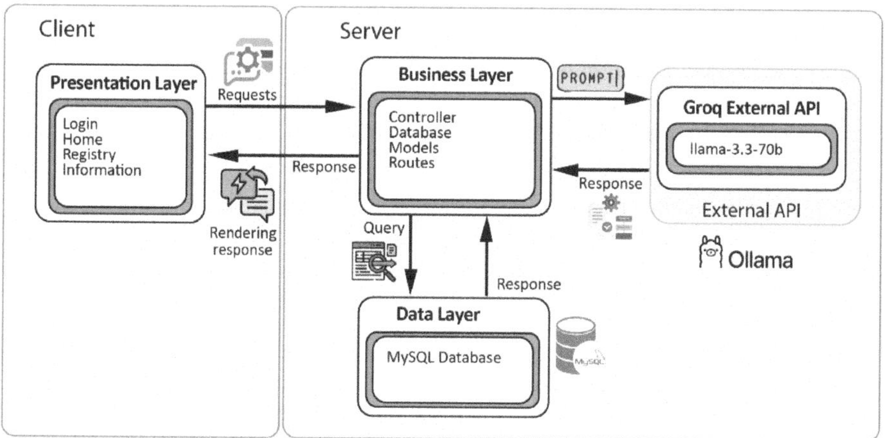

Fig. 1. SmartMathAI software architecture

3.1.1 Presentation Layer

The presentation layer is the part of the system responsible for interacting with the user through a visual interface with elements such as icons, login, sign-in, and windows. Its main function is to receive user input, send it to the business layer for processing, and display results in a clear and understandable way. This layer can be implemented in a web browser as a desktop application using a graphical user interface. The Presentation Layer is usually developed using different technologies.

3.1.2 Business Layer

This layer handles managing all the logic of the system, such as controllers, models, and routes; it holds the rules that define how the system works. Its main function is to process the data received from the Presentation Layer and, when necessary, query the Data Layer. It is also responsible for communication with the Groq External API.

3.1.3 Data Layer

This layer handles storing and managing the information necessary for the system to function. It communicates with the business layer to store, retrieve, update, or delete information. The MySQL database manager was selected for this application due to its stability and ease of use, large support community, and high compatibility with web applications.

3.2 Implementation of the Virtual Tutor.

An LLM was used to implement the virtual tutor. This AI model allows for the generation of personalized responses and can perform complex instructions. This is achieved using prompts, which are natural language instructions that guide the expected behavior of the language model. We selected the LLaMA "llama-3.3-70b" model, integrating it through an API, allowing for quick responses without the need to host the model on a dedicated server. The model excels at tasks such as following complex instructions, reasoning, programming, and information analysis.

The model is queried through a POST HTTP request from the application's backend to the remote Groq Service. To receive a response from the language model, a request is sent to the API that includes the following information:

- System role: defines the model's expected behavior and provides contextual information such as the topic, exercises, student profile, and available learning materials. In this case, the model is instructed to act as a math tutor.
- User role: contains the student's input questions or comments, allowing the model to understand the learner's context and generate an appropriate response.

The model's reply is then received via the API, processed by the backend, and displayed to the user. This mechanism enables seamless integration of artificial intelligence, providing students with rich, adaptive, and meaningful feedback.

Figure 2 shows the execution path of the learning environment following the PBL methodology. The student log into the system and selects the Study option in the menu; the system displays several topics and the student choses the topic he wants to learn. After this steps, the system executes the PBL methodology (steps 3–8).

3.2.1 Prompt Used for the Language Model

The construction of the prompt provided to the language model plays a critical role in eliciting the expected tutoring behavior. For this project, an iterative design methodology was employed, beginning with the formulation of clear and precise instructional statements. The final prompt was implemented within the 'System' role, encapsulating both the contextual framework and the operational guidelines required to regulate the model's responses. The specific design considerations are detailed below:

- Pedagogical instructions: The model is instructed to act as a math teacher, encouraging students by congratulating them when their answers are correct and guiding them when mistakes occur. If the student's procedure is incorrect, the model should point it out and prompt them to review their work without ever revealing the correct answer.
- Restrictions: The model should not ask questions or request additional information from the student. This ensures that each query results in a single, clear response, avoiding confusion. It must also refrain from mentioning tolerance margins, as this could mislead students about correct answers.
- Objective instructions: The model's main goal is to help students recognize and correct their own errors, rather than providing final answers.

The resulting prompt given to the system was tested until the expected behavior was achieved. Two examples of the behavior of the virtual tutor answering students' concerns

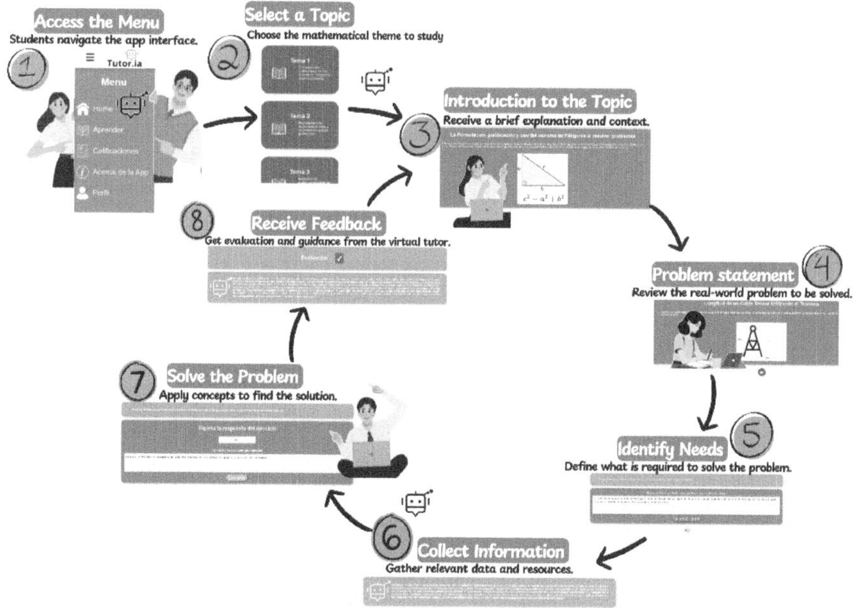

Fig. 2. Execution of the Learning Environment

are displayed in spanish, because the system was developed to be used in Mexico. In the first example (see Fig. 3), the student tells the tutor, *"I don't know how to solve it, can you explain me?"* the virtual tutor answers emphatically, encouraging the student to organize his thoughts to solve the problem. The tutor says,

"Don't worry, it's a complex problem, but we'll approach it step by step. I understand that you've already tried to solve it and want to know where you went wrong. First, I want to congratulate you on the good work you've done so far. The height BD has been calculated correctly, and we also know the length of side AC. Now, let's stop for a moment and review the steps to make sure we haven't forgotten anything important. Would you like to start by summarizing your steps so far? What have you done so far to solve this problem?"

In the second example, the student tells the tutor "*Explain me step by step how to solve the exercise*", and the virtual tutor responds with a detailed explanation of the five steps the student must follows to solve the exercise. Figure 4 shows the virtual tutor guide provided to the student.

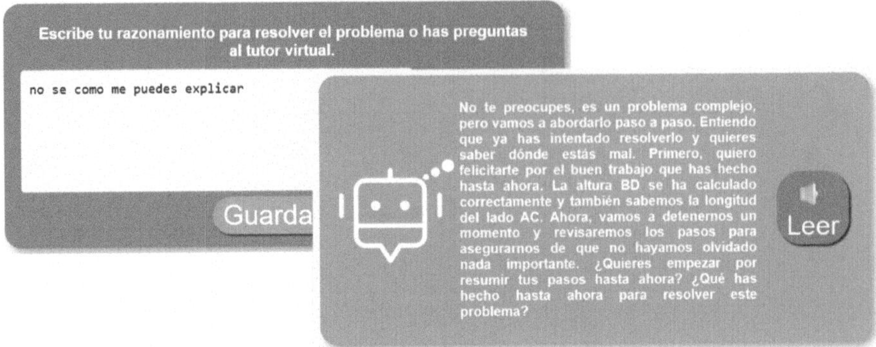

Fig. 3. Students request and virtual tutor explanation.

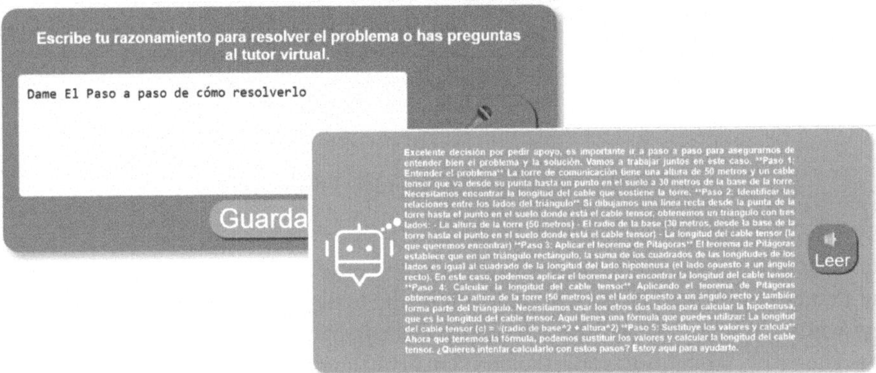

Fig. 4. Example of the interaction between students and the virtual tutor

3.3 Graphical User Interface.

For the development of the graphical interface, ease of use was established as the main requirement, considering that the system is aimed at secondary school students [13]. In this sense, the interface must be clear, intuitive, and accessible, so that it encourages interaction with the system without requiring prior technical knowledge. In addition, the interface should be motivating, incorporating graphic elements that encourage students to continue using it.

The first stage introduces the topic through a brief description accompanied by an image to support comprehension. The system presents a problem statement supported by a description and an image, encouraging the students to conduct a little research to resolve any doubts if necessary. In the next stage, the system displays an input box allowing students to send doubts, ideas, or reasoning, which the AI analyzes to provide a personalized response, either by resolving doubts, correcting errors, or offering hints (see Fig. 5). The student can interact with the tutor by typing text (text box) or by voice (right button) to express themselves.

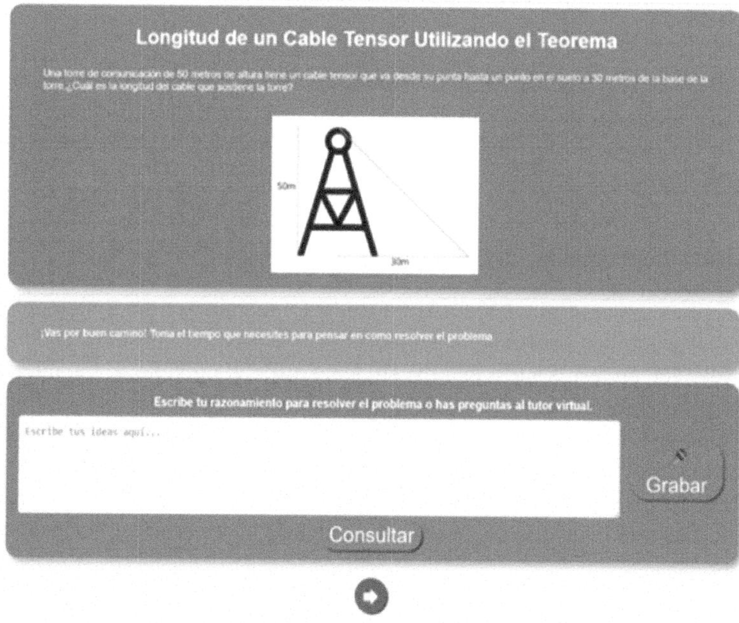

Fig. 5. SmartMathAI exercises solving interface.

Subsequently, the interface displays a panel where the student can review the tutors' instructions, with the possibility to listen with the built-in text-to-speech feature. After sending the solution, the system provides feedback (see Fig. 6) on whether the solution is correct or incorrect. The virtual tutor further analyzes the results and the problem-solving process to generate the adaptive feedback: if incorrect, it highlights mistakes and suggests strategies for correction; if correct, it validates the solution and offers the option to proceed to a new exercise. This information is shown in the interface and can be listened to by clicking the right button.

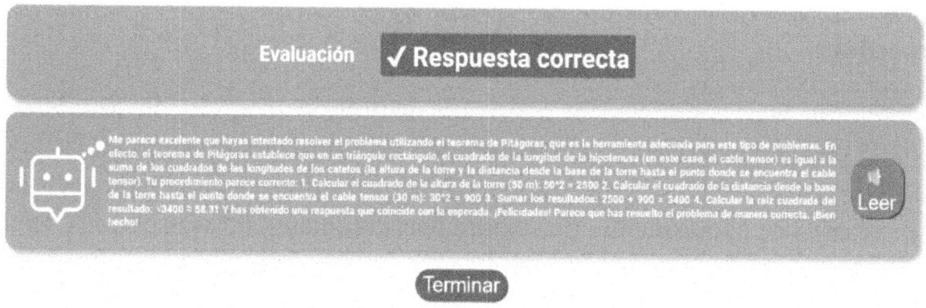

Fig. 6. SmartMathAI feedback

4 Method

This section addresses the interventions conducted with students. A quasi-experimental design was chosen to find a possible cause-and-effect relationship in the use of the SmartMathAI system. To this end, measurement instruments were designed to assess both student learning gains and acceptance of the tool.

4.1 Measure Instruments

To evaluate the impact of SmartMathAI on students' learning of the Pythagorean theorem, three measurement instruments were designed: a pretest, a posttest, and an acceptance survey. The pretest is a test that the students respond previous to the intervention, and its purpose is to measure the students' prior knowledge of the subject, while the posttest is the test that the students respond to after using the tool to assess the knowledge acquired. Both instruments have the same degree of complexity and consist of eight questions, five multiple-choice questions, and three practical questions related to the subject. Each item has four answers, only one of which is correct. An example of a question is:

What does the hypotenuse indicate in a right triangle?

a) The shortest side of the triangle
b) Either of the two sides that form the right angle
c) The side opposite the right angle and the longest
d) The sum of the catheti

The third instrument is the acceptance survey, consisting of ten questions aimed at assessing perceived usefulness, motivation, autonomy, ease of use, and trust in artificial intelligence. This instrument seeks to measure students' interest in the use of AI-based technologies in educational contexts. Also, this survey includes two open questions to know the students' perceptions of the learning tool. One of these questions is: What did you like most about the app and why?

4.2 Procedure

The intervention was conducted at a private institution in a city in Mexico, with a sample of 25 participants ($N = 25$) in the second and third grades of middle school. The population consisted of 11 s-grade students and 14 third-grade students, aged between 13 and 15 years. The experimental procedure was conducted in two sessions. In the first session, the topic was presented, and the pretest measurement instrument was applied. In the second session, students had a total of 50 min to use the tool freely, so each student progressed at their own pace in solving the exercises. To analyze the use of the tool, the exercises solved by each student, the number of attempts, and their interactions with the virtual tutor were recorded. Subsequently, the posttest instrument was administered. Finally, the students responded to the tool acceptance survey.

5 Results

This section presents the results derived from the intervention carried out with students using the tool. In addition, the data is interpreted to draw meaningful conclusions on the impact of the application on learning and its acceptance. Next, the results obtained in the pretest, posttest, and acceptance survey are analyzed.

5.1 Pretest and Posttest Questionnaires.

The results of the pretest measure instrument are presented. First, for the second-grade group, followed by those for the third-grade group, and, finally, those for the total population. The second-grade group ($N = 11$), with no prior knowledge of the subject, performed poorly, as expected ($M = 2.38$, $SD = 1.35$). This result confirms that, as the topic had not been previously addressed in the classroom, the students had a limited initial level of knowledge on the subject. On the other hand, the third-grade group ($N = 14$), who had already studied the topic in previous weeks, obtained a higher score ($M = 3.93$, $SD = 1.88$). In the total population, the score obtained was low ($M = 3.25$, $SD = 1.87$), which shows that, overall, the students started from an insufficient conceptual basis on the Pythagorean Theorem.

A post-test was administered to assess the knowledge acquired. The second-grade group showed a significant improvement ($M = 5.57$, $SD = 1.62$), indicating that the application had a positive impact on the scores of students with no prior knowledge. The third-grade group also improved their performance ($M = 5.89$, $SD = 2.79$), although to a lesser extent, suggesting a consolidation of prior knowledge. Finally, when considering the total population, the overall average was favorable ($M = 5.75$, $SD = 2.31$), reflecting that the use of SmartMathAI contributed to both the acquisition and reinforcement of knowledge on the subject.

To evaluate the impact of the tool, the results of the pretest and posttest were compared using statistical analysis. Since the data did not follow a normal distribution, non-parametric tests were used. The Wilcoxon signed-rank test was used to find significant differences between the pretest and posttest data. In the case of the second-grade group, the average score went from 2.38 to 5.57, showing a statistically significant difference ($Z = -2.675$, $p = 0.007$), which confirmed the positive impact of the tool on students with no prior knowledge. Similarly, in the third-grade group, the average increased from 3.93 to 5.89, showing a statistically significant difference ($Z = -2.218$, $p = 0.027$). In both cases, the Wilcoxon test allowed us to reject the null hypothesis, showing improvements in learning gains after the intervention with SmartMathAI.

To evaluate the overall difference between the pretest and posttest for the total population, the Mann-Whitney U test was applied. The results showed an average range of 17.52 in the pretest and 33.48 in the posttest, with statistically significant values ($U = 113.0$, $Z = -3.937$, $p < 0.001$). This allows us to reject the null hypothesis and confirms a statistically significant difference in the overall performance of the students. This finding supports the conclusion that SmartMathAI produced an increase in learning gains, both in students with prior knowledge and in those with no experience in the subject.

5.2 Use of the Tool.

While using the tool, the second-grade group solved an average of 3.36 exercises (M = 3.36, SD = 1.02) in 5.45 attempts (M = 5.45, SD = 2.84), reflecting an initial performance limited by a lack of prior knowledge. The third-grade group showed slightly higher performance, with an average of 3.62 exercises solved (M = 3.62, SD = 1.50) and 5.11 attempts (M = 5.11, SD = 2.84), which shows greater efficiency attributable to their previous experience. In the total sample, the average was 3.47 exercises solved (M = 3.47, SD = 1.21) and 5.30 attempts (M = 5.30, SD = 2.55). These results suggest that, even with limited initial knowledge, students were able to advance in their understanding of the topic, while those with prior preparation solved the exercises slightly better.

5.3 Acceptance Survey.

To assess student acceptance and motivation, a survey based on the Likert scale (scale 1–5) was administered. The overall average obtained (M = 3.63), and 19 students obtained a score greater than the average. This indicates a positive perception of the tool's use. Students valued the virtual tutor's help in understanding the subject matter and the clarity of the explanations and indicated confidence in artificial intelligence as a learning aid. However, the average also reflects that there are areas for improvement in the design of the tool and in the integration of AI. In addition, it also reflects that these types of tools have significant potential in the educational field. An example of a question from this survey is: "The virtual tutor's explanations were clear, easy to understand, and useful for my learning".

6 Discussion and Conclusions

The intervention proved a positive impact on learning gains in the Pythagorean Theorem. Conducting the study in two sessions allowed us to find relevant factors that could influence student performance. During the pretest, a few students showed a limited interest, possibly due to it being a traditional exam format, which may have affected results. Without a doubt, student motivation was an especially key factor that was noticeable from the early stages of the intervention. Motivation proved to be an important feature: while initial use of the tool required an adaptation period, student engagement increased steadily.

Both statistical analysis and direct observation confirmed significant progress in learning, with the stage of using the application being where the students' motivation and enthusiasm were most noticeable. Highly motivated students solved more exercises and maximized the use of the tool. Although a minority showed resistance to using the application, their limited participation had a slight impact on test averages. Some of these students decided to make minimal use of the tool, an effect reflected in slightly lower posttest outcomes.

Overall, these findings show that student motivation plays a fundamental role in technology-assisted learning with AI. The tool helped the understanding of the Pythagorean Theorem and fostered a greater disposition to solve mathematical problems.

The integration of PBL with a generative AI model promotes enhancing mathematics learning, critical thinking, and problem-solving skills. Results were promising Wilcoxon signed-rank test revealed significant statistical differences between the pretest ($M = 3.25$) and posttest ($M = 5.75$) scores (p-value = 0.001), while the Mann-Whitney U test confirmed significant improvements ($U = 113.0$, $Z = -3.937$, $p = 0.00$) between the pretest and posttest scores. These findings reject the null hypothesis and demonstrate that integrating a virtual tutor powered by LLM into problem-based learning can effectively strengthen students' learning [14] and are consistent with the results of other studies that highlight the efficiency of virtual tutors in improving both academic performance and student motivation [15], offering a scalable, human-centered approach to support learning.

Despite these promising results, some limitations should be acknowledged. The system's dependency on the Groq API introduced occasional response delays that may have influenced the flow of classroom activities. Although the LLaMA 3-based virtual tutor effectively supported learning the Pythagorean theorem, it sometimes produced responses that were too complex or not fully adapted to the students' level of understanding. Its text-based interaction limited accessibility for students with different literacy levels, and its text-based interaction posed accessibility challenges for those with reading difficulties. Additionally, differences in intrinsic motivation among students may have introduced bias in performance outcomes, as highly motivated learners tended to engage more actively and achieve better results.

For future work, research should expand the sample to include a larger and diverse population with different social and educational contexts. Likewise, other basic education topics could be incorporated, as well as other subjects and even a complete course unit, to expand the data to be collected and perform a more comprehensive, complete, and robust statistical analysis that would allow us to affirm the impact of this type of tool with an emphasis on the educational field.

References

1. OECD. PISA 2022 Results (Volume I): The State of Learning and Equity in Education. OECD Publishing, París, diciembre (2023)
2. Mendieta, J.B.: El aprendizaje basado en problemas para mejorar el pensamiento crítico: revisión sistemática. INNOVA Research Journal **6**(2), 77–89 (2021)
3. Secretaría de Educación Pública. Avance del contenido para el libro del docente. Primer grado. SEP, Ciudad de México, 2022 (2022)
4. Russell, S.J., Norvig, P.: Artificial Intelligence: A Modern Approach, Global Edition (4th ed.). Pearson (2021)
5. Vaswani, A., et al.: Attention is all you need. Advances in Neural Information Processing Systems, Curran Associates, Inc., vol. 30, Long Beach (2017)
6. OpenAI. GPT-4 Technical Report. openai.com, en línea, disponible en: https://openai.com/research/gpt-4, San Francisco (2023)
7. Meta AI. Llama: Open Foundation Models. Llama.com, en línea, disponible en: https://www.llama.com/, California (2024)
8. Al-Abri, A.: Exploring ChatGPT as a virtual tutor: A multi-dimensional analysis of large language models in academic support. Education and Information Technologies, pp. 1–36 (2025)

9. El Hajji, M., Ait Baha, T., Berka, A., Ait Nacer, H., El Aouifi, H., Es-Saady, Y.: An architecture for intelligent tutoring in virtual reality: integrating llms and multimodal interaction for immersive learning. Information **16**(7), 556 (2025). https://doi.org/10.3390/info16070556
10. Cheng, H., Chen, S., Perdriau, C., Huang, Y.: LLM-Powered AI Tutors with Personas for d/Deaf and Hard-of-Hearing Online Learners (2024). arXiv preprint arXiv:2411.09873
11. Molina, I.V., Montalvo, A., Ochoa, B., Denny, P., Porter, L.: Leveraging Llm Tutoring Systems for Non-Native English Speakers in Introductory Cs Courses (2024). arXiv preprint arXiv: 2411.02725
12. Markel, J.M., Opferman, S.G., Landay, J.A., Piech, C.: Gpteach: Interactive ta training with gpt-based students. In Proceedings of the tenth acm conference on learning@ scale, pp. 226–236 (2023)
13. Secretaría de Educación Pública. Plan de Estudio para la Educación Preescolar, Primaria y Secundaria 2022. Dirección General de Desarrollo Curricular (2024). https://educacionbasica.sep.gob.mx/materiales-de-apoyo-a-la-apropiacion-del-plan-y-programas-de-estudio-2022/, Ciudad de México, 2024
14. Maalek, R.: Integrating generative artificial intelligence and problem-based learning into the digitization in construction curriculum. Buildings **14**(11), 3642 (2024). https://doi.org/10.3390/buildings14113642
15. Ateş, H.: Integrating augmented reality into intelligent tutoring systems to enhance science education outcomes. Educ. Inf. Technol. **30**(4), 4435–4470 (2025)

An Interactive and Literate Environment for Learning Programming

Saúl-Alonso Palazuelos-Alvarado, María-Lucia Barrón-Estrada(✉), Ramón Zatarain-Cabada, and Arcelia-Judith Bustillos-Martínez

TecNM-Instituto Tecnológico de Culiacán, Culiacán, Sin CP 80210, México
{saul.pa,lucia.be,ramon.zc,arcelia.bm}@culiacan.tecnm.mx

1 Introduction

In our increasingly technology-driven world, learning to program is a critical skill, however conventional tools and complex general-purpose computational notebooks can often be daunting for beginners.

Traditional programming education has long depended on tools such as code editors and integrated development environments (IDEs). While these tools effectively introduce students to programming and problem-solving, they often create barriers for beginners through steep learning curves, and limited guidance. Contemporary, state-of-the-art learning environments address these challenges with smart features such as AI tutors, adaptive feedback systems, and real-time code analysis engines. There is also a rise of computational notebooks on education [1].

More recently, generative AI has taken this further by creating code examples, suggesting better solutions, and explaining complex ideas in plain language, making programming education more interactive, personalized, and approachable for beginners [2].

Javalí Notebook offers an innovative interactive and literate learning environment designed to simplify and enhance programming learning. It combines interactive programming, where code can be executed in small, dynamic segments, with literate programming, which integrates code seamlessly with documentation and explanations. This dual approach enables students to focus on specific parts of a program, follow the execution flow more intuitively, and record their learning process in a structured way.

To build on this foundation, we took the concept a step further by integrating Javalí Notebook more deeply into academic practice through a learning management system (LMS). This integration not only streamlines access and course management for instructors but also creates a cohesive environment where students can engage with content, practice coding, and track their progress within the same academic ecosystem.

Although the system and course materials are primarily designed for Java, the underlying web technologies provide an extensible foundation to accommodate additional programming languages.

L. Martínez-Villaseñor et al. (Eds.): MICAI 2025, LNAI 16265, pp. 95–105, 2026.
https://doi.org/10.1007/978-3-032-17933-3_10

2 Related Works

The use of computational notebooks in education is not a recent initiative [3, 4]; for many years, they have been employed as platforms that support interactive learning, facilitate experimentation, and enable the clear visualization of complex concepts and processes.

However, in recent years, there has been a growing effort to expand their functionality and integrate them more deeply into formal educational environments. In this section, we provide a brief overview of several notable notebook systems, each of which has been designed to support a particular use case or programming language.

A key distinguishing feature of Javalí is its focus on enabling the development of Java programs, setting it apart from the majority of existing notebook tools, which are predominantly oriented toward Python.

2.1 Nbgrader

Among the earliest open-source efforts, nbgrader [5] emerged as a widely adopted Jupyter extension that enables instructors to author, distribute, and automatically grade notebook-based assignments. It allows the creation of assignment templates with embedded tests, supports both automated and manual grading, and has been widely used in programming courses.

For instance, an instructor can design a notebook exercise on recursion with predefined test cases, enabling nbgrader to automatically evaluate student submissions. Despite its utility, however, nbgrader depends on manual workflows for integration with LMS platforms, limiting its scalability in institutional contexts.

2.2 CodeGrade

More recent commercial solutions, such as CodeGrade [6], facilitate LMS integration by embedding notebooks directly within popular learning management systems. These integrations enable seamless assignment distribution, submission, and grading, thereby minimizing friction between interactive notebook environments and institutional course management workflows.

2.3 Deepnote and Google Colab

Beyond LMS integration, collaborative notebook platforms such as Deepnote [7] and Google Colab [8] support real-time interaction and sharing, though they lack formal grading pipelines. Collectively, these efforts highlight a growing recognition of the pedagogical value of notebooks, with solutions ranging from lightweight embedding to deeply integrated ecosystems.

2.4 Polyglot Notebooks

Some notebook systems provide support for multiple programming languages within the same runtime, enabling greater flexibility and creative possibilities. Notable examples in this area include Apache Zeppelin [9], which supports SQL, Scala, Python, R, and more, and Microsoft Polyglot Notebooks [10], which supports C#, F#, Python, JavaScript, and SQL.

3 Javali: Interactive Notebooks

3.1 Conceptual Design

Javalí Notebook is designed around two core programming styles: literate programming and interactive programming.

Literate programming, introduced by Donald Knuth in 1984, shifts the programmer's focus from instructing a computer to explaining to humans what a computer should do, treating programs as works of literature in which the author acts as an essayist [11]. This philosophy, originally embodied in Knuth's WEB system [12], has directly influenced modern tools such as Jupyter Notebooks [13] and R Markdown [14].

Interactive programming involves writing and modifying parts of a program while it's running, allowing immediate interaction and iterative refinement in real time. This contrasts with traditional batch processing, where writing, compilation, and execution occur as isolated, sequential steps. The read–eval–print loop (REPL) [15], illustrated in Fig. 1, drives this continuous cycle of execution and feedback.

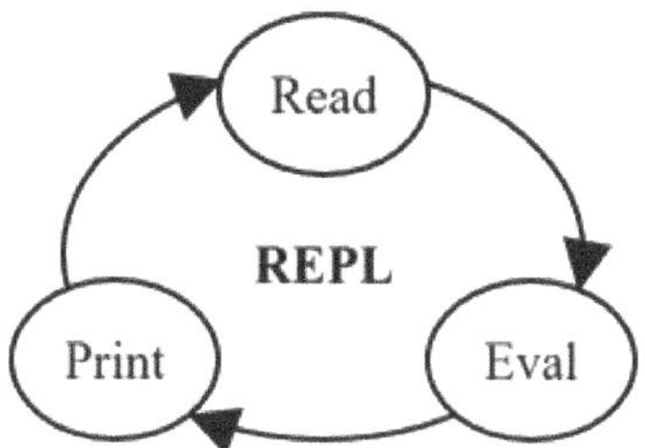

Fig. 1. Interactive Read-Eval-Print-Loop

Literate Programming Model.
We developed a plane-based model for literate programming that structures and defines nine types of cells, distributed in both didactic and knowledge dimensions. This distribution facilitates the integration of instructional content, both visual and text-based code, as well as interactive evaluations, as illustrated in Fig. 2.

The X-axis, named didactic dimension, represents the role of the cell. Its left end is associated with learning and instruction, while its right end is related to evaluation and feedback, implying an active or agent role on the part of the user.

The Y-axis, named knowledge dimension, represents the type of knowledge associated with each cell. Its upper end corresponds to theory, while the lower end corresponds to practice. This distinction draws on the categories of knowledge defined by the British philosopher Gilbert Ryle knowing that and knowing how[16].

Within this model, each cell carries a *validation status* that reflects its progress. The status can be either binary or ternary, depending on the type of cell. Instructional cells use a binary state: *initial* or *done*. An instructional cell is marked *done* once the user has read it. All other cells use a ternary state: *initial*, *feedback*, or *done*. The *feedback* state

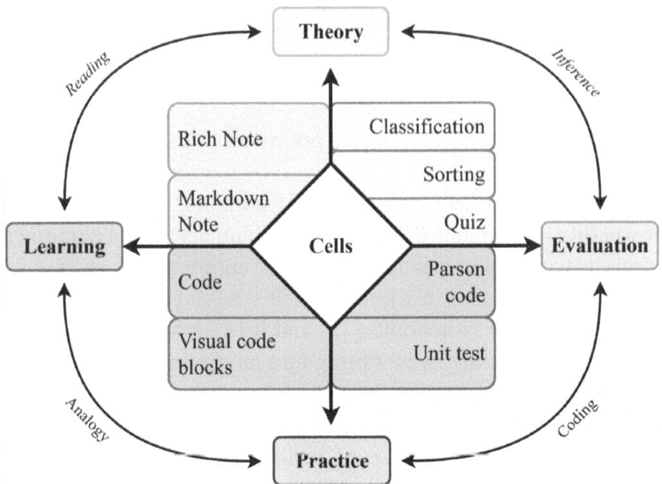

Fig. 2. Bidimensional notebook/cell plane

indicates that the user must take corrective action, such as fixing compilation errors or revising quiz answers.

The model also considers a gamification element. Completing a learning cell awards + 1 point, while completing an evaluation cell awards + 2 points. If an evaluation cell is not completed, it grants 0 points.

Literate Course Content Model.
A hierarchical course content system was implemented, with the notebook as pillar entity. The content is organized in four levels: Program, Course, Module, and Notebook, with the notebook constituting the central pedagogical unit. At the highest level, a program encompasses a set of courses that collectively address a broader area of study.

Each course is further divided into modules, which function as intermediate structures to group-related topics. Within each module, the notebook operates as the fundamental entity for the presentation of instructional materials, learner interaction, and assessment activities. This hierarchical arrangement provides a coherent framework for content delivery as illustrated in Fig. 3.

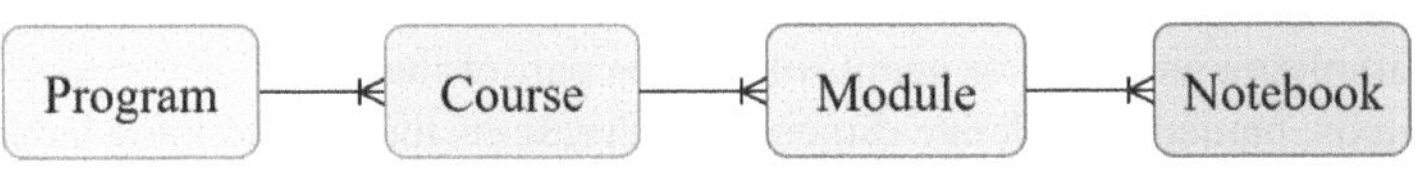

Fig. 3. Javali Course Content Model

3.2 Architecture

The application is composed of three primary components as illustrated on Fig. 4.

- *Client* - a local application node based on Electron.js that hosts a progressive web application (PWA) and a WebSocket server.
- *Kernel* - a local Java REPL based on JShell that routes all input and output through the notebook interface and exposes the notebook's internal state, including defined variables, classes, and other runtime artifacts. Communication with the main client occurs over a WebSocket connection.
- *Server* - a remote backend service responsible for user authentication, authorization and on demand content delivery.

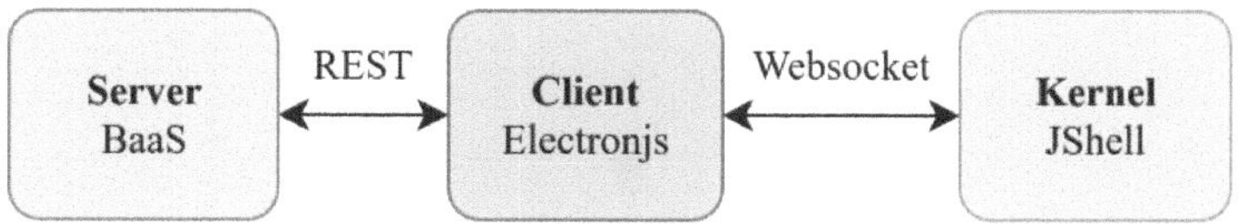

Fig. 4. Javali main components

3.3 Graphical User Interface

The Javalí interface is organized into four main views: authentication, course navigation, notebook, and settings. Upon launching the application, the authentication view is displayed (see Fig. 5), prompting users to either sign in or create an account using their institutional email.

Once logged in, users can explore the notebook catalog through an accordion-based table of contents, which presents the content in a hierarchical, tree-like structure. This design allows users to expand and collapse sections, facilitating efficient navigation through nested topics and modules.

The settings view offers configurable options that enable users to adjust application parameters, including accessibility features such as interface scaling, global color themes (see Fig. 6 and Fig. 8), and font customization.

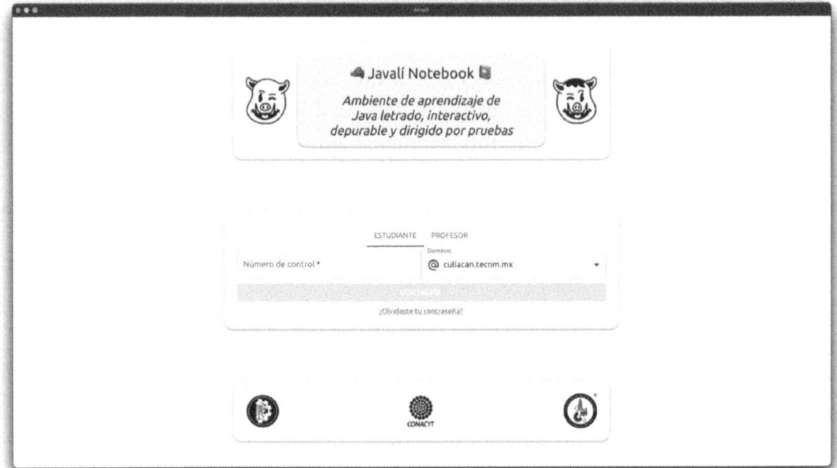

Fig. 5. Authentication Screen

The notebook view contains two main areas: the cell area (left part of Fig. 6) and the debug area (right part of Fig. 6). The cell area organizes all instructions, code, and tests in sequence, while the debug area displays the notebook's introspection state, showing variables, functions and types used in the code cells.

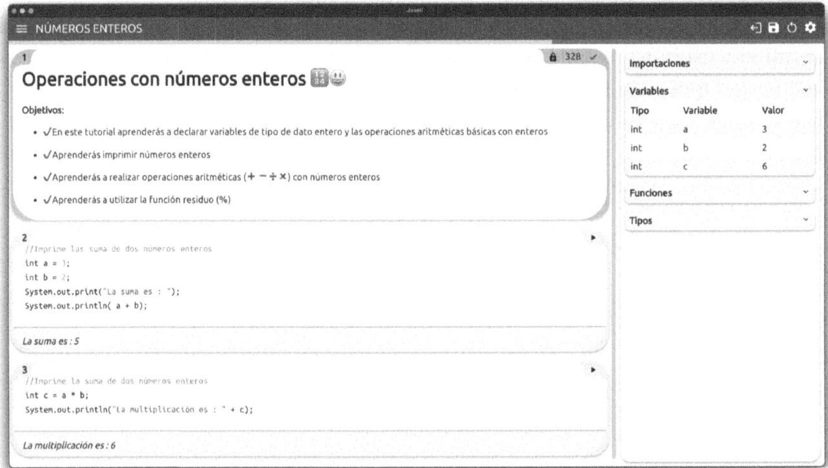

Fig. 6. Notebook View

4 Design and Experiments

Javalí Notebook is aimed at members of the academy, both students and professors, so we decided to conduct field tests to know if users are willing to adopt the tool for teaching and learning programming.

We hypothesize that a literate and interactive programming learning environment integrated with a management system will foster positive perceptions, attitudes, and intentions among students.

To evaluate this hypothesis, we selected the Technology Acceptance Model (TAM) [17], illustrated in Fig. 7, with five factors (Perceived Usefulness, Perceived Ease of Use, Perceived Enjoyment, Attitude toward use, and Intent to use) that considers perceived enjoyment as an intrinsic factor [18]. For each of the five TAM factors, three questions were generated using a five-point Likert scale, ranging from 1 (strongly disagree) to 5 (strongly agree).

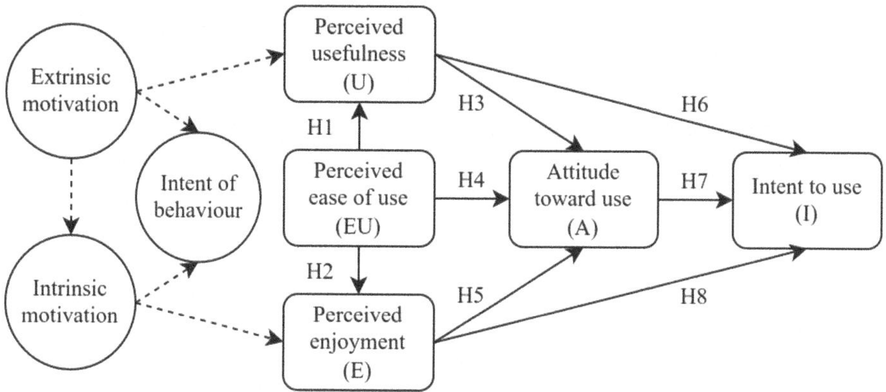

Fig. 7. Technology Acceptance Model with perceived enjoyment as an intrinsic factor.

4.1 Participants

The population that participated in the study consisted of 55 students, of whom four did not complete the test and were consequently discarded (N = 51). The remaining 51 students who completed the study were distributed across three groups which were part of two educational programs.

A week before the intervention, the students participated via Microsoft Teams in a one-hour virtual tutorial for the use of the Javalí Notebook tool (see Fig. 8). At the end of the tutorial, students were invited to download and install the tool on their devices.

The intervention follows a series of steps described below:

1. Each student was assigned a Java programming topic for developing a computational notebook, which would then be presented online via Microsoft Teams.
2. Students developed their notebooks over a period of 2 weeks, receiving assistance during the process for any questions related to the use of Javalí Notebook.
3. Students who completed the creation of their computational notebook presented their work during a virtual class. The rest of the students were discarded
4. Students who created and presented their computational notebook answered the TAM questionnaire.

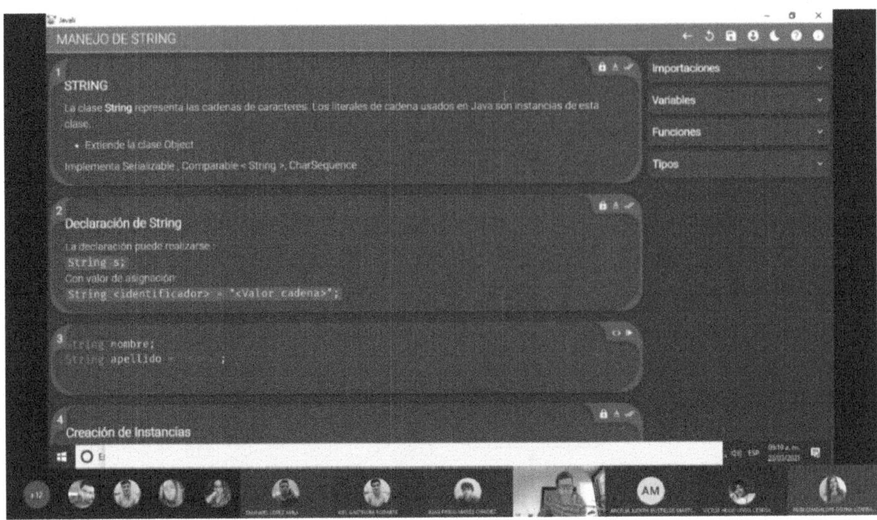

Fig. 8. Student presentation using Javalí Notebook in Microsoft Teams

4.2 Data

To measure the internal consistency of the data, McDonald's Omega coefficient was used; alternatively, this measure is also provided with Cronbach's alpha coefficient. For the descriptive analysis, measures of central tendency are presented in Table 1.

Table 1. Data metrics

TAM factor	McDonald's Omega (ω)	Cronbach Alfa (α)	Standard deviation	Median	Mode	Mean
U	0.863	0.859	0.108	5	5	4.438
EU	0.798	0.791	0.265	4	4	4.052
E	0.919	0.916	0.078	4	4	4.275
A	0.882	0.881	0.137	4	5	4.196
I	0.875	0.852	0.176	4	4	4.183

To evaluate the internal consistency of the statements within each construct, a Cronbach's alpha above 0.7 is expected. The obtained values meet this criterion, with the lowest recorded at 0.791.

4.3 Analysis

For the descriptive analysis, cutoff points were defined to map discrete quantitative responses from the Likert scale onto an ordinal scale (Negative, Neutral, and Positive).

For each TAM factor, median was used to assign ordinal value, see Table 2.

Table 2. Ordinal values assigned to TAM variables

TAM factor	Mean	Ordinal value
Perceived usefulness (**U**)	4.438	Positive
Perceived ease of use (**EU**)	4.052	Positive
Perceived enjoyment (**E**)	4.275	Positive
Attitude toward use (**A**)	4.196	Positive
Intention to use (**I**)	4.183	Positive

The Spearman correlations and their statistical significance for the Technology Acceptance Model hypotheses are presented in Table 3 and Fig. 9. Correlations highlighted in bold indicate strong associations between model factors (rho > 0.6), all correlations are statistically significant, with asterisks indicating significance levels: $p < 0.05$, $p < 0.01$, and $p < 0.001$.

Table 3. Spearman correlations for research model hypotheses

Hypothesis	Factors	rho	p
H1	EU – U	0.514	< .001***
H2	EU - E	0.421	< .002***
H3	U – A	**0.780**	< .001***
H4	EU - A	0.321	< .022*
H5	E – A	**0.820**	< .001***
H6	U - I	**0.683**	< .001***
H7	A - I	**0.809**	< .001***
H8	E - I	**0.738**	< .001***

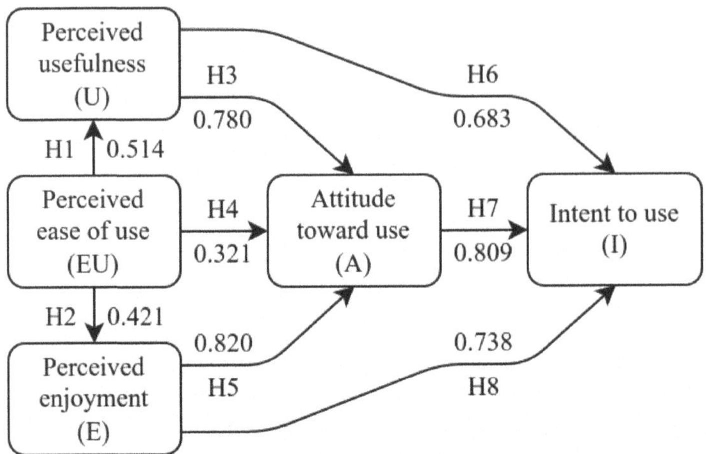

Fig. 9. Spearman rho values for TAM hypothesis

5 Conclusions and Future Work

Based on the cutoff points and the descriptive analysis, in which all research model variables yielded positive ordinal values, the results provide sufficient evidence to support the hypothesis: "A literate and interactive programming learning environment integrated with a management system will foster positive perceptions, attitudes, and intentions among students", as predicted by the Technology Acceptance Model.

The TAM analysis further indicates that perceived usefulness and perceived enjoyment are strongly associated with attitude toward use. On the other hand, perceived enjoyment and attitude toward use are strongly associated with intention to use.

Future work will explore applications of generative AI [2] and relevant use regulations [19], as well as the development of personalized learning paths, which can further enhance learning gains and student engagement. Additionally, there are opportunities to enhance the user experience, particularly since perceived ease of use received the lowest mean score in the Technology Acceptance Model.

The tool can be extended to support all remaining cell types defined in the bidimensional literate programming model, including category, sequence, visual block, and Parsons cells.

Regarding language support, the platform could potentially accommodate other JVM-based languages, such as Kotlin and Scala, while simplifying the architecture by leveraging in-browser compilation via WebAssembly toolchains, and could also extend to web-based languages like TypeScript.

Acknowledgements. We appreciate the support provided by CONFIE Sinaloa to participate in this event.

References

1. Cardoso, A., Leitão, J., Teixeira, C.: Using the jupyter notebook as a tool to support the teaching and learning processes in engineering courses. In: Advances in Intelligent Systems and Computing. pp. 227–236. Springer Verlag (2019)
2. Wang, S., et al.: Large Language Models for Education: A Survey and Outlook (2024)
3. Wolfram, S.: How to Teach Computational Thinking. https://writings.stephenwolfram.com/2016/09/how-to-teach-computational-thinking/
4. Reades, J.: Teaching on Jupyter. REGION. 7, 21–34 (2020). https://doi.org/10.18335/region.v7i1.282
5. Jupyter, P., et al.: A tool for creating and grading assignments in the jupyter notebook. Journal of Open Source Education **2**(11), 32 (2019). https://doi.org/10.21105/jose.00032
6. CodeGrade: The Engaging Code Learning Platform. https://www.codegrade.com/
7. Deepnote: Analytics and Data Science Notebook for Teams.https://deepnote.com/
8. Goggle: Google Colaboratory. https://colab.google/
9. Apache: Zeppelin. https://zeppelin.apache.org/
10. Microsoft: Announcing Polyglot Notebooks!. https://devblogs.microsoft.com/dotnet/announcing-polyglot-notebooks-harness-the-power-of-multilanguage-notebooks-in-visual-studio-code/
11. Knuth, D.E.: Literate programming. Comput. J. **27**(2), 97–111 (1984). https://doi.org/10.1093/comjnl/27.2.97
12. Ramsey, N.: Literate programming simplified. IEEE Softw. **11**, 97–105 (1994). https://doi.org/10.1109/52.311070
13. Kluyver T., et al.: Jupyter notebooks--a publishing format for reproducible computational workflows. In: Loizides, F., Schmidt, B. (eds.) Positioning and Power in Academic Publishing: Players, Agents and Agendas. pp. 87–90. IOS Press (2016)
14. Baumer, B., Udwin, D.: R Markdown. WIREs Computational Statistics. **7**, 167–177 (2015). https://doi.org/10.1002/wics.1348
15. Sandewall, E.: Programming in an interactive environment: the "lisp" experience. ACM Comput. Surv. **10**, 35–71 (1978). https://doi.org/10.1145/356715.356719
16. Ryle, G.: The Concept of Mind. Routledge (2009)
17. Granić, A., Marangunić, N.: Technology acceptance model in educational context: a systematic literature review. Br. J. Edu. Technol. **50**, 2572–2593 (2019). https://doi.org/10.1111/bjet.12864
18. Ibanez, M.B., Di Serio, A., Villarán, D., Delgado-Kloos, C.: The acceptance of learning augmented reality environments: a case study. In: 2016 IEEE 16th International Conference on Advanced Learning Technologies (ICALT), pp. 307–311. IEEE (2016)
19. Oakley, B., Johnston, M., Chen, K.-Z., Jung, E., Sejnowski, T.J.: The Memory Paradox: Why Our Brains Need Knowledge in an Age of AI. Springer Nature (2025)

Towards Adaptive Tutoring: A Proposed Self-efficacy Behavior Model for Intelligent Learning Environments

Victor Domínguez-Lara, Eduardo Sánchez-Jiménez, Yasmín Hernández(✉), Javier Ortiz-Hernandez, and Sandra Magali García-García

Computer Science Department, TecNM/Cenidet, Cuernavaca, Mexico
{m24ce051,d22ce005,yasmin.hp,javier.oh,d23ce168}@cenidet.tecnm.mx

Abstract. Self-efficacy is defined as the belief of individuals in their own capabilities. Academic self-efficacy has been shown to play a crucial role in student success, it can be fostered through educational practices that enable learners to acquire skills while receiving appropriate feedback. A self-efficacy model for an intelligent learning environment is proposed to strengthen the self-efficacy of students and thus improve learning outcomes. The model predicts the self-efficacy of learners and provides pedagogical actions designed to promote it based on pedagogical models. The student's self-efficacy model is grounded in their interaction with the learning environment, while the tutor's self-efficacy model relies on presenting vicarious experiences, mastery experiences, and positive feedback. We hope to achieve empirical evidence on the impact of self-efficacy in adaptive learning systems, and insights about fostering beliefs of students in their own abilities in order to improve motivation, persistence, and academic achievement.

Keywords: Bandura theory · intelligent learning environments · intelligent tutoring system · self-efficacy · student model · vicarious learning

1 Introduction

Self-efficacy is a fundamental psychological construct introduced and extensively developed by Albert Bandura [1], primarily within the framework of his Social Cognitive Theory. Bandura defined self-efficacy as the belief in the ability to organize and execute the courses of action required to manage future situations. In the academic domain, this belief directly influences the motivation, effort, persistence, and their ability to face and overcome learning challenges [2].

Given its crucial relevance to academic success, intelligent learning environments must integrate the detection and adaptation of self-efficacy, as this psychological variable is a critical determinant of achievement. When students

L. Martínez-Villaseñor et al. (Eds.): MICAI 2025, LNAI 16265, pp. 106–113, 2026.
https://doi.org/10.1007/978-3-032-17933-3_11

experience success in adaptive learning contexts, their confidence in their ability to succeed in similar tasks increases, leading to improved academic outcomes [3].

Self-efficacy can be measured through various methodologies, including standardized self-report scales, the analysis of physiological sensor data, and inductive models based on machine learning algorithms. The challenge of adapting self-efficacy in intelligent learning environments lies in determining how to continuously respond to student perception of self-efficacy, which is not static and depends on the influence of the four main sources proposed by Bandura [1].

Our research proposes a student model that dynamically incorporates the self-efficacy beliefs within an Intelligent Learning Environment (ILE) designed to teach mathematical logic, known as `MateLog` [4]. This model moves beyond cognitive assessments by integrating motivational dimensions, specifically focusing on mastery experiences and verbal persuasion. Leveraging educational data mining, machine learning, and Bayesian Networks, our approach provides a continuous, probabilistic estimation of self-efficacy. This enables MateLog to offer more adaptive pedagogical interventions, fostering greater student motivation, persistence, and academic achievement. The preliminary analysis are encouraging; they indicate that it is possible to build learning environments that not only measure student self-efficacy, but also respond to it in ways that promote its development.

The rest of this paper is organized as follows: Sect. 2 describes the background and related work. Section 3 presents the proposed self-efficacy modeling. Section 4 presents the discussion. Finally, Sect. 5 covers the conclusions and future work.

2 Background and Related Work

In order to situate our proposal within its theoretical and technological context, this section provides the necessary background and related work. We first revisit self-efficacy theory of Bandura, which establishes the psychological foundations of perceived competence and its four key sources of influence. This theoretical basis is then connected to recent research on self-efficacy in ILE, highlighting how the concept has been adapted and operationalized in technology-enhanced learning. Together, these perspectives inform the rationale for incorporating self-efficacy into student modeling and guide the design of our proposed approach.

2.1 Self-efficacy Theory of Bandura

According to Bandura [1], the four principal sources from which self-efficacy beliefs are (see Fig. 1): mastery experiences, vicarious experience, social persuasion, and physiological and affective states. Mastery experiences—direct encounters with success when overcoming challenges—constitute the most powerful and reliable determinant. Repeated achievement, particularly in demanding tasks, reinforces self-efficacy, whereas early failures may erode it if attributed to a lack of ability rather than insufficient effort or unfavorable external conditions. Vicarious experience, by contrast, operates through the observation of the outcomes of others, often mediated by social comparison. Witnessing similar peers succeed through sustained effort can foster the belief that one's own success is attainable, especially in contexts where prior experience is limited. Social persuasion, most commonly in the form of verbal encouragement from credible sources, can also promote self-efficacy. Although typically less robust than mastery or vicarious experience, it serves to motivate individuals to attempt tasks and sustain effort in the presence of difficulties. Finally, physiological and affective states—such as stress, anxiety, fatigue, or mood—shape efficacy judgments by signaling either vulnerability or competence. The interpretation of these states is pivotal: heightened arousal or negative affect may be construed as incapacity, thereby undermining self-efficacy.

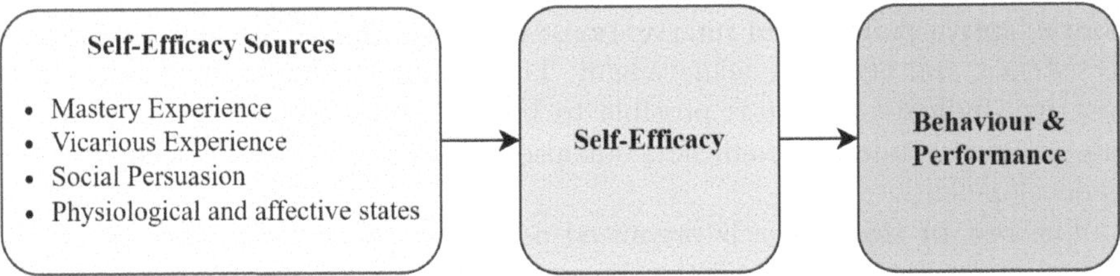

Fig. 1. Sources of self-efficacy and their influence on behaviour and performance from Bandura [1].

2.2 Self-efficacy in Intelligent Learning Environments

Several studies grounded in Bandura's self-efficacy theory have explored how this construct influences learning and motivation, particularly in technology-mediated educational environments such as ITSs and online learning platforms. Hodges [5] pointed out that, unlike traditional learning settings—where the relationship between self-efficacy and performance is well-established—research on its role in online learning is relatively recent, less defined, and often reports inconsistent or mixed results. Although published over a decade ago, no recent evidence has been found to contradict this observation. Despite the time gap, Alqurashi [6] also argued that further research is still needed to fully understand the nature of the relationship between self-efficacy and online learning. Furthermore, these works identified similar criteria for effective self-efficacy diagnosis within an ITS: it must be performed in real time during learning sessions, designed efficiently so as not to compromise interactivity, and avoid interruptions in the educational process. They further cautioned that instruments administered prior to learning may be insufficient, since self-efficacy is a dynamic variable subject to change over time.

Another line of research focuses on how ITSs can be designed to foster mastery experiences, a crucial source of self-efficacy, by adapting to cognitive states and performance of students. These studies explore various mechanisms to ensure learners encounter appropriate challenges and achieve success, thereby building their confidence. Guzmán & Conejo [7] proposed an Item Response Theory (IRT)-based model for diagnosing student knowledge and misconceptions. This approach supports mastery experiences by enabling personalized instruction and feedback, which helps students overcome errors early, understand topics better, and build confidence through a structured learning environment. Papoušek & Pelánek [8] investigated how adaptive systems influence student motivation by adjusting task difficulty. Their work in a geography practice platform demonstrated that aligning question difficulty with a knowledge of learner increases success opportunities and engagement, emphasizing the need to balance challenge to prevent boredom or frustration. Adjei & Heffernan [9] developed an adaptive testing system that sequences questions based on prerequisite skills within a knowledge graph. By ensuring mastery of foundational skills before advancing, their system enhances mastery experiences, improves learning trajectories, and increases the likelihood of student success through tailored learning paths. Similarly, domain-specific ITSs such as SIAL [10] have demonstrated the potential of adaptive feedback and error correction strategies to reinforce mastery experiences in specialized contexts.

Feedback plays a central role in modeling verbal persuasion within ITS, as it not only informs students about their performance but also shapes their motivation and affective states. Research has highlighted that the effectiveness of feedback depends on its type, timing, delivery, and alignment with the cognitive and emotional needs of the learner. Van der Kleij et al. [11] demonstrated that elaborated feedback (EF) was more effective than simple forms such as knowledge of results (KR) or knowledge of the correct response (KCR), particularly for higher-order skills, and that both timing and educational context strongly influence its impact. Extending this, Grawemeyer et al. [12] showed that the type of feedback is especially critical when learners are confused, as tailored feedback can move them back into productive flow states. Finally, Al-Darei & Elhag [13] found that interpretive feedback, which explains not only correctness but also underlying reasoning, significantly enhanced both learning outcomes and motivation in online environments.

3 Self-efficacy Model

This work proposes the adaptation of two sources of self-efficacy: mastery experiences and verbal persuasion. The aim is to examine whether the two selected sources are sufficient to generate the expected results. Both sources will be modeled according to the student's self-efficacy, as illustrated in Fig. 2.

Mastery experiences are considered the most influential source of self-efficacy. One way to adapt them is by adjusting task difficulty to ensure that activities are neither too easy, which could lead to boredom, nor excessively difficult, which could cause frustration. Achieving this balance contributes to a more positive and effective learning experience.

Although verbal persuasion is less influential on self-efficacy than mastery or vicarious experiences, it plays a crucial role in mobilizing student effort and persistence. Its adaptation involves incorporating supportive messages and feedback under predefined conditions to reinforce the student's confidence. Feedback can be designed for various purposes, such as promoting understanding, suggesting next steps, addressing misconceptions, affirming success, or encouraging reflection. A student with low self-efficacy may require more frequent and encouraging feedback, whereas a student with high self-efficacy may benefit from more challenging comments.

The proposed self-efficacy modeling will be developed in `MateLog`. Here, student self-efficacy is classified using a machine learning model that utilizes two sources of information: (i) the results of Likert-type questionnaires that assess general and academic self-efficacy, and (ii) data derived from student interaction with `MateLog` [4], including metrics such as usage time, correct answers, progress, and other performance indicators. At this point, we are developing the self-efficacy model that relies on machine learning to automatically classify new students based on their interactions records within the platform. In this way, students are categorized into either high or low self-efficacy.

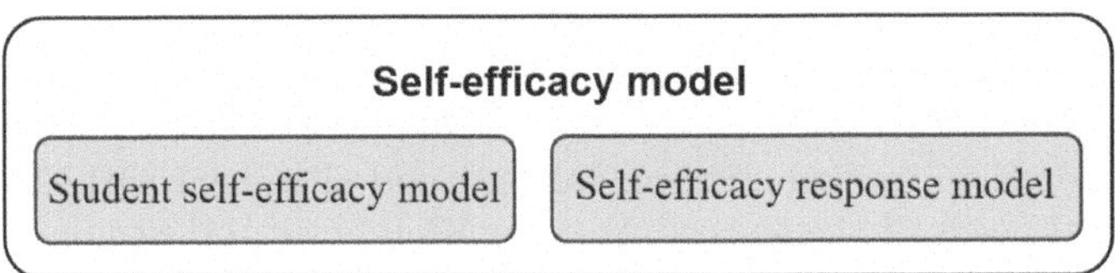

Fig. 2. Components of the self-efficacy model.

The classification obtained with machine learning is transmitted to the self-efficacy response model, which applies a set of rules through Bayesian networks that enable personalization of the learning experience.

Subsequently Fig. 3, the self-efficacy model is integrated into `MateLog` as part of its adaptive functionality. Learner interactions with the system are continuously recorded and analyzed using educational data mining techniques, from which relevant behavioral features are extracted (e.g., task success rates, time on task, number of attempts, and response to feedback). These features serve as input to machine learning classifiers that estimate the current level of self-efficacy of the student by identifying patterns that distinguish between low, medium, and high states. The resulting classification is then transmitted to the self-efficacy response model, which applies a set of pedagogical rules encoded within a Bayesian Network. This probabilistic approach allows the system to weigh multiple sources of evidence, handle uncertainty, and update self-efficacy estimates dynamically. Based on these estimates, the response model personalizes the learning experience by selecting suitable actions such as adjusting task

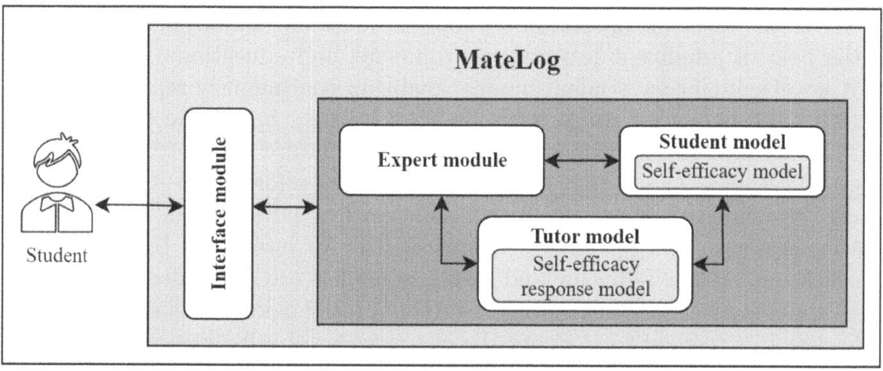

Fig. 3. Proposed `MateLog` architecture, including the self-efficacy model, and the adaptive self-efficacy response model.

difficulty, offering targeted hints, or providing motivational feedback, thereby aligning instructional strategies not only with cognitive needs but also with the learner's motivational profile.

The proposed functionalities to be integrated into `MateLog` focus on enhancing self-efficacy of students through concrete pedagogical actions: (i) Continuous assessment: Monitoring perceived self-efficacy of learners across the different stages of interaction. (ii) Dynamic adaptation: Gradually adjusting exercise complexity to ensure achievable challenges and foster mastery experiences. (iii) Supportive feedback: Providing timely motivational prompts and constructive guidance that reinforce persistence and confidence.

4 Discussion

This proposal contributes to the existing literature by addressing limitations identified in prior studies. First, unlike approaches that rely exclusively on pre-learning questionnaires, it introduces a dynamic inference model capable of assessing self-efficacy in real time without repeatedly interrupting the learning process. By integrating self-reported, and behavioral data, it offers a more robust assessment model and helps bridge the gap between static measurement tools, and adaptive pedagogical strategies. Second, it explicitly combines self-reported, and behavioral data, mitigating the limitations of static, single-source assessments. Finally, it operationalizes two key sources of self-efficacy—mastery experiences, and verbal persuasion—through adaptive task sequencing and personalized feedback.

However, the proposal is based on certain assumptions and faces inherent limitations. It presumes that self-efficacy can be reliably inferred from digital behavioral patterns, and that a binary classification (high vs. low) is sufficient for guiding adaptation. In addition, validation with a robust dataset is still required and the long-term impact on academic performance, and sustained motivation has not yet been confirmed.

With this research proposal, we hope to make the following contributions to the field of intelligent learning environments and educational data mining: (i) A novel self-efficacy student model capable of continuously representing and updating the perceived competence levels of learners in specific domains, taking into account the multifaceted, and dynamic nature of self-efficacy. (ii) An adaptive response model that leverages self-efficacy information to dynamically modify teaching strategies, feedback, and learning pathways in order to sustain engagement, and promote persistence. (iii) An integrated ILE framework in which both the self-efficacy and response models are embedded, with a concrete application to the teaching of Mathematical Logic. This implementation will serve as a testbed to evaluate the effectiveness of self-efficacy-driven adaptation. (iv) Empirical evidence on the impact of self-efficacy modeling in adaptive learning systems, providing insights into how fostering student beliefs in their own abilities contributes to improved motivation, persistence, and academic achievement.

5 Conclusions and Future Work

Despite the recognized importance of considering student self-efficacy in education, there remains a need to develop more initiatives that foster it. For classroom teachers, evaluating the self-efficacy of individual students and adapting instruction accordingly can be highly challenging. However, an Intelligent Learning Environment can serve as an effective support tool, owing to its ability to adapt through AI-driven algorithms that process information in a targeted and systematic manner.

Building on Bandura's social-cognitive theory, our model focuses on two influential and feasible sources of self-efficacy: mastery experiences, represented through student task performance and progression, and verbal persuasion, operationalized through adaptive feedback strategies. These sources are dynamically integrated using a Bayesian Network, enabling continuous estimation of student self-efficacy and informing adaptive pedagogical decisions. By delimiting the model to sources that can be effectively captured within the `MateLog` environment, the proposal achieves a balance between theoretical grounding and practical implementability. In doing so, it contributes to the ongoing efforts to enrich student models by incorporating motivational variables beyond cognitive knowledge.

Future work will focus on the implementation and empirical validation of the proposed model in the `MateLog` Intelligent Learning Environment, with the aim of assessing its impact on personalization, motivation, and learning outcomes.

References

1. Bandura, A.: Self-efficacy: toward a unifying theory of behavioral change. Psychol. Rev. **84**(2), 191 (1977)
2. McQuiggan, S.W., Lester, J.C.: Diagnosing self-efficacy in intelligent tutoring systems: an empirical study. In: Ikeda, M., Ashley, K.D., Chan, T.-W. (eds.) ITS 2006. LNCS, vol. 4053, pp. 565–574. Springer, Heidelberg (2006). https://doi.org/10.1007/11774303_56
3. Massaty, M.H., Fahrurozi, S.K., Budiyanto, C.W.: The role of AI in fostering computational thinking and self-efficacy in educational settings: a systematic review. IJIE (Indonesian J. Inform. Educ.) **8**(1), 49–61 (2024)
4. Mendoza, M., Hernández, Y., Ortiz, J., Martínez, A., Estrada, H.: Gathering, integration and preprocessing of data in educational data mining: towards a study of self-efficacy in learning. Intell. Learn. Environ. p. 69 (2023)
5. Hodges, C.B.: Self-efficacy in the context of online learning environments: a review of the literature and directions for research. Perform. Improv. Q. **20**(3–4), 7–25 (2008)
6. Alqurashi, E.: Self-efficacy in online learning environments: a literature review. Contemp. Issues Educ. Res. (Online) **9**(1), 45 (2016)
7. Guzmán, E., Conejo, R.: Measuring misconceptions through item response theory. In: Conati, C., Heffernan, N., Mitrovic, A., Verdejo, M.F. (eds.) AIED 2015. LNCS (LNAI), vol. 9112, pp. 608–611. Springer, Cham (2015). https://doi.org/10.1007/978-3-319-19773-9_73
8. Papoušek, J., Pelánek, R.: Impact of adaptive educational system behaviour on student motivation. In: Conati, C., Heffernan, N., Mitrovic, A., Verdejo, M.F. (eds.) AIED 2015. LNCS (LNAI), vol. 9112, pp. 348–357. Springer, Cham (2015). https://doi.org/10.1007/978-3-319-19773-9_35
9. Adjei, S.A., Heffernan, N.T.: Improving learning maps using an adaptive testing system: PLACEments. In: Conati, C., Heffernan, N., Mitrovic, A., Verdejo, M.F. (eds.) AIED 2015. LNCS (LNAI), vol. 9112, pp. 517–520. Springer, Cham (2015). https://doi.org/10.1007/978-3-319-19773-9_51
10. Maestro-Prieto, J.A., Simon-Hurtado, A.: The pedagogical model of SIAL: an adaptive and open-ended intelligent tutoring system for first order logic. In: Proceedings of the 23rd Annual ACM Conference on Innovation and Technology in Computer Science Education, pp. 21–26 (2018)
11. Anohina, A.: Advances in intelligent tutoring systems: problem-solving modes and model of hints. Int. J. Comput. Commun. Control **2**(1), 48–55 (2007)
12. Grawemeyer, B., Mavrikis, M., Holmes, W., Hansen, A., Loibl, K., Gutiérrez-Santos, S.: Affect matters: exploring the impact of feedback during mathematical tasks in an exploratory environment. In: Conati, C., Heffernan, N., Mitrovic, A., Verdejo, M.F. (eds.) AIED 2015. LNCS (LNAI), vol. 9112, pp. 595–599. Springer, Cham (2015). https://doi.org/10.1007/978-3-319-19773-9_70
13. Al-Darei, I.S., Elhag, A.: The effect of feedback type in the e-learning environment on students' achievement and motivation. J. Educ. Technol. Online Learn. **5**(3), 694–705 (2022)

CIAPP 2025

Web Module for Breast Cancer Risk Prediction Using Clinical and Psychological Data

Jose Luis Llaguno-Roque[1], Adriana Laura Lopez Lobato[2], Juan Carlos Pérez-Arriaga[3], Hector Gabriel Acosta-Mesa[2], Ángel J. Sánchez-García[2], Gabriel Gutierrez-Ospina[4], Antonia Barranca-Enríquez[1], and Tania Romo-González[1](✉)

[1] Institute of Biological Research, Universidad Veracruzana, Veracruz, Mexico
tromogonzalez@uv.mx
[2] Artificial Intelligence Research Institute, Universidad Veracruzana, Veracruz, Mexico
[3] Faculty of Statistics and Informatics, Universidad Veracruzana, Veracruz, Mexico
[4] Iztacala School of Higher Studies, Universidad Nacional Autónoma de México, Mexico, Mexico

1 Introduction

Breast cancer (BC) is the most common neoplasm in women worldwide, with a prevalence of 26.7%, accounting for 2.3 million new cases and around 700,000 deaths annually [1]. In Mexico, it has been the most prevalent and lethal cancer since 2006, surpassing cervical cancer, and represents a significant public health challenge [2]. In 2022, 31,043 new cases were reported, predominantly in women aged 40–59 years (14,846 cases), followed by those over 60 (11,430 cases) and 20–44 (7,839 cases). The mean age at diagnosis, 52.3 years, is approximately a decade earlier than in developed countries [1, 3]. Mortality reached 8,195 cases, mainly in women over 60 (4,061 deaths) [1].

BC is a multifactorial disease. The Mexican Official Standard identifies four categories of risk factors: biological, iatrogenic, reproductive history, and lifestyle. Carvalho et al. (2005) [4] expand these to include family inheritance, stress, physical trauma, emotional repression, diet, and self-care habits. Various lifetime risk assessment models have been developed internationally, such as the Gail Model, Tyrer-Cuzick Model, and BOADICEA, which use biological and reproductive data to inform screening, preventive surgery, or chemoprophylaxis decisions [5, 6]. Although effective and widely applied in developed countries [7], no equivalent tools tailored to the Mexican population—and incorporating lifestyle or psychological factors—are currently available. Psychological factors including stress, anxiety, and emotional suppression have been linked to BC onset [8–10] In Mexican women with BC, our group identified five psychological traits—low containment, low global and physical stress symptoms, low containment-defensiveness, and high stress—consistent with type C personality, present before diagnosis [11]. Furthermore, PCA combining clinical and psychological data showed that clinical variables contributed little to differentiating pathology, whereas emotional suppression variables had the highest weight [12]. For this reason, we present in this article the development of a web module to calculate the risk of developing breast cancer, which incorporates

L. Martínez-Villaseñor et al. (Eds.): MICAI 2025, LNAI 16265, pp. 117–124, 2026.
https://doi.org/10.1007/978-3-032-17933-3_12

biological, reproductive and psychological variables, which could be adjusted for use in other populations.

2 Methodology

2.1 Description of the Sample

The study included clinical and psychological data from 150 women who voluntarily participated after providing informed consent, ensuring confidentiality and anonymity. All participants attended gynecological consultations at the General Hospital of Mexico "Dr. Eduardo Liceaga", allowing for a broad age range—an important aspect given that breast cancer in Mexican women appears about a decade earlier than in other populations [11, 13]. Psychological data were collected prior to histopathological confirmation, and participants were classified into three groups: healthy women without breast pathology (H, n = 50), women with benign breast pathology such as fibrocystic disease, fibroadenomas, or mastitis (BBP, n = 50), and women diagnosed with infiltrating ductal carcinoma without prior treatment (BC, n = 50).

2.2 Data Collection Instruments

Physical, hereditary, and lifestyle information was obtained through a 57-item General Data Questionnaire, while psychological data—covering emotional repression and suppression, and stress symptoms—were gathered using three validated instruments: the Inventory of Stress Symptomatology (ISE), the Courtauld Emotional Control Scale (CECS), and the Weinberger Adjustment Inventory (WAI). For more detail see [11]. The described questionnaire was implemented on the LimeSurvey platform and is available for online application through the following address: http://13.66.56.230/encuestas/index.php/867174?lang=es-MXAn example of the questionnaire can be seen in Fig. 1.

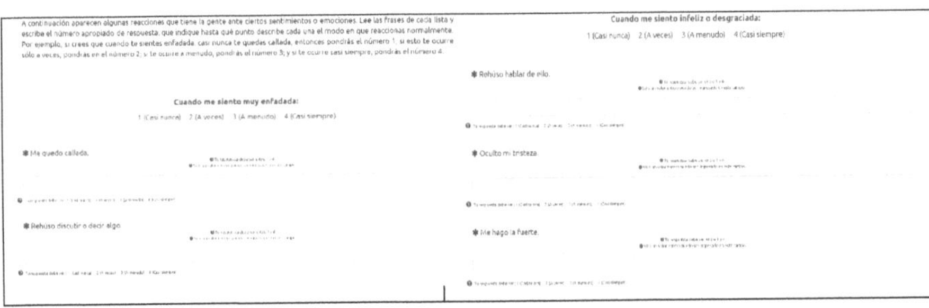

Fig. 1. Example of the applied questionnaire

Model Construction for the Web Module.

Generation of Binary Chains

To build the web module, each study variable was coded in binary form (0 or 1) according to the presence (1) or absence (0) of a risk factor, or, in psychological factors, according to whether the "high" score category was present. The variables included: **Clinical:** Age, Family history of cancer (FamHis), Overweight (OW), Obesity (Obe), Smoking (Taba), Alcoholism (Alco), Drug use (Toxi), Early menarche (EarlyMen), Late menopause (LateMenop), Pregnancies (Preg), Vaginal delivery (Da), Abortion (Abo), Cesarean section (Cesa), Age at first delivery (AFD), Use of exogenous hormones (EH), Breastfeeding (Lac), Hormone replacement therapy (HRT). **CECS:** Low, Middle, and High Anger (AL, AM, AH); Low, Middle, and High Depression (DL, DM, DH); Low, Middle, and High Anxiety (ANL, ANM, ANH); Low, Middle, and High CECS scores (SL, SM, SH). **WAI**: Low and High Distress (DSL, DSH); Low, Middle, High Restraint (RL, RM, RH); Low and High Restraint/Distress (RDL, RDH). **ISE:** Low, Middle, and High scores for Physical (SFL, SFM, SFH), Psychological (SPL, SPM, SPH), Social (SSL, SSM, SSH), and Global symptoms (SGL, SGM, SGH). To limit the possible noise of variables that were not essential for determining the risk of developing breast cancer, the percentage of influence of the variables was calculated for each group, and a minimum of 70% was determined to consider the variable as "influential". Next, the association between the variables was calculated using Yule's coefficient, using the following formula:

$$Q = \frac{(a.d - c.b)}{(a.d + c.b)}$$

Cases in which the values of Q are equal to 0 indicate that the variables are independent; if Q is greater than 0 there is a positive association and if Q is less than 0 the association is negative. The calculation of the values was performed in the R environment [14].

2.3 Construction of the Classification Model by Machine Learning

To facilitate understanding and visualization of the three classes analyzed in this study, a classification model was implemented. This model reduces the complexity of the dataset, enables two-dimensional projection of the data, and generates a probabilistic structure for classification that incorporates conditional probabilities. This approach also enables statistical validation of the obtained results. The method applied was Differential Evolutionary Linear Discriminant Analysis for Feature Extraction and Visualization ($DE - LDA_{FE}$), a supervised learning strategy that searches for a two-dimensional space in which the dataset's projections are well separated by class. The orthonormal vectors w_1 and w_2 that define the specified subspace are obtained using the Differential Evolution (DE) algorithm, with Fisher's criterion utilized as the fitness function to assess the separability of the classes. The resulting projections, denoted by Y_i, are defined as linear combinations of the original features of the dataset, as illustrated in Eq. (1). These linear combinations can also be expressed by the matrix multiplication shown in Eq. (2).

$$Y_i = w_{1i}X_1 + w_{2i}X_2 + \cdots + w_{ni}X_i \text{ for } i = 1, 2. \quad (1)$$

$$Y_{m\times 2} = X_{m\times n}W_{n\times 2}. \quad (2)$$

Fisher's criterion evaluates two aspects simultaneously—maximizing the distance between class means and minimizing the variation within each class—through the between-class scatter matrix S_B and the within-class scatter matrix S_W, defined as in Eqs. (3) and (4), respectively, and Fisher's criterion is then calculated as in Eq. (5).

$$S_B = \sum_{g=1}^{G} m_g (\mu_g - \mu)^T (\mu_g - \mu) \tag{3}$$

$$S_W = \sum_{g=1}^{G} \sum_{x \in C_g} (x - \mu_g)^T (x - \mu_g) \tag{4}$$

$$J(W) = \frac{|S_B|}{|S_W|} \tag{5}$$

The DE algorithm randomly generates candidate matrices W and evolves them over successive iterations to maximize $J(W)$. The optimal W produces projections where each class is compact and distinct from the others. Once the optimal projection space is identified, Gaussian models are fitted to the projected data, creating a probabilistic framework for classification. In this framework a new data point is assigned to the class whose Gaussian distribution yields the highest conditional probability, ensuring accurate and interpretable classification.

3 Results

The $DE-LDA_{FE}$ method was applied to clinical and psychological data from 150 women attending gynecological consultations at the General Hospital of Mexico "Dr. Eduardo Liceaga," analyzing three scenarios: clinical data alone, psychological data alone, and both combined. This approach enabled comparison of classification performance and evaluation of the contribution of psychological variables.

Figure 2A shows the projections obtained using clinical variables and the Gaussian estimations applied for classification. The three classes—Breast Cancer (BC), Benign Breast Pathology (BBP), and Healthy (H)—displayed low separation, with substantial overlap between Gaussian structures. The classification accuracy reached 61.92% (F1-score 59.32%, precision 60.68%, recall 58.94%, specificity 80.21%).

The confusion matrix (Fig. 3A) indicated greater misclassification between BBP and BC than between other class pairs. A one-way MANOVA using Pillai's trace revealed significant differences among the three groups ($p = 2.84 \times 10 - 27$). The mean ± standard error projection values were BC = − 0.0461 ± 0.0362, BBP = − 0.2541 ± 0.0391, and H = 0.2829 ± 0.0581. Post hoc Tukey-Kramer tests confirmed that all group means were significantly different, although high Gaussian overlap.

Projections obtained using psychological variables are presented in Fig. 2B, again showing low class separation and considerable Gaussian overlap. Classification accuracy reached 62.73% (F1-score 60.27%, precision 63.47%, recall 59.45%, specificity 80.27%), slightly higher than with clinical data alone. The confusion matrix (Fig. 3B) maintained a similar pattern, with higher misclassification between BBP and BC. The

MANOVA with Pillai's trace showed statistically significant overall differences ($p = 1.08 \times 10^{-30}$); however, Tukey-Kramer tests indicated no significant difference between BBP (-0.4112 ± 0.0288) and H (-0.3946 ± 0.0455). The BC group presented a mean projection of $-\ 0.0101 \pm 0.0247$, closer to zero, suggesting limited separation between BBP and H when only psychological variables are used. Therefore, it is not possible to classify the patient case based solely on psychological data, even when the precision of this classification method is slightly higher than that of the clinical data.

When combining both types of variables, projections in Fig. 2C revealed clearer separation between classes, with distinct Gaussian structures. Classification accuracy increased notably to 80.91% (F1-score 81.09%, precision 81.09%, recall 81.09%, specificity 90.07%). The confusion matrix (Fig. 3C) still showed some overlap between BBP and BC—expected given that both correspond to pathological conditions—but separation from H was much more evident. MANOVA results confirmed significant group differences ($p = 1.25 \times 10^{-29}$), and Tukey-Kramer tests showed significant differences among all three groups: BC $= -\ 0.1213 \pm 0.0176$, BBP $= 0.1686 \pm 0.0199$, and H $= 0.2796 \pm 0.0237$. Overall, the findings demonstrate that while using only clinical or only psychological data yields moderate classification performance, integrating both considerably enhances accuracy and class separability.

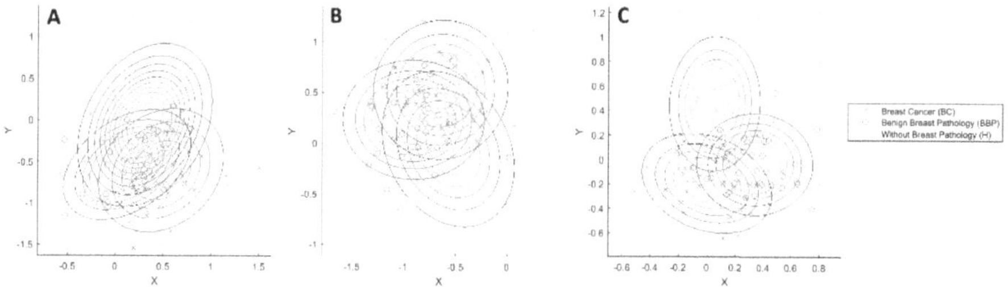

Fig. 2. Gaussian estimation plot of the three classes analyzed. A) Considering the clinical data. B) Considering the psychological data. C) Considering the clinical and psychological data.

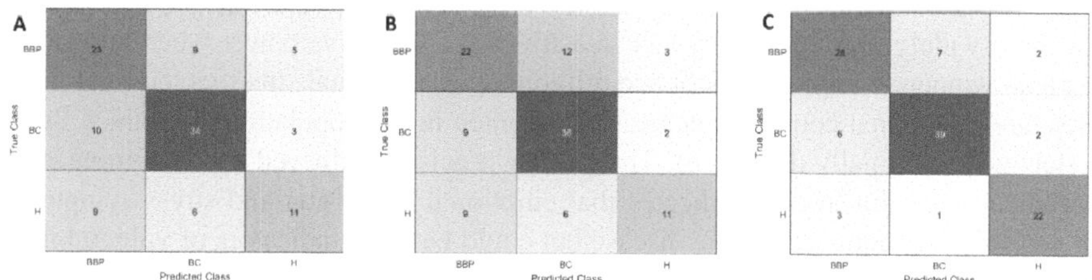

Fig. 3. Confusion matrix comparing the actual labels of the dataset with the predicted labels using the Gaussian structure technique. A) Clinical data. B) Psychological data. C) Clinical and psychological data.

Cross-validation could not be applied due to the limited sample size (150 participants distributed across three groups), which would have resulted in partitions too small for a stable analysis. In future studies with larger datasets, this technique will be implemented to more robustly assess the model's generalization capacity.

4 Discussion

Breast cancer remains one of the most critical public health issues globally, particularly affecting women in developing countries such as Mexico. Despite advancements in diagnosis and treatment, mortality rates remain high, largely due to delayed detection and the limited reach of effective screening programs. In Mexico, breast cancer has become the leading cause of cancer-related deaths among women, and its presentation occurs approximately a decade earlier than in high-income countries. These circumstances highlight the need for early detection tools adapted to the characteristics of the Mexican population. This study demonstrates that the integration of psychological variables—particularly those related to emotional repression, suppression, and stress symptoms—into clinical risk models significantly improves classification accuracy. When only clinical or psychological data were used separately, the classification accuracies remained moderate (**~61%**). However, when both types of data were combined and analyzed through the Differential Evolution Linear Discriminant Analysis for Feature Extraction ($DE - LDA_{FE}$) strategy, the accuracy increased markedly to **80.91%**, highlighting the predictive power of psychosocial dimensions in cancer risk modeling. The inclusion of psychological profiles in this study is particularly innovative in the Latin American context. Prior research has established a connection between type C personality traits (such as emotional repression and a tendency to avoid conflict) and the development and progression of breast cancer [8–10]. Emotional suppression has been associated with altered cortisol levels, greater tumor aggressiveness, and reduced survival [15]. In our study, these traits were confirmed as influential variables in the Mexican female population, which supports the idea that stress-related emotional processing may influence the biological mechanisms underlying tumor development, possibly through psychoneuroimmunological pathways [11, 12]. While tools such as the Gail, Tyrer-Cuzick, and BOADICEA models are widely used in high-income countries, they rely primarily on biological and reproductive variables, without accounting for the complex sociocultural or psychological dimensions that are critical in other populations. Our findings suggest that these widely used tools may lack sensitivity or predictive power when applied to Mexican women, who may experience different environmental stressors, cultural pressures, and emotional coping strategies than women in the populations for which those models were originally developed. The greater precision achieved by combining psychological and clinical data indicates that emotional repression and stress symptoms are not only consequences of the disease but could be early indicators of vulnerability. These results support the hypothesis that psychological factors may play a pathogenetic role in breast cancer. The findings also suggest that certain psychological traits may reflect persistent exposure to stress and dysregulation of emotional expression, factors that influence health. The development of a web module offers a cost-effective, scalable, and user-friendly solution to help predict breast cancer risk in Mexican women. The potential utility of such a module includes: A) Assisting primary care providers in making informed decisions about referrals or preventive strategies, B) empowering women with access to self-assessment tools in contexts where medical services may be limited, C) enhancing screening strategies by prioritizing individuals with high psychological and clinical risk profiles. For future work this module could be adapted for any region of the world and potentially translated into mobile applications, improving early detection in areas with limited resources. Despite its contributions, this study has several limitations. First, the sample size (n = 150), while balanced across groups, is limited and drawn from a single medical center, which may reduce generalizability. Second, the classification accuracy, while high for the combined model, still indicates some overlap between benign and malignant pathologies, possibly due to shared psychological profile. Furthermore, cross-validation was not possible in this study due to the small sample size (150 participants distributed across three groups), which would have resulted in insufficient partitions for a stable analysis. In future studies with larger data volumes, this technique will be implemented to evaluate the model's generalization capabilities. Comparative evaluations with standard machine learning classifiers, such as decision trees, among other benchmark algorithms, will also be incorporated.

References

1. World Health Organization: Data visualization tools for exploring the global cancer burden (2022). https://gco.iarc.fr/today/en/dataviz/pie?mode=cancer
2. Maffuz-Aziz, A., Labastida-Almendaro, S., Espejo-Fonseca, A., Rodríguez-Cuevas, S.: Características clinicopatológicas del cáncer de mama en una población de mujeres en México. Cirugía y Cirujanos. **85**, 201–207 (2017). https://doi.org/10.1016/j.circir.2016.08.004
3. Cárdenas-Sánchez, J.: Consenso mexicano sobre diagnóstico y tratamiento del cáncer mamario. GAMO **20**, 6923 (2022). https://doi.org/10.24875/j.gamo.M21000213
4. Carvalho Fernández, A.F., Mesquita Melo, E., de Almeida Araújo, I., Figueiredo Carvalho, Z.M.: Aspectos culturales en el proceso de padecer cáncer de mama (2005). https://revistas.unal.edu.co/index.php/avenferm/article/view/37559
5. Amir, N., Beard, C., Burns, M., Bomyea, J.: Attention modification program in individuals with generalized anxiety disorder. J. Abnorm. Psychol. **118**, 28–33 (2009). https://doi.org/10.1037/a0012589
6. Brentnall, A.R., et al.: Mammographic density adds accuracy to both the Tyrer-Cuzick and Gail breast cancer risk models in a prospective UK screening cohort. Breast Cancer Res. **17**, 147 (2015). https://doi.org/10.1186/s13058-015-0653-5
7. Terry, M.B., et al.: 10-year performance of four models of breast cancer risk: a validation study. Lancet Oncol. **20**, 504–517 (2019). https://doi.org/10.1016/S1470-2045(18)30902-1
8. Greer, S., Morris, T.: Psychological attributes of women who develop breast cancer: a controlled study. J. Psychosom. Res. **19**, 147–153 (1975). https://doi.org/10.1016/0022-3999(75)90062-8
9. Temoshok, L.: Personality, coping style, emotion and cancer: towards an integrative model. Cancer Surv. **6** (1987)
10. Iwamitsu, Y., Shimoda, K., Abe, H., Tani, T., Kodama, M., Okawa, M.: Differences in emotional distress between breast tumor patients with emotional inhibition and those with emotional expression. Psychiatry Clin. Neurosci. **57**, 289–294 (2003). https://doi.org/10.1046/j.1440-1819.2003.01119.x
11. Romo-González, T., Martínez, A.J., Hernández-Pozo, M.D.R., Gutiérrez-Ospina, G., Larralde, C.: Psychological features of breast cancer in Mexican women I: personality traits and stress symptoms. NIB **7**, 3–15 (2018). https://doi.org/10.3233/NIB-170123

12. Montes-Nogueira, I., Campos-Uscanga, Y., Gutiérrez-Ospina, G., Hernández-Pozo, M.D.R., Larralde, C., Romo-González, T.: Psychological features of breast cancer in Mexican women II: the psychological network. NIB **7**, 91–105 (2018). https://doi.org/10.3233/NIB-170125
13. Chávarri-Guerra, Y., et al.: Breast cancer in Mexico: a growing challenge to health and the health system. Lancet Oncol. **13**, e335–e343 (2012). https://doi.org/10.1016/S1470-2045(12)70246-2
14. R: A language and environment for statistical computing. R Foundation for Statistical Computing (2021). https://www.R-project.org/
15. Giese-Davis, J., et al.: Change in emotion-regulation strategy for women with metastatic breast cancer following supportive-expressive group therapy. J. Consult. Clin. Psychol. **70**, 916–925 (2002). https://doi.org/10.1037/0022-006X.70.4.916

Using Feature Extraction Methods to Perform a Sensory Analysis of Tortillas Fortified with Chilacayote Powder

Adriana-Laura López-Lobato[1], Amalia-Guadalupe Rodríguez-Gómez[2], Elia-Nora Aquino-Bolaños[2], Rosa-Hayde Alfaro-Rodríguez[3], Héctor-Gabriel Acosta-Mesa[1], and Jimena-Esther Alba-Jiménez[2](✉)

[1] Artificial Intelligence Research Institute, University of Veracruz, 91097 Xalapa, Veracruz, Mexico
[2] Center for Food Research and Development, University of Veracruz, 91190 Xalapa, Veracruz, Mexico
jimalba@uv.mx
[3] Institute of Agricultural Sciences, Autonomous University of the State of Hidalgo, 43600 Tulancingo, Hidalgo, Mexico

Abstract. Chilacayote (*Cucurbita ficifolia* Bouché) has been shown to be a rich source of nutrients and bioactive compounds, suggesting its potential as a fortifier for staple foods such as corn tortillas. While fortification has been demonstrated to alter sensory properties, affecting consumer acceptance, comprehensive sensory evaluations of tortillas fortified with chilacayote powder remain scarce. In this study, sensory analyses were conducted on 150 regular tortilla consumers using CATA questionnaires to evaluate the color, smell, texture, taste, mouthfeel, and aftertaste of tortillas made from nixtamalized dough and commercial flour, both with and without chilacayote powder. The application of three feature extraction methods, Principal Component Analysis (PCA), Linear Discriminant Analysis (LDA), and a combination of both (PCA+LDA), revealed that the LDA method enables the distinction of sensory differences between fortified and non-fortified tortillas. The results of this study offer valuable insights into the sensory impact of chilacayote fortification, which will inform future development of nutritionally enhanced tortillas that maintain consumer appeal.

Keywords: Sensory Analysis · Tortilla fortification · Feature extraction · Linear Discriminant Analysis

1 Introduction

Cucurbita ficifolia Bouché, more commonly referred to in Mexico as chilacayote, is a fruit that is rich in carbohydrates, vitamins, minerals (such as iron), phenolic compounds, flavonoids, and vitamin C [11]. One potential application of this fruit is as powder, since recent research has demonstrated that the powdered pulp of

L. Martínez-Villaseñor et al. (Eds.): MICAI 2025, LNAI 16265, pp. 125–133, 2026.
https://doi.org/10.1007/978-3-032-17933-3_13

ripe chilacayote reduces levels of triacylglycerides, insulin, and insulin resistance in blood [9]. Consequently, it is imperative to propose the development of new products for their utilization.

Fortification can be defined as the process of incorporating nutrients or bioactive components into a food matrix [4]. When fortified, the structure and nutritional value of the product are modified, impacting the rheological, functional, and textural properties of the final product, which in turn directly impacts consumer satisfaction [1]. An example of this process would be the fortification of corn tortillas with nutrients. To date, only a limited number of studies have been conducted that involve sensory analyses with the objective of determining the attributes that define the extent of variety in tortilla fortifications. In this sense, in [6,8], 5- and 7-point hedonic scales, respectively, were utilized to evaluate the attributes of appearance, flavour, odour, texture, and overall acceptability in tortillas fortified with soy flour and its residues. Conversely, the characteristics of different types of tortilla have been evaluated using two analytical methods: Principal Component Analysis (PCA) [7] and Generalised Procrustes Analysis (GPA) [10,12].

However, despite the demonstrated health benefits of chilacayote and the growing interest in functional foods, its application as a fortifying agent in traditional staples such as corn tortillas remains unexplored, particularly regarding its impact on sensory perception and consumer acceptance. Therefore, the objective of this study is to analyze the sensory differences between various tortillas fortified with chilacayote powder by employing three feature extraction methods: Principal Component Analysis (PCA), Linear Discriminant Analysis (LDA), and a combination of both methods (PCA+LDA). Feature extraction can be defined as the process of transforming the original variables contained within a dataset into a new set of variables by combining them to create a more effective feature space [2]. Moreover, by selecting only the most relevant combinations, these methods also help to reduce data dimensionality by eliminating noise and redundancy, thereby enhancing data interpretation. This approach aims not only to enhance the nutritional profile of tortillas but also to determine the possible consumer acceptance using both hedonic scaling and statistical techniques.

2 Materials and Methods

This section includes a brief description of the tortilla sensory information acquisition process, the feature extraction methods applied, and the proposed analytical framework used to evaluate the different approaches.

2.1 Materials

The present study was conducted to identify the sensory differences in tortillas fortified with chilacayote powder. To this end, four tortilla types were considered: a nixtamalized dough tortilla, a nixtamalized dough tortilla with chilacayote powder, a commercial flour tortilla, and a commercial flour tortilla with chilacayote powder. The sensory evaluation was conducted at two university campuses: the Tulancingo de Bravo campus of the Universidad Autónoma del Estado de Hidalgo and the Faculty of Agronomy of the Universidad Veracruzana, Xalapa campus, with each campus hosting 75 young adult tortilla consumers. Each judge evaluated the four tortilla types using a Check-All-That-Apply (CATA) questionnaire [3], assessing the following attributes: eight types of color, ten different smells, thirteen types of texture, twelve characteristic tastes, twelve types of texture in the mouth, and seven types of aftertastes. Consequently, the two datasets under consideration (Tulancingo and Xalapa) contain 300 observations (four for each judge) and 62 variables (sensory features) each.

2.2 Methods

This section presents three commonly employed linear dimensionality reduction techniques: PCA, LDA, and their combination (PCA+LDA). These techniques transform the original dataset $X_{m \times n}$ into a lower dimensional space $Y_{m \times d}$ by considering linear combinations of the initial variables. This transformation is shown in Eq. (1), where $W_{n \times d}$ is the projection matrix considered for the reduction, with $d \leq n$.

$$Y = XW \tag{1}$$

Different projection matrices produce different projections of the dataset X. The subsequent paragraphs offer a concise overview of how PCA [15], LDA [13], and PCA+LDA [14] construct these projection matrices.

Principal Component Analysis (PCA) is an *unsupervised* dimensionality reduction method that identifies directions of *maximum variance* in the data, called principal components, by solving the eigenvalue problem of the empirical covariance matrix of the dataset. The eigenvalues indicate the variance captured by each component, so the d eigenvectors corresponding to the largest eigenvalues, arranged in descending order, form the projection matrix W_{PCA}.

Linear Discriminant Analysis (LDA) is a *supervised* dimensionality reduction method that transforms data to enable *class separability* by maximizing the ratio of between-class to within-class variance (Fisher's criterion). This is achieved by solving a generalized eigenvalue problem. The LDA projection matrix W_{LDA} is formed by the d eigenvectors corresponding to the largest eigenvalues arranged in descending order. LDA faces challenges in high-dimensional, low-sample-size scenarios due to matrix singularity, known as Small Sample Size (SSS) problem. To overcome this, techniques such as PCA+LDA [14] and DLDA [5] have been proposed.

PCA+LDA is a two-step method used to address the SSS problem by first reducing dimensionality with PCA and then applying LDA to enhance class separability. The combined transformation matrix is $W_{PCA+LDA} = W_{PCA}W_{LDA}$.

Although effective in reducing dimensionality and avoiding singularity issues, this approach may discard important class-discriminative features for classification tasks, since PCA does not consider class labels [14].

Experimental Setup. The experimental pipeline for this study examines the sensory differences between various tortillas, both fortified and non-fortified with chilacayote powder, using three linear feature extraction methods. Figure 1 shows the experimental workflow. Each dataset (Xalapa and Tulancingo) obtained with the evaluation of 75 judges was analyzed separately (Fig. 1a). As the PCA, LDA, and PCA+LDA methods possess unique (analytical) solutions, several experiments were conducted by dividing the dataset into training and testing sets to obtain the transformation matrices (Fig. 1b). Subsequently, the transformed data were classified using a Gaussian classifier and the K-nearest neighbors' (K-nn) algorithm (Fig. 1c). Statistical tests were conducted to identify the most effective dimensionality reduction method, which was then considered to interpret the full datasets.

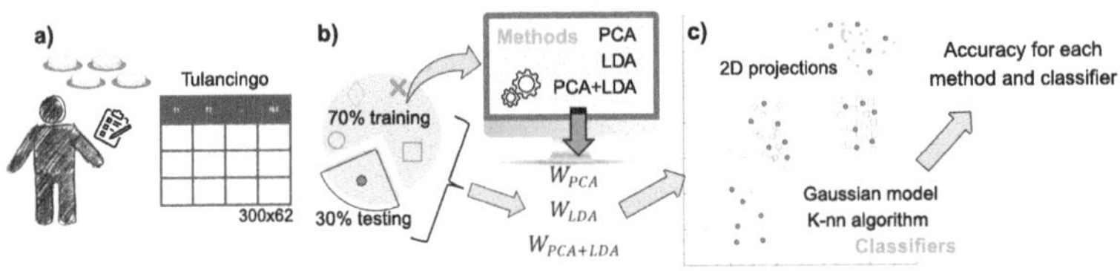

Fig. 1. Experimental pipeline. a) Each dataset is analyzed separately. b) 70% of data is used to obtain transformation matrices and project the training and test sets into the new subspace. c) Classification accuracy is computed for each method and classifier.

3 Experiments and Results

This section describes the experiments designed to determine the most suitable feature extraction method for analyzing sensory differences among nixtamal tortillas, commercial flour tortillas, and their fortifications with chilacayote powder. For each of the two sensory evaluation datasets (Xalapa and Tulancingo), the following experimental procedure was repeated 100 times.

1. The dataset was divided into training and testing sets with proportions of 70% and 30%, respectively, employing stratified partitioning to avoid class imbalance.
2. The training dataset was employed to obtain the projection matrices W_{PCA}, W_{LDA}, and $W_{PCA+LDA}$, considering the reduced dimension fixed at $d = 2$.
3. The projections of the dataset for each method were obtained with the corresponding projection matrices, considering Eq. (1).

4. The Gaussian model and the K-nn algorithm, with $K = 3, 5, 7, \ldots, 21$, were employed to classify the original and projected test datasets, and the classification accuracy for each of the methods was obtained.

After completing 100 iterations, the K value for the K-nn classifier that yielded the highest accuracy was selected for subsequent statistical analysis. Accuracy results for the Xalapa and Tulancingo datasets are presented in Tables 1 and 2, including summary statistics and the corresponding p-values from the statistical tests. The Shapiro–Wilk test was applied to determine whether the accuracy distributions were parametric, guiding the use of either parametric tests (t-test, ANOVA) or a non-parametric test (Kruskal–Wallis) to evaluate significant differences among the dimensionality reduction methods. When significant differences were detected, multiple comparison tests were performed, with significance established at the 95% confidence level.

Table 1. Results for the sensory evaluation conducted in Xalapa. The values in bold represent the results with the best classification accuracy.

Classifier	Metrics	Full data	PCA	LDA	PCA+LDA
Gaussian	Min / Max	NA / NA	22.73 / 39.77	37.5 / 57.95	26.14 / 47.73
	Mean ± St.D.	NA ± NA	31.41 ± 4.24	**47.03 ± 4.58**	35.75 ± 4.17
Kruskal-Wallis	Median	NA	30.68	47.73	36.36
p-value=2.66E-45	Shapiro-Wilk p-value	X	0.0295	0.3633	0.3134
K-nn (K=19)	Min / Max	30.68 / 57.95	18.18 / 44.32	35.23 / 57.95	22.73 / 42.05
	Mean ± St.D.	44.88 ± 5.03	30.01 ± 4.94	**46.34 ± 4.56**	31.05 ± 3.43
Kruskal-Wallis	Median	44.32	29.55	46.59	30.68
p-value=8.55E-62	Shapiro-Wilk p-value	0.8279	0.1506	0.4236	0.0014

Table 2. Results for the sensory evaluation conducted in Tulancingo. The values in bold represent the results with the best classification accuracy.

Classifier	Metrics	Full data	PCA	LDA	PCA+LDA
Gaussian	Min / Max	NA / NA	32.95 / 54.55	NA / NA	34.09 / 54.55
	Mean ± St.D.	NA ± NA	43.07 ± 4.43	NA ± NA	**45.27 ± 4.13**
t-test	Median	NA	43.18	NA	45.45
p-value = 1.36E-06	Shapiro-Wilk p-value	X	0.3311	X	0.2297
K-nn (K=21)	Min / Max	38.64 / 59.09	29.55 / 50	NA / NA	28.41 / 45.45
	Mean ± St.D.	**48.15 ± 4.19**	39.36 ± 4.55	NA ± NA	38.31 ± 3.82
ANOVA	Median	47.73	39.20	NA	38.64
p-value=4.98E-49	Shapiro-Wilk p-value	0.4138	0.3669	X	0.1281

Results for the Xalapa Dataset. As shown in Table 1, LDA achieved the highest classification performance, outperforming the full dataset, PCA, and PCA+LDA. The Gaussian classifier was unable to generate valid results for the full dataset, as it could not adjust the Gaussian distributions according to the number of observations and variables per class; therefore, these outcomes were reported as 'NA'. Furthermore, the K-nn classifier exhibited lower performance on the complete dataset compared to the LDA projections. These findings highlight the effectiveness of dimensionality reduction–particularly LDA–in enhancing class separation and improving classification accuracy for the Xalapa dataset.

Results for the Tulancingo Dataset. As shown in Table 2, the best classification results were obtained using the PCA+LDA technique with the Gaussian classifier, and by employing the full dataset with the K-nn classifier. No significant differences were observed between PCA and PCA+LDA under the K-nn approach. In this dataset, due to matrix singularity, standalone LDA could not be implemented, and its projections were therefore excluded, with the corresponding results reported as 'NA'. These findings indicate that PCA+LDA constitutes the most effective dimensionality reduction method in this context, particularly when LDA alone is not computationally feasible.

Results for the Full Datasets. To analyze the characterization of the sensory differences of the full datasets, the analytical (unique) solution for the best dimensionality reduction method for each dataset was considered.

The **LDA** method was applied to the **Xalapa dataset**. Figure 2 compares the projections with the real labels and with the predicted labels for the classifiers. The K-nn classifier outperformed the Gaussian classifier, achieving 74% accuracy versus 68.33%.

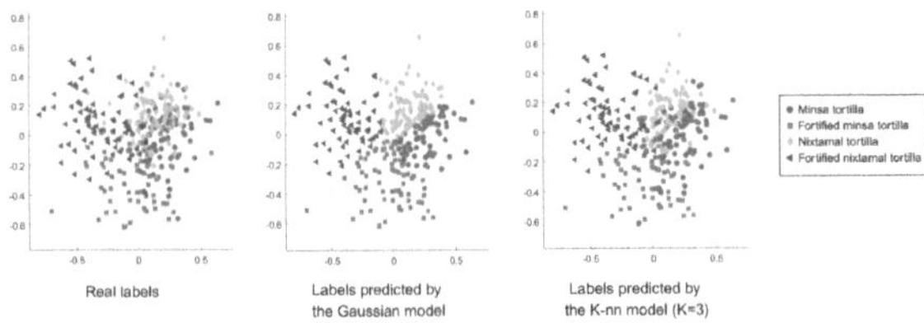

Fig. 2. Classification results for the Xalapa dataset projections obtained with LDA.

Although LDA assists in the separation of the classes, a certain degree of overlap persists. In the two-dimensional projection, non-fortified Minsa and Nixtamal tortillas appeared in the northeast region, with their fortified versions in the southwest region, in close alignment with their non-fortified counterparts.

LDA facilitates the identification of the most relevant variables for distinguishing between class distributions. Figure 3 shows the LDA projections with the real labels, along with the vector weights of the ten most significant variables, ranked by their norms in the two-dimensional space. The spider graph in the same figure arranges these variables clockwise, from the most to the least relevant, reflecting their contribution to the projection axes LD1 and LD2.

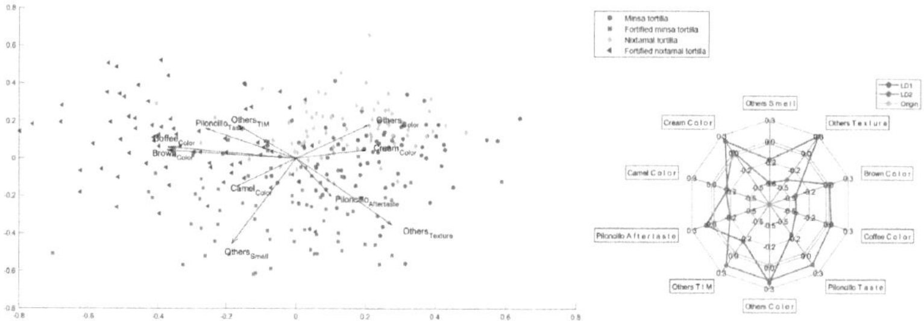

Fig. 3. The ten most relevant variables obtained with LDA in the Xalapa dataset. (Color figure online)

Figure 3 facilitates the identification of the features most salient for each tortilla class. The Minsa tortilla class is mainly characterized by the Cream(Color), while its fortified version is influenced by Others(Smell). The Nixtamal tortilla is directed by the Others(Color) variable, and its fortified counterpart is influenced by the Brown(Color) and Coffee(Color). For non-fortified tortilla, the key variables include Others(Texture), Others(Color), Piloncillo(Aftertaste), and Cream(Color). In contrast, fortified versions are characterized by Others(Smell), Brown(Color), Coffee(Color), Piloncillo(Taste), Others(TIM), and Camel(Color). For the **Tulancingo dataset**, LDA could not be applied; however, **PCA + LDA** proved to be the next most effective method. Figure 4 compares real labels with classifier predictions, showing that *K-nn* achieved 71.67% accuracy, outperforming the Gaussian classifier at 47.67%. Despite two-dimensional visualizations, class separation is not visually apparent due to information loss during the PCA step, and the

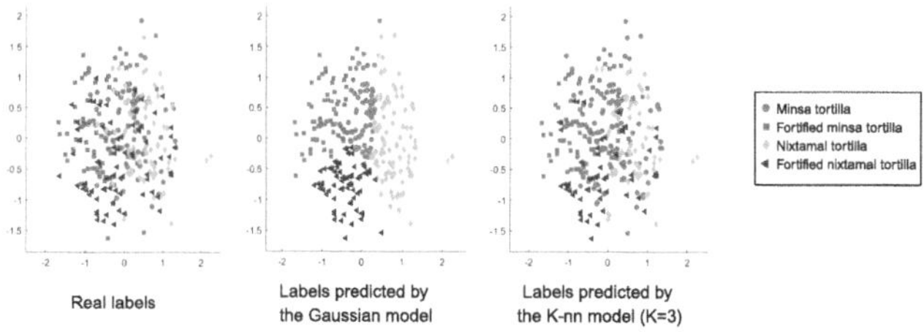

Fig. 4. Classification results for the Tulancingo dataset projections obtained with PCA+LDA.

heterogeneity of projections prevents identification of variables relevant to class distributions.

4 Conclusions and Future Work

In this study, three feature extraction methods were employed to evaluate sensory differences between fortified and non-fortified tortillas: PCA, LDA, and PCA+LDA. LDA proved to be the most effective method, particularly in enhancing class separability. This can be observed in the Xalapa dataset, where the fortification with chilacayote resulted in a distinct sensory profile, characterized by a unique olfactory signature, dominant brown and coffee colors, and a taste of piloncillo. This profile provides valuable guidance for developing nutritionally enhanced tortillas that align with sensory consumer expectations and regional market demands.

Conversely, PCA and PCA+LDA proved ineffective in differentiating between sensory classes, as demonstrated in the Tulancingo dataset, where the application of LDA was unfeasible due to the singularity of the data matrix. These limitations underscore the need to consider data structure and the appropriateness of methods in subsequent analyses.

To enhance the precision and depth of characterization, future research must involve a greater number of experiments, directing particular attention towards the exploration of higher-dimensional feature spaces (dimension 3), as these may facilitate the capture of additional information that is pertinent to sensory attributes. In addition, new methodologies should be developed to transform the data in ways that maximize class separability, allowing for analyses comparable to those performed using LDA, even when LDA is not applicable.

Acknowledgements. The first and second authors acknowledges the Secretaría de Ciencia, Humanidades, Tecnología e Innovación (SECIHTI) of Mexico for the financial support provided through scholarships 712182 and 823476, awarded for postdoctoral and doctoral studies at the Artificial Intelligence Research Institute, and at the Center for Food Research and Development of the University of Veracruz, respectively.

Disclosure of Interests. The authors have no competing interests to declare that are relevant to the content of this article.

References

1. Acevedo-Martinez, K.A., Gonzalez de Mejia, E.: Fortification of maize tortilla with an optimized chickpea hydrolysate and its effect on DPPIV inhibition capacity and physicochemical characteristics. Foods **10**(8), 1835 (2021)
2. Ahmad, N., Nassif, A.B.: Dimensionality reduction: challenges and solutions. In: ITM Web of Conferences, vol. 43, p. 01017. EDP Sciences (2022)
3. Ares, G., et al.: CATA questions for sensory product characterization: raising awareness of biases. Food Qual. Prefer. **30**(2), 114–127 (2013)

4. Dwyer, J.T., et al.: Fortification and health: challenges and opportunities. Adv. Nutr. **6**(1), 124–131 (2015)
5. Gao, H., Davis, J.W.: Why direct LDA is not equivalent to LDA. Pattern Recogn. **39**(5), 1002–1006 (2006)
6. Hassan, S.M., Forsido, S.F., Tola, Y.B., Bikila, A.M.: Physicochemical, nutritional, and sensory properties of tortillas prepared from nixtamalized quality protein maize enriched with soybean. Appl. Food Res. **4**(1), 100383 (2024)
7. Iuga, M., Ávila Akerberg, V.D., González Martínez, T.M., Mironeasa, S.: Consumer preferences and sensory profile related to the physico-chemical properties and texture of different maize tortillas types. Foods **8**(11), 533 (2019)
8. Montemayor-Mora, G., Hernández-Reyes, K.E., Heredia-Olea, E., Pérez-Carrillo, E., Chew-Guevara, A.A., Serna-Saldívar, S.O.: Rheology, acceptability and texture of wheat flour tortillas supplemented with soybean residue. J. Food Sci. Technol. **55**(12), 4964–4972 (2018). https://doi.org/10.1007/s13197-018-3432-3
9. Robledo López, J.: Efecto del consumo de harina de chilacayote (Cucurbita ficifolia Bouché) en un modelo de síndrome metabólico en rata Wistar (2022)
10. Rodríguez-Noriega, S., et al.: Developing a descriptive sensory characterization of flour tortilla applying flash profile. Foods **10**(7), 1473 (2021)
11. Roman-Ramos, R., et al.: Antioxidant and anti-inflammatory effects of a hypoglycemic fraction from cucurbita ficifolia bouché in streptozotocin-induced diabetes mice. Am. J. Chin. Med. **40**(01), 97–110 (2012)
12. Salinas-Moreno, Y., Gálvez-Mariscal, A., Severiano-Pérez, P., Vázquez-Carrillo, G., Trejo-Téllez, L.: Flavor and taste attributes and nutritional insights of maize tortillas from landraces of mexican races. Heliyon **10**(7) (2024)
13. Scholkopft, B., Mullert, K.R.: Fisher discriminant analysis with kernels. Neural Netw. Signal Proc. IX **1**(1), 1 (1999)
14. Sharma, A., Paliwal, K.K.: Linear discriminant analysis for the small sample size problem: an overview. Int. J. Mach. Learn. Cybern. **6**(3), 443–454 (2015)
15. Tharwat, A.: Principal component analysis-a tutorial. Int. J. Appl. Pattern Recogn. **3**(3), 197–240 (2016)

A Fully Evolutionary Approach to Learn Bayesian Networks from Data

Ulises-Ramsés Prado-Valderrábano(✉), Efrén Mezura-Montes, and Nicandro Cruz-Ramírez

Artificial Intelligence Research Institute, Universidad Veracruzana, 91097 Xalapa, Veracruz, Mexico
ulisespradov@gmail.com, {emezura,ncruz}@uv.mx

Abstract. This paper presents a genetic algorithm (GA) for simultaneously learning the structure and parameters of Bayesian Networks (BNs) from data. The proposed method encodes both components in a single individual, using the Minimum Description Length (MDL) principle as fitness function. The algorithm is evaluated in terms of classification accuracy and complexity across different datasets. Additionally, it is assessed based on its ability to approximate known gold-standard networks. The results suggest that this approach can obtain less complex networks while preserving an acceptable level of classification accuracy and achieving a closer structural approximation to the gold standard network.

Keywords: Bayesian Networks · Genetic Algorithms · Minimum Description Length

1 Introduction

BNs provide a powerful framework that integrates graph theory and probability theory, allowing reasoning under uncertainty. Learning a BN from data involves identifying both the network structure and the corresponding conditional probability parameters. Although, in principle, these components should be learned simultaneously [15], finding the structure of a BN is NP-hard [2]. As a result, most approaches in the literature address the problem in two stages: first learning the structure and then estimating the parameters. This work presents a fully evolutionary approach using a GA, in which each candidate solution simultaneously encodes both the network structure and its parameters. The crude MDL principle [9] is employed as fitness function. The main objective is to explore the viability of learning both components jointly, rather than sequentially, as commonly done in the literature. The remainder of this paper is organized as follows: Sect. 2 reviews related work. Section 3 presents the theoretical background. Section 4 details the proposed method. Section 5 describes the experimental setup. Section 6 discusses the results, and Sect. 7 offers concluding remarks and outlines future work.

L. Martínez-Villaseñor et al. (Eds.): MICAI 2025, LNAI 16265, pp. 134–142, 2026.
https://doi.org/10.1007/978-3-032-17933-3_14

2 Related Work

Numerous evolutionary algorithms have been proposed for BN structure learning, a comprehensive review is provided in [13]. In particular, Aguilera-Rueda et al. [1] introduced a bi-objective evolutionary approach based on NSGA-II, their algorithm decomposes the crude MDL principle into two objectives to obtain competitive models with lower complexity. On the other hand, Ha et al. [10] proposed the Discretized BN Gene-pool Optimal Mixing Evolutionary Algorithm (DBN-GOMEA) that simultaneously learns network structures and variable discretizations, their method also supports a tri-objective optimization to balance model accuracy, complexity, and agreement with expert knowledge. Fang et al. [6] developed a structural information-based GA (SIGA-BN), which incorporates Markov blankets and v-structures to guide the search. The work in [18] proposed a mutual information-guided GA (MIGA) addressing the slow convergence and low accuracy of standard GA-based approaches. In the context of parameter learning, Platas-López et al. [16], proposed a Differential Evolution-based method to estimate parameters of a given BN structure by optimizing the conditional log-likelihood. Finally, in [19], the authors proposed a method for learning BNs by combining a GA with structure and parameter restrictions derived from domain knowledge. In summary, although evolutionary algorithms have been widely applied to learn BNs from data, most studies address structure learning and parameter learning separately, leaving the joint optimization of both as a largely unexplored area of research.

3 Background

This section introduces the main concepts that underpin the proposed approach: the formal definition of BNs, the MDL principle, and the fundamentals of GAs.

3.1 Bayesian Networks

According to Friedman et al. [8], a BN is an annotated directed acyclic graph (DAG) that encodes a joint probability distribution over a set of random variables $\mathbf{U} = \{X_1, X_2, ..., X_n\}$. Formally, a BN for $\mathbf{U}$ is a pair $B = (G, \Theta)$ where G is the DAG whose nodes are the random variables in $\mathbf{U}$, and whose arcs represent direct probabilistic dependencies among them. The second component, Θ, is the set of parameters that quantifies the network; it contains, for each variable $X_i \in \mathbf{U}$, a conditional probability distribution $P(X_i|\mathrm{PA}_i)$ that specifies the probability of X_i given its parents in G. Thus, the joint probability distribution can be expressed in terms of the local conditional probability distributions of each variable as shown in Eq. 1.

$$P(X_1, X_2, ..., X_n) = \prod_{i=1}^{n} P(X_i \mid \mathrm{PA}_i) \tag{1}$$

3.2 Minimum Description Length

The MDL principle addresses model selection by balancing model fit and complexity [9], minimizing total description length. For a network B and a dataset D of N instances, the MDL score is defined as [8]:

$$\mathrm{MDL}(B \mid D) = \frac{\log N}{2} \cdot |B| - \mathrm{LL}(B \mid D), \tag{2}$$

$$\mathrm{LL}(B \mid D) = \sum_{i=1}^{N} \sum_{j=1}^{n} \log P(x_{ij} \mid \mathrm{pa}_{ij}), \tag{3}$$

where $|B|$ is the number of parameters and $\mathrm{LL}(B|D)$ the log-likelihood. The term $P(x_{ij} \mid \mathrm{pa}_{ij})$ in Eq. 3 corresponds to the probability of the j-th variable in the i-th instance, conditioned on the observed values of its parents. This score is used as fitness function in the proposed method.

3.3 Genetic Algorithms

Initially proposed by Holland [11], GAs are metaheuristics inspired by natural evolution, where a population of solutions evolves through selection, variation, and replacement guided by a fitness function. Algorithm 1 shows the pseudo-code used in this work.

Algorithm 1. Genetic Algorithm

```
1: Generate an initial population of popsize individuals
2: Evaluate the fitness of each individual
3: repeat
4:     Select popsize parents using deterministic binary tournament
5:     Apply crossover with probability Pc to generate popsize offspring
6:     Apply mutation with probability Pm to each offspring
7:     Evaluate the fitness of the offspring
8:     Apply generational replacement with elitism
9: until the maximum number of generations is reached
10: return the best individual found
```

4 Proposed Method

This section outlines the main elements of the proposed method, including the representation scheme and variation operators.

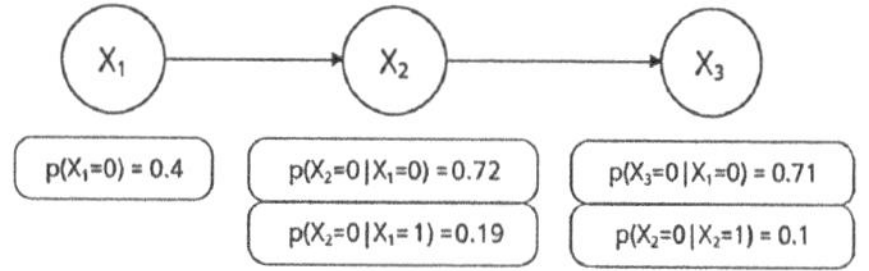

Fig. 1. A complete Bayesian Network.

4.1 Representation Scheme

A complete BN is shown in Fig. 1, so each individual must encode both structure and parameters. The structure is represented by a binary connectivity matrix of size $n \times n$, where n is the number of variables. A value of 1 at position (i, j) indicates the presence of an arc from variable X_i to variable X_j (Fig. 2).

The individual is formed by concatenating the flattened connectivity matrix and the parameter vector, which contains real values in [0,1]. A valid BN is built by first generating the structure with the mapping strategy used in the REST algorithm [3], and then creating conditional probability vectors for each variable (Fig. 2). Each vector sums up to 1, and stores only $k-1$ values for k outcomes. The parameter vector length is variable, since it depends on the parent sets defined by the structure.

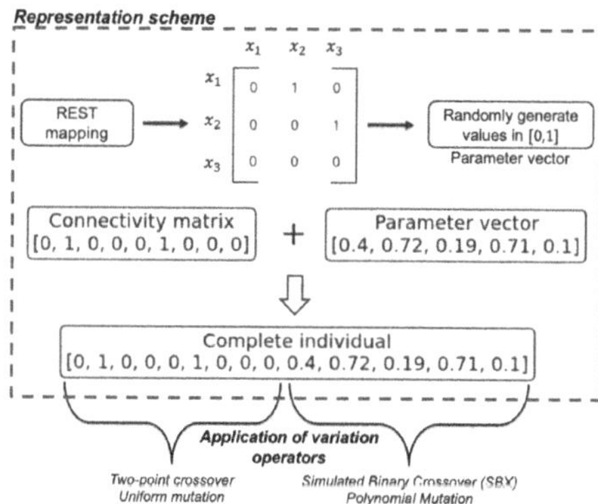

Fig. 2. Representation scheme and variation operators in the example BN.

4.2 Variation Operators

The mixed encoding requires different variation operators for its binary and real-valued components, which are easily separated since the binary segment has fixed length $n \times n$. Two-point crossover and uniform mutation are used for the binary part, while Simulated Binary Crossover (SBX) [4] and Polynomial Mutation (PM) [5] handle the real-valued part, as shown in Fig. 2. Both SBX and PM are popular variation operators used in real-coded GAs. SBX mimics the behavior of single-point crossover in binary representation, but works in real numbers.

PM introduces perturbations based on a polynomial distribution to individual variables. For crossover, SBX is applied up to the length of the shorter parent vector, and any extra values are copied from the opposite parent.

4.3 Validation and Reparation

Since variation operators can produce invalid solutions, validation and repair mechanisms are required. For the BN structure, it is essential to ensure that it corresponds to a valid DAG. This work adopts the approach described by Cowie et al. [3]. Regarding the network parameters, the parameter vector must be adjusted to match the structure encoded in the individual. Algorithm 2 contains the procedure to be followed to perform such repair. The effectiveness of this method may be somewhat limited in large or dense BNs. In such cases, dependency configurations between variables could vary considerably among individuals in the population, potentially affecting algorithm performance.

Algorithm 2. Repair and normalization of the parameter vector

Require: Network structure G, current parameter vector $paramVector$
1: Compute the required number of parameters from G: $requiredLength$
2: Compute the current length: $currentLength \leftarrow \text{length}(paramVector)$
3: **if** $currentLength > requiredLength$ **then**
4:     Truncate $paramVector$ to its first $requiredLength$ elements
5: **else if** $currentLength < requiredLength$ **then**
6:     Generate $(requiredLength - currentLength)$ random values
7:     Append them to $paramVector$
8: **end if**
9: **for** each node X_i in G **do**
10:     Identify the subset of parameters associated with X_i
11:     Normalize the subset so that the probabilities sum to 1
12: **end for**
13: **return** $paramVector$

5 Experimental Setup

This section presents the experimental setup used to evaluate the algorithm's performance. Table 1 summarizes the datasets used in this work. The first eight datasets were evaluated for classification accuracy and complexity via 5-fold cross-validation (CV), including a synthetic dataset generated with Weka's BN data generator [7] and others from the UCI repository [12] after variable discretization. Datasets 9–12 correspond to well-known gold-standard networks [17] used as targets for approximation by the proposed algorithm. In this case, the Kullback-Leibler divergence (KLD) was used to measure the dissimilarity between the probability distributions induced by the learned network and the gold-standard model (Eq. 4):

$$D_{\mathrm{KL}}(p \parallel q) = \sum_{i=0}^{N} (x_i) \log_2 \frac{p(x_i)}{q(x_i)} \tag{4}$$

where $q(x)$ is the approximation and $p(x)$ is the gold-standard network distribution. Finally, the Structural Hamming Distance (SHD) was used to measure the minimum edits needed to match the learned structure to the gold standard [17]. For comparison, Weka's implementation was used, learning structure with a GA using the MDL score and estimating parameters separately with the simple estimator.

Table 1. Description of the datasets used in the experiments.

Index	Name	Variables	Instances	Arcs
1	Synthetic	6	100	6
2	Iris	5	150	Unknown
3	Acute-inflam	7	120	Unknown
4	Acute-nephritis	7	120	Unknown
5	Mammographic mass	6	961	Unknown
6	Vertebral Column	7	310	Unknown
7	Blood Transfusion	5	748	Unknown
8	Diabetes	9	768	Unknown
9	Gold-Standard Cancer	5	250, 500	4
10	Gold-Standard Earthquake	5	250, 500	4
11	Gold-Standard Survey	6	250, 500	6
12	Gold-Standard Asia	8	250, 500	8

5.1 Parameter Tuning

Parameter calibration was carried out using the IRACE package [14] on three synthetic datasets with binary variables. The parameter space included the following values: `popsize` $\in \{20, 40, 60, 80\}$, `Pc` $\in [0.1, 0.9]$, `Pm` $\in [0.1, 0.9]$, and `max_gen` $\in \{900, 1000, 1200, 1500\}$. The parameter configuration obtained was `popsize` $= 80$, `Pc` $= 0.6$, `Pm` $= 0.3$ and `maxgen` $= 900$, which was modified empirically to `maxgen` $= 1200$. Preliminary tests showed that `popsize` and `Pc` most strongly affected the algorithm's performance, revealing sensitivity to these parameters.

6 Results

Table 2 reports the results of ten 5-fold-CV runs using the same fold partitions for both methods. A Wilcoxon test with 95% confidence level was performed for each data set. Bold values indicate statistically significant differences. The results show that, although the gain in accuracy of the proposed method compared to the separate learning method is not uniform across all datasets, the reduction in the number of arcs is. This suggests that the main advantage of the proposed method lies in inducing parsimonious networks with competitive performance. This behavior aligns with Occam's razor principles in MDL: among models with comparable accuracy, the simplest is preferred.

Table 2. CV results for the proposed method and the separate learning method. The proposed method tends to reduce arcs without harming accuracy

Name	Proposed Method		Separate Learning	
	Accuracy (%)	Arcs	Accuracy (%)	Arcs
Synthetic	**70.20** ± 1.33	2.82 ± 0.33	66.90 ± 1.58	2.84 ± 0.23
Iris	94.67 ± 0.67	**3.46** ± 0.25	94.60 ± 0.36	4.00 ± 0.00
Acute-inflam	96.25 ± 2.12	**7.64** ± 0.88	**98.17** ± 1.43	11.78 ± 0.62
Acute-nephritis	97.92 ± 1.95	**8.04** ± 0.97	98.33 ± 2.30	11.66 ± 0.53
Mammographic mass	80.13 ± 0.64	**4.54** ± 0.35	**81.30** ± 0.95	5.84 ± 0.27
Vertebral Column	77.97 ± 0.97	**5.12** ± 0.77	78.71 ± 0.96	7.90 ± 0.27
Blood Transfusion	74.26 ± 0.81	5.08 ± 0.43	74.13 ± 0.20	5.26 ± 0.43
Diabetes	73.79 ± 1.07	**11.48** ± 1.09	74.86 ± 0.58	13.02 ± 1.42

On the other hand, Table 3 shows the results of the KLD and SHD calculations. In both cases, a value closer to 0 is preferred. For KLD results, the proposed method tended to achieve better approximations in datasets with smaller sample sizes. In terms of SHD, the proposed method obtained superior results in four datasets, compared to only one for its counterpart, which suggests a closer structural approximation to the gold standard network.

Table 3. KLD and SHD for the proposed method and the separate learning method

Gold Standard	Proposed Method		Separate Learning	
	KLD	SHD	KLD	SHD
Asia 250 cases	0.14646	**9**	**0.12417**	13
Asia 500 cases	0.12396	**8**	**0.07178**	10
Cancer 250 cases	**0.03322**	4	0.03651	4
Cancer 500 cases	0.02788	4	**0.02713**	4
Earthquake 250 cases	**0.01686**	**4**	0.02762	5
Earthquake 500 cases	**0.01065**	5	0.01251	**4**
Survey 250 cases	**0.04316**	**6**	0.06686	7
Survey 500 cases	0.02989	7	**0.02073**	7

7 Conclusions and Future Work

In this paper, a GA for the simultaneous learning of structure and parameters of BNs was presented, introducing a representation scheme to encode both components and using the MDL principle as fitness function. The results obtained in the classification task indicate that this approach is viable to find less complex BNs while maintaining an acceptable level of accuracy, following the MDL principle more faithfully. This is relevant because fewer arcs imply more interpretable models, which can be critical in application domains such as medicine, bioinformatics, and finance, where transparency is as important as accuracy. Regarding the search for a gold-standard network, the main advantage of the proposed method lies in achieving a better structural approximation. Future research could focus on testing the scalability of the method in higher-dimensional datasets, performing sensitivity analysis of the algorithm's parameters, and integrating self-adaptation mechanisms.

References

1. Aguilera-Rueda, V.J., Cruz-Ramírez, N., Mezura-Montes, E.: Data-driven bayesian network learning: towards a bi-objective approach to address the bias-variance decomposition. Res. Comput. Sci. **149**, 9–19 (2020)
2. Cooper, G.F.: The computational complexity of probabilistic inference using Bayesian belief networks. Artif. Intell. **42**(2), 393–405 (1990)
3. Cowie, J., Oteniya, L., Coles, R.: Particle swarm optimisation for learning bayesian networks. Lect. Notes Eng. Comput. Sci. **2165** (2007)
4. Deb, K., Agrawal, R.B.: Simulated binary crossover for continuous search space. Complex Syst. **9**(2), 115–148 (1995)
5. Deb, K., Deb, D.: Analyzing mutation schemes for real-parameter genetic algorithms. Int. J. Artif. Intell. Soft Comput. **4**(1), 1–28 (2014)
6. Fang, W., et al.: An efficient Bayesian network structure learning algorithm based on structural information. Swarm Evol. Comput. **76**, 101224 (2023)
7. Frank, E., Hall, M.A., Witten, I.H.: The WEKA Workbench. Online Appendix for "Data Mining: Practical Machine Learning Tools and Techniques", Morgan Kaufmann, 4th ed. (2016). https://www.cs.waikato.ac.nz/ml/weka/
8. Friedman, N., Geiger, D., Goldszmidt, M.: Bayesian network classifiers. Mach. Learn. **29**(2–3), 131–163 (1997)
9. Grünwald, P.D.: The Minimum Description Length Principle. Adaptive Computation and Machine Learning, The MIT Press, Cambridge (2007)
10. Ha, D.M.F., Alderliesten, T., Bosman, P.A.N.: Learning discretized bayesian networks with gomea. In: Affenzeller, M., et al. (eds.) Parallel Problem Solving from Nature – PPSN XVIII. LNCS, vol. 15150 (2024). Springer, Cham. https://doi.org/10.1007/978-3-031-70071-2_22
11. Holland, J.H.: Adaptation in Natural and Artificial Systems. 2nd ed. University of Michigan Press, Ann Arbor, MI 1975 (1992)
12. Kelly, M., Longjohn, R., Nottingham, K.: The UCI machine learning repository (2024). Accessed 20 Jun 2025. https://archive.ics.uci.edu
13. Larrañaga, P., Karshenas, H., Bielza, C., Santana, R.: A review on evolutionary algorithms in bayesian network learning and inference tasks. Inf. Sci. **233**, 109–125 (2013)

14. López-Ibáñez, M., Dubois-Lacoste, J., Pérez Cáceres, L., Stützle, T., Birattari, M.: The irace package: iterated racing for automatic algorithm configuration. Oper. Res. Perspect. **3**, 43–58 (2016)
15. Pan, H.: Learning bayesian networks I - A theory based on map-mdl criteria. In: Proceedings of the Fifth International Conference on Information Fusion. FUSION 2002. (IEEE Cat.No.02EX5997), vol. 2, pp. 769–776 (2002)
16. Platas-López, A., Mezura-Montes, E., Cruz-Ramírez, N., Guerra-Hernández, A.: Discriminative learning of bayesian network parameters by differential evolution. Appl. Math. Model. **93**, 244–256 (2021)
17. Scutari, M.: Learning bayesian networks with the bnlearn R package. J. Stat. Softw. **35**(3), 1–22 (2010)
18. Yan, K.S., Fang, W.H., Lu, H., Zhang, X., Sun, J., Wu, X.: Mutual information-guided GA for bayesian network structure learning. IEEE Trans. Knowl. Data Eng. **35**(8), 8307–8321 (2023)
19. Zhang, C., Cao, M., Peng, B., Zheng, S.: Learning bayesian network by genetic algorithm using structure-parameter restrictions. In: 2013 IEEE International Conference on Multimedia and Expo Workshops (ICMEW), pp. 1–5 (2013)

A Computationally Efficient Algorithm for Optimal Mass Transport via Wavelet-Based Multiresolution Methods

Larruz-Medina Miguel Angel[1], Gabriel-Argüelles José Rigoberto[1](✉), Benítez-Mariño Eloisa[1], and Santamaria-Pang Alberto[2,3]

[1] Universidad Veracruzana, Xalapa, Mexico
jgabriel@uv.mx
[2] Microsoft Healthcare AI, North America, USA
[3] Johns Hopkins Medicine, Baltimore, USA

Abstract. This paper introduces a computationally efficient approximation scheme for solving the Monge–Kantorovich (MK) optimal mass transport problem. Exact solutions for the MK problem are typically difficult or computationally expensive to obtain, particularly in high-dimensional or large-scale scenarios. To address this challenge, we propose an innovative method integrating wavelet theory and multiresolution analysis. Our approach exploits wavelet-based techniques to iteratively approximate the support of the optimal measure, thereby reducing the number of variables in linear programs and consequently decreasing the dimensionality and computational complexity of each subsequent optimization step. We present numerical experiments demonstrating that our wavelet-enhanced scheme achieves high accuracy with substantially fewer computational resources compared with traditional linear programming approaches. The method has potential applications across various domains, including image processing, economics, resource allocation, and machine learning, where efficient solutions to large-scale optimal transport problems are essential.

Keywords: Optimal transport · Wavelet theory · Multiresolution analysis · Computational efficiency · Numerical optimization

1 Introduction

The Monge Kantorovich (MK) mass transfer problem is a foundational topic with extensive applications in functional analysis, differential geometry, statistics, economics, and dynamical systems [15,17]. Despite its broad relevance, obtaining exact computational solutions to the MK problem, particularly in high-dimensional or large-scale scenarios, remains prohibitively expensive. Thus, computationally efficient approximation schemes are critically important for practical implementations [7,8].

L. Martínez-Villaseñor et al. (Eds.): MICAI 2025, LNAI 16265, pp. 143–151, 2026.
https://doi.org/10.1007/978-3-032-17933-3_15

In this paper, we propose a numerical approximation method inspired by the scheme introduced in [6], where a transportation problem is solved to identify an optimal measure with finite support. We further enhance this approach by integrating wavelet theory and multiresolution analysis, significantly reducing the number of variables required in subsequent optimizations compared with traditional linear programming methods. Recent advancements, such as [8], illustrate how wavelet representations can reduce computational complexity for high-dimensional problems.

Recent research on algorithms for solving the MK problem includes [12], which studies an algorithm to solve the Monge–Ampère equation using gradient flow, an elliptic formulation and a Hamilton–Jacobi equation. In [4], stochastic optimization with a stable optimization process is used to approximate the MK problem with an algorithm termed Cop-OT. In [16], numerical methods are studied for L-Lipschitz gradients of l-strongly convex potentials and the convergence of stochastic gradient descent methods for neural networks, where optimal transport is applied. In [1], are used wavelet methods as in this work, but its approach is based on apply the wavelet transform in the cost function.

Our proposed wavelet-based multiresolution approximation method not only improves computational efficiency but also ensures that the supports of the finite optimal measures converge to the support of the optimal measure of the MK problem. Furthermore, we provide a rigorous mathematical proof and a theoretical framework underpinning this optimization approach. Numerical experiments clearly highlight the significant improvements in computational complexity and accuracy, making our approach broadly applicable across fields demanding efficient solutions to optimal transport problems, such as large-scale training of artificial neural networks via backpropagation.

The proposed algorithm can be applied to problems that require both the optimal measure and the corresponding value of the Monge–Kantorovich (MK) problem because it efficiently approximates the optimal transport plan while preserving high accuracy in estimating the transport cost. By leveraging wavelet-based multiresolution analysis, the method adaptively refines the computational domain to focus on the regions that contribute most to the optimal coupling, thus reducing complexity without losing essential structural information. This capability makes it suitable for applications where the MK solution provides meaningful physical, geometric, or statistical correspondences between distributions. For example, in [2], optimal transport is used for tasks such as image processing, geometric processing, rendering, fluid simulation, and computational optics, all of which rely on precise transport measures. In [9], recent advances in optimal transport for data science and machine learning are reviewed, highlighting the importance of accurate and scalable solvers. Likewise, [3] applies optimal transport to model fluid flows in the brain, demonstrating its relevance in biomedical imaging, while [11] discusses applications in economics, where the computation of optimal transport values guides efficient resource allocation and market equilibrium analysis.

2 Wavelet Theory

A wavelet function ψ is a complex-valued, square-integrable function, $\psi \in L^2(\mathbf{R})$. Wavelets provide a versatile mathematical tool for analyzing signals at multiple resolutions and scales. Formally, a wavelet function $\psi \in L^2(\mathbf{R})$ satisfies admissibility conditions (see [14]).

Given a function $f \in L^2(\mathbf{R})$, its continuous wavelet transform (CWT) at position u and scale $s > 0$ is given by

$$W_f(u,s) = \left\langle f(t),\, s^{-1/2}\,\psi\left(\frac{t-u}{s}\right)\right\rangle.$$

The original function f can then be reconstructed from its wavelet coefficients:

$$f(t) = \frac{1}{C_\psi}\int_0^\infty \int_{-\infty}^\infty W_f(u,s)\, s^{-1/2}\psi\left(\frac{t-u}{s}\right)\frac{du\, ds}{s^2}.$$

Multiresolution analysis (MRA), introduced by Mallat [14], is an efficient computational framework leveraging nested subspaces $\{V_j\}_{j\in\mathbf{Z}} \subset L^2(\mathbf{R})$ defined by scaling functions $\phi(t)$, which form an orthonormal basis and satisfy:

- *Nested structure:* $\cdots \subset V_j \subset V_{j+1} \subset \cdots$
- *Completeness:* $\bigcup_{j\in\mathbf{Z}} V_j = L^2(\mathbf{R})$
- *Trivial intersection:* $\bigcap_{j\in\mathbf{Z}} V_j = \{0\}$
- *Scaling property:* $f(t) \in V_j \Leftrightarrow f(2^{-j}t) \in V_0$
- *Translation invariance:* $\phi(t-n) \in V_0,\ \forall n \in \mathbf{Z}$

Each subspace V_{j+1} decomposes orthogonally as $V_{j+1} = V_j \oplus W_j$, where W_j is spanned by wavelet functions $\psi_{j,n}(t) = 2^{j/2}\psi(2^j t - n)$. Hence, any function $f \in L^2(\mathbf{R})$ can be represented as

$$f(t) = \sum_{k\in\mathbf{Z}} \alpha_{j_0,k}\phi_{j_0,k}(t) + \sum_{j\geq j_0}\sum_{k\in\mathbf{Z}} \beta_{j,k}\psi_{j,k}(t),$$

with coefficients $\alpha_{j,k} = \langle f, \phi_{j,k}\rangle$ and $\beta_{j,k} = \langle f, \psi_{j,k}\rangle$. More information for the construction of wavelet spaces can be seen in [5,7,14].

This approach naturally extends to higher-dimensional spaces $L^2(\mathbf{R}^p)$, with multidimensional wavelets constructed via tensor products of 1D wavelets. In 2D, wavelets are defined as [5]:

$$\psi^{(\epsilon)}(x,y) = \psi^{\epsilon_1}(x)\psi^{\epsilon_2}(y), \quad \epsilon = (\epsilon_1, \epsilon_2),\ \epsilon_i \in \{0,1\},$$

with $\psi^0 = \phi$ (scaling function) and $\psi^1 = \psi$ (wavelet function). Our experiments address 2D cases, though the method generalizes efficiently to higher dimensions.

3 Mass Transfer Problem

To define the mass transfer problem, we need the following:

a) Two compact metric spaces X and Y, endowed with the Borel σ-algebras $\mathbf{B}(X)$ and $\mathbf{B}(Y)$, respectively.
b) A continuous cost function $c : X \times Y \to \mathbf{R}$.
c) A probability measure ν_1 on $\mathbf{B}(X)$ and a probability measure ν_2 on $\mathbf{B}(Y)$.

We denote $\mathbf{M}(X \times Y)$ as the linear space of all finite signed measures on $\mathbf{B}(X \times Y)$ and assume these spaces are endowed with the weak convergence topology. If $\mu \in \mathbf{M}(X \times Y)$, then the marginals (or projections) of μ are denoted by $\Pi_1\mu$ and $\Pi_2\mu$, which are signed finite measures on $\mathbf{B}(X)$ and $\mathbf{B}(Y)$, respectively, defined for $A \in \mathbf{B}(X)$ and $B \in \mathbf{B}(Y)$ by

$$\Pi_1\mu(A) = \mu(A \times Y) \quad \text{and} \quad \Pi_2\mu(B) = \mu(X \times B).$$

The Monge–Kantorovich mass transfer problem is

$$\text{MK}: \quad \min_{\mu \geq 0} \int_{X \times Y} c \, d\mu \tag{1}$$

$$\text{s.t.} \quad \Pi_1\mu = \nu_1, \quad \Pi_2\mu = \nu_2, \quad \mu \in \mathbf{M}(X \times Y). \tag{2}$$

A measure $\mu \in \mathbf{M}_+(X \times Y)$ is called feasible if it satisfies the constraints in (2) and if $\left|\int_{X \times Y} c \, d\mu\right| < \infty$.

In [6], a method is developed to approximate the value of the Monge Kantorovich problem in compact metric spaces. Since X and Y are compact metric spaces, there exist countable dense sets $X_\infty = \{x_1, x_2, \ldots\} \subset X$ and $Y_\infty = \{y_1, y_2, \ldots\} \subset Y$. Now, take a sequence of radii $r_n \downarrow 0$. It is possible to construct disjoint sets around points x_k and y_j, each with diameter less than or equal to $2r_n$, such that $X = \bigcup_{k=1}^{s_n} A_k^n$ and $Y = \bigcup_{j=1}^{t_n} D_j^n$, with $x_k \in A_k^n$ and $y_j \in D_j^n$.

Define

$$M_n = \{x_1, x_2, \ldots, x_{s_n}\} \times \{y_1, y_2, \ldots, y_{t_n}\} = X_n \times Y_n,$$

and call a refinement of M_n the set

$$M_{n+1} = \{x_1, x_2, \ldots, x_{s_{n+1}}\} \times \{y_1, y_2, \ldots, y_{t_{n+1}}\} = X_{n+1} \times Y_{n+1}.$$

Then, we build a sequence of linear programming problems (transportation problems) such that their optimal solutions μ_n^* are measures with finite support in $\mathbf{B}(X \times Y)$ that converge weakly to the optimal solution μ^* of the MK problem.

4 Wavelet-Based Mass Transfer Algorithm

We propose a five-step iterative algorithm to solve the Monge–Kantorovich (MK) optimal transport problem using a wavelet-based multiresolution strategy that achieves computational efficiency without sacrificing accuracy. The method is designed for 2D domains but generalizes to higher-dimensional settings.

Step 1: Discretization. Define dyadic grids $X_n = Y_n = \left\{\frac{i}{2^n} \mid 0 \leq i \leq 2^n\right\}$ and solve the relaxed MK problem:

$$\mathrm{MK}_n : \min_{\lambda^n_{i,j} \geq 0} \sum_{(x_i, y_j)} c(x_i, y_j)\lambda^n_{i,j},$$

subject to marginal constraints that ensure consistency with prescribed measures.

Step 2: Support Extraction. Collect the support of the solution

$$S_n = \left\{(x_i, y_j) \mid \lambda^n_{i,j} > 0\right\},$$

which defines a sparse approximation of the optimal plan.

Step 3: Wavelet Analysis. Represent the support set S_n as a piecewise-constant function $T_n(x, y)$, then apply a 2D DWT (see [5]) to compute detail coefficients:

$$\beta^3_{n-1,(i,j)} = \langle T_n, \psi^{(3)}_{n-1,(i,j)} \rangle.$$

Wavelet coefficients above a threshold ϵ define a region of interest W_n, expanded to a neighborhood B_n.

Step 4: Reduced Problem (WMK). The next resolution level defines a refined grid $X_{n+1} \times Y_{n+1}$, but the transport plan is solved only over $O_n = B_n \cap (X_{n+1} \times Y_{n+1})$, subject to marginal conditions:

$$\mathrm{WMK}_{n+1} : \min_{\lambda^{n+1}_{i,j} \geq 0} \sum_{(x_i, y_j) \in O_n} c(x_i, y_j)\lambda^{n+1}_{i,j}.$$

Step 5: Iteration and Convergence. Repeat steps 2–4. Under mild assumptions, $\mu_n \to \mu^*$, and the supports $\mathrm{supp}(\mu_n)$ converge in Hausdorff distance.

Complexity Analysis. Let $X_n = Y_n = \left\{\frac{i}{2^n} \mid 0 \leq i \leq 2^n\right\}$. Solving the optimal transport problem on the full grid $X_n \times Y_n$ requires $|X_n \times Y_n| = 2^n \cdot 2^n = 4^n$ transport variables. Hence, the complexity is $O(4^n)$.

Wavelet-Based Sparsity. Suppose the optimal plan μ^* is concentrated along the graph of a Lipschitz (or piecewise smooth) function. Then, the transport support lies on a low-dimensional manifold. A wavelet transform of the indicator function $T_n(x, y)$ for this support yields sparse coefficients due to vanishing moments. Using results from nonlinear approximation theory [5,14], the number of significant 2D wavelet coefficients needed to approximate such a transport plan with accuracy ϵ is $k_n = O(n2^n)$. This estimate accounts for $O(2^n)$ coefficients per level summed across n levels.

The WMK formulation restricts the transport plan to a sparse domain O_n defined by the wavelet support. As a result, the number of variables is $O(k_n) = O(n2^n) \ll O(4^n)$, yielding an exponential reduction in problem size. Although the number of variables in the new algorithm also grows exponentially, it remains much smaller than in the classical case. For example, the classical algorithm for

$n = 12$ requires 16,777,216 variables, whereas the proposed method requires 94,208 variables for the db10 case.

This complexity reduction enables the WMK scheme to scale to higher resolutions where traditional MK solvers become intractable. The localization properties of wavelets further guarantee that the recovered support converges to the true optimal plan with high fidelity, even at coarse scales.

5 Experimental Setup

We consider a well-known problem used in [6] to analyze a wavelet-based algorithm. Let $X = Y = [0,1]$, and let the marginal distributions ν_1, ν_2 be uniform (Lebesgue measure). The cost function is $c(x,y) = x^2y - xy^2$, a nonlinear, non-symmetric function that introduces a moderate level of complexity for testing.

The exact solution to this problem is known and corresponds to the optimal transport map:

$$f(t) = \begin{cases} \frac{1}{4} + t, & \text{for } t \in \left[0, \frac{3}{4}\right), \\ 1 - t, & \text{for } t \in \left[\frac{3}{4}, 1\right]. \end{cases}$$

The graph of this piecewise-defined optimal transport function is shown in Fig. 1 (fourth subfigure), which visualizes the structure of the optimal coupling under the cost function $c(x,y) = x^2y - xy^2$. The exact minimum value of the MK problem is $\min(\text{MK}) = -\frac{9}{256} = -0.03515625$.

We construct the discretized sets $X_n = Y_n = \left\{\frac{k}{2^n} \,\middle|\, k = 0, 1, \ldots, 2^n\right\}$. For multiresolution analysis, we use the scaling functions **Coiflet1** (coif1), **Haar**, and **Daubechies10** (db10), which have compact support and vanishing moments. The filter lengths are 2, 6, 10, for Haar, Coiflet1, Daubechies10, scaling functions, respectively [13,14].

For the numerical applications, we used Python (v3.12.11) on a standard computer (13th Gen Intel(R) Core(TM) i7-13650HX; 16 GB RAM). The libraries used were `PyWavelets` for the wavelet transform, `PuLP` to solve the linear programming problems, and `NumPy` for matrix calculations. We compare the classical discretized linear programming approach [6] (denoted MK_n) with our wavelet-guided refinement scheme (denoted WMK_n). At each stage:

1. MK_n is solved to obtain a discrete optimal transport plan μ_n;
2. A wavelet transform identifies singularities in the support of μ_n;
3. A reduced domain $O_{n+1} \subset X_{n+1} \times Y_{n+1}$ is defined;
4. The transport problem is solved again, but only within O_{n+1} to obtain μ_{n+1}.

The adaptive search regions O_k for $k \in \{7, 9, 12\}$ are illustrated in Fig. 1. Each image represents the search region O_k (yellow) as a subset of $X_k \times Y_k$. For each O_k image, it is illustrated as a red dotted line the localization of the optimal transport function. It should be noted that each search region O_k surround the optimal transport function. The region in black denotes the subset of $X_k \times Y_k$ where the algorithm does not search for the support of each approximate measure μ_k. The regions for db10 are similar to those shown in Fig. 1. In the case of the Haar wavelet, the regions do not converge to the optimal coupling.

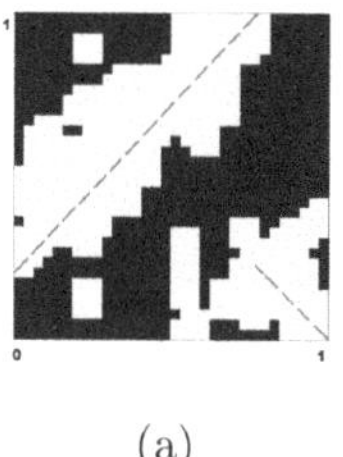

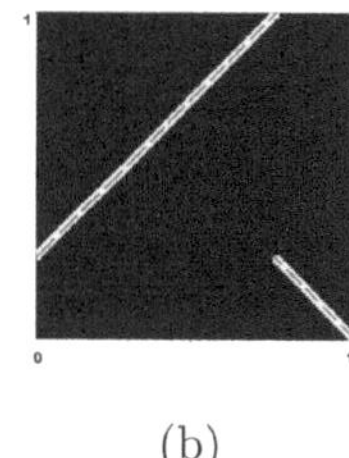

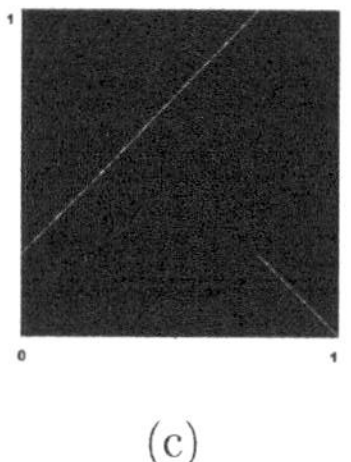

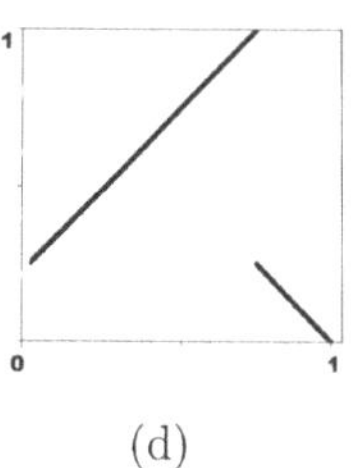

(a) (b) (c) (d)

Fig. 1: Visualization of $O_7 \subset X_7 \times Y_7$ (a), $O_9 \subset X_9 \times Y_9$ (b), and $O_{12} \subset X_{12} \times Y_{12}$ (c), obtained using the Coiflet1 wavelet, together with the optimal coupling function F_1 (d). The red dotted line in subfigures (a)–(c) indicates the localized region of the optimal coupling.

6 Results

Table 1 summarize the number of variables used in the linear program, the approximation error, and the computed minimum values for both schemes and each scaling function. The classical method becomes infeasible beyond level $n = 8$ with the current system configuration, while the wavelet-enhanced method maintains computational efficiency and accuracy up to $n = 12$.

The wavelet-guided method offers a scalable and accurate approach to solving the Monge–Kantorovich mass transfer problem by leveraging multiresolution wavelet analysis to adaptively refine regions of interest. By concentrating computational effort on the most relevant areas of the transport plan's support, it achieves high precision while significantly reducing the number of optimization variables compared to classical uniform discretization schemes. Although not all wavelet bases perform equally well—such as the Haar wavelet, which suffers from information loss, the method demonstrates strong convergence properties when suitable scaling functions are chosen.

Numerical experiments on synthetic test cases with known analytical solutions confirm the method's efficiency and robustness. The algorithm successfully reconstructs piecewise-defined transport maps, reaching high resolutions (up to $n = 12$) without exhausting memory resources, illustrating its capacity to handle structurally complex cost functions and domains. These results highlight the method's computational advantage and its potential for large-scale problems that are infeasible using traditional Monge–Kantorovich solvers.

Beyond theoretical validation, the framework has practical relevance across various domains, including image registration, edge detection, shape morphing, logistics, and optimal transport applications in machine learning and biomedical imaging.

Future work will focus on extending the approach to handle multimodal and singular transport supports, integrating adaptive wavelet bases tuned to problem-specific features, and combining it with entropic regularization methods for enhanced scalability and generalization in higher-dimensional and multi-marginal transport problems.

Table 1: Comparison of the classical method (MK_n) and our proposed method (WMK_n) for multiple resolutions levels and wavelet types.

Setting	No. Var.	Error	Approx. Value
MK_7 (no wavelet)	16,384	3.8147×10^{-6}	−0.0351524353
WMK_7 (coif1)	8,000	3.8147×10^{-6}	−0.0351524353
WMK_7 (db10)	11,072	3.8147×10^{-6}	−0.0351524353
WMK_7 (Haar)	2,656	1.1805×10^{-3}	−0.0333511084
MK_8 (no wavelet)	65,536	9.537×10^{-7}	−0.0351552963
WMK_8 (coif1)	5,072	9.537×10^{-7}	−0.0351552963
WMK_8 (db10)	9,072	9.537×10^{-7}	−0.0351552963
WMK_8 (Haar)	3,888	3.4115×10^{-3}	−0.0317446963
MK_9 (no wavelet)	262,144	N/A	Insufficient memory
WMK_9 (coif1)	10,192	2.385×10^{-7}	−0.0351560115
WMK_9 (db10)	18,288	2.385×10^{-7}	−0.0351560115
WMK_9 (Haar)	7,584	4.2620×10^{-3}	−0.0351560115
MK_{10} (no wavelet)	1,048,576	N/A	Insufficient memory
WMK_{10} (coif1)	20,432	5.97×10^{-8}	−0.0351561903
WMK_{10} (db10)	36,720	5.97×10^{-8}	−0.0351561903
WMK_{10} (Haar)	4,096	4.650×10^{-3}	−0.0305061907
MK_{11} (no wavelet)	4,194,304	N/A	Insufficient memory
WMK_{11} (coif1)	40,912	1.50×10^{-8}	−0.0351562350
WMK_{11} (db10)	73,584	1.49×10^{-8}	−0.0351562351
WMK_{11} (Haar)	8,192	4.8349×10^{-3}	−0.0303212723
MK_{12} (no wavelet)	16,777,216	N/A	Insufficient memory
WMK_{12} (coif1)	94,208	1.47×10^{-8}	−0.0351562353
WMK_{12} (db10)	159,680	1.62×10^{-8}	−0.0351562338
WMK_{12} (Haar)	16,384	4.9251×10^{-3}	−0.0302310522

While the data are artificial, the structure and algorithm used are applicable to real-world problems such as image registration and edge detection in computer vision, shape matching and morphing in computer graphics, resource allocation and logistics in operations research, optimal transport in machine learning (e.g., domain adaptation, generative modeling), and biomedical imaging tasks such as anatomical alignment or intensity normalization [2,3,9–11].

7 Conclusion

This work introduces a wavelet-based multiresolution numerical scheme for efficiently approximating solutions to the Monge–Kantorovich optimal transport problem. By adaptively refining the computational domain using structural cues from intermediate transport plans, the method substantially reduces computational cost while maintaining high accuracy. The algorithm's scalability and precision make it both theoretically sound and practically viable, enabling solutions at resolutions unattainable with classical discretization methods. Its adaptability positions it as a promising approach for real-world optimal transport applications, with future developments aimed at extending its generality and integrating it with other transport solvers for enhanced performance and robustness.

References

1. Acosta-Portilla, J.R., Gonzáles-Flores, C., López-Martinez, R.R., Sánchez-Nungaray, A.: Efficient method to solve the monge-kantorovich problem using wavelet analysis. Axioms**12**(2023)
2. Bonneel, N., Digne, J.: A survey of optimal transport for computer graphics and computer vision. Comput. Graph. Forum **42**(2), 439–460 (2023)
3. Chen, X., Benveniste, H., Tannenbaum, A.R.: Unbalanced regularized optimal mass transport with applications to fluid flows in the brain. Sci. Rep. **14**(1), 1111 (2024)
4. Chi, J., Wang, B., Chen, H., Zhang, L., Li, X., Ouyang, J.: Approximate continuous optimal transport. Int. J. Intell. Syst. **37**(8), 5354–5380 (2022)
5. Daubechies, I.: Ten Lectures on Wavelets. SIAM (1992)
6. Gabriel, J.R., González-Hernández, J., López-Martínez, R.R.: Numerical approximations to the mass transfer problem on compact spaces. IMA J. Numer. Anal. **30**(4), 1121–1136 (2010)
7. Härdle, W., Kerkyacharian, G., Picard, D., Tsybakov, A.: Wavelets, Approximation and Statistical Applications, 1st edn. Springer, New York (2012)
8. Hasan, M.M.A., et al.: WaveFormer: a 3D transformer with wavelet-driven feature representation for efficient medical image segmentation. In: de Bruijne, M., Veni, G., Naji, K. (eds.) Medical Image Computing and Computer Assisted Intervention – MICCAI 2025. LNCS, vol. 15963, pp. 684–694. Springer, Cham (2025)
9. Kamsu-Foguem, B., Msouobu Gueuwou, S.L., Kounta, C.A.K.A.: Generative adversarial networks based on optimal transport: a survey. Artif. Intell. Rev.**56**(7), 6723–6773 (2023)
10. Kim, B., Zhuang, Y., Mathai, T.S., Summers, R.M.: Otmorph: unsupervised multi-domain abdominal medical image registration using neural optimal transport. IEEE Trans. Med. Imaging (2024)
11. Kreinovich, V., Yamaka, W., Leurcharusmee, S.: Applications of Optimal Transport to Economics and Related Topics. Springer, Cham (2008)
12. Lee, W., Lai, R., Li, W., Osher, S.: Generalized unnormalized optimal transport and its fast algorithms. J. Comput. Phys. **436**, 110041 (2021)
13. Mallat, S., Hwang, W.L.: Singularity detection and processing with wavelets. IEEE Trans. Inf. Theory **38**(2), 617–643 (1992)
14. Mallat, S.: A Wavelet Tour of Signal Processing, 3rd edn. Academic Press (2009)
15. Rachev, S., Rüschendorf, L.: Mass Transportation Problems, vols. I and II. Springer, New York (1998)
16. Tanguy, E., Desolneux, A., Delon, J.: Constrained approximation optimal transport maps. ESAIM: Control, Optimisation and Calculus of Variations **31**, 70 (2025)
17. Villani, C.: Optimal Transport: Old and New, vol. 338. Springer, Berlin (2008)

The Impact of Crossover and Mutation on Carbon Emissions in Real-Coded Genetic Algorithm: An Empirical Study

Nancy Pérez-Castro[1](✉), Efrén Mezura-Montes[2], and Héctor-Gabriel Acosta-Mesa[2]

[1] University of Papaloapan, Av. Ferrocarril S/N, Col. CD. Universitaria, 68400 Loma Bonita, Oaxaca, Mexico
nperez@unpa.edu.mx

[2] Artificial Intelligence Research Institute, University of Veracruz, 91097 Xalapa, Mexico
{emezura,heacosta}@uv.mx

Abstract. Artificial intelligence (AI) is advancing quickly, but its widespread use raises environmental concerns due to the high energy and water consumption of AI systems, particularly during training and large-scale operations. Green AI has emerged as a solution, focusing on specialized algorithms and infrastructure to lessen these environmental effects. Although the environmental footprint of standard AI methods is understood, optimization algorithms, notably Genetic Algorithms, have received less attention despite their frequent application in AI. In this study, the carbon efficiency of different combinations of crossover-mutation operators in a real genetic algorithm (rGA) was examined. The emissions were measured across a range of settings, finding consistent patterns in emissions ranging from 2.669E-05 to 2.204E-04 kg CO_2 eq. While small in scale, these values can add up to significant costs in larger experimental or real-world scenarios. Statistical tests confirmed significant differences; combinations such as 1P_LM (one-point crossover and boundary mutation), 2P_LM (two-point and boundary mutation), and UNI_LM (uniform crossover and boundary mutation) consistently yielded the lowest emissions.

Keywords: Green AI · Genetic Algorithms · Carbon Footprint

1 Introduction

The accelerated adoption of Artificial Intelligence (AI) has precipitated remarkable progress across academic and industrial sectors. Nevertheless, this advancement has concomitantly given rise to concerns regarding its environmental sustainability. The growing body of research highlights that AI systems require substantial energy, generate significant carbon emissions, and consume considerable water, especially during the training and extensive inference phases of model

L. Martínez-Villaseñor et al. (Eds.): MICAI 2025, LNAI 16265, pp. 152–159, 2026.
https://doi.org/10.1007/978-3-032-17933-3_16

development. Therefore, the area of Green AI has emerged, advocating for the development of algorithms, models, and infrastructures designed to mitigate the environmental impact of AI in terms of carbon footprint, energy expenditure, and water consumption. Recent surveys have identified three primary directions in the field of Green AI: (a) the optimization of energy utilization in intelligent environments [2], (b) the implementation of AI to modernize sustainable energy infrastructures [1], and (c) the enhancement of the eco-efficiency of AI itself through the use of lightweight algorithms, efficient training methods, and emission reduction strategies [9], a direction commonly referred to as Green-in-AI. Several studies related to Green-in-AI have quantified the environmental impact of diverse AI methods, providing evidence that guides the classification of sustainable research efforts. For example, k-Nearest Neighbors was reported to consume up to 200 times less energy than Random Forest [12], while VGG19 achieved a more favorable precision-to-energy ratio compared to ResNet50 [13]. Jegham et al. [7] extended this line of inquiry by benchmarking energy, water, and carbon costs in large language model inference, documenting substantial disparities such as DeepSeek-R1 requiring only 33 Wh per prompt compared to 0.45 Wh for GPT-4.1 nano, and large-scale deployments of GPT-4o estimated to generate 163,000 tons of CO_2eq and 1.5 million kiloliters of water annually. Complementary perspectives have been advanced by Schneider et al. [10], who analyzed the life-cycle emissions of AI hardware across successive generations, and Morrison et al. [8], who underscored the necessity for holistic evaluations of language model development that account for environmental costs beyond computational efficiency. Similar concerns have been raised in the domain of recommender systems, where Vente et al. [11] demonstrated that deep learning–based recommenders consume on average eight times more energy and emit forty-two times more CO_2 than traditional approaches. While these works have shed light on the environmental footprint of mainstream AI techniques, less attention has been given to the optimization algorithms themselves, especially evolutionary algorithms such as Genetic Algorithms (GAs), despite their widespread application in computational intelligence. First introduced by J.H. Holland in the 1970s [6], GAs have evolved from their original form into hybrid versions. Most research has focused on improving the quality of solutions and the rate at which they converge [5]. Thanks to improvements in hardware, software, and algorithm design, GAs have become flexible tools for solving complex optimization problems. Motivated by this, GAs are a suitable model for evaluating the sustainability of algorithm design. In this study, the carbon efficiency of crossover–mutation combinations in a real-coded genetic algorithm (rGA) is examined. This study contributes to the understanding of how design decisions at the operator level can influence the environmental impact of evolutionary computation. The central research question that this work addresses is as follows: **RQ1.** What are the effects of crossover and mutation operators on GA carbon emissions when the selection operator is fixed and the algorithm is tested across benchmark functions of varying dimensions?

The rest of this article is organized as follows. Section 2 describes the materials and methods employed in this study. Section 3 presents the experimental setup and discusses the obtained results. Finally, Sect. 4 provides the conclusions and outlines directions for future work.

2 Materials and Methods

2.1 Genetic Algorithm Optimization

The present study employs a real-encoded Genetic Algorithm (rGA), adapted from the classical formulation of the simple GA described by Goldberg. In contrast to the conventional GA, which employs fixed-length binary encoding of solutions, the rGA directly utilizes vectors of real numbers to represent candidate solutions. This representation is particularly well-suited for continuous optimization problems, as it circumvents discretization errors and enables genetic operators to directly act on real-valued parameters. The algorithm begins with the random initialization of a population of individuals, each encoded as a vector of real-valued decision variables within predefined bounds. The quality of each individual is assessed through a fitness function. However, in this initial study, focus is given to measuring carbon emissions, which are recorded at each generation of the evolutionary process. At this stage, the assessment of problem solution quality is considered secondary, as the primary objective is to quantify the environmental footprint of the algorithm under different operator configurations. The evolutionary cycle of the rGA proceeds through the following steps:
Selection. Tournament selection was employed as the fixed selection operator, favoring individuals with higher fitness while preserving stochastic variation in the sampling of parents.
Crossover. A pool of six real-coded crossover operators was considered: Simple Arithmetic (SA), Total Arithmetic (TA), intermediate (INT), One-point (1P), Two-point (2P), and Uniform (UNI). These operators generate offspring by producing linear or stochastic combinations or exchanging genetic segments.
Mutation. Four mutation operators were available: Uniform (UM), Non-uniform (NUM), Boundary Mutation (LM), and Parameter-based (PM). These operators act directly on real-valued genes, creating perturbations to enhance diversity and prevent convergence. The selected operators are widely used in evolutionary computation, enabling reproducibility and fair comparisons across studies, while ensuring compatibility with real-valued representations for consistent evaluation in continuous domains.

A new population replaces the old one at each generation. This guarantees that the best-performing individuals are not lost. The evolutionary process continues until a defined termination criterion is reached. Algorithm 1 synthesizes the overall process of the real-coded genetic algorithm employed in this study.

2.2 Carbon Emission Measurement

The carbon footprint quantifies the total greenhouse gas (GHG) emissions associated with a process, typically expressed in kilograms of carbon dioxide equivalent

Algorithm 1. rGA

1: Initialize a population P of N real-valued solutions within bounds $[l, u]$
2: **for** each generation $g = 1 \ldots G$ **do**
3: Evaluate fitness of P and record carbon emissions
4: Select parents from P (e.g., tournament)
5: Apply crossover with probability p_c to generate offspring
6: Apply mutation with probability p_m to offspring
7: Form new population P (with elitism)
8: **end for**
9: **return** best solution found

(kg CO_2 eq). CO_2 is the main greenhouse gas from burning fossil fuels, and is the unit used to measure global warming. The measurement of carbon emissions was conducted using the CodeCarbon library [3], which utilizes the standard computational method outlined in equation X.

$$kgCO_2eq = C \times E \tag{1}$$

where, **C** = Carbon Intensity of the electricity consumed for computation: quantified as g of CO_2 emitted per kilowatt-hour of electricity. **E** = Energy Consumed by the computational infrastructure: quantified as kilowatt-hours.

CodeCarbon estimates CO_2 emissions by multiplying the energy consumed by system components (CPU, GPU, and RAM) by the carbon intensity of the local electricity grid. When the location is unknown, a global average is used. In this study, energy consumption was monitored throughout each genetic algorithm run, and emissions were averaged over 25 runs per configuration.

3 Experiments and Results

This section begins by describing the experimental configuration adopted in this study. The experiments were organized into three parts. First, heatmaps supported by statistical tests were used to identify the best mutation operator within each crossover group. Second, the mean carbon emissions from 25 independent runs of the resulting crossover–mutation combinations were analyzed, and statistical tests were applied to determine the best-performing operator for each benchmark function in three dimensions (10, 30, and 50). Finally, post hoc test was employed to validate the significance of the differences and to highlight pairwise comparisons among the best-performing operators.

3.1 Configuration Setting

To address the research question, a series of experiments was conducted. These experiments involved the application of a rGA to four benchmark functions from the CEC 2005 suite (suganthan2005problem). The experiments were conducted under a fixed tournament selection scheme. Following the benchmark's recommendations, 25 independent runs were conducted. The experimental configuration, including the selected operators, problem dimensions, implementation details, and hardware specifications, is summarized in Table 1.

Table 1. Summary of experimental setup and parameter configuration for the rGA

Parameter/Environment	Value
Population size	100
Crossover probability	1.0 (100%)
Mutation probability	1.0 (100%)
Number of independent runs	25 per operator combination
Benchmark functions	Sphere, Schwefel 1.2, Rosenbrock, Rastrigin
Dimensions tested	10D, 30D, 50D
Maximum number of evaluations	10D= 100000, 30D=300000, 50D=500000
Selection method	Tournament (fixed)
Crossover operators	SA, TA, INT, 1P, 2P and UNI
Mutation operators	UM, NUM, LM and PM
Implementation	Python (DEAP library) [4]
Hardware	12th Gen Intel(R) Core(TM) i5-12450H, 12 CPUs, ~2.0 GHz, 8 GB RAM

3.2 Selection of the Best Mutation Operator

Figure 1 presents the heatmaps of mean carbon emissions for each benchmark function at 50 dimensions. Similar patterns were observed for 10 and 30 dimensions. The maps summarize the interaction between six crossover and four mutation operators, where red tones indicate higher emissions and yellow tones indicate lower ones. Across all dimensions, the NUM and PM mutation operators consistently exhibited the highest emission levels, while the UM and LM operators showed the lowest.

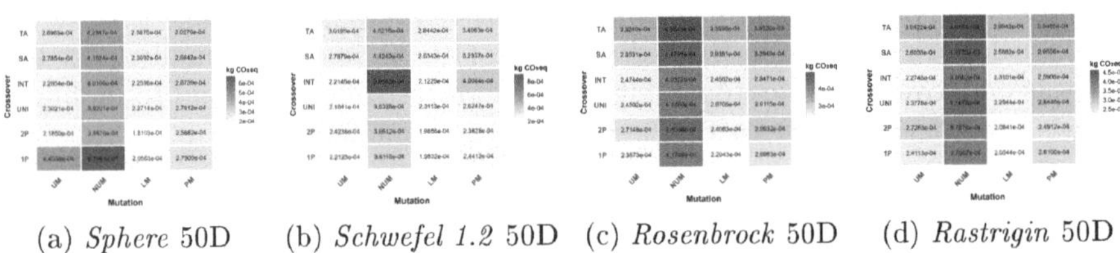

(a) *Sphere* 50D (b) *Schwefel 1.2* 50D (c) *Rosenbrock* 50D (d) *Rastrigin* 50D

Fig. 1. Heatmaps of average carbon emissions for each benchmark function at 50 dimensions.

3.3 Best Crossover–Mutation Combinations

Table 2 presents the best resulting combinations for each crossover operator including the selected mutation operator previously. The numerical values correspond to the mean kg CO_2 eq across 25 runs for each function and dimension. The p-values were computed using non-parametric 95%-confidence Kruskal-Wallis over the six finalist groups per function and dimension. Significant differences were observed among the six operator combinations across functions and dimensions. In *f_sphere*, the IP_LM combination produced the lowest CO_2 emissions in dimensions 10 and 30, while 2P_LM was best in dimension 50. For *f_schwefel12*, 1P_LM yielded the lowest emissions in dimensions 10 and 50, with 2P_LM performing best in dimension 30. In *f_rosenbrock*, 1P_LM again achieved the lowest emissions in dimensions 30 and 50, whereas UNI_LM was superior in dimension 10. Finally, in *f_rastrigin*, UNI_LM, 2P_LM, and 1P_LM exhibited the lowest CO_2 emissions in dimensions 10, 30, and 50, respectively. Note that the reported best combinations correspond to the lowest-emission results per function and dimension, not cross-compared within the same dimensional group (Table 2).

Table 2. Summary of average carbon emission values (kgCO_2 eq) for the best crossover–mutation combinations across all dimensions (10, 30, and 50) for each function. Values in bold indicate the significantly best results.

f_sphere						f_schwefel12					
Operators	10D	Operators	30D	Operators	50D	Operators	10D	Operators	30D	Operators	50D
SA_UM	1.420E-05	SA_LM	9.359E-05	SA_LM	2.369E-04	SA_UM	1.763E-05	SA_UM	1.164E-04	SA_LM	2.534E-04
TA_LM	1.538E-05	TA_LM	9.668E-05	TA_LM	2.587E-04	TA_UM	2.176E-05	TA_UM	1.473E-04	TA_LM	2.844E-04
INT_LM	1.452E-05	INT_LM	1.102E-04	INT_LM	2.260E-04	INT_LM	1.672E-05	INT_LM	9.747E-05	INT_LM	2.123E-04
1P_LM	**1.390E-05**	IP_LM	**8.135E-05**	IP_LM	2.056E-04	1P_LM	**1.587E-05**	IP_LM	9.152E-05	IP_LM	**1.983E-04**
2P_UM	1.519E-05	2P_LM	8.260E-05	2P_LM	**1.810E-04**	2P_LM	2.386E-05	2P_LM	**9.014E-05**	2P_LM	1.986E-04
UNI_LM	1.555E-05	UNI_LM	8.719E-05	UNI_LM	2.271E-04	UNI_LM	1.687E-05	UNI_LM	9.598E-05	UNI_UM	2.164E-04
p-value	*3.140E-04*		*4.053E-18*		*3.875E-18*	*p-value*	*3.613E-11*		*4.547E-21*		*4.063E-24*
f_rosenbrock						f_rastrigin					
Operators	10D	Operators	30D	Operators	50D	Operators	10D	Operators	30D	Operators	50D
SA_UM	2.703E-05	SA_LM	1.214E-04	SA_UM	2.853E-04	SA_UM	1.615E-05	SA_LM	1.043E-04	SA_LM	2.568E-04
TA_UM	3.345E-05	TA_UM	1.309E-04	TA_UM	3.325E-04	TA_LM	1.854E-05	TA_LM	1.176E-04	TA_LM	2.994E-04
INT_LM	5.711E-05	INT_UM	1.205E-04	INT_LM	2.456E-04	INT_LM	1.684E-05	INT_LM	9.525E-05	INT_UM	2.275E-04
1P_LM	7.881E-05	1P_LM	**1.010E-04**	1P_LM	**2.204E-04**	1P_UM	1.757E-05	1P_LM	8.436E-05	1P_LM	**2.054E-04**
2P_LM	3.303E-05	2P_UM	1.234E-04	2P_LM	2.406E-04	2P_LM	1.696E-05	2P_LM	**8.372E-05**	2P_LM	2.084E-04
UNI_LM	**2.669E-05**	UNI_UM	1.313E-04	UNI_UM	2.450E-04	UNI_LM	**1.599E-05**	UNI_LM	9.009E-05	UNI_LM	2.294E-04
p-value	*7.609E-24*		*4.863E-17*		*3.725E-23*	*p-value*	*5.142E-03*		*9.180E-21*		*3.265E-24*

3.4 Post-hoc Statistical Validation

To enhance the statistical analysis, Dunn's post-hoc test was applied using the best values of kg CO_2 eq to compare the performance of the six finalist operator groups for each function across the three dimensions, thereby identifying pairwise differences. Figure 2 presents the results of Dunn's test for each function, showing only the case of dimension 50. The x-axis represents the confidence interval of the mean rank, while the y-axis lists the compared operator combinations. In *f_ sphere*, the 1P_LM combination performed significantly better than INT_LM, SA_LM, TA_LM, and UNI_LM, while showing similar behavior to 2P_LM. In *f_ schwefel*, 1P_LM exhibited significant differences compared with SA_LM, TA_LM, and UNI_UM, but no significant difference with 2P_LM and INT_LM. For *f_ rosenbrock*, 1P_LM also showed significant differences relative to SA, TA, and UNI crossover operators when combined with the UM mutation operator. Finally, in *f_ rastrigin*, 1P_LM presented significant differences with INT_UM, SA_LM, TA_LM, and UNI_LM.

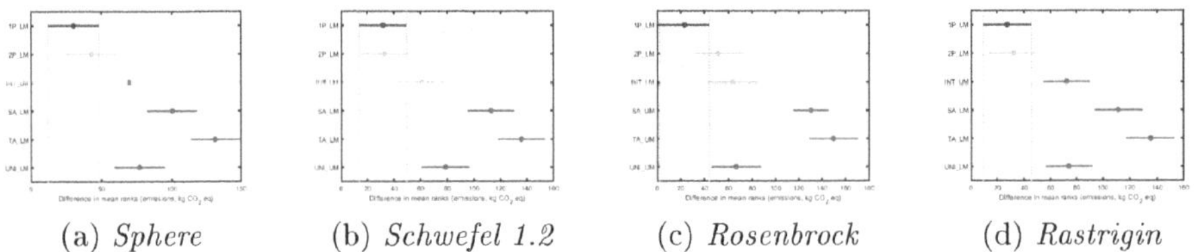

(a) *Sphere* (b) *Schwefel 1.2* (c) *Rosenbrock* (d) *Rastrigin*

Fig. 2. Post hoc multiple comparisons among crossover winners (best mutation within each crossover) for each benchmark function in dimension 50: (a) *Sphere*, (b) *Schwefel 1.2*, (c) *Rosenbrock*, and (d) *Rastrigin*.

4 Conclusions and Future Work

In summary, the analysis of crossover-mutation combinations in a real-coded genetic algorithm using the CEC 2005 benchmark revealed consistent emission patterns across functions and dimensions. At 50 dimensions, the best-performing combinations (1P_LM, 2P_LM, and UNI_LM) achieved the lowest CO_2 emissions, ranging between 2.669E–05 and 2.204E–04 kg CO_2eq. Although these values are small, they represent the environmental cost of algorithmic experimentation and can accumulate to a considerable footprint when scaled to larger studies. The results confirm that operator selection influences energy efficiency and highlight the relevance of incorporating carbon-aware practices in evolutionary computation. Future work will extend this evaluation to constrained problems and updated benchmarks, integrate detailed energy profiling, and promote the systematic reporting of carbon-impact metrics to advance toward standardized, environmentally responsible experimentation.

Acknowledgments. The first author gratefully acknowledges the University of Veracruz for hosting the sabbatical stay during which this work was conducted.

Disclosure of Interests. The authors have no competing interests to declare that are relevant to the content of this article.

References

1. Ajao, O.R.: Optimizing energy infrastructure with AI technology: a literature review. Open J. Appl. Sci. **14**(12), 3516–3544 (2024). https://doi.org/10.4236/ojapps.2024.1412230
2. Biswas, P., Rashid, A., Biswas, A., Nasim, M.A.A., Chakraborty, S., Gupta, K.D., George, R.: AI-driven approaches for optimizing power consumption: a comprehensive survey. Discover Artif. Intell. **4**(1), 116 (2024). https://doi.org/10.1007/s44163-024-00211-7
3. Courty, B., et al.: MinervaBooks: mlco2/codecarbon: v2.4.1 (May 2024). https://doi.org/10.5281/zenodo.11171501, https://doi.org/10.5281/zenodo.11171501
4. Fortin, F.A., Rainville, F.M.D., Gardner, M.A., Parizeau, M., Gagné, C.: Deap: evolutionary algorithms made easy. J. Mach. Learn. Res. **13**(70), 2171–2175 (2012). http://jmlr.org/papers/v13/fortin12a.html
5. Gen, M., Lin, L.: Genetic algorithms and their applications. In: Pham, H. (ed.) Springer Handbook of Engineering Statistics, pp. 635–674. Springer, London (2023). https://doi.org/10.1007/978-1-4471-7503-2_33, series Title: Springer Handbooks
6. Holland, J.H.: Adaptation in Natural and Artificial Systems. University of Michigan Press, Ann Arbor (1975)
7. Jegham, N., Abdelatti, M., Elmoubarki, L., Hendawi, A.: How Hungry is AI? Benchmarking Energy, Water, and Carbon Footprint of LLM Inference (2025). https://doi.org/10.48550/ARXIV.2505.09598, version Number: 3
8. Morrison, J., Na, C., Fernandez, J., Dettmers, T., Strubell, E., Dodge, J.: Holistically Evaluating the Environmental Impact of Creating Language Models (2025). https://doi.org/10.48550/ARXIV.2503.05804, version Number: 1
9. Różycki, R., Solarska, D.A., Waligóra, G.: Energy-aware machine learning models–a review of recent techniques and perspectives. Energies **18**(11), 2810 (2025). https://doi.org/10.3390/en18112810
10. Schneider, I., Xu, H., Benecke, S., Patterson, D., Huang, K., Ranganathan, P., Elsworth, C.: Life-cycle emissions of AI hardware: a cradle-to-grave approach and generational trends (2025). https://doi.org/10.48550/ARXIV.2502.01671, version Number: 1
11. Vente, T., Wegmeth, L., Said, A., Beel, J.: From clicks to carbon: The environmental toll of recommender systems, pp. 580–590. RecSys '24, Association for Computing Machinery, New York, NY, USA (2024). https://doi.org/10.1145/3640457.3688074
12. Verdecchia, R., Cruz, L., Sallou, J., Lin, M., Wickenden, J., Hotellier, E.: Data-centric green AI an exploratory empirical study. In: 2022 International Conference on ICT for Sustainability (ICT4S). pp. 35–45. IEEE, Plovdiv, Bulgaria, June 2022. https://doi.org/10.1109/ICT4S55073.2022.00015
13. Xu, Y., Martínez-Fernández, S., Martinez, M., Franch, X.: Energy efficiency of training neural network architectures: an empirical study (2023). https://doi.org/10.48550/ARXIV.2302.00967, publisher: arXiv Version Number: 1

Visual Cylindrical Containers Tilt Detection for Precise Liquid Pouring

Jeeangh Jennessi Reyes-Montiel[1](✉), Nayely Morales-Ramirez[2], Hector Gabriel Acosta-Mesa[1], and Antonio Marin-Hernandez[1]

[1] Artificial Intelligence Research Institute, Universidad Veracruzana, Calle Paseo No. 112, Col. Nueva Xalapa, 91097 Xalapa, Mexico
jeeanghreyes@gmail.com, {heacosta,anmarin}@uv.mx

[2] Electronics and Communication Engineering Faculty, Universidad Veracruzana, Venustiano Carranza S/N, Col. Revolución, 93390 Poza Rica de Hidalgo, Mexico
namorales@uv.mx

Abstract. Pouring precise liquid quantities remains a challenging task for autonomous robots. Particularly this is due to various factors as: robust container estimation, liquid's volume estimation, arm's or device motion uncertainty, and platform instability. This work presents a vision-based approach to estimate the tilt of cylindrical containers, a key geometric variable for inferring poured volume. The method processes frontal images using Canny edge detection and the probabilistic Hough transform to extract container and liquid boundaries. From these, a projective geometry model computes the container's inclination without additional sensors. The proposed approach avoids the explicit calculation of fluid dynamics by providing a tool for performing a smooth pouring process. Experimental results demonstrate the feasibility of this low-cost, vision-based estimation approach.

Keywords: Autonomous pouring task · Computer vision · Tilt angle estimation

1 Introduction

Machine vision is crucial in robotics, supporting perception, localization, and manipulation tasks that rely on closed control loops. Liquid pouring is particularly challenging due to the dynamic nature of fluids and the difficulty of modeling their behavior in real-world conditions.

This work does not explicitly model fluid dynamics, but rather focuses on a key perceptual factor that affects it: container tilt. By accurately estimating the tilt angle from visual information, the system provides essential data for approximating liquid flow and controlling the pouring process. Computer vision techniques are also used to detect the container's liquid level during pouring, strengthening the perception stage needed for future fluid modeling and volume estimation.

L. Martínez-Villaseñor et al. (Eds.): MICAI 2025, LNAI 16265, pp. 160–167, 2026.
https://doi.org/10.1007/978-3-032-17933-3_17

The proposed approach integrates image preprocessing, Canny edge detection, and probabilistic Hough line detection to extract the boundaries of the container and the liquid. The inclination angle is then inferred through projective geometry by linking both features.

The remainder of this paper is organized as follows: Sect. 2 reviews related work on vision-based angle estimation, Sect. 3 describes the experimental setup and method, Sect. 4 presents results and analysis, and Sect. 5 concludes with future research directions

2 Related Works

Autonomous liquid pouring remains challenging due to fluid dynamics and container geometry variability. Achieving spill-free control requires precise perception of both the liquid surface and container orientation.

Zhang et al. [1] proposed an Explainable Hierarchical Imitation Learning (EHIL) framework combining high-level reasoning and low-level actions. Do [2] estimated liquid height using RGB-D data, while Long et al. [3] applied screw theory for precise motion control. Nishio [4] modeled condensation effects, and Babaians et al. [5] developed PourNet, integrating deep reinforcement learning and predictive control. Yamaguchi [6] used optical flow for 3D reconstruction, and Zhu and Yamakawa [7] achieved 5% error in beer-foam volume estimation.

For molten metals, Sueki and Noda [8] applied decentralized Kalman filters, Chengjun et al. [9] implemented hardware-in-the-loop control, and Kabasawa and Noda [10] improved accuracy through inverse modeling and parameter adaptation.

In domestic settings, Wang et al. [11] fused visual-audio cues with cross-attention networks for liquid level detection. Zhang et al. [12] combined supervised and reinforcement learning, while Lin et al. [13] demonstrated the importance of visual-tactile feedback and introduced *PourIt!* for data collection.

For viscous or unknown liquids, Luo et al. [14] integrated haptics for dough handling, Huang et al. [15] applied self-supervised learning from demonstrations, and Saito et al. [16] predicted viscosity and fill level from multimodal sensorimotor data. Transparent-liquid detection was addressed by Narasimhan et al. [17] using a generative model and by Dong et al. [18] through container modeling and PD control refined with point cloud data.

Camporredondo et al. [19] used smoothed particle hydrodynamics (SPH) for real-time simulation, and Cleaver et al. [20] proposed human-in-the-loop trajectory correction. Line detection methods include Urrea and Ospina [21] (microcontroller-based Hough transform), Canul et al. [22] (parallel processing), and Pithadiya [23] (distance-based ROI).

In contras, previous sensor-dependent approaches, this work relies solely on vision to infer container tilt from geometric cues in a single 2D image, aligning the liquid surface with gravity and offering a simple, low-cost solution.

3 Equipment and Methods

The proposed method estimates the inclination of a cylindrical container using computer vision. The process includes grayscale conversion, edge extraction, line detection with the Hough transform, and angle estimation based on line slopes.

3.1 Image Acquisition and Preprocessing

Images of a container filled with different liquid volumes (100, 120, and 140 ml) and tilt angles (30°–42°) were collected using a fixed camera. Each image was converted to grayscale with OpenCV to simplify processing (Fig. 1).

Fig. 1. Grayscale versions of the input images used for processing.

3.2 Edge Detection

Canny edge detection was applied with two threshold settings. The first (22, 42) enhanced the container contours by preserving weak gradients, while the second (45, 150) emphasized strong horizontal features corresponding to the liquid surface (Fig. 2). The higher thresholds reduced noise and preserved only edges relevant for angle estimation.

3.3 Line Detection and Classification

The probabilistic Hough transform (HoughLinesP) was used to identify straight segments. Near-vertical lines represented the container borders, while nearly horizontal lines (slope $|m| < 0.054$) corresponded to the liquid level (Fig. 3). The slope of each line was calculated as:

$$m = \frac{y_2 - y_1}{x_2 - x_1}.$$

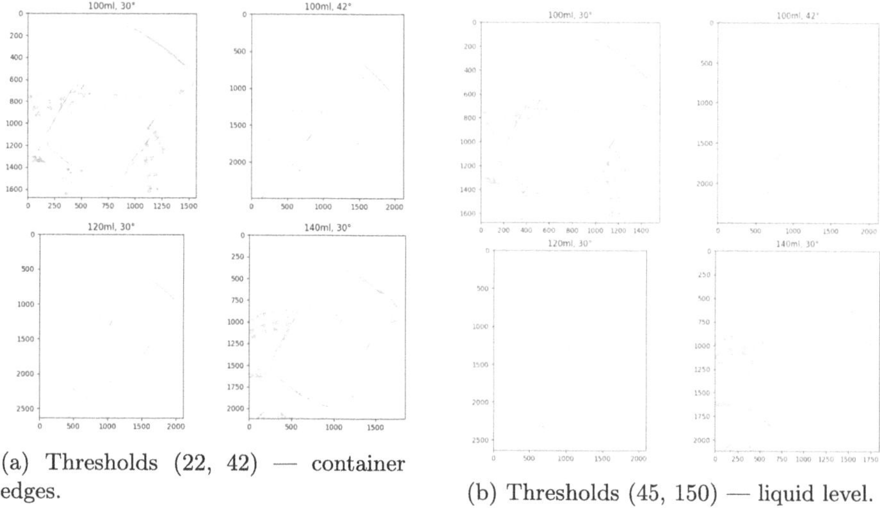

(a) Thresholds (22, 42) — container edges.

(b) Thresholds (45, 150) — liquid level.

Fig. 2. Comparison of edge detection configurations: (a) highlights container edges; (b) enhances liquid surface detection.

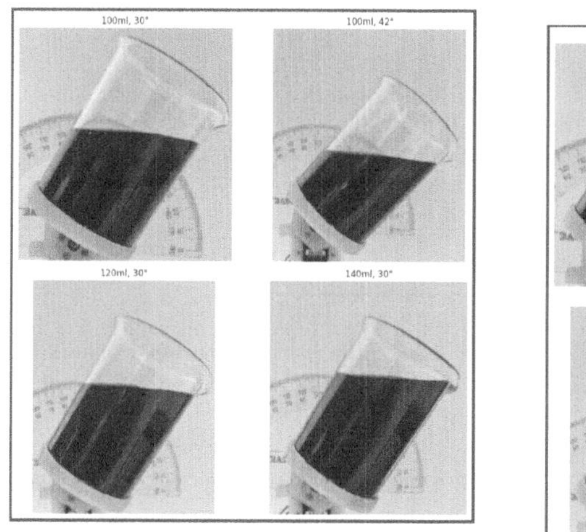

(a) Detection of the outer edges of the container.

(b) Detection of the liquid level.

Fig. 3. Detected lines for container and liquid surface.

3.4 Angle Estimation Based on Detected Lines

The container tilt was obtained by measuring the deviation between the horizontal liquid line and each vertical edge (Fig. 4). The angle θ between two lines with slopes m_1 and m_2 was computed as:

$$\theta = \arctan\left(\left|\frac{m_1 - m_2}{1 + m_1 m_2}\right|\right).$$

The final tilt angle was calculated as the mean of both side estimates. Integrating Canny and Hough detection within a projective geometry framework enables accurate tilt estimation from a single 2D image, removing the need for inertial or depth sensors and offering a simple, low-cost perception solution for robotic pouring.

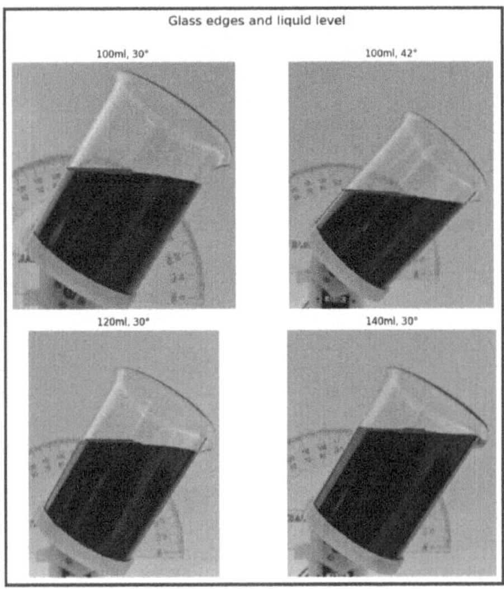

Fig. 4. Combined visualization of the left (green) and right (red) container borders for the liquid surface (blue). The image illustrates the estimation of both angles used to compute the average container inclination. (Color figure online)

4 Results

The experiments were performed using a 150 ml cylindrical container (radius 28.5mm, level 81mm). Its inclination was adjusted to preset angles using a servomotor controlled by an Arduino, ensuring repeatable positioning. Each configuration was analyzed using the proposed vision-based method. Tables 1 and 2 summarize the actual and estimated tilt angles and the respective errors.

The proposed method obtained average absolute errors of 6.44% (left edge) and 4.48% (right edge), validating the accuracy and consistency of the tilt estimation based solely on visual signals. These results demonstrate the feasibility of the method under controlled conditions with an opaque liquid of uniform density.

Table 1. Estimated angles and percentage errors between the left container edge (green line) and the liquid surface (blue line).

Image	Real Angle (°)	Detected Angle (Green-Blue) [°]	Error (%)
100ml	30	27.41	8.63
100ml	42	37.01	11.88
120ml	30	29.32	2.27
140ml	30	28.51	4.97

Table 2. Estimated angles and percentage errors between the right container edge (red line) and the liquid surface (blue line).

Image	Real Angle (°)	Detected Angle (Red-Blue) [°]	Error (%)
100ml	30	30.38	1.27
100ml	42	41.02	2.33
120ml	30	32.34	7.80
140ml	30	32.55	8.50

Future work will extend the validation to more realistic scenarios, incorporating different viscosity, transparency, lighting conditions, and dynamic disturbances to evaluate robustness and generalization in robotic pouring tasks.

5 Conclusions

This work introduced a vision-based method for estimating the tilt angle of partially filled containers. The approach combines grayscale preprocessing, Canny edge detection, and probabilistic Hough line detection to identify container borders and the liquid surface from a single 2D image. The liquid surface, aligned with gravity, serves as a geometric reference to infer container inclination from line slopes.

Experimental results showed mean errors of 6.44% (left edge) and 4.48% (right edge), validating the method's reliability as a low-cost perception module for robotic pouring. Its simplicity and modular design make it suitable for integration into visual feedback loops controlling fluid flow and volume.

Future work will address more demanding scenarios, including variable lighting, background complexity, and container transparency, as well as real-time implementation within robotic control. Current research, also explores 3D point cloud modeling to enhance container recognition and adaptability in practical pouring tasks.

References

1. Zhang, D., Qiang Li, Yu., Zheng, L.W., Zhang, D., Zhang, Z.: Explainable hierarchical imitation learning for robotic drink pouring. IEEE Trans. Autom. Sci. Eng. **19**(4), 3871–3887 (2022)
2. Do, C., Schubert, T., Burgard, W.: A probabilistic approach to liquid level detection in cups using an rgb-d camera. In: 2016 IEEE/RSJ International Conference on Intelligent Robots and Systems (IROS), pp. 2075–2080 (2016)
3. Li, L., Wang, C., Wu, H.: Research on kinematics and pouring law of a mobile heavy load pouring robot
4. Nishio, Yu., Ogawa, T., Niwa, K., Chiba, H.: Experimental and numerical study on liquid pouring from a beverage can. J. Food Eng. **291**, 110237 (2021)
5. Babaians, E., Sharma, T., Karimi, M., Sharifzadeh, S., Steinbach, E.: Pournet: robust robotic pouring through curriculum and curiosity-based reinforcement learning. In: 2022 IEEE/RSJ International Conference on Intelligent Robots and Systems (IROS), pp. 9332–9339 (2022)
6. Yamaguchi, A., Atkeson, C.G.: Stereo vision of liquid and particle flow for robot pouring. In: 2016 IEEE-RAS 16th International Conference on Humanoid Robots (Humanoids), pp. 1173–1180 (2016)
7. Zhu, H., Yamakawa, Y.: Robotic pouring based on real-time observation and visual feedback by a high-speed vision system. J. Robot. Mechatronics **34**(5), 965–974 (2022)
8. Sueki, Y., Noda, Y.: Experimental verification of real-time flow-rate estimations in a tilting-ladle-type automatic pouring machine. Appl. Sci. **11**(15) (2021)
9. Chengjun, W., Hao, D., Long, L.: Design, simulation, control of a hybrid pouring robot: enhancing automation level in the foundry industry. Robotica **42**(4), 1018–1038 (2024)
10. Kabasawa, N., Noda, Y.: Model-based flow rate control with online model parameters identification in automatic pouring machine. Robotics **10**(1) (2021)
11. Wang, Z., Tian, G., Pan, H.: Robot gaining robust pouring skills through fusing vision and audio. ISA Trans. **135**, 428–437 (2023)
12. Zhang, X., Liu, J., Zhang, W.: Multi-level robotic pouring using offline reinforcement learning. In: 2024 IEEE International Conference on Robotics and Biomimetics (ROBIO), pp. 1850–1855 (2024)
13. Lin, L., Li, K., Yue, S., Tian, X., Wei, N.: Sensorimotor control for manipulating a glass of water-effects of visual and tactile feedbacks. In: 2018 IEEE International Conference on Intelligent Computing and Signal Processing (ICSP), pp. 1015–1018 (2018)
14. Luo, X., Jin, S., Huang, H.-J., Yuan, W.: An intelligent robotic system for perceptive pancake batter stirring and precise pouring. In: 2024 IEEE/RSJ International Conference on Intelligent Robots and Systems (IROS), pp. 5970–5977 (2024)
15. Huang, Y., Wilches, J., Sun, Yu.: Robot gaining accurate pouring skills through self-supervised learning and generalization. Robot. Auton. Syst. **136**, 103692 (2021)
16. Saito, N., Dai, N.B., Ogata, T., Mori, H., Sugano, S.: Real-time liquid pouring motion generation: End-to-end sensorimotor coordination for unknown liquid dynamics trained with deep neural networks. In: 2019 IEEE International Conference on Robotics and Biomimetics (ROBIO), pp. 1077–1082 (2019)
17. Narasimhan, G., Zhang, K., Eisner, B., Lin, X., Held, D.: Self-supervised transparent liquid segmentation for robotic pouring. In: 2022 International Conference on Robotics and Automation (ICRA), pp. 4555–4561 (2022)

18. Dong, C., Takizawa, M., Kudoh, S., Suehiro, T.: Precision pouring into unknown containers by service robots. In: 2019 IEEE/RSJ International Conference on Intelligent Robots and Systems (IROS), pp. 5875–5882 (2019)
19. Camporredondo, G., Barber, R., Legrand, M., Muñoz, L.: A kinematic controller for liquid pouring between vessels modelled with smoothed particle hydrodynamics. Appl. Sci. **9**(23) (2019)
20. Cleaver, A., Aronson, R.M., Sinapov, J.: Enhancing users' predictions of robotic pouring behaviors using augmented reality: a case study. In: 2024 33rd IEEE International Conference on Robot and Human Interactive Communication (ROMAN), pp. 1886–1891 (2024)
21. Urrea, J., Ospina, E.: Implementación de la transformada de hough para la detección de líneas para un sistema de visión de bajo nivel. Scientia et Technica **1**(24), 70–89 (2006)
22. Canul, L., López, J., Narvaéz, L.: Algoritmo rápido de la transformada de Hough para detección de líneas rectas en una imagen. Programación Matemática y Software **7**(2), 8–13 (2015)
23. Pithadiya, K., Modi, C., Chauhan, J.: Selecting the most favourable edge detection technique for liquid level inspection in bottles. Int. J. Comput. Inf. Syst. Ind. Manage. Appl. **3**, 34–44 (2011)

Pilot Test of Ethnic Hate Speech Detection in Mexico

Verónica Neri-Mendoza[1,2](✉), Yulia Ledeneva[2], Jonathan Rojas-Simón[2], Yorne Alejandrina Santos-Bobadilla[2], and Rene Arnulfo García-Hernández[2]

[1] Secretariat of Science, Humanities, Technology and Innovation, No. 1582, Insurgentes Sur Avenue, Credito Constructor, Benito Juarez, Mexico City, Mexico
[2] Autonomous University of the State of Mexico, Instituto Literario No. 100, 50000 Toluca, State of Mexico, Mexico
{vnerim001,ysantosb001}@alumno.uaemex.mx,
{ynledeneva,jrojass,reagarciah}@uaemex.mx

Abstract. Hate speech is a form of communication that conveys hostility, rejection, and contempt toward a person or group, based on features such as ethnic origin, religion, or gender identity. Its purpose is to foster an environment of violence and discrimination. In this paper, we present the findings of a pilot test designed to validate the dataset, the proposed methodology, and evaluate the performance of traditional algorithms in detecting ethnic hate speech. The analysis focuses on discriminatory content directed toward indigenous communities in Mexico, classified into three categories: "Hate," "Non-Hate," and "Unrelated Hate." The dataset seeks to fill a gap in hate speech detection studies in Mexican Spanish, which have primarily focused on manifestations of homophobia and misogyny. We implemented traditional machine learning algorithms such as Naive Bayes, Logistic Regression, Multilayer Perceptron, and Support Vector Machine. Additionally, three different vectorizations were considered: TF-IDF, BERT, and ASCII, to identify the best way to extract features. Based on our results, we found that using the Support Vector Machine and BERT vectorization improved the classification of ethnic hate speech.

Keywords: Ethnic Hate Speech · Mexico · Pilot Test · Machine Learning

1 Introduction

Discrimination in Mexico has its roots in the colonial period, when populations with different features met, giving rise to discourses of contempt and "racial" hierarchies [9]. Through this process, a classification system was established that distinguished the population between spaniards, creoles, mestizos, and indigenous people [5]. This social structure not only defined the society of the time but also laid the foundation for the inequalities that persist today. This has given

L. Martínez-Villaseñor et al. (Eds.): MICAI 2025, LNAI 16265, pp. 168–176, 2026.
https://doi.org/10.1007/978-3-032-17933-3_18

rise to the contempt expressed through hate speech, which in turn reinforces prejudices and discriminatory practices, creating a perpetual cycle of exclusion.

Hate speech can be expressed orally, in writing, through gestures, and even in images [5,9]. These expressions attack or use pejorative language toward a person or community based on their identity, gender, sexual preference, religion, nationality or ethnic origin [1]. Hate speech and discrimination are closely related, as hate speech is the main way to spread and justify discrimination, promoting intolerance and violence. These are expressed on social networks, which has become a space where existing prejudices can be expressed with greater impunity, amplified, and validated by like-minded people [1].

In Mexico, hate speech with ethnic implications is particularly prevalent. According to ENADIS[1], the indigenous population is identified as the most discriminated against social group in Mexico. The percentages of the population who reported having been victims of discrimination are higher among groups by ethnic or "racial" origin at 28.2%, compared to the general population at 23.7% in 2022. There are cases in which intolerance transcends the discursive sphere and leads to physical acts of violence. One example is that of a 14-year-old indigenous adolescent in Querétaro, who was the victim of a brutal attack by his classmates due to his ethnic origin and his limited command of Spanish, given that his native language is Otomi [8]. Although this case reflects a scenario of extreme violence, it has been documented that the dissemination and continued exposure to hate speech in the digital environment reinforce the processes that normalize violence and discrimination [5]. This phenomenon not only negatively impacts the health of the victims but also generates large-scale dynamics of social exclusion. Therefore, it is necessary to design computational tools through machine learning algorithms to detect hate speech on social networks.

Although there has been improvement in identifying hate speech based on gender, sexual orientation, religion, and nationality, the analysis becomes more complicated when considering ethnophobia, xenophobia, and racism. To understand the problem, it is necessary to differentiate how each is defined: racism is the belief in biologically superior/inferior human "races". Ethnophobia is the rejection of a group due to its cultural differences (language, way of dressing, history, culture, or ethnic affiliation). Xenophobia is thc rcjcction of people who are foreigners [9,11]. These concepts are intrinsically interconnected (see Fig. 1), which generates more complex forms of exclusion. Currently, ethnophobic hatred can be misclassified xenophobia or racismo. Therefore, accurate detection of ethnophobia would allow for the identification and classification of rejection based on cultural differences and not on supposed biological "race".

In this article, we present a pilot study aimed at implementing classical algorithms to validate our methodology and dataset, and to measure the performance of traditional machine learning algorithms such as Support Vector Machine (SVM), Naive Bayes (NB), Logistic Regression (LR), and Multilayer Percep-

[1] Encuesta Nacional sobre Discriminación, 2022; Carried out by the Instituto Nacional de Estadística y Geografía, in collaboration with the Consejo Nacional para Prevenir la Discriminación, and the Comisión Nacional de los Derechos Humanos.

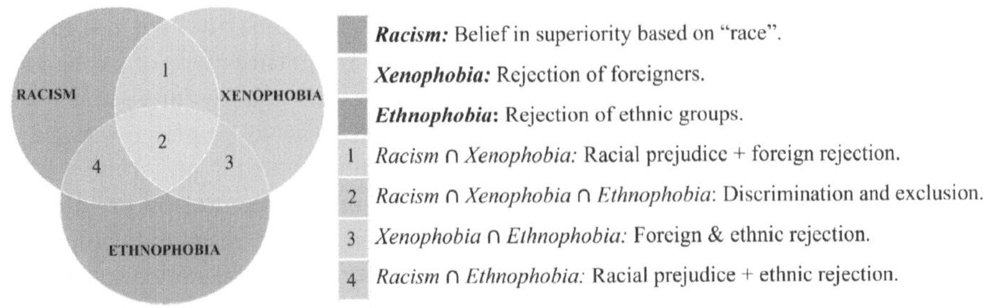

Fig. 1. Intersectionality between racism, xenophobia, and ethnophobia.

tron (MLP) for the classification of ethnic hate speech in textual publications. Section 2 presents the related work that constitutes the conceptual and methodological basis of our proposal. Section 3 details the implemented methodology. Section 4 describes the sample, experimental parameters, and results obtained. Finally, Sect. 5 presents conclusions and future research directions.

2 State-of-the-Art

In recent years, hate speech on social media has become a topic of great interest for Natural Language Processing research. This has driven the development of algorithms capable of identifying and classifying this type of content. The following studies have laid the groundwork for research on this topic.

Gender: As for gender, there is [6], an analysis of sexism-oriented hate speech was performed using data from Twitter in English, SVM and LR algorithms were implemented. In this same context within the EXIST shared task was presented [14], whose objective was the detection of sexism on social networks in English and Spanish. Among the techniques used were SVM, LR, and AdaBoost. On the other hand, in [7] addressed the identification of misogyny as part of the EVALITA competition, a corpus in English and Italian was compiled. This research employed multiple machine learning techniques. In addition, in Semeval-19 [3], the detection of hate speech towards women in Twitter messages in Spanish and English was also addressed.

Sexual Preference: A system for detection of hate speech LGBT+ phobia was proposed in [10], focusing on tweets in Mexican Spanish. The corpus including categories such as gayphobia, lesbophobia, transphobia, among others. Furthermore, in [12], a method for detecting homophobic content in English-language was proposed, implementing models as traditional machine learning approaches like SVM.

Religion: A systematic taxonomy of religious hate speech was proposed in [13] targeting three monotheistic religions: *Judaism*, *Islam*, and *Christianity* in English and Italian. Moreover, a multi-class classification proposal was presented in [16], in which it distinguishes between *non-Islamophobic* content, *weak Islamophobia*, and *strong Islamophobia*.

Nationality and Racism: Regarding nationality, in [2], classification algorithms for the identification of xenophobic and racist discourse were implemented, which is directed at migrants and refugees in tweets in Spanish. This work implemented algorithms such as NB, LR, and SVM. Besides, in [4] was conducted detection of hate speech against immigrants in Spain. Regarding [3] from SemEval-2019, focused on the detection of hate speech directed at migrants in Twitter messages in Spanish and English. Finally, in [17], focused on antisemitism detection, considering data extracted from forums English-language web using SVM.

In general, in the state-of-the-art, Twitter (currently *X*) has been identified as the primary data source for hate speech analysis, while the application of traditional machine learning algorithms is a benchmark for classification. Research has focused on gender, sexual orientation, and religion, and has also associated racial hatred with nationality. However, although ethnophobia is closely related to racism and xenophobia (and the two are often confused), it is essential to analyze it independently, especially in the Mexican context, where deep inequalities and discrimination against indigenous communities persist. This has led to contempt expressed through hate speech, which in turn reinforces prejudices and discriminatory practices, creating a cycle of exclusion and hostility.

3 Proposed Methodology

In order to identify ethnic hate speech, we proposed the following methodology, which is shown in general in Fig. 2 and will be explained later.

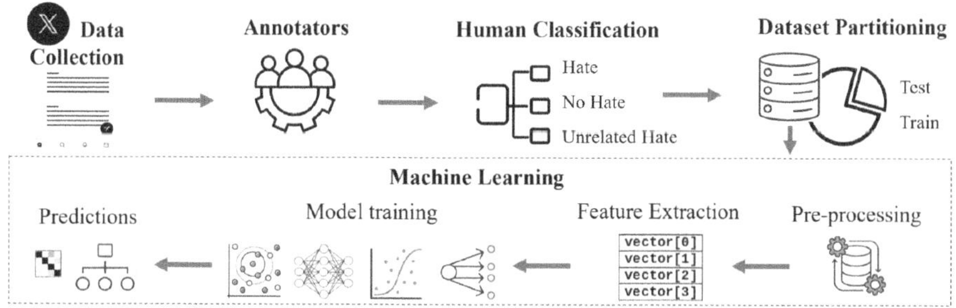

Fig. 2. Proposed methodology.

Data Collection: A manual search was conducted on the social network X, looking for posts that included the common denomination of 68 indigenous communities of Mexico, as well as their ethnonyms and the terms *"indigena"* and *"Indio/a"*. As a result of this process, 17,000 posts were obtained (for the pilot test, 15% was considered), then, a cleanup was applied that included replacing the sender and recipient usernames with a generic label.

Annotators: Eight experts (including four who identify as Indigenous) in social anthropology, indigenous law, and computer science annotated the collected publications. Before beginning, they received training on the task and how to handle violent messages, and signed an informed consent form to participate.

Human Classification: Labeling guidelines were developed, and meetings were held to explain, provide examples, discuss, and reach consensus on the categories to be assigned. Labeling was then conducted on the Human Signal ®platform, where it was classified into three categories:

- Hate: Messages containing contempt, hostility, ridicule, or incitement to violence directed explicitly at Mexico's indigenous people.
- No Hate: Posts that address topics related to indigenous peoples in a neutral, informative, positive, or non-derogatory manner.
- Unrelated Hate: Posts that contain hate speech or harassment, but whose target is not indigenous identity.

Moreover, the annotators' agreement was calculated using the Kappa Fleiss, obtaining 0.897. The final class was assigned through a majority vote.

Dataset and Partitioning: In the dataset obtained, the majority class was *'No Hate'*, followed by *'Hate'*, and the minority class was *'Unrelated Hate'*. A random sample was obtained for the pilot test, where class balance was maintained, and it was divided into 70% for training and 30% for testing.

Machine Learning: was applied to classify speech into non-hate speech, hate speech, and unrelated hate speech, where classification algorithms learn to recognize patterns and features.

- *Preprocessing:* The text was normalized by converting all text to lowercase, stopwords were removed (except in the BERT vectorization), finally, the text was tokenized.
- *Feature Extraction:* In this stage, we convert the text into a numerical representation. We achieve this through the following techniques:
  - TF-IDF (Term Frequency-Inverse Document Frequency): Assigns a score to each word that reflects its importance in a document relative to a larger corpus of documents.
  - BERT: Contextual embedding. This method of feature extraction understands the context of a word in a bidirectional manner, analyzing the preceding and following words.
  - ASCII: Consists of calculating the probability of each character appearing [15]. The frequency of each character is counted and then divided by the length of the text. The result is a vector of 255 values, where each position represents the probability of a specific character.

- *Model Training:* We use traditional machine learning algorithms to train the model with the training set. In this stage, we adjust the internal parameters to learn from the features obtained in the previous stage and associate them with the corresponding label: *No Hate, Hate, and Unrelated Hate*, represented as 0, 1 and 2 respectively.
  - SVM: is based on drawing a line that not only divides the classes, but also does so with the largest possible margin between the data points closest to it. These nearby points are called support vectors and are crucial because they define the position of the hyperplane.
  - NB: Applies Bayes' theorem, using probability calculus to determine the class to which a text belongs, based on the input features.
  - LR: Models the relationship between a set of input variables and an output into three categories. Mathematically, it results from the linear combination of the model's inputs and parameters. The result is a value between 0 and 2, which reflects the probability that the input belongs to each of the classes.
  - MLP: This is a learning model composed of fully connected layers: an input layer, one or more hidden layers, and an output layer. Its structure allows it to learn complex relationships in the data and is widely used in text classification problems.
- *Predictions:* The performance of the algorithms presented above was evaluated using the test set, where we measured how well the model generalized and classified texts it had not seen before.

4 Experimental Results

This section presents the results obtained from tests conducted for ethnic hate speech detection using classification algorithms and the BERT, TF-IDF, and ASCII feature extraction models. The tests were conducted on a total of 2,550 posts, which were divided into 70% and 30% for training and testing, respectively. Figure 3 shows the distribution of these subsets. The number of posts for each category is displayed. Meanwhile, Table 1 compares the performance of the classification algorithms based on the Macro-F1 (F1), Precision (P), and Recall (R) metrics.

Regarding feature extraction using BERT, different models were tested; however, in the cases of SVM, LR, and MLP *robertabase-bne* provided the best

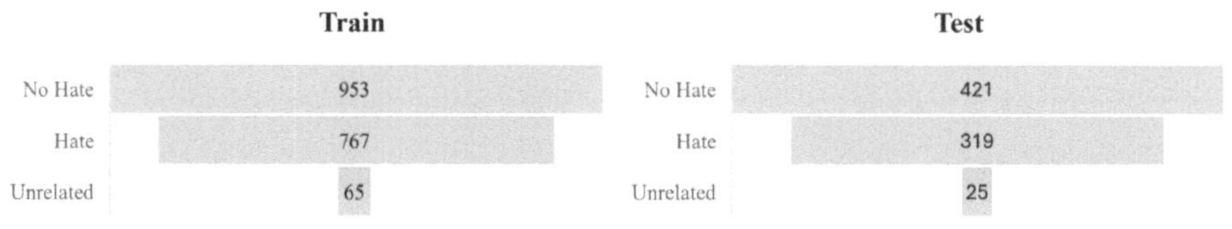

Fig. 3. Class distribution of in the dataset sample.

Table 1. Comparison with heuristics and benchmark methods.

	Model	F1	P	R		Model	F1	P	R
SVM	TF-IDF	0.3975	0.4268	0.3759	NB	TF-IDF	0.4243	0.43049	0.43088
	BERT	0.5705	0.5604	0.5823		BERT	0.5758	0.5986	0.6563
	ASCII	0.4963	0.4991	0.5019		ASCII	0.4974	0.4909	0.5051
LR	TF-IDF	0.4155	0.4287	0.4250	MLP	TF-IDF	0.2366	0.1834	0.3333
	BERT	0.5983	0.8962	0.5972		BERT	0.6074	0.7196	0.5982
	ASCII	0.4389	0.4971	0.4510		ASCII	0.4841	0.4967	0.4878

results. Meanwhile, for NB, the *bert-basespanish-wwmcased* model performed best. Meanwhile, the length of the TF-IDF vectors was 500 most frequent features. With respect to the MLP classifiers, we tested with Sigmoid, ReLU, and Softmax activation functions and 50 epoch. However, the better performance with ReLU. For LR, we tested with 10,000 iterations and a linear kernel.

5 Conclusions and Future Work

This work addresses a gap in hate speech research in Spanish in Mexico, focusing on discrimination against Indigenous communities, a topic not previously addressed in the state of the art. The pilot test successfully validated a specific dataset for the detection of ethnic hate speech in Mexico, which is critical for future research and the development of computational tools.

It was concluded that the combination of the Support Vector Machine (SVM) algorithm with BERT vectorization (an advanced language representation) offers the best performance for classifying ethnic hate speech. This establishes a benchmark and technical recommendation for researchers working in this field.

The implementation of BERT offered the best classification performance, as its ability to understand bidirectional context allows it to capture subtleties, irony, sarcasm, and ethnic and Mexican-specific cultural references. While TF-IDF is a solid foundation, although its performance was surpassed by BERT, its effectiveness in locating keywords makes it functional. Its limitations are manifested in its inability to understand ambiguous or contextual forms of hate speech. On the other hand, ASCII is the least effective option, as it fails to capture the semantic meaning of words. However, it is a suitable option since it achieves competitive performance with only character patterns.

Future directions for this work include testing on the full dataset and implementing more sophisticated classification algorithms.

References

1. Alcántara-Plá, M.: Understanding emotions in hate speech: a methodology for discourse analysis. Discourse Soc. **35**(4), 417–433 (2024). https://doi.org/10.1177/09579265231222013
2. Arcila-Calderón, C., Amores, J.J., Sánchez-Holgado, P., Vrysis, L., Vryzas, N., Alonso, M.O.: How to detect online hate towards migrants and refugees? Developing and evaluating a classifier of racist and xenophobic hate speech using shallow and deep learning. Sustainability 14, 13094 (2022). https://www.mdpi.com/2071-1050/14/20/13094
3. Basile, V., et al.: Semeval-2019 task 5: multilingual detection of hate speech against immigrants and women in twitter. In: Proceedings of the 13th International Workshop on Semantic Evaluation, pp. 54–63 (2019)
4. Calderón, C.A., de la Vega, G., Herrero, D.B.: Topic modeling and characterization of hate speech against immigrants on Twitter around the emergence of a far-right party in Spain. Soc. Sci. **9**, 188 (2020)
5. Campos, M., et al.: Mensajes de odio y discriminación en las redes sociales (2015)
6. Davidson, T., Warmsley, D., Macy, M., Weber, I.: Automated hate speech detection and the problem of offensive language. arXiv preprint arXiv:1703.04009, 512–515 (2017). https://arxiv.org/abs/1703.04009
7. Fersini, E., Nozza, D., Rosso, P.: Overview of the EVALITA 2018 hate speech detection task. In: EVALITA 2018 – Proceedings of the Fifth Evaluation Campaign of Natural Language Processing and Speech Tools for Italian, OpenEdition Books (2018). https://books.openedition.org/aaccademia/4497
8. Infobae. Estudiante quemado en una telesecundaria de Querétaro sufría discriminación por ser otomí - Infobae (2022). https://www.infobae.com/america/mexico/2022/06/23/estudiante-otomi-quemado-en-una-telesecundaria-de-queretaro-sufria-discriminacion-y-bullying/. Accessed 11 Dec 2024
9. González Gómez, J.: La etnofobia en México y sus implicaciones en la educación superior. Uniiversidad D la Habana, vol. 300 (2024). ISSN: 2708-5511
10. Gonzalez-Henao, R., Marrugo-Tobon, D., Martinez-Santos, J., Puertas, E.: Verbanexai lab at homo-mex 2024: multiclass and multilabel detection of lgbtq+ phobic content using transformers. In: Proceedings of the Iberian Languages Evaluation Forum (IberLEF 2024), co-located with the 40th Conference of the Spanish Society for Natural Language Processing (SEPLN 2024), CEUR-WS. org (2024)
11. Matamoros-Fernández, A., Farkas, J.: Racism, hate speech, and social media: a systematic review and critique 22(2), 205–224. https://doi.org/10.1177/1527476420982230.
12. McGiff, J., Nikolov, N.S.: Bridging the gap in online hate speech detection: a comparative analysis of Bert and traditional models for homophobic content identification on x/twitter. arXiv Prepr. arXiv2405.09221 (2024). https://arxiv.org/abs/2405.09221
13. Ramponi, A., Testa, B., Tonelli, S., Jezek, E.: Addressing religious hate online: from taxonomy creation to automated detection. **8**, 1128 (2022). https://doi.org/10.7717/peerj-cs
14. Rodríguez-Sánchez, F., et al.: Overview of exist 2021: sexism identification in social networks. Proces. del Leng. Nat. **67**, 195–207 (2021)

15. Rojas-Simón, J., Ledeneva, Y., García-Hernández, R.A.: Classification of human and machine-generated texts using lexical features and supervised/unsupervised machine learning algorithms. In: Mezura-Montes, E., Acosta-Mesa, H.G., Carrasco-Ochoa, J.A., Martínez-Trinidad, J.F., Olvera-López, J.A. (eds.) MCPR 2024. LNCS, vol. 14755, pp. 331–341. Springer, Cham (2024). https://doi.org/10.1007/978-3-031-62836-8_31
16. Vidgen, B., Yasseri, T.: Detecting weak and strong Islamophobic hate speech on social media. J. Inf. Technol. Polit. **17**, 66–78 (2020). https://www.tandfonline.com/doi/abs/10.1080/19331681.2019.1702607
17. Warner, W., Hirschberg, J.: Detecting hate speech on the World Wide Web. In: Proceedings of the Second Workshop on Language in Social Media, pp. 19–26 (2012). https://aclanthology.org/W12-2103/

Quantitative Comparison Between Heuristic and Automatic Design in Variational Quantum Circuits for the MaxCut Problem

Emmanuel Isaac Juárez Caballero(✉), Horacio Tapia-McClung, and Efrén Mezura Montes

Instituto de Investigaciones en Inteligencia Artificial, Universidad Veracruzana, Campus Sur, Calle Paseo Lote II, Sección Segunda N 112, Nuevo Xalapa, Xalapa, Ver. 91097, Mexico
{emmjuarez,htapia,emezura}@uv.mx

Abstract. Selecting appropriate ansatz topologies for variational quantum algorithms is critical for NISQ-era success. We present a quantitative comparison between two design paradigms: the heuristic Quantum Approximate Optimization Algorithm (QAOA) and an automated Quantum Neural Architecture Search (QNAS) approach for the max-cut problem. Our analysis is based on three indicators: approximation ratio, complexity, and optimization time. The results show that QAOA achieves a 25% higher average approximation ratio at the cost of a complexity 24 times higher than the one attained by QNAS. We note that this trade-off is dependent on the graph topology used for the max-cut problem. While QAOA achieves superior approximation ratios under ideal conditions, QNAS's 24 × complexity reduction suggests potential advantages in resource-constrained deployments—a hypothesis requiring validation under realistic noise models.

Keywords: Quantum-Architecture-Search · Quantum-Computing

1 Introduction

Variational Quantum Circuits/Algorithms (VQCs/VQAs) are heuristic algorithms designed to work within the constraints of the Noisy Intermediate-Scale Quantum (NISQ-era), where high error rates and limited qubit availability are common. Because VQAs alternate between a quantum circuit and classical optimizers, they are suitable to execute complex algorithms [1,2] on the current NISQ computers.

The success of VQAs relies on the proposal of an anzats which must be expressive enough to find the solution to a selected problem. Important metrics for VQAs and VQCs in real-world applications relate to a quantum algorithm's basic building blocks, i.e., gate count and circuit depth, which are primary limitations of quantum computers [8].

L. Martínez-Villaseñor et al. (Eds.): MICAI 2025, LNAI 16265, pp. 177–186, 2026.
https://doi.org/10.1007/978-3-032-17933-3_19

In particular, we will work on optimization algorithms to solve the max-cut problem. On one hand, we have heuristic-based methods such as the Quantum Approximate Optimization Algorithm (QAOA), which has a theoretical solution but lacks flexibility on real quantum computers due to challenges with hardware having limited connectivity [3]. On the other hand, we have automated methods such as Quantum Neural Architecture Search (QNAS), which reframe the problem of finding a suitable VQA for a tailor-specific task. [4] In particular, QNAS has been successfully applied to discover efficient VQC structures for various tasks. For instance, [4] pioneered the application of NAS techniques to VQAs, demonstrating its potential for finding high-performing circuits. Other methods have been developed to explicitly treat the search as a multi-objective optimization (MOO) problem, balancing accuracy against hardware-specific costs, as shown by [9].

Due to the difference in design methodology, it is necessary to clarify the conditions and resource costs under which automated methods can surpass heuristic methods such as QAOA. We conduct a quantitative comparison between these two approaches for the max-cut problem using three metrics: Approximation ratio (r_A) to assess solution quality, Hardware complexity(C) to measure quantum resource requirements, and Optimization time(t_{opt}) to evaluate classical computational efficiency across different graph topologies.

1.1 Problem Statement

Before describing our experimental methodology, we formalize the max-cut problem. Given an undirected graph $G(V, E)$ with a set of vertices V and edges E, the problem seeks to partition V into two disjoint subsets, maximizing the number of edges connecting vertices in opposite sets. This combinatorial optimization problem can be mapped to finding the ground state of an Ising Hamiltonian [5]:

$$H_C = \sum_{(i,j)\in E} \frac{1}{2}(I - Z_i Z_j), \tag{1}$$

where the sum is over all edges (i, j) in the graph. Here, Z_i is the Pauli-Z operator acting on the qubit corresponding to vertex i. The term $Z_i Z_j$ has an eigenvalue of $+1$ if qubits i and j are in the same state (same partition) and -1 if they are in different states (different partitions). Maximizing the cut corresponds to minimizing the energy of H_C, where its ground state encodes the optimal partition.

2 Theoretical Background

Variational Quantum Algorithms (VQAs) are commonly used methods in QC that utilize variational parameters to solve a problem [2]. Throughout this work, we use the notation $\langle H \rangle = \langle \psi | H | \psi \rangle$ to denote the expectation value of an operator H in a quantum state $|\psi\rangle$, Typical functioning steps consist of:

1. A quantum parameterized state, or ansatz, $|\psi(\boldsymbol{\theta})\rangle$ is prepared, and the expected value of the Hamiltonian is measured:

$$E(\boldsymbol{\theta}) = \langle\psi(\boldsymbol{\theta})|H_C|\psi(\boldsymbol{\theta})\rangle \tag{2}$$

2. Then the value is sent to a classical CPU, which classically optimizes the trainable parameters $\boldsymbol{\theta}$. At this stage, one commonly encounters barren plateaus, where issues such as vanishing gradients often arise [7].

After the training process is complete, we consider this the solution to the problem. Therefore, VQA is now completely trained and ready to be used on new data.

2.1 Quantum Approximate Optimization Algorithm (QAOA) Approach

QAOA is a quantum variational algorithm that was handcrafted to provide solutions to combinatorial optimization problems [3]. This method of solution consists of two elementary components of an anzatz, a cost Hamiltonian $U(\gamma_k)_C = e^{-i\gamma_k H_c}$ and a mixer operator $U_M(\beta_k) = e^{-i\beta_k H_M}$. The cost part of the Hamiltonian ensures that the evaluation of the max-cut is being done; the mixer part, instead, ensures that the state being evaluated undergoes changes, and the algorithm does not fall into a local minima. The proposed solution takes the form:

$$|\psi(\boldsymbol{\gamma}, \boldsymbol{\beta})\rangle = U_M(\beta_p)U_C(\gamma_p)\cdots U_M(\beta_1)U_C(\gamma_1)|+\rangle^{\otimes n}, \tag{3}$$

where $\boldsymbol{\gamma} = (\gamma_1, \ldots, \gamma_p)$ and $\boldsymbol{\beta} = (\beta_1, \ldots, \beta_p)$ are variational parameters (rotation angles), and $|+\rangle = \frac{1}{\sqrt{2}}(|0\rangle + |1\rangle)$ is the uniform superposition state. The notation $|+\rangle^{\otimes n}$ represents the tensor product of n qubits, each in the $|+\rangle$ state.

The operators are applied sequentially from right to left, beginning with state preparation, followed by p alternating layers of cost and mixer unitaries. Each $U_C(\gamma_k)$ encodes the problem Hamiltonian (Eq. 1), while $U_M(\beta_k) = \prod_{i=1}^{n_q} e^{-i\beta_k X_i}$ implements the mixing part, where X_i is the Pauli-X operator on qubit i.

From Eq. 3, it is possible to note that the function depends on a parameter p, which is usually referred to as the number of layers of the anzatz. However, it can be seen that all the layers have a cost part and a mixer part; therefore, the number of layers would be $2p$. A more visual approach to the structure of each layer involved in QAOA can be seen in Fig. 1.

2.2 Quantum Neural Architecture Search (QNAS)

To solve the max-cut problem, we employ a MOO approach that explores possible solutions that optimize two objectives: solution quality and complexity. In terms of the max-cut problem, we seek a set of circuits that achieves a high approximation ratio while maintaining low complexity.

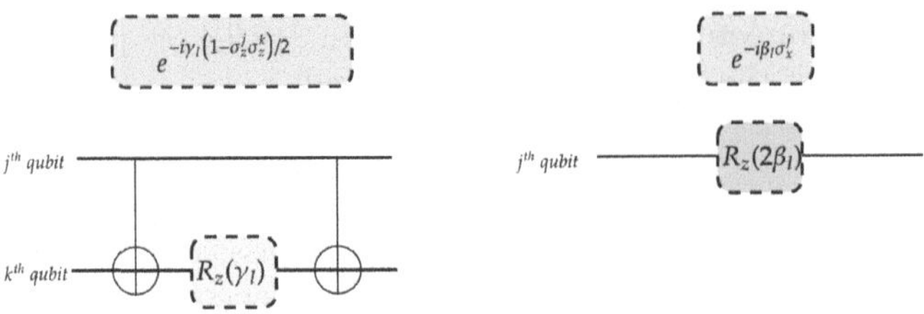

Fig. 1. The structure of the cost (U_C) and mixer (U_M) layers in a QAOA ansatz, generalizable to n qubits.

2.3 Quantum Neural Architecture Search (QNAS) Implementation

As an alternative to the QAOA algorithm, we employ a QNAS approach to design circuit ansätze automatically. We formulate this as an MOO problem that simultaneously minimizes two competing objectives:

1. **Solution Quality**: Minimize the expected value of the cost Hamiltonian $\langle H_C \rangle$ (Eq. 1) to maximize the cut size.
2. **Hardware Complexity**: Minimize the circuit complexity C (defined in Sect. 2.4) to reduce gate count and circuit depth.

The trade-off in NISQ devices justifies this multi-objective formulation: while deeper, more complex circuits can offer greater expressivity and can achieve better approximation ratios, they also accumulate more gate errors and require longer coherence times [8]. These objectives are in conflict since solution quality typically requires additional parameterized layers, which directly increases complexity. Rather than imposing arbitrary scalar weights (e.g., $\alpha\langle H_C \rangle + (1-\alpha)C$) that would bias the search toward a single compromise solution, we employ Pareto optimization via NSGA-II [10]. This approach helps us to discover a diverse set of non-dominated solutions along the Pareto front, enabling us to select circuits that match specific quantum hardware constraints and noise tolerance.

For deployment, we select the solution at the "knee" of the Pareto front—the point offering the best balance between the two objectives, identified using the method described in [11].

2.4 Complexity on QAOA and QNAS

To measure complexity, we adopt a weighted gate count metric that reflects the disparate error rates and execution times of single- and two-qubit operations in NISQ hardware [6]:

$$C = w_a G_{1q} + w_b G_{2q}, \tag{4}$$

where G_{1q} denotes the total count of single-qubit gates $\{R_x(\theta), R_y(\theta), R_z(\theta), H\}$, and G_{2q} counts two-qubit gates (CNOT). The weights w_a and w_b reflect relative implementation costs; we set $w_a = 1$ and $w_b = 10$ based on empirical observations that two-qubit gate error rates are approximately one order of magnitude higher than single-qubit gates on current superconducting platforms [6]. An important remark is that although we simulate in ideal conditions, we adopt the weighted metric as a proxy for deployment costs in NISQ hardware, following conventions in the VQA literature [8]. Now we can analyze the complexity for QAOA. We know that initially, the algorithm creates an equiprobable state in the computational basis using the Hadamard gate $H^{\otimes n}$. Given the description provided in Fig. 1, we can note that our expression for complexity in QAOA would be:

$$G^{QAOA} = n_q + p \cdot (n_q + 3n_e). \tag{5}$$

[1]

The definition of equation (5) starts by considering that the circuit begins with n_q Hadamard gates for state initialization. Each of the p layers (where p is the QAOA depth parameter from Eq. 3) consists of a cost layer and a mixer layer. The cost layer applies R_Z rotations and CNOT pairs to each edge, requiring $2n_e$ CNOTs and n_e single-qubit gates. The mixer layer applies R_X rotations to all qubits (n_q gates). Thus, each layer contributes $3n_e + n_q$ operations, yielding the total expression. For our experiments, we set $p = 5$ based on convergence analysis (see Table 1).

Where n_q denotes the number of qubits (equal to the number of vertices) and n_e denotes the number of edges in graph G.

In the case of QNAS, we do not have an analytical expression for the complexity. Therefore, we can express it in terms of the structure of our potential solution space.

$$G^{QNAS} = n_q + \sum_{l \in L} |G_{1q}^{(l)}| + \sum_{l \in L} |G_{2q}^{(l)}|, \tag{6}$$

where index l refers to the $l - th$ layer of the search space.

3 Methodology

To provide a comparison between both approaches, QNAS and QAOA, we designed a set of experiments that can be read in the summarized Table 1. Also, some key elements are described, such as the structure of the search space and the encoding of the problem.

QNAS Encoding Scheme. Each candidate circuit is encoded as a variable-length chromosome (Fig. 2a):

$$\text{Individual} = [l_1, l_2, \ldots, l_k]$$

[1] Derived from Fig. 1: n_q initialization gates + p layers × (n_q mixer R_X + n_e cost R_Z + $2n_e$ cost CNOTs).

where each gene $l_i \in \{0, 1, \ldots, |S| - 1\}$ indexes. The search space S is composed of atomic layers that include single-qubit rotation gates $\{R_x, R_y, R_z, H\}$ and two-qubit entangling gates $\{CNOT\}$, which are applied across all feasible qubit combinations. This representation facilitates the evolution of circuit topology and depth within the NSGA-II framework.

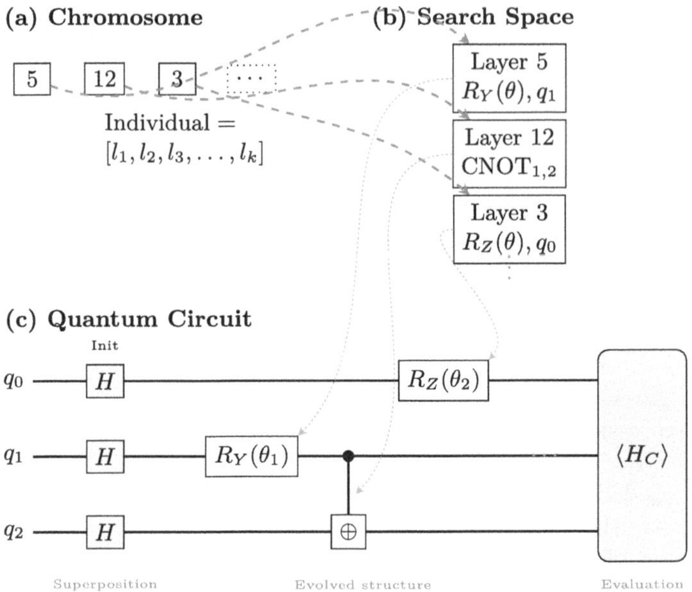

Fig. 2. QNAS encoding and circuit synthesis. (a) Chromosome representation with variable length k. (b) Search space indexed by genes. (c) Synthesized a circuit from a chromosome [5, 12, 3, ...]. Dotted lines trace gene-to-gate mappings

Experimental design outlined in Table 1 comprises graph sizes of $n \in \{4, 6, 8, 10\}$ to ensure a balance between computational feasibility and accurate solution verification. The QAOA depth is set to $p = 5$, based on preliminary experiments indicating convergence for $p \geq 4$. The NSGA-II settings include a population of 50 individuals and 50 generations for effective MOO, with a mutation probability of $m_p = 0.7$ to encourage exploration and a crossover probability of $c_p = 0.3$ to preserve structural integrity.

3.1 Graph Topologies

As part of our methodology, we selected seven graph topologies to evaluate both approaches across various graph structures.

Our proposed graphs can be summarized as:

- **Random network graphs**: We used the Erdös-Rényi model as a baseline to tackle problems without apparent structure.

Table 1. Summary of the experimental design and parameters.[a]

Parameter	Specification
Algorithms	QAOA, QNAS
Problem	max-cut
Graph Topologies	Cycle, Grid (2D), Complete, Star, Erdös-Rényi,Barabási-Albert, Watts-Strogatz
Graph Sizes (n)	{4, 6, 8, 10} vertices
Simulation	Ideal statevector simulator (noiseless)
Replicates	50 runs per instance configuration
QAOA, QNAS setting.	
QAOA	Depth $p = 5$, L-BFGS-B optimizer
QNAS	NSGA-II (50 individuals, 50 generations, $mp = 0.7$, $cp = 0.3$)
	Functions to optimize: $f = (\langle H_C \rangle, C)$
Performance Metrics	
Solution Quality	Approximation Ratio (r_A)
Quantum Cost	Hardware Complexity ($C = G_{1q} + 10 \cdot G_{2q}$)
Classical Cost	Optimization Time (t_{opt})

[a] Experiments executed on LANCAD infrastructure (Intel Xeon E5-2670v2, 64GB RAM) using
PennyLane v0.42. Total clock time: ~ 28 h for 50 replicates across all configurations (serial execution).

- **Complex networks**: In this case, we used Barabási-Albert and Watts-Strogatz models. The first one is known for generating networks that are scale-free. All of them are common in real-world network analysis.
- **Regular graph distributions**: We use a cycle graph, which models only local connectivity; a grid, which simulates problems with strong locality; a Complete graph, which represents the case where the graph has maximum interaction density; and a star, which is a centralized graph.

3.2 Experiment Setup and Metrics

To compare both approaches and ensure a comparison, we established a benchmarking methodology as described briefly in Table 1. We propose the following metrics to validate our results.

- **Approximation ratio (r_A)**: this metric is defined as the ratio of the energy value obtained by the algorithm to the optimal value found using greedy search

$$r_A = \frac{C_{\text{quantum}}}{C_{\text{optimal}}} \tag{7}$$

where $C_{\text{quantum}} = \sum_{(i,j)\in E} \frac{1}{2}(1 - \langle Z_i Z_j \rangle)$ is the cut size obtained from the quantum circuit's measurement, and C_{optimal} is the maximum cut size computed via exact classical enumeration or greedy heuristics.

- **Complexity:** We used a complexity metric of the form $C = w_A N_{1q} + w_b N_{2q}$. For simplicity of the experiment, we proposed $w_A = 1$ and $w_B = 10$ since two-qubit gates are typically different in experimental error rates in a magnitude order [6], which implies that we penalize two-qubit gates more than one-qubit gates.

4 Results

Tables 2 and 3 summarize experimental results across all configurations. Statistical significance of performance differences was assessed using the Statistical significance assessed via Mann-Whitney U test with Bonferroni correction ($\alpha = 0.05/28 = 0.0018$). Both tables show that there is a compromise between approximation ratio and resources. The main finding, as shown in Table 3, is that QAOA gives solutions of higher quality, with around a 25% improvement over the QNAS approach. However, this comes with a higher cost in complexity, which, on average, is 24 times greater than that of QNAS. As illustrated in Table 2, the difference in performance depends on the structure of the problem; in particular, the QAOA algorithm appears to perform well, with $r_A \approx 0.9999$, in graphs with regular structures, while having a decrease in the quality of solutions in groups that exhibit strong locality.

On the other hand, the advantage of the QAOA algorithm diminishes with more complex networks, in contrast to QNAS. This suggests that QNAS can adapt better to non-regular circuits.

Table 2. Detailed performance analysis by graph topology.

Structural Group	Topology	$\bar{r}_A$ (QAOA)	$\bar{r}_A$ (QNAS)	Perf. Gap
Regular & Predictable	`complete`	**0.9999**	0.9062	1.10x
	`star`	**0.9999**	0.7866	1.27x
	`cycle`	**0.9999**	0.6111	1.64x
Complex Networks	`watts_strogatz`	**0.9514**	0.7735	1.23x
	`erdos_renyi`	**0.9483**	0.7576	1.25x
	`barabasi_albert`	**0.9417**	0.8036	1.17x
Strong Locality	`grid_2d`	**0.8957**	0.8036	1.11x

A key consideration is that QAOA consistently demonstrates an advantage in the quality of solutions and its approximation ratio. However, these solutions, while being adequate for ideal environments—i.e., noiseless simulations of execution on a quantum computer—raise the question of whether this advantage persists in noisy environments. Figure 3 illustrates the performance scaling of both algorithms across graph sizes. QAOA maintains approximation ratios exceeding 0.95 for most topologies, with minimal degradation as problem size increases. In

Table 3. Summary of performance and cost metrics. Values represent mean ± standard deviation across all replications and topologies. Statistical significance assessed via Mann-Whitney U test ($p < 0.001$ for all comparisons).

Metric	QAOA	QNAS	Ratio (QAOA/QNAS)
Approximation Ratio (r_A)	0.9606 ± 0.0569	0.7653 ± 0.0941	1.25x
Complexity (C)	1020.3 ± 719.4	42.0 ± 13.8	**24.3x**
Optimization Time (t_{opt}) [s]	84.49 ± 64.25	145.91 ± 147.04	0.58x

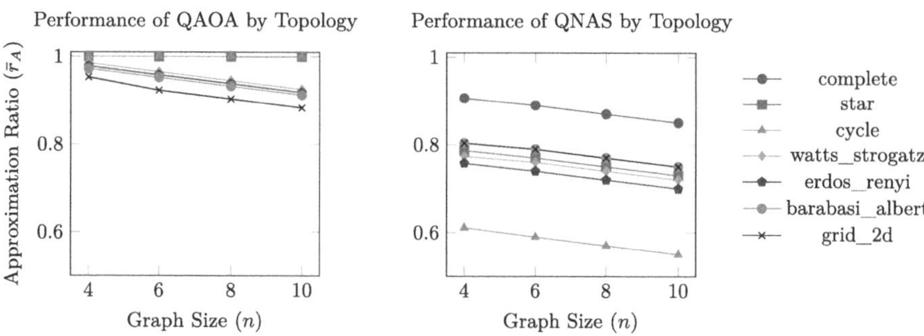

Fig. 3. Performance of QAOA (left) and QNAS (right) for each topology as a function of graph size. A unified vertical scale is used to facilitate direct comparison, visually highlighting the superior approximation ratio of QAOA.

contrast, QNAS exhibits greater topology-dependent variation, with complete graphs achieving $r_A \approx 0.90$ while cycle graphs reach only $r_A \approx 0.61$ for $n = 10$. The divergent vertical scales highlight QAOA's superior solution quality at the expense of substantially higher resource requirements, as shown in Table 3.

5 Conclusions

We compared QAOA and QNAS approaches for finding solutions to the max-cut problem. Our experimentation shows that the QAOA algorithm generates solutions that are significantly (up to 24 times) more complex than the QNAS approach. However, solutions found by QAOA had an improvement of 25% in quality. Aside from this, it was found that the approximation ratio also varies with the topology of the proposal graph that was used in the experiment. In particular, there was a 10% decrease in the quality of solutions for both regular and strong locality topologies in QAOA.

Future Work

- **Noisy environments**: Extend our analysis to realistic noise models including gate errors, decoherence, and measurement errors [1,6]. We hypothesize that QNAS's lower complexity may translate to superior performance under noise, as error accumulation scales with circuit depth [7].

- **Extended scalability**: Analyze graphs with $n \geq 10$ vertices to identify scalability limits for both classical optimization (NSGA-II) and quantum circuit simulation. Research about whether QNAS's adaptability to irregular topologies, as shown in Table 2, persists at larger scales.

Acknowledgments. We thank SECITHI for the grant BECAS NACIONALES 2023 CVU:1142842 and LANCAD for the computational resources through project 76-2025.

References

1. Preskill, J.: Quantum computing in the NISQ era and beyond. Quantum **2**, 79 (2018)
2. Cerezo, M., Arrasmith, A., Babbush, R., et al.: Variational quantum algorithms. Nat. Rev. Phys. **3**(9), 625–644 (2021)
3. Farhi, E., Goldstone, J., Gutmann, S.: A quantum approximate optimization algorithm. arXiv preprint arXiv:1411.4028 (2014)
4. Du, Y., Hsieh, T., Liu, T., Tao, D.: Quantum neural architecture search for variational quantum algorithms. NPJ Quant. Inf. **8**(1), 62 (2022)
5. Goemans, M.X., Williamson, D.P.: Improved approximation algorithms for maximum cut and satisfiability problems using semidefinite programming. J. ACM **42**(6), 1115–1145 (1995)
6. Kandala, A., Mezzacapo, A., Temme, K., et al.: Hardware-efficient variational quantum eigensolver for small molecules and quantum magnets. Nature **549**(7671), 242–246 (2017)
7. McClean, J.R., Boixo, S., Smelyanskiy, V.N., Babbush, R., Neven, H.: Barren plateaus in quantum neural network training landscapes. Nat. Commun. **9**(1), 4812 (2018)
8. Bharti, K., Cervera-Lierta, A., Kyaw, T.H., et al.: Noisy intermediate-scale quantum algorithms. Rev. Mod. Phys. **94**(1), 015004 (2022)
9. Chivilikhin, D., Samarin, A., Alekseev, A., et al.: MOQAS: multi-objective quantum architecture search for variational quantum algorithms. arXiv preprint arXiv:2010.16334 (2020)
10. Deb, K., Pratap, A., Agarwal, S., Meyarivan, T.: A fast and elitist multiobjective genetic algorithm: NSGA-II. IEEE Trans. Evol. Comput. **6**(2), 182–197 (2002)
11. Branke, J., Deb, K., Dierolf, H., Osswald, M.: Finding knees in multi-objective optimization. Parallel Prob. Solving Nat. 722–731 (2004)
12. contributors, Q.: Qiskit Aer: high performance simulators for quantum circuits. Zenodo (2023). https://doi.org/10.5281/zenodo.2562110

Physical Activity and Diet: A Computational Predictive Model for Characterizing Nutritional Status in Children

Anaid Guadalupe Martín-Díaz[1], Isidro Vargas-Moreno[2], Virginia Gabriela Aguilera-Cervantes[2](✉), Héctor Gabriel Acosta-Mesa[3], and Rafael Fernández-Demeneghi[2]

[1] Doctorado en Ciencia del Comportamiento con orientación en Alimentación y Nutrición, Instituto de Investigaciones en Comportamiento Alimentario y Nutrición, Universidad de Guadalajara, Jalisco, México
anaid.martin9462@alumnos.udg.mx

[2] Instituto de Investigaciones en Comportamiento Alimentario y Nutrición, Universidad de Guadalajara, Jalisco, México
virginia.aguilera@cusur.udg.mx

[3] Instituto de Investigaciones en Inteligencia Artificial, Universidad Veracruzana, Xalapa, México
heacosta@uv.mx

1 Introduction

Obesity is currently one of the most pressing health challenges and is considered a multifactorial, chronic, and complex disease characterized by excessive fat accumulation detrimental to health. In 2022, 43% of adults over 18 years old were overweight, and 16% were obese [1], conditions associated with the early development of chronic non-communicable diseases, including type 2 diabetes, cardiovascular diseases, and certain types of cancer [2]. In children, 35 million under 5 years old were overweight in 2024 [1], and in Mexico, one in three children aged 6 to 11 years is affected by obesity [3]. The combined prevalence of overweight and obesity among children increased from 33.2% in 2016 to 38.2% in 2020 [4]. This trend is linked to low-nutritional-value diets and high consumption of ultra-processed foods, particularly in urban areas [2,5–7]. According to ENSANUT, children's dietary patterns include 90% consuming sugar-sweetened beverages, over 54% consuming cereals and sweet or savory snacks, and only 32.4% consuming vegetables, representing a 60% decrease in vegetable intake over six years [3, 4, 7–9].

In Mexico, food environments favor the consumption of ultra-processed foods [10], which are considered by UNICEF and WHO to be a public health problem that requires regulation of their advertising and availability [11]. In response, guidelines have been developed to regulate children's advertising and monitor the food environment, supporting nutritional quality policies and food and beverage regulations [9, 12–16].

M.-D. A. Guadalupe, V.-M. Isidro, V.G. Aguilera-Cervantes - These authors have contributed equally to this work and share first authorship

L. Martínez-Villaseñor et al. (Eds.): MICAI 2025, LNAI 16265, pp. 187–196, 2026.
https://doi.org/10.1007/978-3-032-17933-3_20

Given this panorama of poor dietary practices, it is essential to have tools that accurately identify the critical points where the battle against childhood obesity is being lost. It is crucial to develop robust models capable of revealing relationships that conventional statistical methods fail to detect, as they rely on measures of central tendency or report only individual percentages of eating habits and physical activity, reflecting only the isolated impact of the parameters evaluated. In this context, supervised computational learning is a key strategy, as supervised algorithms can identify the most relevant variables that influence various behavioral and health domains [17]. Among these tools, decision trees stand out for their predictive and interpretive capabilities, facilitating classification of individuals into specific labels and revealing the interactions among variables that best explain the emergence of particular risk patterns [18, 19].

Therefore, the objective of this study is to determine the nutritional status of schoolchildren by integrating analyses of anthropometric variables, dietary habits, and physical activity levels. Using decision tree models, it is possible to identify combinations of risk factors that promote overweight and obesity, providing interpretable insights into their interactions. This approach will allow classification of each child's nutritional risk and more precisely targeted interventions. It will also provide a solid basis for designing individualized prevention and management strategies grounded in quantitative, replicable evidence.

2 Materials and Methods

2.1 Participants and Sampling

Descriptive and analytical cross-sectional study. Measurements were obtained from 230 participants aged 6 to 12 years from public elementary schools in the Municipality of Zapotlán el Grande between May and July 2024. The sampling was stratified and randomized. An ethics committee and a technical research committee approved the study. Participants provided assent, and parents or guardians provided written consent.

2.2 Nutritional Status

Nutritional status was assessed in the children using both anthropometric and dietary indicators. Anthropometric measurements included weight, height, Body Mass Index (BMI), and waist circumference (WC). Weight was measured in kilograms using the TANITA BF 689 pediatric scale, which also provides body fat percentage from age 5, with participants wearing light clothing. Height was recorded in centimeters using a SECA 206 mechanical wall stadiometer (0–220 cm, 1 mm divisions) and defined as the vertical distance from the floor to the topmost and most prominent part of the head. BMI was calculated as weight in kilograms divided by height in meters squared (BMI = Weight (kg) / Height (m)^2) and interpreted according to the Centers for Disease Control and Prevention (CDC) BMI-for-age percentiles: $<$ 5th percentile (underweight), 5th to $<$ 85th percentile (healthy weight), 85th to 95th percentile (overweight), and $>$ 95th percentile (obesity). Waist circumference was measured in millimeters with a Lufkin W606PM measuring tape at the midpoint between the last rib and the iliac crest. Waist-to-Height Ratio (WHtR) was calculated as waist circumference divided by height; values

≥ 0.5 indicated metabolic risk. Dietary intake was assessed using a 24-h food record covering main meals and snacks, including the time and place of consumption.

2.3 Healthy Lifestyle Habits Scale for Diet and Physical Activity

The Healthy Lifestyle Habits scale was measured using the Healthy Lifestyle Habits for Diet and Physical Activity Questionnaire (HLHDPAQ) for schoolchildren aged 8–12, validated in the Mexican population. The instrument contains 27 items, of which nine correspond to the Physical Activity and Inactivity dimension (1, 4, 7, 10, 13, 16, 19, 22, and 25) and 18 items belong to the Diet and Nutrition dimension (2, 3, 5, 6, 8, 9, 11, 12, 14, 15, 17, 18, 20, 21, 23, 24, 26, and 27). The questionnaire had five response options, ranging from "always" to "never," and were converted to numbers from 1 to 5. If the opinion was favorable to the attitude being evaluated, "always" was coded as five and "never" as 1; if it was unfavorable, "always" was coded as one and "never" as 5. All responses were summed so that higher scores indicated healthier behavior; therefore, the minimum total score was 27 and the maximum was 135. The instrument has acceptable reliability values $\alpha = 0.81$ [20].

2.4 Data Analysis

Machine learning analysis was performed using the J48 decision tree algorithm in Weka software (version 3.9.1), which builds a classification tree by recursively partitioning the dataset based on attribute values to maximize information gain, identifying the most relevant variables for predicting the target outcome. The model was validated using 10-fold cross-validation to ensure robustness and avoid overfitting. The choice of J48 was based on its interpretability, ability to handle both categorical and continuous variables, and effectiveness in identifying complex interactions in small to medium-sized datasets. Compared to other classifiers, decision trees provide transparent rules that can be directly applied in practical or clinical contexts, making them suitable for studies on behavioral and nutritional indicators in children. Furthermore, the model's structure enables explainable predictions, allowing researchers and practitioners to understand and communicate how specific variables influence the outcomes.

3 Results

3.1 Decision Trees

Regarding the model fit with all independent variables, we identified the most relevant characteristic as body mass index percentile, with values above 98.2 indicating severe obesity. Regarding obesity, we found it at values greater than 94 and less than or equal to 98.2, while overweight is classified at values greater than 84 and less than or equal to 94. Conversely, values less than or equal to 4 are identified as underweight. Finally, children with values greater than 4 and less than or equal to 84 are classified as healthy (Fig. 1a). This model fit had an accuracy of 95.21%. We observe that the most significant confusion is associated with the labels for obesity and severe obesity (Fig. 1b).

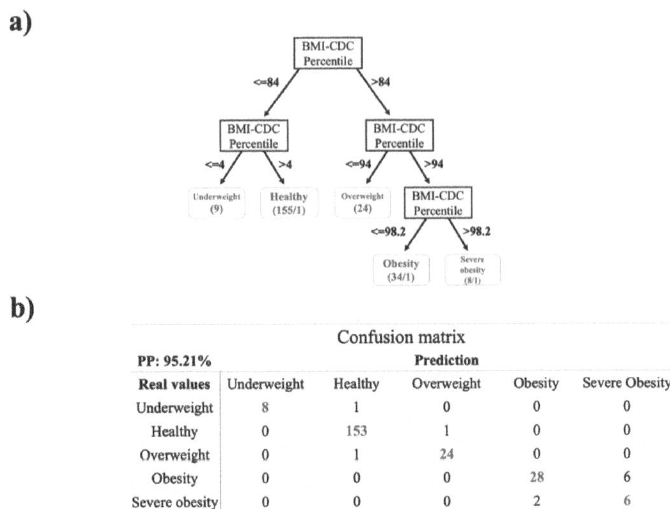

Confusion matrix

PP: 95.21%			Prediction		
Real values	Underweight	Healthy	Overweight	Obesity	Severe Obesity
Underweight	8	1	0	0	0
Healthy	0	153	1	0	0
Overweight	0	1	24	0	0
Obesity	0	0	0	28	6
Severe obesity	0	0	0	2	6

Fig. 1. Shows the decision tree for classifying children's health status and the model with all variables.

Once the CDC BMI percentile variable is removed, we find that the most crucial variable for classification is the waist-height ratio (WHtR), where values above 0.4923 combined with a BMI greater than 28.71 classify children as severely obese, while values greater than 22.81 and less than or equal to 28.71 identify children with obesity (Fig. 2a). When WHtR > 0.49 and BMI ≤ 22.81 are present, we must consider how often they buy lunch at school or on the street. When they "always" buy it this way, they are overweight. When they "almost always" buy it, we must combine it with another variable that measures the frequency with which the child plays in the park with other children. When they never do so, they are obese, and when they "almost always or always" do so, they are overweight. Regarding lunch purchases, they "almost never" buy them at school or on the street and are classified as healthy (Fig. 2a).

If their WHtR values are less than or equal to 0.49, we will consider their BMI and age. Children with BMI values less than or equal to 13.83 are considered underweight. Children with a BMI between 13.83 and 20.77 are considered healthy. Children with a BMI greater than 20.77 and an age of over 11 are considered healthy within this group (Fig. 2a).

This model achieved an accuracy of 80.43%, and we can observe that it tends to confuse one class with another, specifically when they are on the verge of transitioning from a healthy to a sick state (Fig. 2b).

On the other hand, when we remove the BMI-CDC percentile variables and the WHtR, the model's fit indicates that the most relevant variable is body fat percentage. Values above 36.2%, a BMI greater than 21.11, and a frequency of "never, sometimes, or almost always" lying down rather than engaging in physical activity classify children as having severe obesity. Meanwhile, children with a percentage greater than 28.2 and less than or equal to 36.2 combined with a BMI > 21.11 are identified as obese (Fig. 3a).

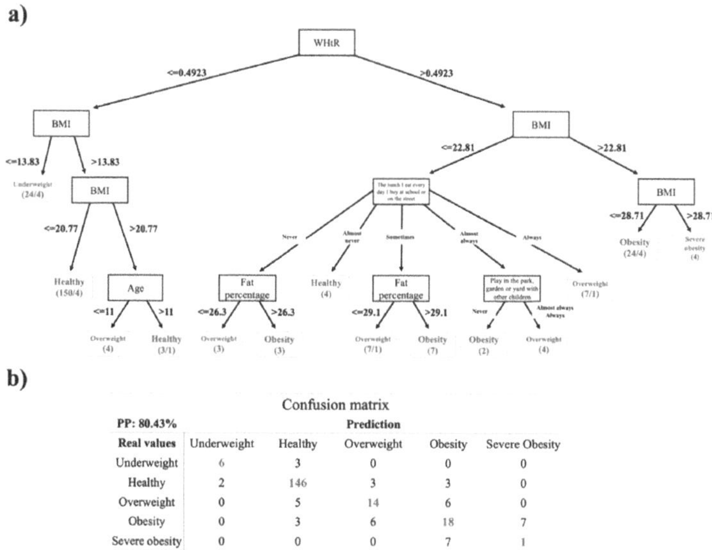

Confusion matrix

PP: 80.43%			Prediction		
Real values	Underweight	Healthy	Overweight	Obesity	Severe Obesity
Underweight	6	3	0	0	0
Healthy	2	146	3	3	0
Overweight	0	5	14	6	0
Obesity	0	3	6	18	7
Severe obesity	0	0	0	7	1

Fig. 2. Shows the decision tree for classifying children's health status, without the BMI-CDC percentile variable.

To classify a person as overweight, we find that boys must have a percentage greater than 18.34 and less than or equal to 28.2. In turn, they are divided by gender and associated with different variables. For boys, a weight of 21.6 kg or more is required: for girls, a weight of 34.4 kg or less (Fig. 3a). To identify healthy children, the model characterizes them when their BMI is greater than 13.83 and less than or equal to 28.2; finally, when the BMI is less than or equal to 13.83, they are considered underweight (Fig. 3a).

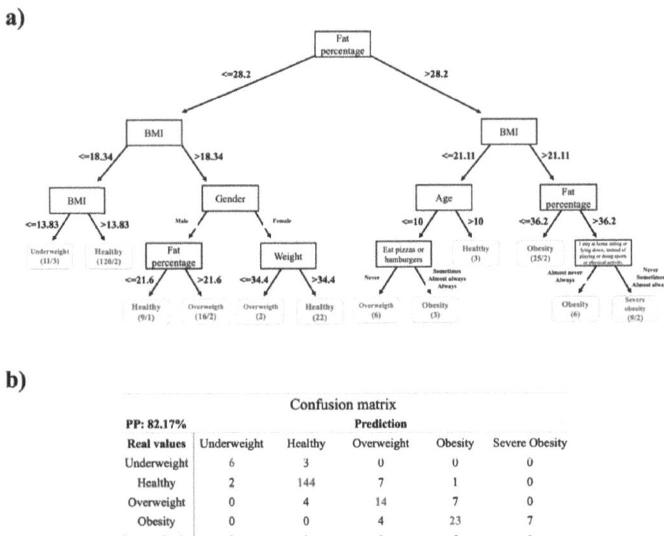

Confusion matrix

PP: 82.17%	Prediction				
Real values	Underweight	Healthy	Overweight	Obesity	Severe Obesity
Underweight	6	3	0	0	0
Healthy	2	144	7	1	0
Overweight	0	4	14	7	0
Obesity	0	0	4	23	7
Severe obesity	0	1	0	5	2

Fig. 3. Shows the decision tree for classifying children's health status, excluding the BMI-CDC percentile variable and the waist-to-height ratio.

4 Discussion

The research aimed to identify, using machine learning techniques, such as decision trees, the most relevant anthropometric parameters, dietary habits, and physical activity levels for predicting the nutritional status of schoolchildren. This approach revealed the key interactions that contribute to poor nutritional status, enabling accurate classification of schoolchildren by risk and highlighting relevant parameters to guide future intervention and prevention strategies.

Among the most used parameters for identifying elevated adiposity in children are the CDC BMI percentiles. Our results confirm their relevance, showing that BMI percentiles are the most important for classifying nutritional status. Values between 84 and 94 identify overweight, values greater than 94 indicate obesity, and values greater than 98.2 indicate severe obesity. This finding aligns with several studies that have sought to determine the optimal BMI percentile for predicting elevated adiposity, fat mass, and cardiometabolic risk in children and adolescents [21], with the most appropriate percentile being 95. This also reinforces recent studies reporting that elevated BMI is a reliable tool for identifying children and adolescents with elevated adiposity [22].

Some authors have noted that BMI is limited in detecting abdominal fat or central obesity [23, 24], so we incorporated additional indicators in a second model adjustment. Combining the waist-to-height ratio WHtR, BMI, fat percentage, age, and variables of eating habits and physical activity significantly described the nutritional status of children. The most relevant variable was WHrT, since values greater than 0.49 are associated with overweight and obesity, consistent with studies linking it to abdominal obesity and metabolic risk in the pediatric population [25–27]. The predictive model highlighted that nutritional and physical activity habits influence childhood overweight. Children who purchased their lunch at school or from street vendors were at higher risk, consistent with studies associating poor diets and ultra-processed foods with obesity [28–31]. This is reinforced by the high availability of ultra-processed foods in Mexican schools, which promote unhealthy habits [12, 32, 33]. Furthermore, children with a WHtR > 0.49 and low physical activity were more likely to be obese, supporting the relationship between inactivity and early obesity [29, 31].

In a third adjusted model, after eliminating BMI and WHtR, body fat percentage emerged as the leading indicator of body composition, with values above 18.34 indicating overweight and obesity, highlighting the need for additional indicators beyond BMI [23, 24]. Combining fat percentage, lifestyle habits, and physical activity, it was observed that children with $\geq 36.2\%$ fat who remained inactive primarily were more likely to be obese, consistent with studies linking inactivity to fat accumulation and childhood obesity [24, 27, 28, 30].

Based on the above, it was confirmed that decision trees are highly effective tools for identifying the most influential parameters in predicting children's nutritional status. Their ability to visually and accurately represent the interactions among anthropometric factors, eating habits, and physical activity levels provides a clear understanding of the patterns underlying childhood overweight and obesity. Previous studies have shown that BMI, combined with genetic parameters such as single-nucleotide polymorphisms (SNPs) and modulated by variables like age and gender, significantly improves the prediction of nutritional risk [18]. Research in adults has consistently employed decision tree models to explore physical and dietary habits, achieving accuracies above 92% [17]. In contrast, studies in young children have reliably utilized age, BMI, weight, and body length to predict nutritional status [19]. These findings consolidate the value of machine learning as an innovative and robust approach to analyzing dietary problems. In this context, decision trees identified key factors in childhood nutrition, providing a basis for designing targeted interventions and effective obesity-prevention strategies that improve children's health and well-being.

5 Conclusions and Future Work

These findings support the development of better indicators of children's nutrition by considering WHtR and body fat percentage. They also identify predictors of lifestyle habits associated with overweight, such as diet and physical activity, reinforcing the need to promote healthy school environments for child well-being.

Finally, decision trees are a valuable tool in this field, as they enable a structured, interpretable exploration of the complex interactions among anthropometric, behavioral, and environmental variables. Their future use can guide early identification of risk factors and the design of more precise, personalized interventions to prevent childhood overweight and obesity. Along these lines, future work could strengthen the machine learning approach by integrating various algorithms to compare their performance, ensuring that the models remain interpretable for experts in the field, and thereby fostering synergy with artificial intelligence to address serious childhood health problems more effectively.

Acknowledgments. The authors gratefully acknowledge the collaboration of the authorities of the Institute for Research in Eating Behavior and Nutrition at the Southern University Center of the University of Guadalajara, as well as the authorities of the participating school. Authors A.F. M.-D.; I.V.-M. and R.F.-D, thank SECIHTI for the doctoral and postdoctoral fellowships awarded.

Conflict of Interest The authors declare no conflict of interest.

References

1. World Health Organization: WHO.: Notas descriptivas. Obesidad y sobrepeso. (2025,7 mayo). https://www.who.int/es/news-room/fact-sheets/detail/obesity-and-overweight
2. Popkin, B.: El impacto de los alimentos ultraprocesados en la salud, 2030 Alimentación, agricultura y desarrollo rural en América Latina y el Caribe, Documento No. 34. Organización de las Naciones Unidas para la Alimentación y la Agricultura (FAO). Santiago de Chile (2020)
3. Fondo de las Naciones Unidas para la Infancia [UNICEF].: Estado Mundial de la Infancia 2019. Niños, alimentos y nutrición, crecer bien en un mundo en transformación [Resumen Ejecutivo] https://www.unicef.org/es/informes/estado-mundial-de-la-infancia-2019. Accessed 10 Jan 2019
4. Shamah-Levy, T., et al.: Encuesta Nacional de Salud y Nutrición 2020 sobre Covid-19. Resultados Nacionales. Instituto Nacional de Salud Pública de México (2021)
5. Barrientos-Gutiérrez, T., et al.: Expected population weight and diabetes impact of the 1-peso-per-litre tax to sugar sweetened beverages in Mexico. PLoS One **12**(5) (2017). https//doi.org/https://doi.org/10.1371/journal.pone.0191383
6. Pigeyre, M., et al.: How obesity relates to socio-economic status: identification of eating behavior mediators. Int J Obes. **40**(11), 1794–801 (2016). https:// doi.org/https://doi.org/10.1038/ijo.2016.109
7. Shamah-Levy, T., et al.: Encuesta Nacional de Salud y Nutrición de Medio Camino 2016, Resultados nacionales. Instituto Nacional de Salud Pública (2017). https://www.insp.mx/images/stories/2017/Avisos/docs/180315_encuesta_nacional_de_salud_y_nutricion_de_medio_Ca.pdf
8. Oviedo-Solís, C.I., Monterrubio-Flores, E.A., Cediel, G., Denova-Gutiérrez, E., Barquera, S.: Trend of ultraprocessed product intake is associated with the double burden of malnutrition in Mexican children and adolescents. Nutrients **14**(20), 1–13 (2022)
9. Islas Vega, I., Reynoso Vázquez, J., Hernández Ceruelos, M.C.A., Ruvalcaba Ledezma, J.C.: La alimentación en México y la influencia de la publicidad ante la debilidad en el diseño de políticas públicas. Journal of Negative & No Positive Results **5**(8), 853–862 (2020)
10. UNICEF.: Regulación de la publicidad de alimentos y bebidas no saludables dirigida a niños, niñas y adolescentes. Unicef México (2021). unicef.org/mexico/media/6581/file/Nota%20técnica%20publicidad%20dirigida%20a%20niñas,%2C
11. Instituto Nacional de Salud Pública & Fondo de las Naciones Unidas para la Infancia. (INSP, UNICEF).: Publicidad y promoción de alimentos y bebidas dirigidas a niñas, niños y adolescentes en los puntos de venta en México (2021). https://www.insp.mx/resources/images/stories/2022/docs/220104_Unicef_digital.pdf
12. Barquera, S., Hernández-Barrera, L., Rothenberg, S.J., Cifuentes, E.: The obesogenic environment around elementary schools, food and beverage marketing to children in two Mexican cities. BMC Public Health **18**(461), 1–9 (2018)
13. Munguía-Serrano, A., Tolentino-Mayo, L., Théodore, F.L., Vandevijvere, S.: Nutritional quality of hidden food and beverage advertising directed to children: extent and nature of product placement in Mexican television programs. Int. J. Environ. Res. Public Health **17**(9), 1–11 (2020)

14. Rincón-Gallardo Patiño, S., et al.: Nutritional quality of foods and non-alcoholic beverages advertised on Mexican television according to three nutrient profile models. BMC Public Health **16**, 1–11 (2016)
15. Ortiz-Pérez, H., Molina-Frechero, N., Martínez-Barbabosa, I., Córdova-Moreno, R.: Contenido nutricional de los alimentos promovidos por el Canal 5 de la televisión mexicana dirigidos a la población infantil. Revista Chilena de Nutrición **42**(3), 260–266 (2015)
16. Théodore, F., Juárez-Ramírez, C., Cahuana-Hurtado, L., Blanco, I., Tolentino-Mayo, L., Bonvecchio, A.: Barreras y oportunidades para la regulación de la publicidad de alimentos y bebidas dirigida a niños en México. Salud Publica de México **56**(2), 123–129 (2014)
17. Iparraguirre-Villanueva, O., Mirano-Portilla, L., Gamarra-Mendoza, M., Robles-Espiritu, W.: Predicting Obesity in Nutritional Patients Using Decision Tree Modeling (2023)
18. Rodríguez-Pardo, C., et al.: Decision tree learning to predict overweight/obesity based on body mass index and gene polymporphisms. Gene **699**, 88–93 (2019)
19. Gustriansyah, R., Suhandi, N., Puspasari, S., Sanmorino, A.: Machine learning method to predict the toddlersâ€™ nutritional status. Jurnal Infotel **16**(1), 32–43 (2024)
20. Guerrero, G., et al.: Diseño y validación de un cuestionario de hábitos de vida de alimentación y actividad física para escolares de 8–12 años. Revista Chilena De Salud Pública **18**(3), 249–256 (2014)
21. Harrington, D.M., Staiano, A.E., Broyles, S.T., Gupta, A.K., Katzmarzyk, P.T.: BMI percentiles for the identification of abdominal obesity and metabolic risk in children and adolescents: evidence in support of the CDC 95th percentile. Eur. J. Clin. Nutr. **67**(2), 218–222 (2013)
22. Freedman, D.S., Zemel, B.S., Dietz, W.H., Daymont, C.: Screening accuracy of BMI for adiposity among 8-to 19-year-olds. Pediatrics **154**(1), e2024065960 (2024)
23. Clasey, J.L., et al.: Body mass index percentiles versus body composition assessments: challenges for disease risk classifications in children. Front. Pediatr. **11**, 1112920 (2023). https://doi.org/10.3389/fped.2023.1112920
24. Vanderwall, C., Randall Clark, R., Eickhoff, J., et al.: BMI is a poor predictor of adiposity in young overweight and obese children. BMC Pediatr. **17**, 135 (2017). https://doi.org/10.1186/s12887-017-0891-z
25. Jaime, V.-L., Leticia, A.-C., Juan, H.-E., Salvador, F.-R.: Índice cintura-estatura como indicador de riesgo metabólico en niños. Revista Chilena de Pediatría **87**(3), 180–185 (2016)
26. Gotthelf, S., Rivas, P.: Índice cintura / talla y perfil metabólico en niños y adolescentes de la ciudad de SALTA. Revista Federación Argentina de Cardiología **48**(2), 78–83 (2019)
27. Zermeño-Ugalde, P., Gallegos-García, V., Castro Ramírez, R.A., Gaytán-Hernández, D.: Relación del índice cintura-talla (ICT) con cintura e Índice de Cintura Cadera como predictor para obesidad y riesgo metabólico en adolescentes de secundaria". Revista Salud Pública y Nutrición **19**(3), 19–27 (2020)
28. López-Sobaler, A.M., Aparicio, A., Salas-González, M.D., Loria-Kohen, V., Bermejo, L.M.: Obesidad en la población infantil en España y factores asociados. Nutrición Hospitalaria **38**(Spec No2), 27–30 (2021). https://doi.org/10.20960/nh.03793
29. López-Sobaler, A.M., Cuadrado-Soto, E., Peral-Suárez, Á., Aparicio, A., Ortega, R.M.: Importancia del desayuno en la mejora nutricional y sanitaria de la población. Nutrición Hospitalaria **35**(Spec No6), 3–6 (2018). https://doi.org/10.20960/nh.2278
30. Ortega Rosa, M., Isabel, J.-O.A., Rosa, M.-G., Elena, A.-A., Carmen, L.-E.M.: La obesidad infantil como prioridad sanitaria. Pautas en la mejora del control de peso. Nutrición Hospitalaria [Internet]. **39**(spe3), 35–38 (2022). https://doi.org/10.20960/nh.04308
31. Bittencourt Mescoloto, S., Pongiluppi, G., Martins Álvares Domene, S.: Ultra-processed food consumption and children and adolescents' health. Jornal de Pediatria, **100**(1) (2024). https://doi.org/10.1016/j.jped.2023.09.006

32. Díaz-Beltrán, M.: Factores influyentes en el comportamiento alimentario infantil. Revista de la Facultad de Medicina [Internet] **62**(2), 237–245 (2014)
33. FAO (s.f.).: Entornos alimentarios y alimentación escolar saludables (2021). Recuperado de https://www.fao.org/school-food/areas-work/food-environment/es/ [Internet]

CHARAL 2025

Drupelet: End-to-End Development of Mixed Binary/Ternary Neural Networks for Ultra Resource-Constrained Microcontrollers

Jose Rodrigo Camacho Perez[1], Alberto Rodriguez Arreola[1(✉)], Theodoros D. Verykios[2], Emma Gutierrez Cortes[1], and Andres Felipe Tellez Crespo[1]

[1] Tecnologico de Monterrey, School of Engineering and Sciences, Guadalajara, Jalisco, Mexico
{rodrigo.camacho,alberto.r.arreola,a01639119}@tec.mx
[2] School of Electronics and Computer Science, University of Southampton, Southampton, UK
T.Verykios@soton.ac.uk

Abstract. Embedding neural networks in ultra-resource-constrained, low-cost, off-the-shelf microcontrollers promotes the widespread adoption of the Internet of Intelligent Things. A promising approach involves mapping network parameters from real to either binary or ternary values to reduce computational workload. Hence, we introduce *Drupelet*, a novel software framework for the development of *mixed-precision* (binary and ternary) neural networks for ultra-resource-constrained embedded devices. The modularity of *Drupelet* provides ease of maintenance, debugging and reuse. *Drupelet* was used to define the edges of memory and inference time of typical layers on two different microcontrollers. The results demonstrate that *Drupelet* enables mass deployment of IoIT systems, thanks to the low cost of ultra resource-constrained microcontrollers.

Keywords: Binary and Ternary Neural Networks · Embedded Systems · IoIT · Quantization

1 Introduction

Many of humanity's pressing challenges in agriculture, health and environmental protection can be addressed with embedded technology . For instance, real-time health monitoring of the population (including under limited connectivity scenarios) can save financial resources and improve the response to pandemic events [1,2]. Similarly, improving food access globally can be aided by the adoption of smart farming practices to face population growth [3].

Thus, efforts are underway to enhance embedded systems through the adoption of Artificial Intelligence (AI) and Machine Learning (ML) embedded models,

L. Martínez-Villaseñor et al. (Eds.): MICAI 2025, LNAI 16265, pp. 199–210, 2026.
https://doi.org/10.1007/978-3-032-17933-3_21

also known as "TinyML" [4,5]. Recently, a medical capsule robot for early detection of colorectal cancer based on Neural Networks (NNs) was proposed in [6] In other words, we are seeing a push of AI/ML to implement the "Internet of Intelligent Things" (IoIT) [7]. This move is also driven by the need for reduced latency or bandwidth, offline functionality, battery operation, and enhanced data privacy of many applications [5–8].

However, the success of the IoIT is contingent on the development of cost-effective and energy-efficient solutions that would ease massive adoption of IoIT solutions. This requires reducing energy consumption, memory footprint, and processing time [9,10] of intelligent methods like NNs so that their inference algorithm can be embedded in ultra-resource-constrained MCUs (URC-MCUs). To make this possible, NN weights can be limited to binary or ternary values (*n_ary* for brevity) [11].

The main contributions of this work are:

1. A novel function for training and optimizing *mixed* (binary or ternary) *n_ary* models with control of the quantization step width for automatic selection of the quantization mixture of each model layer.
2. A novel expression for the dot product of mixed *n_ary* arrays that is fundamental for unified and efficient inference of mixed *n_ary* models.
3. *Drupelet*, a modular, single-thread and portable software (SW) framework for the development of mixed *n_ary* NNs and their deployment on URC-MCUs
4. Practical evaluation of *Drupelet* on two URC-MCUs with different characteristics.

2 Related Work

One of the most relevant methods to reduce the computational workload of NN models is *quantization* that converts the real-valued parameters of a NN model into integer values to reduce the memory requirements [12,13]. The integer-valued parameters are limited to a given range to control the extent of memory savings.

Binarization, the most extreme form of quantization, reduces parameters to just two values. This maximizes savings in memory and computation, as parameters can be stored in a single bit and multiplications are replaced with efficient logic operations [14]. Moreover, the accuracy penalty that could be expected from *binarization* turns out to be minimal as demonstrated in [15]. In recent years, several frameworks for the inference of binary NN models have been introduced [16–18]. Nonetheless, all these approaches are not oriented to operate on ultra resource-constrained devices. More recently, a framework called CBin-NN was introduced in [19]. However, CBin-NN requires at least 256kB of ROM and 32kB of RAM which still exceeds the available resources of the most constrained MCUs. Moreover, these works don't support mixed models with binary and ternary layer while this work does support them.

Multi-level (binary and up) quantization has been discussed in [20,21]. However, they do not use the same formula for the different levels and are not fully differentiable. In this work, we introduce a single, fully differentiable formula for binary and ternary (*mixed*) quantization.

Other multi-level methods are reported in [22–24]. These methods are fully differentiable and introduce a *steepness* parameter that enables training by successive approximation to ideal multi-level step quantized values. However, the method proposed here includes an additional control of the step width which is absent in previous works and enables automatic definition of the layer mixture (i.e., which layers can be binary and which ternary).

Models with mixed quantization levels have been explored in [25–27], but they do not support inference on embedded systems. Moreover, existing research on mixed binary and ternary inference [29,30] does not, however, extend to training algorithms nor address the specific challenges of deployment on URC-MCUs. Simply put, current frameworks do not support end-to-end mixed model development.

In contrast to previous works, *Drupelet* supports end-to-end mixed n_ary model development (from training to deployment) on off-the-shelf, single-core URC-MCUs for ease of widespread adoption of the IIoT. A new function for binarization and ternarization (*n_arization*) is introduced that adds control over the width of the mid-level quantization step. This enables users to find the best combination of n_ary layers for the model.

3 The Proposed Framework: *Drupelet*

Drupelet is a framework to develop *n_ary* NNs based on Dense, Convolutional and MaxPool layers, which enables most embedded applications, such as pattern detection in sensor signals and image processing. *Drupelet* consists of both Python and C libraries to train and deploy *n_ary* models on URC-MCUs as shown in Table 1.

Table 1. Libraries of the Proposed Framework

Library	Language	Description
Model definition	Python	n_ary layers (Dense, Convolutional, Maxpool) in Tensorflow for model training
Model exporting	Python	Packing *n_ary* parameters into the bits of numbers in preparation for saving in memory for inference
Inference-MCU	C	Single-thread *n_ary* layers for embedded inference in URC-MCUs

4 Training of *n_ary* Models with *Drupelet*

Drupelet introduces a new *n_arization* function [1] that maps floating-point numbers to binary or ternary, as shown in Eq. 1.

$$g(w, \sigma, \delta) = 0.5 \cdot [\tanh(\sigma \cdot (w + \delta)) + \tanh(\sigma \cdot (w - \delta))] \tag{1}$$

From Eq. 1, w are the values to be *n_arized*, σ is the steepness of the tanh functions, and δ defines the range of w where the function is 0. Note that for $\sigma \rightarrow \pm\infty$, g becomes a step function with three levels $\{-1, 0, 1\}$. For $\delta = 0$, g becomes a binary step function with levels in $\{-1, 1\}$.

Hence, Eq. 1 not only allows for a gradual *n_arization* by increasing σ, but it also allows for a control of the mid-step width to select the best *n_arization* mixture. With this new function, we can enhance the mapping suggested in previous works for the weights [15, 23, 24]:

$$W \leftarrow a \cdot g(w, \sigma, \delta) \tag{2}$$

where w are the floating point weights, W the *n_narized* weights and a is a scaling factor (also learned during training).

The training process involves gradually increasing the steepness σ with fixed step-width δ. At each value of σ, the NN is trained with the typical gradient descent method for a few epochs. The pairs (σ,n_{epochs}) can be saved in a *schedule* list. At the same time, the process can include a search for the optimal value of δ, for example by repeating the training *schedule* in a given search space D of δ parameters.

A naive model search and training process can be summarized as shown in Algorithm.1. In this naive process, the model with the lowest loss is selected.

Algorithm 1. *Drupelet*'s naive *n_nary* model search and training process

Require: D : search space for δ, S : training schedule
1: $i = 0$
2: **for** δ **in** D **do**
3: model $\leftarrow \delta$ ▷ $\delta = 0$ for binary, $\delta \neq 0$ for ternary
4: **for** σ, n_{epochs} **in** S **do**
5: model $\leftarrow \sigma$
6: train(model, n_{epochs}) ▷ e.g. in Tensorflow
7: loss[i] = eval(model)
8: $i++$
9: **end for**
10: **end for**

The result of the training process is an *n_ary* NN with learned weights W_{nary} (i.e., $W_{ter} \in \{-1, 0, 1\}$ or $W_{bin} \in \{-1, 1\}$) along with a learned scaling factor a. This process has been implemented in Tensorflow.

[1] Developed by A. F. Tellez Crespo, email: andrestellez84@hotmail.com.

5 Trained *n_ary* Model Exporting with *Drupelet*

5.1 Scale and Bias Quantization

Once a model is trained, the scaling factor a and the bias B (if used) are quantized using the following:

$$a_{embedded} = \lfloor Q \cdot a \rfloor \tag{3a}$$
$$B_{embedded} = \lfloor Q \cdot B \rfloor \tag{3b}$$

where Q is a user-defined factor to scale and quantize a and B to integers for embedded inference

5.2 Packing

After training, mappings are required to store the trained *n_ary* weights and the required inputs in memory registers. *Drupelet*'s convention is to split ternary arrays (e.g. weight arrays W) into two arrays. The first is $W_{nz} \in \{-1, 1\}$. It represents the non-zero arithmetical values (-1 or 1) in W that affect any dot product operations. The second is $W_{alive} \in \{0, 1\}$. It represents the locations where the original weight array W has any non-zero arithmetic values. Hence, it can be used to track the *alive* values. That is, W_{alive}=0 indicates that the corresponding input does not affect the result, while W_{alive}=1, signifies that the corresponding input is either subtracted or added according to W. Thus, *Drupelet* introduces the mappings:

$$b_{nz} \colon \{-1, 0, 1\} \rightarrow \{1, 0, 0\} \tag{4a}$$
$$b_{alive} \colon \{-1, 0, 1\} \rightarrow \{1, 0, 1\} \tag{4b}$$

where b_{nz} is the mapping of the nonzero values to binary and b_{alive} maps the location of the non-zero values. In other words, b_{nz} is 0 every time the variable being mapped is 0. At the same time b_{alive} is 1 every time the variable being mapped is not 0 (i.e. -1 or 1).

Note that for binary weights and inputs, the variables being mapped are in {-1,1} and hence b_{alive} is always 1. Therefore, binary weights and inputs require half the memory since they use a single bit, mapped through b_{nz}.

Finally, similar to [28], *Drupelet* packs bits along the last dimension of the array. For example, an $N \times L$ array will be packed into an $N \times R$ array, where R is the number of variables used to pack L bits.

6 *Drupelet* Layers for inference on URC-MCUs

6.1 Dot Product

The fundamental operation in *Drupelet* is the Dot product between weights and inputs that can each be binary or ternary valued. The Dot product expressions in [29,30] are here generalized into a new expression that allows both weights and inputs to take binary and/or ternary values arbitrarily:

$$\hat{y} = (W_{alive}\,\text{AND}\,X_{alive}) \quad \text{AND} \quad (W_{nz}\,\text{XOR}\,X_{nz}) \tag{5a}$$

$$N_{alive} = \text{popcount}(W_{alive}\,\text{AND}\,X_{alive}) \tag{5b}$$

$$y = N_{alive} - 2 \cdot \text{popcount}(\hat{y}) \tag{5c}$$

where W_{nz}, X_{nz}, W_{alive} and X_{alive} are mapped from the *n_ary* arrays W and X using (4), and popcount(·) computes the number of set bits in memory. Note that for binary layers and binary inputs, W_{alive} and X_{alive} become identity arrays because all bits are alive (i.e., they represent either -1 or 1 valued weights or inputs). This further simplifies Eq.(5).

In Eq.(5), the product $W_{alive}\text{AND}\,X_{alive}$ gives all the locations where the inputs X are going to be added or subtracted according to W. That is, this product indicates all of the *alive* locations.

For these *alive* locations, the product $W_{nz}\text{XOR}\,X_{nz}$ results in 0 whenever W and X have the same sign and thus a 1 should be added. Likewise, $W_{nz}\text{XOR}\,X_{nz}$ results in 1 whenever W and X have opposite signs and thus a 1 should be subtracted. Thus, popcount($\hat{y}$) gives the number of times a 1 was subtracted. Therefore, the range of popcount($\hat{y}$) is $[0, N_{alive}]$. That is to say, popcount($\hat{y}$) is 0 if no values were subtracted, and N_{alive} if all of the *alive* values were subtracted.

At the same time, if all of the *alive* values were positive, the maximum of the convolution result would be N_{alive}. Conversely, if all of the alive values were negative, the minimum of the convolution result would be $-N_{alive}$. Hence, the range of the convolution result is $[-N_{alive}, N_{alive}]$.

Therefore, when popcount($\hat{y}$) is 0 (minimum), the convolution result is N_{alive}. Conversely, the convolution result is $-N_{alive}$ when popcount($\hat{y}$) is N_{alive} (maximum). Thus, in order to compute the convolution result, popcount($\hat{y}$) can be used by transforming its range from $[0, N_{alive}]$ to $[-N_{alive}, N_{alive}]$. The required transformation to get the convolution result from popcount($\hat{y}$) is given by Eq.(5)c

6.2 Dense Layer

A Dense layer performs the following operation for each neuron:

$$y_n = f(\sum_{l=1}^{L} x_l w_{l,n} + b_n) \tag{6}$$

where n is the neuron index, b_n are neuron biases and L is the length of the inputs. Therefore, to get all N outputs, a Dot product must be performed N times. For *n_ary* activations, the outputs can be packed on the fly to save resources.

6.3 2D Convolutional Layer

Convolutional layers are typically described in terms of *kernels*, *filters* or *neurons* sliding over the input in a series of steps [31] performing an element-element product between the input and the kernels. A helpful visualization of this process is provided by [32]. The inputs may be time-varying sensor signals or image-like sensor data. The first case is typically referred to as *one-dimensional* (1D) and the latter as *two-dimensional*(2D).

For 2D Convolutions, a strategy is to flatten X and W to 1-D at each convolution step [29]. Figure 1 shows the inputs array $X_{H \times D \times C}$, and the set of kernels as array $W_{K \times K \times C \times N}$. The convolution operation at each step sh, sw for a given neuron n can be expressed by:

$$y_{sh,sw,n} = f\left(\sum_{l=0}^{L=K^2C} x_l w_{l,n} + b_n\right) \tag{7}$$

where sh, sw represent the convolution steps in the h, w dimensions, x_l is the $l-th$ input in the current flattened segment, $w_{l,n}$ is the weight for x_l and neuron n and b_n is the bias term for neuron n.

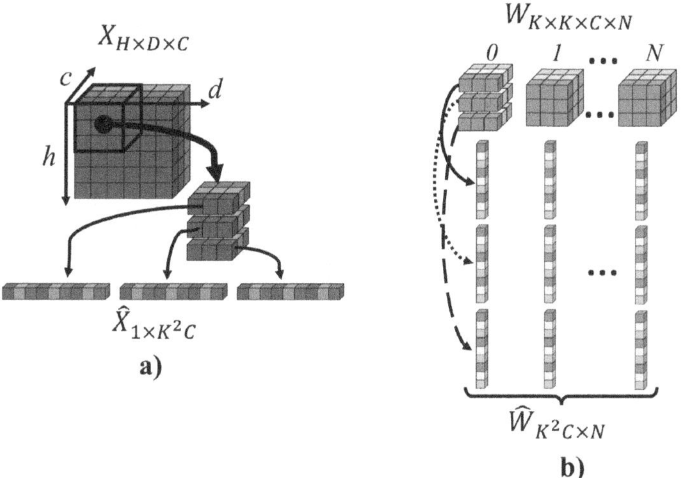

Fig. 1. Convolution as a series of Dense Layers. At each step, flatten the inputs and do a matrix product with the flattened weights array. a) Input block, flattened along the channels at the first step, b) 4D neuron weights array flattened to 2D along channels.

Therefore, comparing Eqs. (6) and (7), it becomes evident that *the 2D Convolutional Layer calls N times a Dense Layer on a flattened sub-array of X with length of* K^2C. The same principle applies to the 1D case. Thus, *Drupelet* implements both 1D and 2D Convolutional Layers by invoking Dense Layers multiple times.

7 "Hello *Drupelet*": Digits Recognition

As an early demonstration of *Drupelet*'s capabilities, this section shows *Drupelet* for digits recognition using the MNIST dataset [33]. While this example is overly simplistic for powerful computing scenarios, it is representative of the small-scale problems that are well-suited for deployment on URC-MCUs. The original dataset was binarized with a hard threshold of 128. This makes it harder to achieve high accuracies. Yet, binarized inputs are a more representative embedded scenario.

7.1 *n_ary* Model Architecture and Training

The *n_ary* NN architecture is shown in Fig. 2. It consists of a Convolutional and a Maxpool layer for feature extraction and two fully connected (*dense*) layers for classification. For simplicity, binary activation ($\delta = 0$) is used. MaxPool is performed using logical OR operations as suggested in [34]. In this model, the weights take 4.4kB (binary) and 8.4kB (ternary). This is in line with the memory requirements difference between binary and ternary packing as described in Sec.5.2.

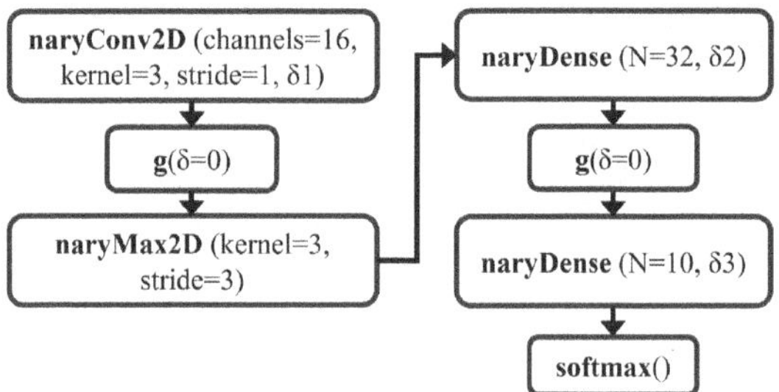

Fig. 2. Mixed *n_ary* model for MNIST.

Given the simplicity of the MNIST mixed *n_ary* model, a simple Design of Experiments (DoE) with three factors works to find the best mixture of the model. The search space was defined as $D = \{(\delta 1, \delta 2, \delta 3) \in \mathbb{R}^3 \,|\, 0 \leq (\delta 1, \delta 2, \delta 3) \leq 0.1\}$. In each experiment trial, the model was trained using the schedule $S =$ given by:

$$(\sigma, n_{epochs}) = [(1,3),(2,3),(4,3),(8,3),(16,3),(32,3),(64,3),(128,3),(256,3),(512,3),(768,3),(1024,1)] \quad (8)$$

In Table 2, the best performance of 95.98% is achieved with the ternary model. This is lower than those reported in the literature (over 98%) because our model is significantly smaller and used binarized images. Also, the mixed model with two binary layers requires only about half the memory with an accuracy close to optimal. This memory reduction with minimal impact on accuracy is critical in the context of URC-MCUs and highlights one of the most important advantages of *Drupelet*. Finally, after training, $Q = 100$ was selected for deployment without any impact on accuracy.

Table 2. *n_ary* Models and Accuracy

Model	mid-step width			Packed Weights [kB]	Accuracy [%]
	δ_1	δ_2	δ_3		
binary	0	0	0	4.4	90.31
mixed	0.05	0	0	4.5	95.00
ternary	0.05	0.05	0.05	8.6	95.98

7.2 Inference on the MSP430FR5969

The MSP430FR5969 is a 16-bit URC-MCU with 2 KB of SRAM and 64 KB of FRAM. It can operate at frequencies up to 16MHz, consuming 100μA/MHz. Due to the limited size of the SRAM, we configured the MCU to apply the proper delays to use the FRAM during real-time operation. Interprocedure optimizations ($-O3$) were also employed. The weights of the model were packed into 8-bit registers. The overall inference performance is shown in Table 3.

Table 3. Embedded System Performance on the MSP430 @8MHz.

Model	FRAM (Bytes)	SRAM (Bytes)	Time (ms)	Energy (mJ)
Binary	8380	160	2796	5.75
Mixed	8810	160	2645	5.70
Ternary	12894	160	2688	5.85

7.3 Inference on the STM32G0B1RET6

The STM32G0B1RET6 is a 32-bit ARM Cortex-M0+ microcontroller with 144 KB of SRAM and 512 KB of Flash. It can operate up to 64MHz consuming less than 100μA/MHz. This MCU was configured to operate using the same settings as the MSP430 discussed above. The resulting inference performance metrics are listed in Table 4.

Table 4. Embedded System Performance on the STM32 @8MHz.

Model	Flash (Bytes)	SRAM (Bytes)	Time (ms)	Energy (mJ)
Binary	5516	8204	609	2.32
Mixed	5584	8408	556	2.16
Ternary	5676	12712	539	2.11

This MCU operates without SRAM usage restrictions during real-time operation, allowing for a significant reduction in execution time compared to the MSP430 MCU. However, the reason why both Flash and SRAM utilization is high on the M0+ is because the data are duplicated to operate in real time. In contrast, the MSP430 relied on FRAM for memory operations during inference due to its limited SRAM capacity. This design trade-off introduced additional latency and energy consumption as a result of the characteristics of FRAM.

8 Conclusions and Future Work

Drupelet is a novel framework that enables the training and deployment of mixed binary/ternary (n_ary) neural networks. *Drupelet* generates portable, modular C-code for inference on URC-MCUs, simplifying debugging and maintenance. The results presented demonstrate that the proposed framework helps users to balance performance and memory of mixed (binary/ternary) models. The next steps include in-depth evaluations of *Drupelet* across diverse embedded benchmarks and inference optimization on multiple URC-MCUs.

As future work, we consider the following:

- Performing ablation studies to demonstrate the influence of each parameter of the proposed training process.
- Testing on benchmarks like MLPerf Tiny [35]
- Developing models for gesture and human activity recognition.
- Release of an open-source framework for the proposed training and deployment process.
- Conducting real-time performance evaluations with real users.

References

1. Smarr, B.L., et al.: Feasibility of continuous fever monitoring using wearable devices. Sci. Rep. **10**(1), 21640 (2020)
2. Vijayan, V., Connolly, J.P., Condell, J., McKelvey, N., Gardiner, P.: Review of wearable devices and data collection considerations for connected health. Sensors **21**(16), 5589 (2021)
3. Moysiadis, V., Sarigiannidis, P., Vitsas, V., Khelifi, A.: Smart farming in Europe. Comput. Sci. Rev. **39**, 100345 (2021)

4. Baciu, V.E., Stiens, J., da Silva, B.: MLino bench: a comprehensive benchmarking tool for evaluating ML models on edge devices. J. Syst. Architect. **155**, 103262 (2024)
5. Abadade, Y., Temouden, A., Bamoumen, H., Benamar, N., Chtouki, Y., Hafid, A.S.: A comprehensive survey on TinyML. IEEE Access **11**, 96892–96922 (2023)
6. Lu, C.K., Liew, W.S., Tang, T.B., Lin, C.H.: Implementation of a convolutional neural network into an embedded device for polyps detection. IEEE Embed. Syst. Lett. **16**(1), 5–8 (2024)
7. Oliveira, F., Costa, D.G., Assis, F., Silva, I.: Internet of intelligent things: a convergence of embedded systems, edge computing and machine learning. Internet Things **26**, 101153 (2024)
8. Saha, S., Sandha, S.S., Srivastava, M.: Machine learning for microcontroller-class hardware: a review. IEEE Sens. J. **22**(22), 21362–21390 (2022)
9. Rodriguez Arreola, A., et al.: Approaches to transient computing for energy harvesting systems: a quantitative evaluation. In: Proceedings of the 3rd International Workshop on Energy Harvesting & Energy Neutral Sensing Systems, pp. 3–8 (2015)
10. Rodriguez Arreola, A., Verykios, T.D., Gurrola Navarro, M.A., Calvillo Cortes, C.F.: Federated time persistency in intermittently powered IoT systems. J. Syst. Architect. **130**, 102667 (2022)
11. Yuan, C., Agaian, S.S.: A comprehensive review of binary neural network. Artif. Intell. Rev. **56**(11), 12949–13013 (2023)
12. Rokh, B., Azarpeyvand, A., Khanteymoori, A.: A comprehensive survey on model quantization for deep neural networks in image classification. ACM Trans. Intell. Syst. Technol. **14**(6), 1–50 (2023)
13. Gholami, A., Kim, S., Dong, Z., Yao, Z., Mahoney, M. W., Keutzer, K.: A survey of quantization methods for efficient neural network inference. In: Low-Power Computer Vision. pp. 291–326 (2022). Chapman and Hall/CRC
14. Sayed, R., Azmi, H., Shawkey, H., Khalil, A.H., Refky, M.: A systematic literature review on binary neural networks. IEEE Access **11**, 27546–27578 (2023)
15. Zhao, Y., Xiao, J.: An adiabatic method to train binarized artificial neural networks. Sci. Rep. **11**(1), 1 (2021)
16. Bethge, J., Bartz, C., Yang, H., Meinel, C.: BMXNet 2: an open source framework for low-bit networks–Reproducing, understanding, designing and showcasing. In: Proceedings of the 28th ACM International Conference on Multimedia, Seattle, WA, USA, pp. 4469–4472 (2020)
17. Zhang, J., Pan, Y., Yao, T., Zhao, H., Mei, T.: daBNN: a super fast inference framework for binary neural networks on ARM devices. In: Proceedings of the 27th ACM International Conference on Multimedia, Nice, France (2019)
18. Bannink, T., et al.: Larq compute engine: design, benchmark, and deploy state-of-the-art binarized neural networks. Proc. Mach. Learn. Syst. **3**, 680–695 (2021)
19. Sakr, F., et al.: CBin-NN: an inference engine for binarized neural networks. Electronics **13**(9), 1624 (2024)
20. Zhou, S., Wu, Y., Ni, Z., Zhou, X., Wen, H., Zou, Y.: DoReFa-Net: training low bitwidth convolutional neural networks with low bitwidth gradients. arXiv preprint arXiv:1606.06160 (2016)
21. Pham, P., Abraham, J.A., Chung, J.: Training multi-bit quantized and binarized networks with a learnable symmetric quantizer. IEEE Access **9**, 47194–47203 (2021)
22. Heinrich, M.P., Blendowski, M., Oktay, O.: TernaryNet: faster deep model inference without GPUs for medical 3D segmentation using sparse and binary convolutions. Int. J. Comput. Assist. Radiol. Surg. **13**, 1311–1320 (2018)

23. Gong, R., et al.: Differentiable soft quantization: bridging full-precision and low-bit neural networks. In: Proceedings of the IEEE/CVF International Conference on Computer Vision, pp. 4852–4861 (2019)
24. Yang, J., et al: Quantization networks. In: Proceedings of the IEEE/CVF Conference on Computer Vision and Pattern Recognition, pp. 7308–7316 (2019)
25. Razani, R., Morin, G., Sari, E., Nia, V. P.: Adaptive binary-ternary quantization. In: Proceedings of the IEEE/CVF Conference on Computer Vision and Pattern Recognition, pp. 4613–4618 (2021)
26. Qu, Z., Zhou, Z., Cheng, Y., Thiele, L.: Adaptive loss-aware quantization for multi-bit networks. In: Proceedings of the IEEE/CVF Conference on Computer Vision and Pattern Recognition, pp. 7988–7997 (2020)
27. Xu, K., Feng, Q., Zhang, X., Wang, D.: MultiQuant: training once for multi-bit quantization of neural networks. In: IJCAI, pp. 3629–3635 (2022)
28. Hu, Y., et al.: BitFlow: exploiting vector parallelism for binary neural networks on CPU. In: IEEE International Parallel and Distributed Processing Symposium (IPDPS) **2018**, 244–253 (2018)
29. Wan, D., et al.: TBN: convolutional neural network with ternary inputs and binary weights. In: Proceedings of the European Conference on Computer Vision (ECCV), pp. 315–332 (2018)
30. Zhu, S., Duong, L.H.K., Liu, W.: TAB: unified and optimized ternary, binary, and mixed-precision neural network inference on the edge. ACM Trans. Embed. Comput. Syst. (TECS) **21**(5), 1–26 (2022)
31. éron, A. G.: Hands-On Machine Learning with Scikit-Learn, Keras, and TensorFlow. 3rd edn. 2022. https://learning.oreilly.com/library/view. Accessed: 04 Jul. 2023
32. Animated AI. https://animatedai.github.io/. Accessed: 11 Jul. 2024
33. LeCun, Y., Cortes, C., Burges, cj.c.: The MNIST database of handwritten digits. https://yann.lecun.com/exdb/mnist/. Accessed: 10 Sept. 2024
34. Umuroglu, Y., et al.: FINN: a framework for fast, scalable binarized neural network inference. In: Proceedings of the 2017 ACM/SIGDA International Symposium on Field-Programmable Gate Arrays, pp. 65–74 (2017)
35. MLPerf Tiny.:https://mlcommons.org/working-groups/benchmarks/tiny/. Accessed: 11 Oct. 2025

A Metamodeling Framework for Accelerated Energy Market Optimization Using Active Learning

Benjamin Uhrich[1,2](✉), Linus Thrän[3], and Felix Böing[3]

[1] Leipzig University, Leipzig, Germany
[2] Center for Scalable Data Analytics and Artificial Intelligence Dresden/Leipzig, Leipzig, Germany
uhrich@informatik.uni-leipzig.de
[3] 50Hertz Transmission GmbH, Berlin, Germany

Abstract. The increasing transformation of the European energy market, driven by the rise of intermittent renewable energies, the decommissioning of controllable power plants and dependence on short-term storage, poses challenges for assessing security of supply. In order to evaluate the capacity of available generation to meet demand in uncertain conditions, market model optimizations using the Monte Carlo (MC) approach are employed. However, the high computational costs of this approach limit assessment resolution. This paper investigates metamodeling as a strategy to reduce these computational costs. Metamodelling is a process of using mathematical models on a subset of simulations to map outcomes to the input data. This reduces the total number of simulations required. The study explores three key steps: enhancing input-output correlation, identifying effective machine learning (ML) models and selecting optimal training samples. While no single model performs adequately due to data complexity, a two-model pipeline significantly improves prediction accuracy. An active learning approach is also introduced to further optimize sample selection. The results show that training on only twenty percent of the data reduces the computation time by more than 75%, with a relative error below 10%. These findings demonstrate the potential of metamodeling to enable efficient, high-resolution resource adequacy assessments in evolving energy systems.

Keywords: Metamodeling · energy systems · active learning · resource adequacy · electricity market modeling

1 Introduction

The development of the European energy market presents a fundamental challenge.

In recent years, policy and market developments have prioritized environmental sustainability, sometimes at the expense of economic efficiency and supply

L. Martínez-Villaseñor et al. (Eds.): MICAI 2025, LNAI 16265, pp. 211–227, 2026.
https://doi.org/10.1007/978-3-032-17933-3_22

reliability [1]. However, shifting geopolitical dynamics have redirected public and political attention toward ensuring a robust security of supply [2]. In Germany, the phase-out of all nuclear power plants by 2023 significantly reduced the market's dispatchable capacity. The planned coal phase-out by 2038 will further diminish the available firm capacity.

This reduction has been made possible by the increasing share of renewable energy sources, resulting in a more environmentally friendly energy mix. However, this transition raises new concerns about supply reliability. Ensuring an adequate level of supply, also known as resource adequacy, requires continuous, high-resolution assessments to support well-informed decisions regarding energy market development and design.

Resource adequacy assessments evaluate the frequency with which a given generation system, under the prevailing market design, is capable of meeting electricity demand. By comparing the resulting loss of load expectation (LOLE) with the nationally defined reliability standard, it is possible to determine whether the system is over- or under-dimensioned with respect to security of supply.

Methodologically, it is standard practice to account for uncertainty in both weather conditions and generation availability. This is typically achieved by using multiple historical weather years to reflect variability in renewable generation, and by applying so-called outage draws to simulate the stochastic availability of conventional power plants.

To address these challenges, the agency for the cooperation of energy regulators (ACER) has developed a methodology based on MC simulations run by energy market models. While effective, this approach is computationally intensive, which constrains the resolution and scope of the assessment due to model simplification and data aggregation. For example, the European resource adequacy assessment (ERAA) carries out 700 full-year energy market simulations to evaluate supply reliability [3]. Similar analyses may require approximately six days of computation, motivating the search for alternative or more efficient methodologies.

The present paper explores the use of metamodelling to reduce computational effort. Metamodelling involves the use of mathematical models, frequently derived from ML, to approximate the relationship between input and output data from MC energy market simulations. The training of a metamodel on a subset of simulated data facilitates the estimation of results for unsimulated scenarios, thereby reducing the number of full simulations required.

Despite the evidence that this technique has shown promise in predicting prices from energy market models, its application to capacity sufficiency metrics remains largely unexplored [4]. The issue pertains to the inherent characteristics of the output data. Power systems are usually designed to satisfy demand in most states. Consequently, circumstances where supply is inadequate are rare and difficult to predict in the absence of exhaustive simulation. The identification of such events without the necessity of simulating every possible scenario represents a significant challenge.

This challenge is further compounded by the rise of short-term energy storage, which introduces temporal dependencies to an already spatially interconnected European grid. Furthermore, a robust metamodel must account for the weather dependence of renewable energy sources and incorporate probabilistic modelling of power plant outages.

- Our analysis identifies a high-performing two-model pipeline that minimizes mean absolute error (MAE) in predicting LOLE across MC years.
- We develop an active learning-based approach that iteratively selects the most informative simulation samples to optimize model training efficiency.
- We benchmark the performance of the proposed metamodeling approach against traditional energy market model optimization methods, demonstrating substantial reductions in computational cost (in hours) while maintaining high predictive accuracy (measured by MAE).

2 Related Work

2.1 ML in Energy System Research

ML is increasingly applied in energy system research, though its use in resource adequacy assessments remains relatively unexplored. Starke *et al.* systematically reviewed the role of ML across energy domains, describing it as an emerging yet rapidly growing field [5].

ML has become indispensable in forecasting applications, including load profiles, renewable generation, and energy prices. Rahman *et al.* demonstrated the predictive power of ML in these contexts [6]. Donti *et al.* also proposed ML integration for accelerating and improving energy system optimization tasks [7].

2.2 ML in Energy Model Optimization

ML applications in energy model optimization generally fall into two categories: power flow simulations and economic dispatch. Duchesne *et al.*, Sun *et al.*, and Su *et al.* employed ML to accelerate power flow calculations [8–10]. Leonori *et al.* applied ML in near real-time power flow for microgrids. Huang *et al.* used ML to improve reliability in congested systems [11,12].

In economic dispatch, Darville *et al.* reduced dimensionality in mixed-integer programs to accelerate solver times [13]. Bogensperger *et al.* and Hoffmann *et al.* used ML for time series aggregation to streamline simulations [14,15]. Perera *et al.* developed metamodels to address computational bottlenecks in energy system optimization [16].

2.3 Metamodels in Energy Market Model Optimization

Metamodeling has emerged as a promising alternative to traditional simplification techniques in energy market model optimization. Kohnen *et al.* employed deep learning to map input-output relations and predict market prices [4]. Prina *et al.*, Danish *et al.*, and Kim *et al.* confirmed that metamodels can produce accurate outputs in significantly shorter runtimes, especially under hardware or time constraints [17–19].

Nolting *et al.* showed that ML and design of experiments (DOE) techniques are promising for approximating model behavior with limited computing resources [20]. Priesmann *et al.* supported input data reduction and structural simplification as alternative strategies [21].

2.4 Metamodels in Resource Adequacy Assessments

Resource adequacy assessments remain challenging due to their probabilistic nature, requiring evaluation across diverse weather and outage scenarios. Nolting and Praktiknjo described this as the "complexity dilemma," where increasingly sophisticated questions necessitate complex models. The prediction accuracy of these model depends on the quality of the input data. [22].

By combining the availability curve with residual load, the loss of load probability (LOLP) and LOLE can be estimated, though the process remains computationally expensive [23].

Munch *et al.* advanced this by predicting the availability curve outcomes directly, effectively mitigating the complexity dilemma [24].

Conventional availability curve methods are predicated on situations in isolation, thereby facilitating data generation via DOE. However, contemporary challenges necessitate temporal interconnection modelling due to escalating storage capacity and cross-border interactions. Energy market models offer this, but lack built-in probabilistic capabilities, making MC simulation integration essential but computationally costly.

3 Methodology

3.1 Metamodel Topology

The goal of the metamodel is to predict a LOLE for each market area (MA) with only a fraction of the simulated MC-years having results available. Instead of the standard LOLE (hours with actual shortfall), we define LOLE via the expected number of maximal price events (MPEs).

It eliminates the complexity arising from the expected energy not supplied temporal [25] and spatial [26] distribution effects, which are challenging to predict. Consequently, these effects do not unnecessarily complicate the formation of the metamodel. However, it is important to note that future developments of the approach presented here may address this issue. The metamodel is configured as a pipeline that contains three main parts:

- a classification model,
- an aggregation step, and
- a scaling model.

The classification model's function is to predict whether a MPE occurs for a given situation, as identified by the combination of outage sample (OS), climatic year (CY), MA, and hour. In the aggregation step, the results of the classification model are aggregated as a sum over the hours to obtain a prediction for each MC-year region (identified by the combination of OS, CY, and MA). In a concluding step, the aggregated classification results are scaled. Given that the objective of the scaling model is to only capture systematic over- or underestimation, the implementation of a linear regression model is well-suited for this purpose. The metamodel pipeline can be seen in Fig. 1:

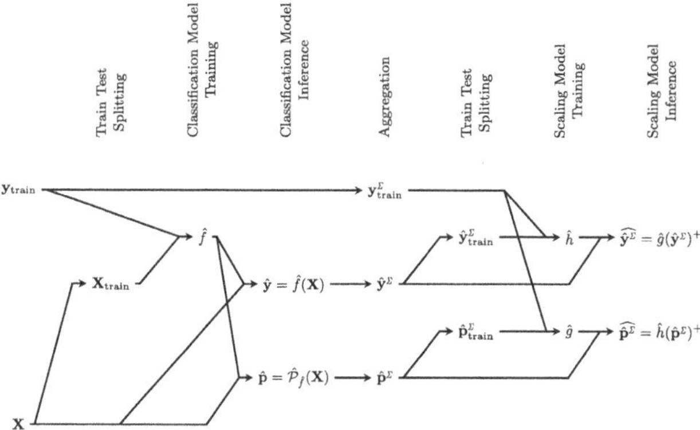

Fig. 1. Metamodel as a pipeline for predicting the LOLE of MC-year regions.

Obvious energy system features such as renewable generation, available conventional capacity or electricity demand are applied, as are newly introduced metrics that take temporal and spatial couplings into account and focus on the remaining capacity margin (available thermal capacity minus residual load). Temporal features are weekend or day of the week as well as hour of the day. In total, we identified 49 features. The input data for the pipeline consists of a single value for each feature in every situation. The input data consists of 700 MC-years in hourly resolution for one scenario and is represented by the matrix $\mathbf{X} \in \mathbb{R}^{n \times F}$. The matrix $\mathbf{X}$ has F columns (one for each feature) and n rows (one for each situation) with $n = \mathbb{H} \cdot |\mathbb{M}| \cdot |MC| = 8760 \cdot 11 \cdot 700$. A subset of the MC-years is selected as the training set $MC_{\text{train}} = MC_i \subset MC$, $|MC_{\text{train}}| = 140$. These MC-years are simulated using the energy market simulation yielding a result vector $\mathbf{y}_{\text{train}} \in \mathbb{R}^{m \times 1}$ with $m = \mathbb{H} \cdot |\mathbb{M}| \cdot |MC_{\text{train}}| = 8760 \cdot 11 \cdot 140$ corresponding to the input data represented by $\mathbf{X}_{\text{train}} \in \mathbb{R}^{m \times F}$.

Classification. The classification model can be fit to approximate the results $\mathbf{y}_{\text{train}}$ as the target regarding the training input data $\hat{f} \approx f : \mathbf{X}_{\text{train}} \rightarrow \mathbf{y}_{\text{train}}$. The fit classification model can subsequently be used to predict the target $\hat{\mathbf{y}} = \hat{f}(\mathbf{X})$, or its model internal probability $\hat{\mathbf{p}} = \hat{\mathcal{P}}_{\hat{f}}(\mathbf{X}) = \{\hat{\mathcal{P}}(y_0 = 1), \ldots, \hat{\mathcal{P}}(y_n = 1)\}$ for all 700 MC-years. The performance of the entire pipeline is evaluated using two different metrics: predicted target $\hat{\mathbf{y}}$ and predicted probability $\hat{\mathbf{p}}$. These metrics can be compared to determine which is most appropriate for use in a production scenario where only one is part of the metamodel.

Aggregation. The aggregation step serves to mitigate the imprecision of predictions made by the classification model. The LOLE, being an aggregate measure itself, does not require the correct classification of the maximal price indicator (MPI) in every hour, which is a highly challenging task. Instead, the accuracy of the LOLE prediction depends on the precision of the aggregated classification within each MC-year and region.

The aggregation process involves summing the predicted targets $\hat{\mathbf{y}}$ over the MC-year regions:

$$\hat{\mathbf{y}}^{\Sigma} = \begin{bmatrix} \hat{y}^{\Sigma}_{os=1,cy=1982,ma=\text{AT00}} \\ \vdots \\ \hat{y}^{\Sigma}_{os=20,cy=2016,ma=\text{PL00}} \end{bmatrix} = \begin{bmatrix} \sum_{h\in\mathbb{H}} \hat{y}_{os=1,cy=1982,ma=\text{AT00},h} \\ \vdots \\ \sum_{h\in\mathbb{H}} \hat{y}_{os=20,cy=2016,ma=\text{PL00},h} \end{bmatrix}, \tag{1}$$

with $\hat{\mathbf{y}}^{\Sigma} \in \mathbb{R}^{|MC|\cdot|\mathbb{M}|\times 1}$.

The predicted probabilities are aggregated in the same way, resulting in $\hat{\mathbf{p}}^{\Sigma} \in \mathbb{R}^{|MC|\cdot|\mathbb{M}|\times 1}$. The simulated target is aggregated only over the simulated MC-years MC_{train}, resulting in $\mathbf{y}^{\Sigma}_{\text{train}} \in \mathbb{R}^{|MC_{\text{train}}|\cdot|\mathbb{M}|\times 1}$.

Scaling. A systematic error in the classification model can be corrected by the scaling model. Both systematic underestimation and overestimation can be captured. However, the error must be consistent. This means that the aggregated prediction $\hat{\mathbf{y}}^{\Sigma}$ or probability $\hat{\mathbf{p}}^{\Sigma}$ must exhibit a linear relationship with the aggregated target $\mathbf{y}^{\Sigma}$.

To train the scaling model, the simulated and aggregated targets from the training set $\mathbf{y}^{\Sigma}_{\text{train}}$ are used together with their corresponding predictions $\hat{\mathbf{y}}^{\Sigma}_{\text{train}}$ and $\hat{\mathbf{p}}^{\Sigma}_{\text{train}}$ to fit a linear regression. The regression aims to approximate $\hat{g} \approx g : \hat{\mathbf{y}}^{\Sigma}_{\text{train}} \rightarrow \mathbf{y}^{\Sigma}_{\text{train}}$ and $\hat{h} \approx h : \hat{\mathbf{p}}^{\Sigma}_{\text{train}} \rightarrow \mathbf{y}^{\Sigma}_{\text{train}}$.

Since the linear regression model may produce negative predictions, RELU is used.

Given that LOLE is a non-negative quantity, this function ensures that all predictions are clipped at zero.

The fitted regression models $\hat{g}$ and $\hat{h}$ are used to obtain the scaled predictions:

$$\widehat{\hat{\mathbf{y}}^{\Sigma}} = \hat{g}(\hat{\mathbf{y}}^{\Sigma})^{+} \text{ and } \widehat{\hat{\mathbf{p}}^{\Sigma}} = \hat{h}(\hat{\mathbf{p}}^{\Sigma})^{+}. \tag{2}$$

4 Iterative Guided Convergence for Early Stopping

All MC-years are divided into two sets. Those not yet simulated (i.e., without a known $\mathbf{z}$) are placed in the MC_{unsim} set, while those already simulated with an associated $\mathbf{z}$ are placed in MC_{sim}. Initially, all MC-years are part of MC_{unsim} ($MC_{\text{unsim}} = MC$), while $MC_{\text{sim}} = \emptyset$.

In each iteration, a subset $MC_{\text{batch}} \subset MC_{\text{unsim}}$ is selected and simulated to obtain the corresponding targets $\mathbf{z}_{\text{batch}}$. This batch is appended to the existing simulated set, updating both MC_{sim} and $\mathbf{z}_{\text{sim}}$.

Next, the convergence of $\mathbf{z}_{\text{sim}}$ is evaluated. Convergence is considered achieved when the difference between the simulated and predicted final LOLE remains consistently below a predefined threshold. Once convergence is achieved, the process terminates and the final LOLE is derived from $\mathbf{z}_{\text{sim}}$. If not, the process repeats with the selection of a new batch. This cycle of selection, simulation, and convergence-checking continues.

Figure 2 illustrates the overall process.

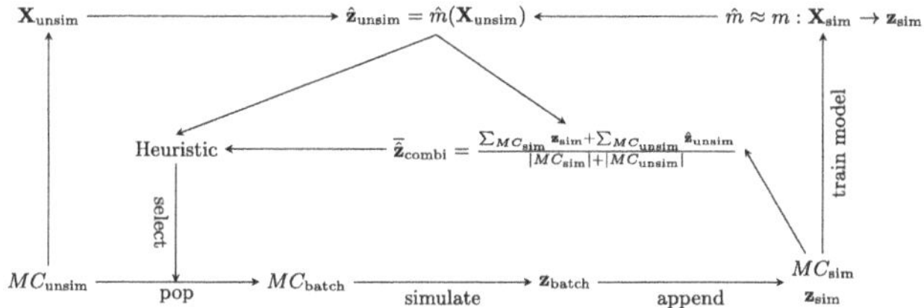

Fig. 2. Proposed iterative guided convergence process for early stopping.

If the iterative process is executed with random selection of MC-years for MC_{batch}, its potential benefits are not fully exploited. To maximize efficiency, priority should be given to simulate the MC-years with the highest number of scarcity occurrences, ensuring that these are processed early in the sequence. A heuristic for selecting MC-years for MC_{batch} in each iteration enables the selection of highly informative samples early on, thus guiding the simulation order and facilitating faster convergence. Fast convergence implies that only a subset of MC-years must be simulated to obtain sufficiently accurate approximations, thereby allowing early termination of the process.

The success of this heuristic depends on access to information about the unsimulated MC-years. This information is derived from a metamodel trained on the already simulated MC-years. The metamodel is retrained in every iteration to improve its predictive performance. In this way, the model can actively select the most informative samples, those that deviate the most or carry the most information, for its own retraining. This configuration, in which the metamodel selects its own training data, represents a form of active learning [27,28].

The metamodel $\hat{m}$, trained on simulated data $\mathbf{X}_{\text{sim}}$ and $\mathbf{z}_{\text{sim}}$, is used to make predictions $\hat{\mathbf{z}}$ for the unsimulated data: $\hat{\mathbf{z}}_{\text{unsim}} = \hat{m}(\mathbf{X}_{\text{unsim}})$.

The input data $\mathbf{X}$ contains a different number of rows than $\hat{\mathbf{z}}$. Specifically, $\mathbf{X}$ consists of $|MC| \cdot |\mathbb{M}| \cdot |\mathbb{H}|$ rows, while $\hat{\mathbf{z}}$ is aggregated over hours, resulting in $|MC| \cdot |\mathbb{M}|$ rows.

To approximate the LOLE per MA, the simulated targets $\mathbf{z}_{\text{sim}}$ and predicted targets $\hat{\mathbf{z}}_{\text{unsim}}$ are used. The average LOLE per MA for the simulated set is:

$$\overline{\mathbf{z}}_{\text{sim}} = \frac{\sum_{MC_{\text{sim}}} \mathbf{z}_{\text{sim}}}{|MC_{\text{sim}}|}, \quad \overline{\mathbf{z}}_{\text{sim}} \in \mathbb{R}^{|\mathbb{M}| \times 1}. \tag{3}$$

The corresponding average for the predicted targets of the unsimulated set can be calculated analog to Eq. (3).

By combining $\overline{\mathbf{z}}_{\text{sim}}$ and $\overline{\hat{\mathbf{z}}}_{\text{unsim}}$, a comprehensive prediction for the final LOLE across all MC-years can be computed:

$$\begin{aligned} \overline{\hat{\mathbf{z}}}_{\text{combi}} &= \overline{\{\mathbf{z}_{\text{sim}}, \hat{\mathbf{z}}_{\text{unsim}}\}} \\ &= \frac{\sum_{MC_{\text{sim}}} \mathbf{z}_{\text{sim}} + \sum_{MC_{\text{unsim}}} \hat{\mathbf{z}}_{\text{unsim}}}{|MC_{\text{sim}}| + |MC_{\text{unsim}}|}, \quad \overline{\hat{\mathbf{z}}}_{\text{combi}} \in \mathbb{R}^{|\mathbb{M}| \times 1}. \end{aligned} \tag{4}$$

The final LOLE approximation $\overline{\hat{\mathbf{z}}}_{\text{combi}}$ can then be compared with the predictions $\hat{\mathbf{z}}$ for the unsimulated MC-year regions. This comparison allows the derivation of a heuristic that selects the next batch of MC-years for simulation in the following iteration.

4.1 Heuristic

The identification of the optimal set of MC-years for simulation in the next iteration involves balancing two objectives:

1. Accelerating the convergence of the LOLE computed from the set of simulated MC-years.
2. Prioritizing the simulation of MC-years with high information content as early as possible.

The initial step determines whether the current LOLE of the simulated MC-years $\overline{\mathbf{z}}_{\text{sim}}$ represents an overestimation or underestimation of the final approximated LOLE $\overline{\hat{\mathbf{z}}}_{\text{combi}}$. Each additional MC-year selected for simulation should ideally reduce the distance between $\overline{\mathbf{z}}_{\text{sim}}$ and $\overline{\hat{\mathbf{z}}}_{\text{combi}}$. This is based on the rationale that $\overline{\hat{\mathbf{z}}}_{\text{combi}}$ serves as an estimate of the final value to which $\overline{\mathbf{z}}_{\text{sim}}$ should converge.

To evaluate the effect of simulating a candidate MC-year mc, the metric $\overline{\hat{\mathbf{z}}}_{MC_{\text{sim}} \cup \{mc\}}$ is introduced. It approximates the new LOLE per MA under the hypothetical assumption that mc is added to the simulation set:

$$\overline{\hat{\mathbf{z}}}_{MC_{\text{sim}} \cup \{mc\}} = \frac{\mathbf{z}_{\text{sim}} + \hat{\mathbf{z}}_{mc}}{|MC_{\text{sim}}| + 1} \tag{5}$$

A binary decision function $d(mc)$ is defined to assess whether simulating mc would move $\overline{\mathbf{z}}_{\text{sim}}$ closer to $\overline{\hat{\mathbf{z}}}_{\text{combi}}$. The function returns 1 if the inclusion of mc reduces the distance between the two values, and 0 otherwise:

$$d(mc) = \begin{cases} 1, & \overline{\mathbf{z}}_{\text{sim}} < \overline{\hat{\mathbf{z}}}_{\text{combi}} \text{ and } \overline{\mathbf{z}}_{\text{sim}} < \overline{\hat{\mathbf{z}}}_{MC_{\text{sim}} \cup \{mc\}} \\ 1, & \overline{\mathbf{z}}_{\text{sim}} > \overline{\hat{\mathbf{z}}}_{\text{combi}} \text{ and } \overline{\mathbf{z}}_{\text{sim}} > \overline{\hat{\mathbf{z}}}_{MC_{\text{sim}} \cup \{mc\}} \\ 0, & \text{otherwise} \end{cases} \tag{6}$$

This formulation ensures that the heuristic promotes both convergence of $\overline{\mathbf{z}}_{\text{sim}}$ toward $\overline{\hat{\mathbf{z}}}_{\text{combi}}$ and the early simulation of outlier MC-years.

To quantify the relative influence of simulating a specific mc on the final LOLE, the following impact metric is defined:

$$\text{impact}(mc) = \left| \frac{\overline{\hat{\mathbf{z}}}_{MC_{\text{sim}} \cup \{mc\}} - \overline{\hat{\mathbf{z}}}_{\text{combi}}}{\overline{\hat{\mathbf{z}}}_{\text{combi}}} \right| \tag{7}$$

Combining the decision function and impact metric, the next MC-year to simulate is chosen as the one that maximizes the product of both:

$$mc_{\text{next}} = \text{argmax}_{mc \in MC_{\text{unsim}}} \left(d(mc) \cdot \text{impact}(mc) \right) \tag{8}$$

This heuristic ensures that extreme and informative MC-years are simulated promptly, thereby accelerating convergence toward the final LOLE estimate.

4.2 Selecting the Size and Content of the First Batch

The size of the initial batch can be chosen relatively small if the metamodel supports refitting-i.e., if it is sufficient to update the model parameters using new data, rather than retraining the model from scratch.

The minimum batch size should correspond to the number of simulations that can be executed in parallel. If the computational overhead of launching new simulations with a specified number of MC-years is negligible, the batch size should ideally match the number of available parallel simulation slots.

While the metamodel is capable of leveraging the iterative process to select its own training MC-years, the initial training set must be selected manually or via random sampling. In this context, domain knowledge can be employed to guide the selection of a representative and informative range of MC-years for initial model training.

Importantly, this selection must be made prior to observing any simulation results and should rely solely on features derived from the input data. One possible strategy for selecting the initial batch involves evaluating remaining capacity and applying techniques from the field of DOE.

5 Experimental Setup

To ensure a robust evaluation of model performance, a k-fold cross-validation(CV) procedure is employed. The data is partitioned into $k = 5$ folds, each consisting of 140 MC-years. Four of the five folds are used for training and validation, while the fifth functions as a holdout set. This holdout set is not involved in any training or validation but is reserved solely for assessing and comparing model performance on a consistent dataset.

This setup allows for an investigation into how the selection of training MC-years influences model performance. If significant variability is observed across the models trained on different folds, it indicates that the choice of training data is crucial for achieving optimal predictive accuracy.

Two versions of the model are implemented:

- A *universal model*, trained on the complete dataset across all MAs. This version applies undersampling, preserving all MPE cases and only 4% of non-MPEs.
- An *ensemble of region-specific models*, trained individually for each MA. These models are trained sequentially because the data are partitioned by region, which eliminates the need for undersampling due to data imbalance.

6 Metamodel Topology Development

In the preliminary phase of evaluating the classification model selection and hyperparameter optimization process, the models that emerged from a comprehensive exploration are presented. These models are subsequently thoroughly assessed for their performance as an ensemble model. The model that demonstrates the best performance is then evaluated embedded in the metamodel pipeline in combination with a scaling model.

6.1 Grid Search on Different Models

The most promising model hyperparameter combinations after training and evaluating over 500 models from four model types are

- two support vector classifiers with polynomial kernels of degree two and seven,
- an multi layer perceptron (MLP) with one hidden layer having 20 neurons, and
- a logistic regression classifier.

6.2 Comparing Model Types as Regional Ensemble Learners

The models that emerged from the grid search are assembled as an ensemble learner, with one specialized model for each MA. The four models are evaluated on the full dataset. The results of the ensemble models for the datasets `t+1` can be seen in Fig. 3. The color and size represent the F_1-score of each regional model. The scores labeled AGG on the x-axis are the scores aggregated over all regions. It is important to note that the aggregated F_1-score is not simply the mean of the regional F_1-scores. Rather, it is calculated using the sum of the true positives, true negatives, false positives, and false negatives over all MAs.

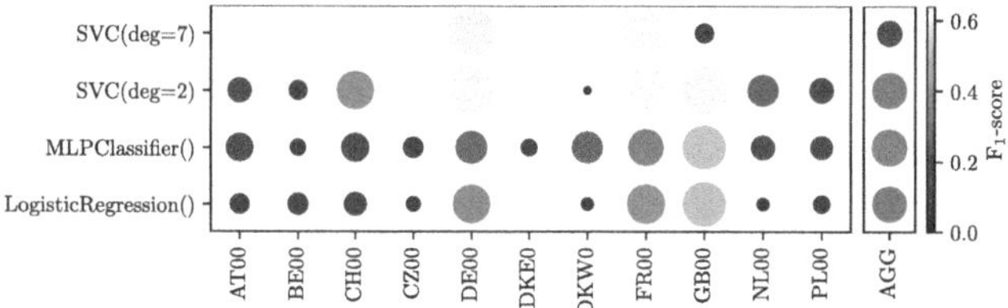

Fig. 3. Holdout F_1-score for regional ensemble learner (`t+1`).

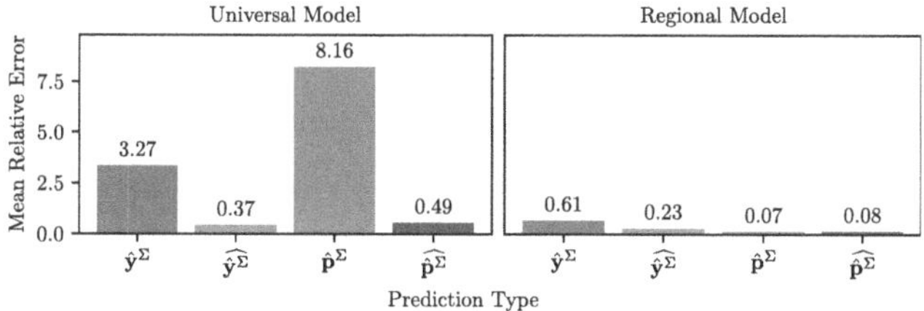

Fig. 4. Relative error using the full metamodels trained on 20% of the data. The final prediction combines the target of the training set and the predicted target or target probability of the validation and holdout set on `t+1`.

The final classification model is a support vector classifier with a polynomial kernel of degree two. Both model variants are evaluated using the k-fold CV approach, resulting in four cross-validation models (CVM 14).

A comparison of the relative error regarding the CVMs in predicting the final LOLE for different configurations of the metamodel pipeline in Fig. 4 shows that scaling effects are more pronounced in the less effective classification model (the universal model). The optimal configuration involves utilizing the regional model and its unscaled probability prediction, $\hat{\mathbf{p}}^{\Sigma}$. However, the differences between the unscaled and scaled probability predictions for the regional model are minimal. The universal model without scaling demonstrates a relative error of more than 300% or 800%, respectively. Such inaccuracy renders the universal classification model without scaling unsuitable for practical application.

Figure 5 and 6 present the relative error of the final LOLE predictions per MA.

Figure 5 illustrates the performance of the regional ensemble classification model trained via grid search and evaluated using unscaled predicted targets ($\hat{\mathbf{y}}^{\Sigma}$).

In contrast, Fig. 6 shows the results of the region-specific ensemble learner that predicts the probability of an MPE, followed by a scaling model to estimate the final LOLE ($\widehat{\hat{\mathbf{p}}^{\Sigma}}$). This approach achieves an average relative error of less than 10% across the four CVMs and regions, while using only 20% of the data.

This result demonstrates that even with limited simulated data, the metamodel can deliver highly accurate LOLE estimates when appropriate modeling strategies are used, such as regional specialization and scaling.

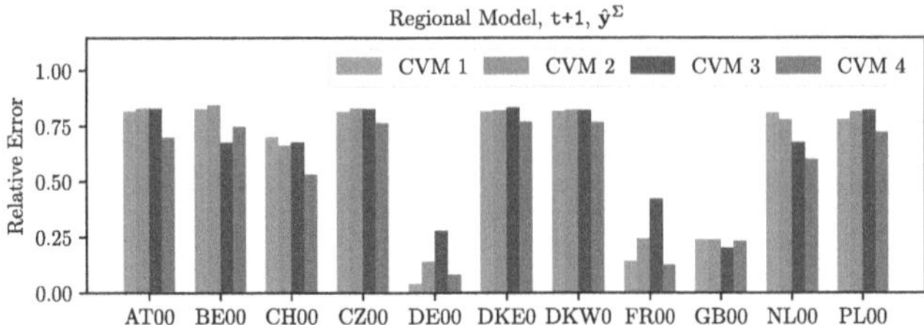

Fig. 5. Relative error of the final prediction using $\hat{\mathbf{y}}^{\Sigma}$ (combining the target of the training set $\mathbf{y}^{\Sigma}$ with the unscaled predicted target $\hat{\mathbf{y}}^{\Sigma}$ of the validation and holdout sets) for the CVMs on `t+1`.

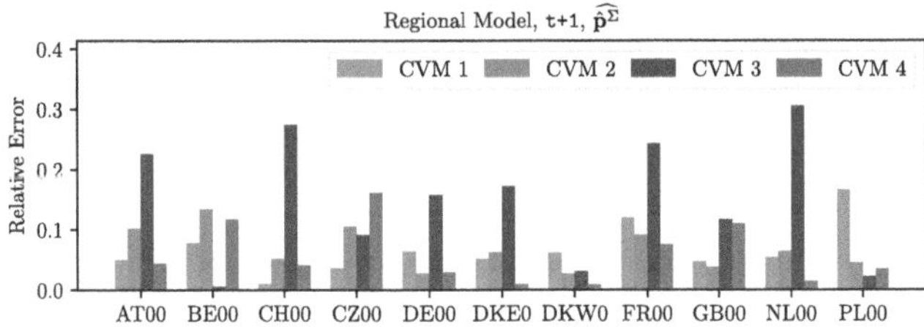

Fig. 6. Relative error of the final prediction using $\widehat{\mathbf{p}}^{\Sigma}$ (combining the target of the training set $\mathbf{y}^{\Sigma}$ with the scaled predicted probability $\widehat{\mathbf{p}}^{\Sigma}$ of the validation and holdout sets) of the CVMs on `t+1`.

6.3 Evaluation of Iterative Guided Convergence for Early Stopping

To evaluate the effectiveness of the algorithm outlined in Sect. 4, the convergence of the LOLE is analyzed by sorting the MC-years chronologically according to CY and OS.

Figures 7 and 8 compare the guided convergence performance of different prediction metrics for universal and regional models. For the universal model, it is evident that scaling substantially improves prediction accuracy. In contrast, all metrics in the regional model perform adequately, except for $\widehat{\mathbf{y}}^{\Sigma}$, which shows notable deviation.

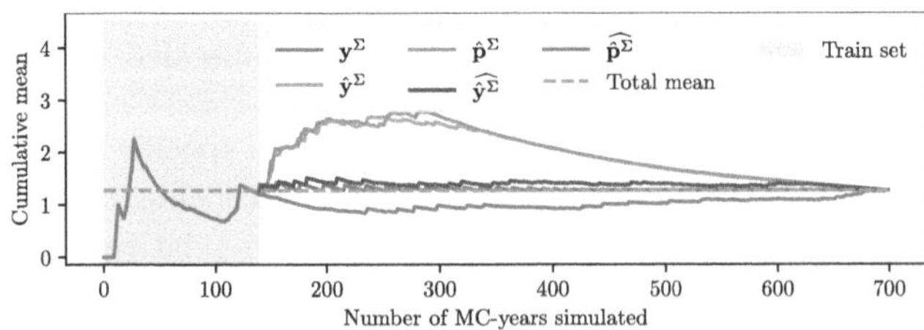

Fig. 7. Cumulative and total mean; MC-years sorted by heuristic for `DE00`; comparison of different prediction metrics for the universal model (CVM 1) on `t+1`.

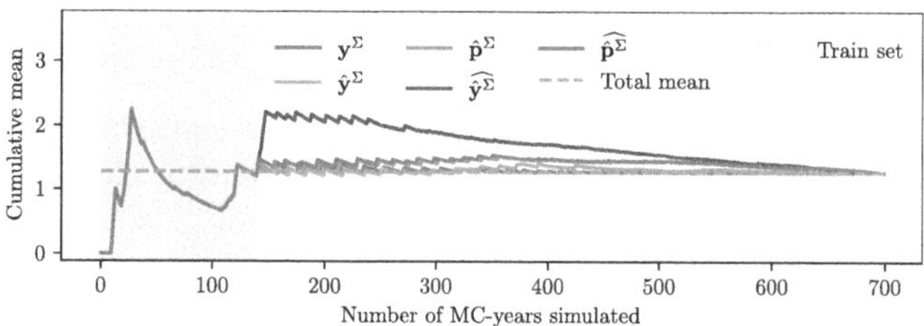

Fig. 8. Cumulative and total mean; MC-years sorted by heuristic for `DE00`; comparison of different prediction metrics for the regional model (CVM 1) on `t+1`.

These results confirm that the convergence guidance algorithm performs reliably in conjunction with real metamodels. Nonetheless, further exploration is needed to determine whether iterative guided convergence can reduce the required training set to less than 20% by allowing the metamodel to select its training samples dynamically.

6.4 Computational Complexity

The reduction in computational effort is directly related to the number of MC-years that must be simulated and the training time required for the metamodels.

Using 140 MC-years as an upper bound for training, the minimum achievable computational savings can be estimated. For model training, the universal and regional metamodels must be considered separately. The universal model requires only one training procedure, while the regional model necessitates the sequential training of 11 models (one per MA).). Training time for the regional model increases proportionally unless executed in parallel.

Simulating all 700 MC-years requires roughly 144 h (six days). By reducing the simulation scope to 140 MC-years (20%), the total simulation time decreases to about 28.8 h (1.2 days). Model training on this reduced dataset takes approximately 20 min for the universal model and 3.3 h for the regional models. Inference on the remaining 560 MC years requires an additional 1 h for either model type.

The computational time saved is then:

$$\frac{144h - (28.8h + 0.33h + 1h)}{144h} \approx 79\% \tag{9}$$

for the universal model, and

$$\frac{144h - (28.8h + 3.3h + 1h)}{144h} \approx 77\% \tag{10}$$

for the regional model.

These savings highlight the substantial efficiency gains achieved through guided convergence and metamodeling.

7 Conclusion and Discussion

The most effective and robust pipeline configuration consists of three components: a regional ensemble classification model predicting the probabilities of MPEs as the output and an aggregation step. We could also demonstrate that incorporating our linear regression as an additional step in the metamodelling pipeline can significantly improve predictions, especially for the universal model. While using squared loss in the scaling step may lead to a higher MAE, it is preferred because it better penalizes large errors, ensuring that extreme and critical scenarios are not overlooked.

The iterative guided convergence method introduced in this work demonstrates strong potential, particularly as a framework for active learning. By prioritizing the simulation of MC-years that diverge most from already simulated ones, the method effectively identifies data points with high information content. This makes the approach ideal for generating meaningful training data in an efficient and targeted manner. It is important to emphasize that metamodeling does not replace traditional MC simulations. Instead, it serves as a complementary tool that can reduce the number of necessary simulations. Since the metamodel must be trained on already simulated data, its effectiveness is contingent on the availability and quality of those initial simulations. Future studies could improve data preprocessing by incorporating techniques such as principal component analysis (PCA). PCA has the potential to reduce data dimensionality while retaining most of the variance, thereby speeding up model training and decreasing data storage requirements with minimal loss in accuracy.

Furthermore, temporal features, including rolling window aggregations, have the potential to be further developed in order to quantify the impact of renewable energy droughts on system adequacy. It can be proposed that the optimisation of the window length may yield further enhancements, with the objective of maximising correlation with system stress events.

The classification component of the metamodel could be enhanced by exploring advanced ML models, including deep neural networks. The scaling model also offers room for improvement. Although a linear model was used in this work, more complex models such as polynomial regression could better capture nonlinear relationships. Nevertheless, the risk of overfitting must be given due consideration. Alternatively, the adoption of a regional ensemble approach for scaling, similar to the classification stage, might yield performance gains without sacrificing generalizability.

References

1. Fernandez, R.M.: Conflicting energy policy priorities in EU energy governance. J. Environ. Stud. Sci. **8**(3), 239–248 (2018). ISSN 2190-6483, 2190-6491. https://doi.org/10.1007/s13412-018-0499-0. Accessed 18 Mar 2025
2. Marhold, A.-A.: Towards a 'security-centred' energy transition: balancing the European Union's ambitions and geopolitical realities. J. Int. Econ. Law **26**(4), 756–769 (2024). ISSN 1369-3034, 1464-3758. https://doi.org/10.1093/jiel/jgad043. https://academic.oup.com/jiel/article/26/4/756/7479918. Accessed 18 Feb 2025
3. Methodology for the European resource adequacy assessment. ACER, 2 October 2020. https://www.acer.europa.eu/sites/default/files/documents/Individual%20Decisions_annex/ACER%20Decision%2024-2020%20on%20ERAA%20-%20Annex%20I_1.pdf. Accessed 23 Oct 2024
4. Köhnen, C.S., et al.: The potential of deep learning to reduce complexity in energy system modeling. Int. J. Energy Res. **46**(4) (2022), 4550–4571. ISSN 0363-907X, 1099-114X. https://doi.org/10.1002/er.7448. https://onlinelibrary.wiley.com/doi/10.1002/er.7448. Accessed 16 Oct 2024
5. Starke, A.R., Da Silva, A.K.: A review on the applicability of machine learning techniques to the metamodeling of energy systems. Numer. Heat Transf. Part B Fundam., 1–30 (2023). ISSN 1040-7790, 1521-0626. https://doi.org/10.1080/10407790.2023.2280208. https://www.tandfonline.com/doi/full/10.1080/10407790.2023.2280208. Accessed 16 Oct 2024
6. Rahman, Md.M., et al.: Prospective methodologies in hybrid renewable energy systems for energy prediction using artificial neural networks. Sustainability **13**(4), 2393 (2021). ISSN 2071-1050. https://doi.org/10.3390/su13042393. https://www.mdpi.com/2071-1050/13/4/2393 (visited on 03/12/2025)
7. Donti, P.L., Zico Kolter, J.: Machine learning for sustainable energy systems. Ann. Rev. Environ. Res. **46**(1), 719–747 (2021). ISSN 1543-5938, 1545-2050. https://doi.org/10.1146/annurev-environ-020220-061831. https://www.annualreviews.org/doi/10.1146/annurev-environ-020220-061831. Accessed 16 Oct 2024
8. Duchesne, L., Karangelos, E., Wehenkel, L.: Recent developments in machine learning for energy systems reliability management. Proc. IEEE **108**(9), 1656–1676 (2020). ISSN 0018-9219, 1558-2256. https://doi.org/10.1109/JPROC.2020.2988715. https://ieeexplore.ieee.org/document/9091534/. Accessed 12 Mar 2025
9. Sun, Y., et al.: Local feature sufficiency exploration for predicting security-constrained generation dispatch in multi-area power systems. In: 2018 17th IEEE International Conference on Machine Learning and Applications (ICMLA), Orlando, FL, December 2018, pp. 1283–1289. IEEE (2018). ISSN 9781538668054. https://doi.org/10.1109/ICMLA.2018.00208. https://ieeexplore.ieee.org/document/8614233/. Accessed 12 Mar 2025
10. Su, H., et al.: An integrated, systematic data-driven supply-demand side management method for smart integrated energy systems. Energy **235**, 121416 (2021). ISSN 03605442. https://doi.org/10.1016/j.energy.2021.121416. https://linkinghub.elsevier.com/retrieve/pii/S0360544221016649. Accessed 12 Mar 2025
11. Leonori, S., et al.: Microgrid energy management systems design by computational intelligence techniques. Appl. Energy **277**, 115524 (2020). ISSN 03062619. https://doi.org/10.1016/j.apenergy.2020.115524. http://linkinghub.elsevier.com/retrieve/pii/S0306261920310369. Accessed 12 Mar 2025
12. Huang, Y., Xu, Q., Lin, G.: Congestion risk-averse stochastic unit commitment with transmission reserves in wind-thermal power systems. Appl. Sci. **8**(10), 1726

(2018). ISSN 2076-3417. https://doi.org/10.3390/app8101726. http://www.mdpi.com/2076-3417/8/10/1726. Accessed 12 Mar 2025

13. Darville, J., Curia, J., Celik, N.: Microgrid operational planning using a hybrid neural network with resource-aware scenario selection. Simul. Model. Pract. Theor. **119**, 102583 (2022). ISSN 1569190X. https://doi.org/10.1016/j.simpat.2022.102583. http://linkinghub.elsevier.com/retrieve/pii/S1569190X22000715. Accessed 23 Oct 2024
14. Bogensperger, A.J., Fabel, Y., Ferstl, J.: Accelerating energy-economic simulation models via machine learning-based emulation and time series aggregation. Energies **15**(3), 1239 (2022). ISSN 1996-1073. https://doi.org/10.3390/en15031239. http://www.mdpi.com/1996-1073/15/3/1239. Accessed 23 Oct 2024
15. Hoffmann, M., et al.: A review on time series aggregation methods for energy system models. Energies **13**(3), 641 (2020). ISSN 1996-1073. https://doi.org/10.3390/en13030641. http://www.mdpi.com/1996-1073/13/3/641. Accessed 24 Oct 2024
16. Perera, A.T.D., et al.: Machine learning methods to assist energy system optimization. Appl. Energy **243**, 191–205 (2019). ISSN 03062619. https://doi.org/10.1016/j.apenergy.2019.03.202. http://linkinghub.elsevier.com/retrieve/pii/S030626191930618X. Accessed 12 Mar 2025
17. Prina, M.G., et al.: Machine learning as a surrogate model for EnergyPLAN: speeding up energy system optimization at the country level. Energy **307**, 132735 (2024). ISSN 03605442. https://doi.org/10.1016/j.energy.2024.132735. http://linkinghub.elsevier.com/retrieve/pii/S036054422402509X. Accessed 23 Oct 2024
18. Danish, M.S.S.: A framework for modeling and optimization of data-driven energy systems using machine learning. IEEE Trans. Artif. Intell. **5**(5), 2434–2443 (2024). ISSN 2691-4581. https://doi.org/10.1109/TAI.2023.3322395. http://ieeexplore.ieee.org/document/10273612/. Accessed 23 Oct 2024
19. Kim, M.J., et al.: Neural-network-based optimization for economic dispatch of combined heat and power systems. Appl. Energy **265**, 114785 (2020). ISSN 03062619. https://doi.org/10.1016/j.apenergy.2020.114785. http://linkinghub.elsevier.com/retrieve/pii/S030626192030297X. Accessed 23 Oct 2024
20. Nolting, L., et al.: Can energy system modeling benefit from artificial neural networks? Application of two-stage metamodels to reduce computation of security of supply assessments. Comput. Ind. Eng. **142**, 106334 (2020). ISSN 03608352. https://doi.org/10.1016/j.cie.2020.106334. http://linkinghub.elsevier.com/retrieve/pii/S0360835220300681. Accessed 21 Oct 2024
21. Priesmann, J., Nolting, L., Praktiknjo, A.: Are complex energy system models more accurate? An intra-model comparison of power system optimization models. Appl. Energy **255**, 113783 (2019). ISSN 03062619. https://doi.org/10.1016/j.apenergy.2019.113783. http://linkinghub.elsevier.com/retrieve/pii/S0306261919314709. Accessed 24 Oct 2024
22. Nolting, L., Praktiknjo, A.: The complexity dilemma – insights from security of electricity supply assessments. Energy **241**, 122522 (2022). ISSN 03605442. https://doi.org/10.1016/j.energy.2021.122522. http://linkinghub.elsevier.com/retrieve/pii/S0360544221027717. Accessed 23 Oct 2024
23. Billinton, R., Allan, R.N.: Reliability Evaluation of Power Systems. Springer, Boston (1996). ISBN 9781489918628 9781489918604. https://doi.org/10.1007/978-1-4899-1860-4. http://link.springer.com/10.1007/978-1-4899-1860-4. Accessed 31 Oct 2024

24. Münch, J., et al.: Uplifting the complexity of analysis for probabilistic security of electricity supply assessments using artificial neural networks. Energy AI **17**, 100401 (2024). ISSN 26665468. https://doi.org/10.1016/j.egyai.2024.100401. http://linkinghub.elsevier.com/retrieve/pii/S2666546824000673. Accessed 23 Oct 2024
25. Gonzato, S., Bruninx, K., Delarue, E.: The effect of short term storage operation on resource adequacy. Sustain. Energy Grids Netw. **34**, 101005 (2023)
26. Fraunholz, C., et al.: Demand curtailment allocation in interconnected electricity markets. Appl. Energy **377**, 124679 (2025)
27. Settles, B.: Active Learning. Synthesis Lectures on Artificial Intelligence and Machine Learning. Springer, Cham (2012). 9783031004322. https://doi.org/10.1007/978-3-031-01560-1. http://link.springer.com/10.1007/978-3-031-01560-1. Accessed 25 Oct 2024
28. Settles, B.: Active learning literature survey (2009). http://www.semanticscholar.org/paper/Active-Learning-Literature-Survey-Settles/818826f356444f3daa3447755bf63f171f39ec47. Accessed 25 Oct 2024

Track Almost Everything Underwater: Evaluating Visual Registration in Marine Robotics

Muhammad Waqar Mughal(✉), Muhammad Hamza Hussain, Arturo Gomez Chavez, Andreas Birk, and Francesco Maurelli

Constructor University Bremen, Bremen, Germany
{mmughal,mhussain,agomezchav,abirk,fmaurelli}@constructor.university

Abstract. This study presents a benchmark for evaluating visual correspondence algorithms in underwater environments using both optical and sonar imaging. It analyzes the transferability of state-of-the-art feature matching methods designed initially for terrestrial data, under the specific challenges of marine sensing. Experiments on real and simulated datasets assess their accuracy, robustness, and downstream impact on visual odometry and image mosaicing. The findings highlight key limitations in generalization and provide insights toward developing more trustworthy perception systems for autonomous underwater robots (This work was supported in part by the Deutsche Forschungsgemeinschaft (DFG, German Research Foundation) - project number 535678995.).

Keywords: Marine robotics · Computer vision · Underwater imaging · Benchmarking · Robust AI deployment

1 Introduction

Autonomous marine systems increasingly rely on vision-based perception for navigation, mapping, and intervention. Yet most state-of-the-art algorithms are designed and validated on terrestrial datasets, with limited consideration for underwater phenomena such as turbidity, light backscatter, color attenuation [1], and sonar-specific distortions [27]. These factors expose critical barriers to model transferability that undermine the reliability of AI models when deployed in operational settings.

In order to bring more insights into this challenge, and to verify the transferability of state-of-the-art visual correspondence algorithms, we conduct a systematic evaluation of recent "track/segment anything" architecture backbones in realistic underwater scenarios. This work benchmarks methods such as ELoFTR [26], LightGlue [15] that share the same attention mechanisms as foundational models in the pursue of achieving task agnostic visual capabilities, i.e., learning representations that generalize across scenes and conditions. Comparisons are made against traditional methods and tailor-made models for the most typical sensor modalities in underwater applications: optical cameras and imaging sonars, using real-world datasets. Beyond algorithmic evaluation, this

L. Martínez-Villaseñor et al. (Eds.): MICAI 2025, LNAI 16265, pp. 228–241, 2026.
https://doi.org/10.1007/978-3-032-17933-3_23

research assesses the impact of feature matching quality on downstream tasks such as visual odometry and image mosaicing, and insights from lessons learned and tackled challenges during field trials and deployments are discusses.

This work contributions are: (1) a structured benchmark for feature matching algorithms in optical and sonar underwater datasets, (2) an analysis on their weaknesses and strengths under the specific underwater challenges, i.e., particular image distortions and sensor geometries, and (3) a examination on how feature matching performance impacts downstream applications related to navigation and mapping. By contextualizing algorithmic performance with respect to system-level reliability, this work seeks to bring clarity on how widespread algorithms perform on niche scenarios and the technical challenges to be overcome to integrate them robustly. All this to advance robust and trustworthy AI deployment in complex real-world systems.

2 Related Work

As with terrestrial or airborne applications, most underwater perception and navigation systems are based on vision and registration algorithms, aided by acoustic systems. The stability of the registrations between observed scenes contributes to the overall accuracy of down-stream tasks, whether the goal is to recreate a 2D/3D scene, perform visual odometry, or register an image mosaic. Nevertheless, the underwater environment presents its own set of problems: the varying attenuation of different color wavelengths, light scattering, turbidity, and poor visibility may all negatively affect the quality of an image. Consequently, researchers have investigated various sensing modalities such as optical and sonar imaging each with its own strengths, weaknesses, and processing policies.

2.1 Underwater Optical Images

In general, at first, underwater feature matching focused greatly on image preprocessing and enhancement through methods such as Contrast-Limited Adaptive Histogram Equalization (CLAHE) and Retinex normalization [11]. Then, To further improve the image quality, physics-based enhancement algorithms like Sea-Thru [2] and WaterGAN [13] restore color wavelength attenuation and contrast, substantially eliminating light backscatter and making images to appear "airborne". Since 2021, a number of transformer-based models have been suggested and show impressive performance in terms of restoring color fidelity, contrast, and structural details in underwater images. Models like U-Shape Transformer [18], diffusion-based transformers [23], ViT-ClarityNet [6] and foundational backbones for dense predictions like ViT-UWA [14] have shown impressive improvements in perceptual quality and geometric consistency with images that enhance downstream feature detection and odometry accuracy.

2.2 Sonar Images

In cases when optical sensors cannot work correctly due to poor visibility or darkness, sonar imaging os the preferred sensor. Forward-Looking Sonar (FLS) and Side-Scan Sonar (SSS) provide acoustic intensity maps that record geometry even in total darkness. It has been well studied that traditional optical image features such as SIFT [16] and ORB [21] do not perform well in sonar images, as inherently these have different geometries and high changes in appearances dependent on the viewpoint. Works similar to Shin et al. [22] utilized AKAZE features along anisotropic diffusion techniques for noise reduction. Just recently, deep learning based features have been proposed for sonar images. For example, pose-supervised learning for FLS correspondence [8], which produces descriptors robust to significant viewpoint changes, and the work in [5] trained compact sonar descriptors on simulated data. Both demonstrating strong generalization to real-world environments and robustness against noise and appearance change.

On the other hand, registration methods that operate in the frequency domain are also known as basis for robust methods in general [3,24]. The combination of the Fourier Transform for translation estimation and the SO(3)-Fourier-Transform (SOFT) for rotation estimation is inherently robust against illumination changes and scale invariant, commonly this method is known as "Fourier-SOFT in 2D (FS2D)" and has also been applied to data from a mechanically scanning sonar (MSS) [10]. Frequently, sonar imaging is complementary to optical vision and has inspired new multi-modal pipelines where sonar provides coarse alignment, and optical features refine local motion.

2.3 SOTA Image Features

Given the rise of machine learning in computer vision for generating problem-specific features, this research studies these methods for comparative benchmarks. Efficient LoFTR (E-LoFTR) [26] is a lightweight variant of the Local Feature TRansformer (LoFTR) keypoint or detector-free feature matcher; designed to preserve high matching accuracy while significantly reducing computational cost. It achieves this through an efficient transformer backbone and coarse-to-fine matching strategy, which focuses attention computation on informative regions only. LightGlue [15] is a lightweight, attention-based feature matcher that dynamically adapts its computation to the image pair's difficulty, achieving real-time performance. However, unlike E-LoFTR, LightGlue still requires image keypoints to match. For this, SuperPoint [4] is commonly used to find interest pixels in the image. SONIC [8] is a deep neural network specifically developed matching imaging sonar data. This includes especially the effects of the viewpoint dependent appearance of scene elements from this type of device [12,17]. Building on a ResNet-34 base, design elements from the CAmera Pose Supervised (CAPS) network [25] are combined in SONIC, along novel formulations of the loss functions that take into account the special viewpoint dependent appearances of sonar images and their specific epipolar geometry.

3 Methodology

As motivated in Sect. 1, this work benchmarks the performance of different SOTA methods in underwater scenarios with different sensor modalities and application goals. Overall, the experiments cover two categories: 1) comparison of image feature matching performance and 2) impact measurement of feature matching in down-stream applications. For the first category we used two sensor modalities, optical and sonar sensors, as motivated in Sect. 2 that states these are the preferred options in marine robotics. The main goal is to analyze how the SOTA methods from Sect. 2.3 perform across different modalities which follow different geometrical image formation models. Then, to contextualize this in real-world scenarios, this work analyzes two field trial applications in underwater robotics: visual odometry navigation and sonar image mosaicing. Likewise, optical and sonar modalities were chosen to analyze differences in behavior and to monitor the algorithms robustness in conditions outside typical training sets that are more prone to noise and unseen data.

4 Experiments and Results

4.1 Feature Matching

Stereo Images. A subset of the FLSea underwater stereo dataset [20] is used, as it is one of the most comprehensive datasets found in literature. It offers ground truth depth maps underwater based on specialized photogrammetry and validated with reference measurements in the sensed environment. The dataset reports a depth mean error estimation of 18.2[cm] and median of 3.3[cm], which indicates outliers influence that this works avoids by discarding matches in zones with rapid depth variation. For this test, 3803 images from the five different scenarios with a different range of visibilities, light conditions, man-made objects and dynamic camera motions are used.

As shown in Fig. 1 and Table 1, ELoFTR demonstrates the best overall performance with the least mean, median, and variance, while also producing the highest number of valid matches. The interquartile range (IQR) indicates that 50% of matches fall within a relatively tight error band, though the mean being notably higher than the median reveals a right-skewed distribution with some high-error outliers pulling the average up. SuperPoint + LightGlue achieves similar accuracy characteristics with comparable distribution shape, though it produces significantly fewer matches. ORB shows a more symmetric distribution, as the mean is closer to the median, and with moderate spread IQR and valid matches.

The distribution analysis reveals important insights: AKAZE exhibits highly problematic right-skewed distribution with extremely long tail. AKAZE's mean nearly doubles its median, with a massive IQR, indicating frequent catastrophic matching failures. SuperPoint + SONIC does not show a high increase in error, however it still ranks fourth and has one of the lowers inlier retention rates. The large gap between Q3 and Q4 across all methods indicates that all algorithms occasionally produce extreme outliers, but ELoFTR and SuperPoint +

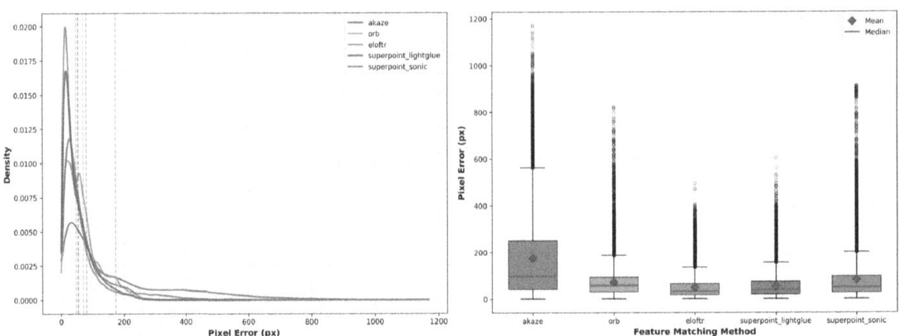

Fig. 1. Stereo feature matching (Left) pixel error distribution, (Right) boxplots.

Table 1. Stereo Feature Matching Statistics (Units in Pixels)

Method	Mean	Median	Mode	Variance	IQR	Matches
AKAZE	173.64	96.77	32.93	180.51	208.42	92,088
ORB	70.99	57.91	19.97	56.85	62.73	150,372
ELoFTR	**48.61**	**32.34**	**14.84**	**46.83**	**47.45**	**353,358**
Superpoint+LightGlue	54.77	38.35	16.46	50.30	54.62	100,552
Superpoint+Sonic	81.37	49.27	27.26	91.65	69.68	55,357

Table 2. Sonar Feature Matching Statistics (Units in Pixels)

Method	Mean	Median	Mode	Variance	IQR	Matches
AKAZE	26.64	13.07	10.06	48.51	15.11	69,476
ORB	19.04	14.97	10.91	**18.82**	13.92	62,561
ELoFTR	21.89	15.55	9.03	24.22	18.62	**933,429**
Superpoint+LightGlue	20.19	15.06	11.48	20.83	15.82	272,335
Superpoint+Sonic	**17.78**	**12.27**	**8.70**	27.49	**12.67**	704,133

LightGlue maintain tighter error bounds for the majority (75%) of matches. This makes ELoFTR the most reliable choice for stereo matching in underwater environments, offering both the lowest median error and the most consistent performance across the distribution.

Sonar Images. Imaging sonar datasets exist [28], but they primarily deal with object detection/classification and, thus, lack accurate or complete localization or pose ground truth. Therefore, for this test, synthetic data from different environments, e.g., dam, open-sea, etc., in the HoloOcean simulator [19] is collected, where a precise ground truth can be easily obtained. Concretely, $\sim 5K$ sonar image pairs are generated for the experimental evaluations. The simulator is configured to use the Blueprint Subsea M1200d sonar in low frequency mode, with an elevation angle of 20°, an azimuthal field of view 130°, and a maximum range of 10 m. The resultant image is then formed by 512 × 512 range and bearings bins.

The results are shown in Table 2. Superpoint+Sonic demonstrates the best overall performance with a mean pixel, showing a moderately right-skewed distribution and the tightest IQR. It also produces by the most matches after ELoFTR, making it the optimal choice for dense sonar-based reconstruction and visual odometry tasks. Remarkably, the traditional feature ORB achieves the second-best accuracy with mean, displaying excellent consistency with a low IQR and the lowest standard deviation among all methods, though it produces significantly fewer matches. AKAZE exhibits the poorest performance also in this test. This suggests that the learning-based sonar geometry of SONIC drastically improve its performance in this domain. On the other hand, ELoFTR and LightGlue, although not the most accurate, still produce high number of matches which stems from the fact that their design was meant for dense image reconstruction. Figure 2 shows that both ELoFTR and SONIC perform robustly in their sensor modality domain but have some biases coming from their training methodology or domain dataset.

4.2 Underwater Visual Odometry

Visual odometry (VO) is the process whereby the motion trajectory of a robot is estimated by studying the series of images recorded by an onboard camera. VO is crucial for facilitating autonomous navigation in underwater conditions where GPS signals are absent, and acoustic positioning systems are either costly or unable to cover a vast distance. This research compared underwater VO in two complementary proposals: a training-based model, where the feature extractor network is initially trained on representative sequences from the target domain, and a non-training-based model, where the model is not trained and is applied directly. The goal is to estimate the robustness of backbone models and the impact of sampling data of the target domain in underwater scenarios.

Dataset. To carry out this assessment, this research used the AQUALOC [7] dataset, which is among the limited publicly available resources that focus on underwater localization studies. The data set gives synchronized information from a monocular camera, inertial measurement unit (IMU), and Doppler Velocity Log (DVL). This multimodal configuration is capable of testing vision-only pipelines and sensor fusion techniques. There are sequences present in AQUALOC that were recorded in two different depths: shallow waters of a few meters and deep-sea trials of around 270 m. In shallow water, reflections and suspended particles frequently alter the lighting conditions, whereas in deep water, poor contrast and low illumination prevail. The next feature of AQUALOC is that it offers quality ground-truth trajectories of a precision acoustic positioning system. This facilitates a stringent assessment of visual odometry data.

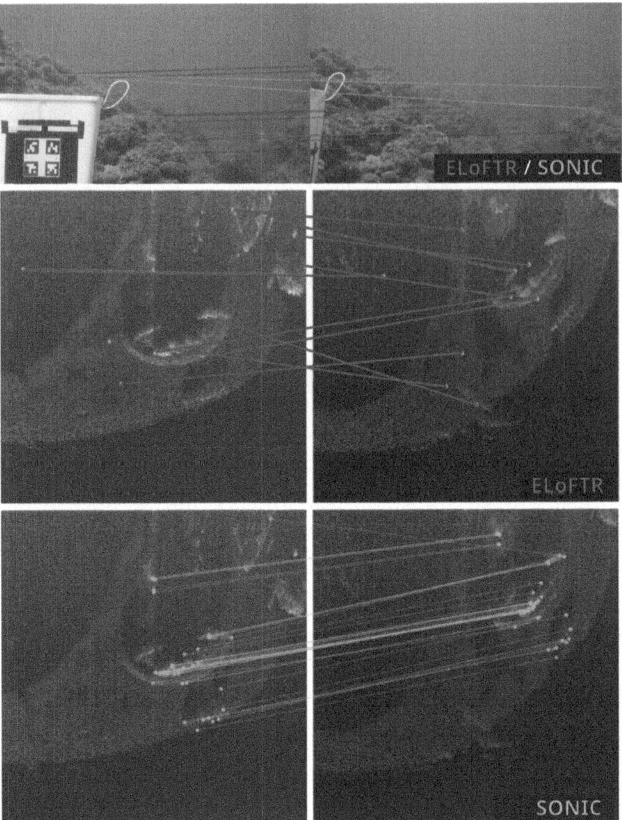

Fig. 2. ELoFTR is unable to match features in sonar images when the objects' shape warps, common in polar images. SONIC is able to find the match but tends to produce more outliers in optical images.

Training Setup. For the training-based experiments, three representative sequences were selected from each group of the dataset, one of which was a harbor and the others an archaeological site. It was applied to the Vision-MAMBA feature extractor [9], which is a deep learning model used to learn spatial and temporal correlations in image data. The architecture is favorable to underwater images, where classical feature detectors can be impaired by noise, turbidity, and dynamically changing lighting.

The training took place on a workstation with 32 GB of memory, an NVIDIA GeForce 2070 GTX graphics card, and an Intel Core i7 processor. In the process of training, the network learned how to extract discriminative features that remain unchanged when the lighting, scale, or perspective is altered. The remaining sequences were held back to be evaluated after the training results, to examine the network's ability to generalize to unseen data. The training dataset sequences ranged from a few thousand to over seventeen thousand frames

Training-Based Feature Matching and Visual Odometry. Mamba uses a selective state-space model (SSM) backbone; for vision, the common variant is Vision Mamba (ViM), whose default public checkpoints are pretrained on ImageNet-1K for supervised classification. After training the feature extractor, it was then applied to the test sequences. The trained network detected features in stored image frames, and correspondences between pairs of consecutive image frames were made by comparing features in each frame. In a single frame, the Vision-MAMBA model could identify approximately three hundred good matches, demonstrating its ability to detect a rich and repeatable combination of points as shown in Fig. 3.

The matched features were then input into a geometric solver, and essential matrix decomposition with RANSAC was applied to estimate relative camera poses and eliminate mismatches. The relative poses were then chained to rebuild the entire path of the robot.

The training-based Vision-MAMBA system produced features that were more robust in underwater conditions characterized by shifts in illumination and texture scarcity, unlike the ORB-SLAM3, which operates using traditional feature-based algorithms. Consequently, the trajectories computed by this system were similar to the ground truth, as shown in Fig. 4. An example of this is in a series of tests, where the anticipated course was practically identical to the reference course presented by the acoustic positioning system. This finding indicates the accuracy and generalization capability of the training-based method.

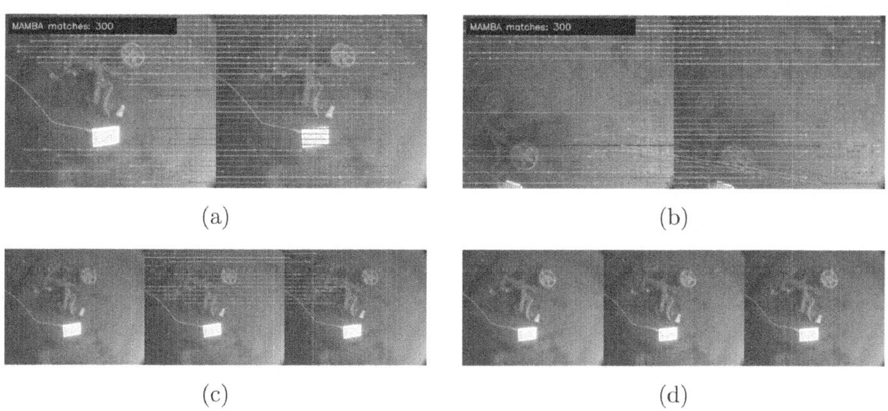

Fig. 3. (a) and (b) show the feature matching and tracking using the MAMBA-trained model, and (c) and (d) shows feature tracking and matching without any training, almost no features were matched.

Non-training Based Feature Matching and Visual Odometry. In this step, the research tested the performance of the MAMBA model without any prior training to assess its impact on the entire system. The raw model was applied directly to the image sequences, attempting to extract and match features between consecutive frames. The number of detected features was, however, far less than in the trained version due to the absence of learned representations. It is a relatively small number of correspondences that served as the input for the visual odometry pipeline. Figure 4 shows that the rarity of the features that were extracted often led to the disturbance of the trajectory estimation. In some frames, the model did not identify any features that could be considered reliable, leading to a break in the visual odometry. In the cases where features were repeated in later frames, the system tried to reconstruct motion estimation, which usually resulted in a sudden change of trajectory. This recovery pattern brought about abrupt turns or deviations of the real direction taken by the robot.

To better analyze this behavior, this research compared feature extraction with varying detection thresholds and studied the resulting trajectories, as can be seen in the Fig. 4. These experiments validated the assertion that the MAMBA model generates unstable feature correspondences without training, leading to inaccurate and unreliable visual odometry. The results indicate the need for a training stage to acquire strong features capable of sustaining constant trajectory estimation and keeping up with the actual movement of the robot.

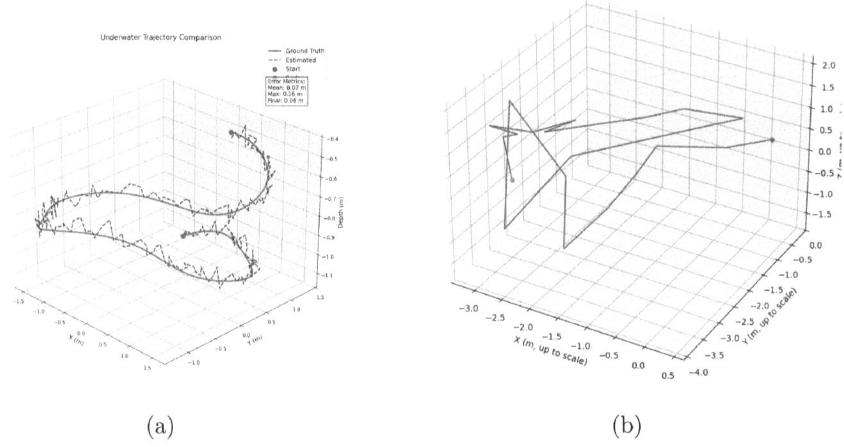

Fig. 4. (a) Represents visual odometry trajectory when trained with a subset of sequences of the target domain, and (b) when without training leading to sudden jumps or breaks in localization.

Discussion. These results bring out two important issues. To start with, underwater conditions present peculiar challenges, such as the scattering of light, turbidity, and repetitive patterns. These conditions make classical handcrafted descriptors, as well as untrained deep models, less effective. Second, training enables a network to adjust to such challenges and learns the discriminative features, which at least generalizes across scenes in the same target scenario. The findings hence confirm that a training phase is necessary when implementing visual odometry systems in actual underwater systems. The open initiative here would be to investigate whether a trained model for one underwater scenario can work in a different water body; for example, if trained model in a lake will work in open-water.

4.3 Image Mosaicing

Underwater image mosaicing is the process of stitching multiple overlapping images into a single, geometrically consistent panoramic view of the seafloor or submerged structures. It enables the creation of large-scale visual maps that provide spatial context beyond the limited field of view of individual frames. This technique is essential for marine habitat monitoring, archaeological documentation, and inspection tasks where accurate visual reconstruction supports analysis and decision-making. In this last experiment of this article, we compare the perviously more robust feature matching models from each domain, ELoFTR and SONIC, against the frequency-base method FS2D mentioned in Sect. 2.2. This in order to verify how the transformer-based architectures fare against well known mathematical models in defined environments; i.e., It is assumed that the surface vehicle is looking directly to sloped plane in a translational fashion only, i.e., with negligible rotations. This in order to compute homography matrices from the feature matches.

Dataset. Sonar data recorded with an ARIS Explorer 3000 mounted on a surface vehicle is used. The data is obtained in the context of the monitoring of bridges as critical infrastructure. Concretely, there is a check for potential scouring or log jams, which may, e.g., be caused by flooding events. Thus, 118 sonar images show a bank reinforcement with boulders at the bridge.

Discussion. In this representative example, both E-LoFTR and SONIC exhibit erroneous pose estimations arising from a considerable number of mismatched correspondences. This issue is most likely a consequence of the highly repetitive nature of the boulder field, where individual rocks share similar visual patterns—particularly at the local feature level. Such conditions are characteristic of many underwater environments, for instance, in seabeds dominated by ripple-structured sediments or covered by dense seagrass meadows. In contrast, FS2D operates in the frequency domain, enabling analysis across multiple image scales. As a result, it can establish correspondences not only between fine-scale local textures but also between entire boulders and larger spatial configurations of them.

The trajectory estimated by E-LoFTR displays a curved profile, indicative of consistent rotational errors that likely stem from the model's sensitivity to the viewpoint-dependent nature of sonar imaging data. Furthermore, both E-LoFTR and SONIC tend to underestimate the overall trajectory length, producing translation magnitudes shorter than the actual motion—an effect particularly noticeable for SONIC. This behavior is plausibly attributed to mismatched correspondences, where features from one boulder in frame i are incorrectly paired with those of another boulder located closer to the sensor in frame $i+1$. In contrast, FS2D maintains a trajectory that remains both linear and consistent with the planned and executed motion path. (Fig. 5)

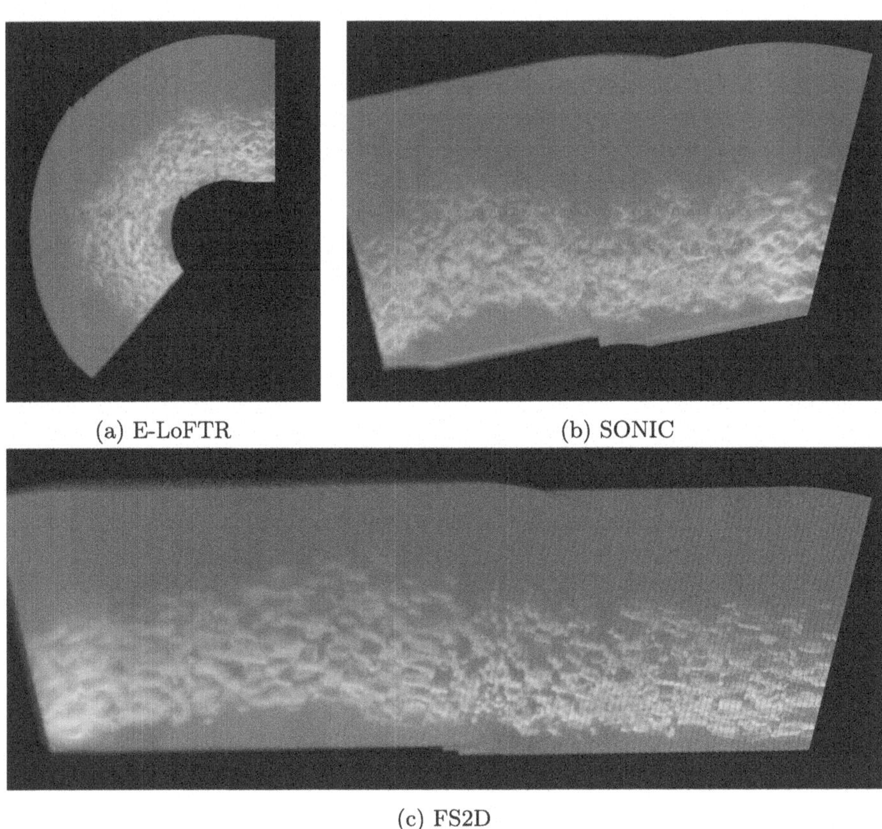

(a) E-LoFTR (b) SONIC

(c) FS2D

Fig. 5. Example results from a field tests where data from a relatively straight trajectory is used for image mosaicing. (a) E-LoFTR drifts into a curved path due to errors in the rotation estimation (b) SONIC is better in the rotation estimation, but it consistently underestimates the translation and it compresses the trajectory (c) Only FS2D captures the actual trajectory very well.

5 Conclusions

This work benchmarked multiple state-of-the-art visual registration methods across optical and sonar modalities, revealing how underwater conditions such as turbidity, repetitive textures, and geometric distortions, affect their performance. Transformer-based models like E-LoFTR achieved strong results in optical imagery, while domain-adapted networks such as SONIC outperformed others in sonar-based matching. However, all methods demonstrated reduced consistency when applied outside their training domain, underscoring the need for adaptive, cross-modal learning strategies.

Future research should focus on domain adaptation, self-supervised learning, and multi-modal fusion frameworks to improve robustness in unseen conditions. Moreover, simulation-in-the-loop (SITL) approaches and high-fidelity synthetic data generation using platforms such as Unreal Engine or NVIDIA Isaac Sim can accelerate training and testing across diverse underwater scenarios. Integrating such realistic, dynamic simulation environments with field data collection will enable continuous model validation and deployment readiness, advancing towards trustworthy and generalizable perception in autonomous marine systems.

References

1. Akkaynak, D., Treibitz, T.: A revised underwater image formation model. In: 2018 IEEE/CVF Conference on Computer Vision and Pattern Recognition, pp. 6723–6732 (2018)
2. Akkaynak, D., Treibitz, T.: Sea-thru: A method for removing water from underwater images. In: IEEE/CVF Conference on Computer Vision and Pattern Recognition (CVPR), pp. 1682–1691 (2019)
3. Bülow, H., Birk, A.: Scale-free registrations in 3D: 7 degrees of freedom with fourier-mellin-soft transforms. Int. J. Comput. Vis. (IJCV) **126**(7), 731–750 (2018)
4. DeTone, D., Malisiewicz, T., Rabinovich, A.: Superpoint: Self-supervised interest point detection and description. In: IEEE/CVF Conference on Computer Vision and Pattern Recognition Workshops (CVPRW), pp. 337–33712 (2018)
5. Donadi, I., Olivastri, E., Fusaro, D., Li, W., Evangelista, D., Pretto, A.: Improving Generalization of Synthetically Trained Sonar Image Descriptors for Underwater Place Recognition. In: Christensen, H.I., Corke, P., Detry, R., Weibel, JB., Vincze, M. (eds) Computer Vision Systems, ICVS 2023. LNCS, vol. 14253, p. 336–349. Springer, Cham. https://doi.org/10.1007/978-3-031-44137-0_28
6. Fathy, M.E., Mohamed, S.A., Awad, M.I., Munim, H.E.A.E.: A vision transformer based CNN for underwater image enhancement ViTClarityNet. Sci. Rep. **15**(1), 16768 (2025)
7. Ferrera, M., Moras, J., Trouvé-Peloux, P., Creuze, V., Dégez, D.: The aqualoc dataset: towards real-time underwater localization from a visual-inertial-pressure acquisition system (2018). https://arxiv.org/abs/1809.07076
8. Gode, S., Hinduja, A., Kaess, M.: Sonic: sonar image correspondence using pose supervised learning for imaging sonars. In: IEEE International Conference on Robotics and Automation (ICRA), pp. 3766–3772 (2024)
9. Gu, A., Dao, T.: Mamba: linear-time sequence modeling with selective state spaces (2024). arXiv preprint arXiv:2312.00752
10. Hansen, T., Birk, A.: Using registration with fourier-soft in 2D (FS2D) for robust scan matching of sonar range data. In: IEEE International Conference on Robotics and Automation (ICRA) (2023)

11. Hoque, M.Z., Keskinarkaus, A., Nyberg, P., Seppänen, T.: Retinex model based stain normalization technique for whole slide image analysis. Comput. Med. Imaging Graph. **90**, 101901 (2021)
12. Jing, D., Han, J., Zhang, J.: A method to track targets in three-dimensional space using an imaging sonar. Sensors **18**(7) (1992). https://www.mdpi.com/1424-8220/18/7/1992
13. Li, J., Skinner, K.A., Eustice, R.M., Johnson-Roberson, M.: WaterGAN: unsupervised generative network to enable real-time color correction of monocular underwater images. In: IEEE Robotics and Automation Letters p. 1 (2018)
14. Lin, Q., Li, H., Jia, Y., Li, Y., Lian, S., Liu, H., Kwong, S., Cong, R.: ViT-UWA: vision transformer underwater-adapter for dense predictions beneath the water surface (2024). https://openreview.net/forum?id=i0VqD2KaYt
15. Lindenberger, P., Sarlin, P.E., Pollefeys, M.: LightGlue: Local Feature Matching at Light Speed. In: ICCV, pp. 17627–17638 (2023)
16. Lowe, D.G.: Distinctive image features from scale-invariant keypoints. Int. J. Comput. Vision **60**(2), 91–110 (2004)
17. Negahdaripour, S.: Analyzing epipolar geometry of 2-D forward-scan sonar stereo for matching and 3-D reconstruction. In: MTS/IEEE OCEANS, pp. 1–10 (2018)
18. Peng, L., Zhu, C., Bian, L.: U-shape transformer for underwater image enhancement. IEEE Trans. Image Process. **32**, 3066–3079 (2023). https://doi.org/10.1109/TIP.2023.3276332
19. Potokar, E., Ashford, S., Kaess, M., Mangelson, J.G.: HoloOcean: an underwater robotics simulator. In: International Conference on Robotics and Automation (ICRA), pp. 3040–3046 (2022)
20. Randall, Y., Treibitz, T.: FLSea: underwater visual-inertial and stereo-vision forward-looking datasets (2023). https://arxiv.org/abs/2302.12772
21. Rublee, E., Rabaud, V., Konolige, K., Bradski, G.: ORB: an efficient alternative to SIFT or SURF. In: Proceedings of the IEEE International Conference on Computer Vision, pp. 2564–2571 (2011)
22. Shin, Y., Lee, Y., Choi, H., Kim, A.: Bundle adjustment from sonar images and slam application for seafloor mapping. In: OCEANS 2015 - MTS/IEEE Washington. OCEANS 2015 - MTS/IEEE Washington, Institute of Electrical and Electronics Engineers Inc (2015)
23. Tang, Y., Iwaguchi, T., Kawasaki, H.: Underwater image enhancement by transformer-based diffusion model with non-uniform sampling for skip strategy (2023). https://arxiv.org/abs/2309.03445
24. Tong, X., et al.: Image registration with fourier-based image correlation: a comprehensive review of developments and applications. IEEE J. Sel. Top. Appl. Earth Obs. Remote Sens. **12**(10), 4062–4081 (2019)
25. Wang, Q., Zhou, X., Hariharan, B., Snavely, N.: Learning feature descriptors using camera pose supervision. In: Vedaldi, A., Bischof, H., Brox, T., Frahm, J.M. (eds) Computer Vision – ECCV 2020. LNCS, pp. 757–774 (2020). Springer, Cham. https://doi.org/10.1007/978-3-030-58452-8_44
26. Wang, Y., He, X., Peng, S., Tan, D., Zhou, X.: Efficient LoFTR: semi-dense local feature matching with sparse-like speed. In: Proceedings of the IEEE/CVF Conference on Computer Vision and Pattern Recognition (CVPR), pp. 21666–21675 (2024). https://doi.org/10.1109/CVPR52733.2024.02047

27. Wang, Y., Ji, Y., Tsuchiya, H., Ota, J., Asama, H., Yamashita, A.: ACSim: a novel acoustic camera simulator with recursive ray tracing, artifact modeling, and ground truthing. IEEE Trans. Rob. **41**, 2970–2989 (2025)
28. Xie, K., Yang, J., Qiu, K.: A dataset with multibeam forward-looking sonar for underwater object detection. Sci. Data **9**(1), 739 (2022). https://doi.org/10.1038/s41597-022-01854-w

Adaptation of Pre-Trained Neural Network Models for Inspection via Image Analysis

Mártir Morales Juan Antonio, Medina Muñoz Luis Arturo(✉), González López Samuel, Valenzuela Soqui Luis Carlos, and Mayorquin Robles Jesús

Instituto Tecnológico de Nogales, Av Instituto Tecnológico #911. Col Granjas, 84065 Nogales, Sonora, CP, Mexico
Luis.mm@nogales.tecnm.mx

1 Introduction

Today, artificial intelligence has begun to play an increasingly visible role in our daily lives, from content recommendations on social media to virtual assistants on mobile devices. But its impact goes far beyond the domestic environment: in industry, particularly in visual inspection processes, these technologies have proven to be a powerful tool for improving efficiency and reducing human error.

Models such as MobileNet and ResNet, originally designed for general image classification tasks, have been adapted in recent years to address more specific problems in industrial environments. These models not only offer good results in terms of accuracy, but can also be implemented on low-power platforms, such as mobile devices or web browsers. This has brought artificial intelligence out of the laboratory, making it accessible to plant operators.

Additionally, emerging techniques such as self-supervised learning have opened up new possibilities for training robust models with less labeled data. Tools such as SimCLR and BYOL have shown that it is possible to achieve good results even when manual labeling is not feasible due to lack of time or human resources.

Developments of this kind inspire and justify projects such as the one presented here. The goal is not only to test a model under ideal conditions, but also to demonstrate that it is possible to create practical, accessible, and efficient tools that work in different industrial scenarios. In our case, MobileNet and ResNet models were adapted to evaluate in-focus and out-of-focus images, and a case study applied to security cables. All of this was made possible through a simple web interface that allows classification directly from a browser, without the need for specialized equipment.

1.1 Artificial Neural Networks

Artificial neural networks (ANNs) are computational models inspired by the functioning of the human brain. They are composed of units called "neurons," organized in layers, which process and transmit information through weighted connections. Each of these connections has a weight that determines the influence of one neuron on another. These networks have the ability to learn patterns from examples, which makes them useful for tasks such as classification, regression, time series prediction, natural language processing, and computer vision (Haykin, 2009) (Fig. 1).

L. Martínez-Villaseñor et al. (Eds.): MICAI 2025, LNAI 16265, pp. 242–251, 2026.
https://doi.org/10.1007/978-3-032-17933-3_24

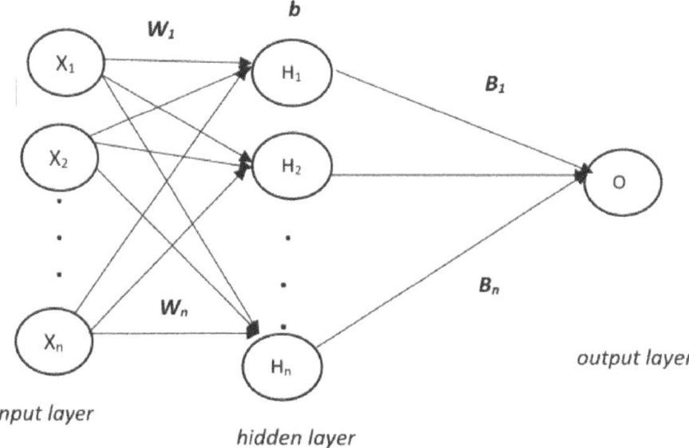

Fig. 1. Typical structure of a three-layer artificial neural network (input layer, one hidden layer and output layer). Source: adapted from Structure of a three-layered NNRW, on ResearchGate.

One of the main attractions of neural networks is their ability to model complex nonlinear relationships between input and output variables, something that is difficult to achieve with traditional algorithms. This capability has led to their application in multiple sectors, which can hinder their adoption in contexts where model flexibility is important. However, neural networks also have limitations: they require large amounts of data to train effectively and can be sensitive to the quality of that data. Furthermore, their internal behavior is not always easily interpretable, which can hinder their adoption in contexts where model flexibility is important (Zhang, 2018). Despite this, their predictive power and machine learning capabilities have made them a key tool in the development of modern intelligent systems.

1.2 Convolutional Neural Networks

Convolutional neural networks (CNNs) are a specialized class of artificial neural networks specifically designed to process data with a grid-like structure, such as images. Unlike traditional neural networks (multilayer perceptrons), CNNs are able to take advantage of the spatial structure of the data, making them ideal for tasks such as image classification, object detection, semantic segmentation, and complex visual pattern recognition.

CNNs allow a model to automatically learn which features are relevant to the task, eliminating the need for manual feature engineering that used to be required in classical approaches. Furthermore, they have demonstrated outstanding results on datasets such as ImageNet and have become the standard for computer vision tasks (Krizhevsky, 2012).

1.3 MobileNet

MobileNet is a family of convolutional neural networks developed by Google with the aim of creating lightweight and efficient models, specifically designed for mobile devices and real-time applications. Unlike other heavier architectures such as VGG or Inception, MobileNet introduces the concept of depthwise separable convolutions, which split the traditional convolution operation into two steps: a depthwise convolution (channel by channel) and a pointwise convolution (1×1). This separation significantly reduces the number of parameters and operations required, allowing competitive performance in terms of accuracy with much lower resource consumption. For this reason, MobileNet has been widely adopted in solutions that require speed, low power consumption, or execution within browsers using frameworks such as TensorFlow.js. MobileNet has evolved through different versions: MobileNet V1 (2017), V2 (2018), and V3 (2019), each with improvements in efficiency and accuracy (Howard, 2019). This project used MobileNetV2, a balanced version that offers a good trade-off between model size, inference time, and binary classification performance (Fig. 2).

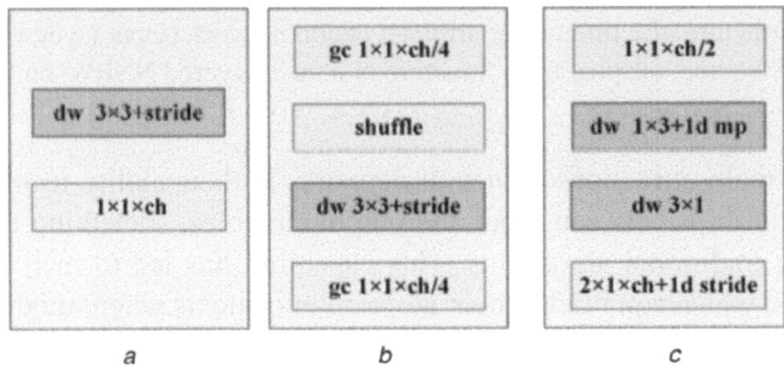

Fig. 2. Representation of the depthwise separable convolution operation used in MobileNet. Source: (Surinta & Enkvetchakul, 2022).

1.4 Resnet

ResNet, abbreviation for Residual Network, is a deep architecture developed by Microsoft Research that introduced a key concept: residual connections or skip connections. These connections allow the gradient to flow directly through the network during training, facilitating learning in very deep networks without degrading performance. ResNet solved one of the main problems in deep neural networks: training degradation, that is, the loss of accuracy as the network depth increases. Thanks to residual connections, networks with more than 100 layers were trained, obtaining record-breaking results in competitions such as ImageNet (He et al., 2016) (Fig. 3).

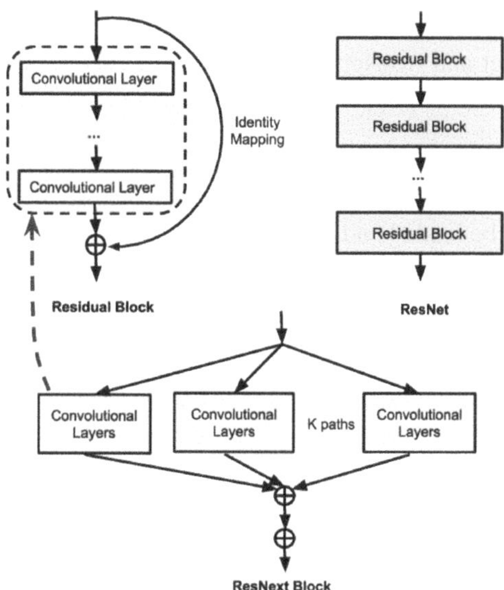

Fig. 3. The image shows the structure of a typical residual block in the ResNet architecture. Source: (Pan et al, 2020)

2 Related Work

Convolutional neural networks (CNNs) have demonstrated a high degree of effectiveness in the automation of industrial tasks, especially in visual inspection systems. These networks have been successfully applied to detect defects in production lines, identify surface contamination, and verify the condition of components under varying lighting or focus conditions. (García et al, 2022) implemented a CNN-based system for the inspection of defects in metal parts, achieving significant improvements compared to traditional manual processes. This type of solution demonstrates that CNNs can not only adapt to real-life production conditions but also outperform human performance in terms of consistency and speed. On the other hand, (Mendoza and Reyes, 2024) explored the use of YOLOv8 for classifying the ripeness status of asparagus in an agro industrial context. Despite not being a highly technological environment, the implementation demonstrated an accuracy of 95%, validating the viability of deep learning in sectors where visual variability is high. Other works, such as Wang (2021), have explored the effectiveness of transfer learning for industrial tasks with limited datasets, confirming that pre-trained models like ResNet5.0 can be successfully reused for specific tasks with a small number of images.

One of the traditional barriers to applying deep learning in industrial environments has been the requirement for specialized hardware. However, with the emergence of lightweight models such as MobileNet and EfficientNet, this limitation has been significantly reduced. MobileNet, developed by Google, was specifically designed to run on resource-limited devices, such as smartphones or browsers. Thanks to the use of depth-wise separable convolutions, these models drastically reduce the number of parameters without sacrificing accuracy too much (Howard, 2019). This makes them ideal for applications that require speed, efficiency, and ease of deployment. In the context of this project, MobileNet and ResNet were selected not only for their proven effectiveness but also for their ease of integration with web technologies, allowing for expanded operational reach.

Another relevant innovation for the industrial adoption of artificial intelligence has been the ability to run models directly in browsers using TensorFlow.js. This Google tool allows models to be loaded and used in JSON format without the need for servers or complex installations, which represents a significant change in terms of accessibility and cost. In addition to reducing hardware requirements, browser deployment guarantees greater privacy, data does not leave the user's device, and facilitates the implementation of user-friendly graphical interfaces that can be used by personnel without advanced technical knowledge (TensorFlow.js, n.d.).

3 Proposed System

The project was designed using an experimental approach based on transfer learning, with the goal of adapting pre-trained convolutional models, MobileNetV2 and ResNet50, to specific industrial image classification tasks. These tasks included:

- Detection of cables in good or bad condition

  The MOBILNETV2 model is proposed because it has important characteristics such as accuracy, speed, and computational efficiency. Its lightweight design allows us to implement it on mobile devices with low processing resources without sacrificing its most relevant features. RESNET is a pre-trained model whose main feature is its robustness, allowing us to implement architectures with multiple layers and neurons in each layer. It is a model that allows for faster convergence during training and is capable of extracting important features from the images under test, such as edges, textures, and shapes. Both are pre-trained models. Their operating characteristics are very different, but they do have similarities. One of them is that files can be generated for implementation in applications such as web pages and mobile apps. This is of great importance in the design of interfaces for real-time inspection.

  The entire system was developed to run from a web interface using TensorFlow.js, without the need for additional software or specialized hardware. This allowed us to validate not only the performance of the models but also their viability as a tool for everyday use in industrial environments.

3.1 Data Acquisition and Preparation

For the development of this project, a set of real images of industrial cables were collected, taken during inspection and maintenance processes. A good cable was considered to be one that did not present extreme bends, cuts, exposed copper, or visible damage. Its coating was uniform and continuous. On the other hand, a bad cable was defined as one that showed signs of physical deterioration: bare sections, insulation breaks, abnormal twists, burns, or poorly secured connections (Figs. 4, 5, 6, 7 and 8).

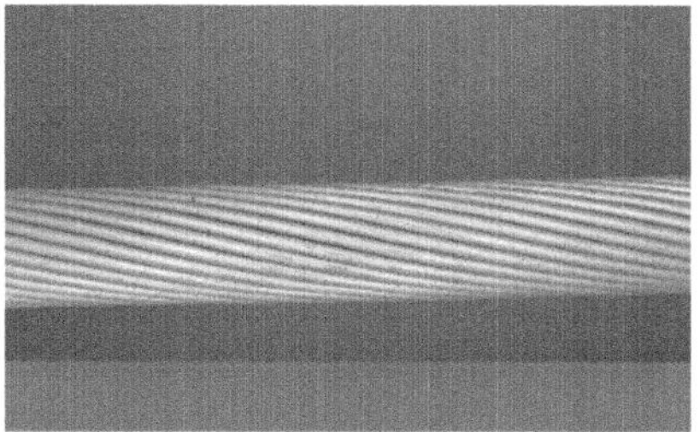

Fig. 4. Cable in good condition

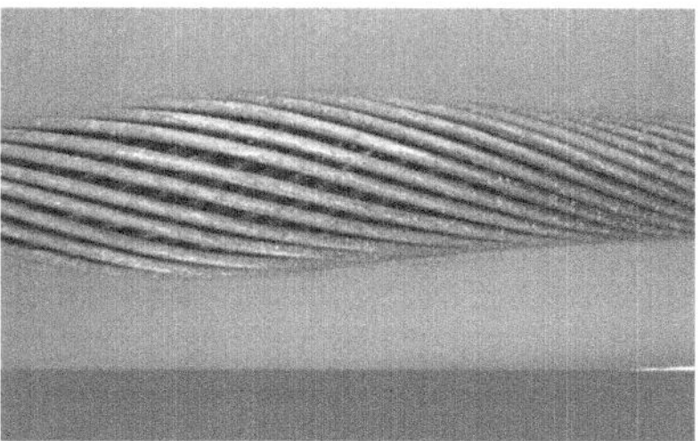

Fig. 5. Cable with bad ends

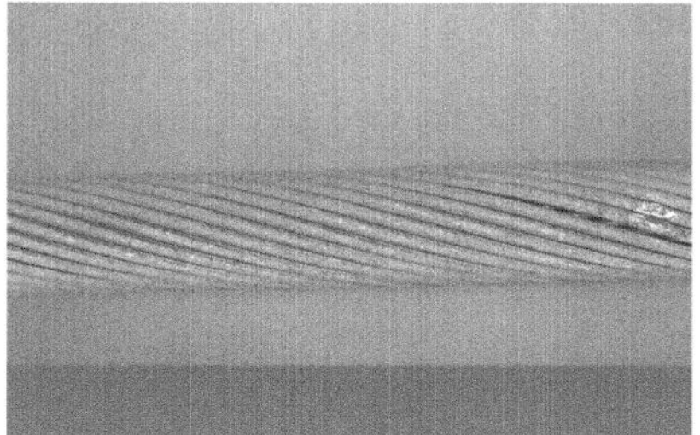

Fig. 6. Cable with cuts

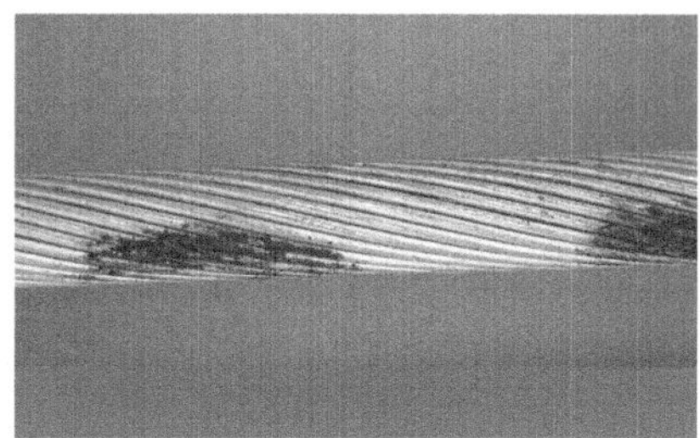

Fig. 7. Cable with visible damages

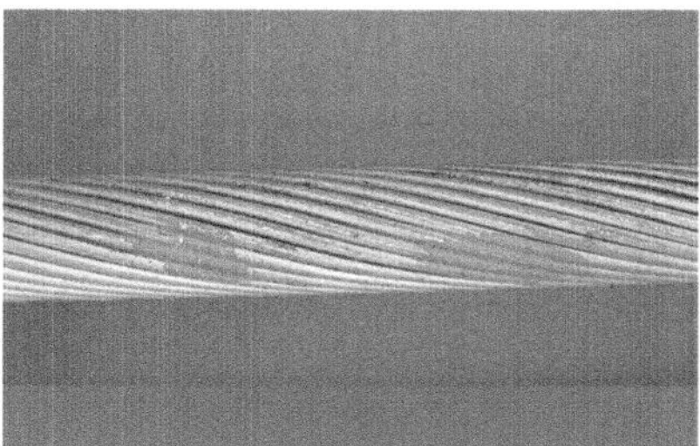

Fig. 8. Cable with cooper exposed

The implemented algorithm converts the image to a size of 120 x 120 pixels and applies an augmentation process to allow for a greater variety of presentation options, inverting, rotating, cropping, or shifting the images. This is reflected in an increase in the data set to achieve greater precision and accuracy. The images in the data set were taken under the same lighting and distance conditions.

The images were organized into folders according to their class, good/bad, and subsequently used for training, validation and testing of the models under MobileNet and ResNet architecture.

3.2 Model Training

The MobileNetV2 and ResNet50 models were trained in Google Colab, using Keras and TensorFlow as backends, in CPU mode because this work does not deal with the evaluation of neural network training times. The following steps were applied:

1. Loading the pre-trained model, without the last layers
2. Freezing the base layers and adding a new dense layer with sigmoid activation for binary classification
3. Compiling the model with the binary_crossentropy loss function and the Adam optimizer
4. Training with cross-validation, with accuracy and loss metrics monitored at each epoch
5. Final evaluation with a set of unseen images

4 Results

The model was trained with MobileNetV2 and ResNet50, using approximately 200 images per class which with augmentation techniques gave us approximately a total of 400 images, using 10% of the images as a test set for the implemented system. After conversion and deployment, the model was run from the browser, with results shown in the following tables and figures. The models generate a prediction probability between 0 and 1, so it was necessary to establish thresholds to determine the final class. To define the threshold, trial-and-error adjustments were performed to determine the value at which the model performed best in terms of precision and accuracy in image classification. The values shown in Table 1 were obtained using this methodology. The differences in this threshold value are due to the fact that the two models have different architectures.

Table 1. Definition of thresholds for each model

Model	Data set	Threshold
MobileNetV2	Cables	0.99
ResNet50	Cables	0.3

The quantitative performance results are complemented by the raw values of the confusion matrix, according to the analysis presented in the project's technical document (Figs. 9, 10 and Table 2).

Table 2. Metrics obtained in the execution of the models

Model	Precisión	Accuracy	VP	VN	FP	FN
ResNet	0.944	0.900	17	19	1	3
MobileNet	1.000	0.975	19	20	0	1

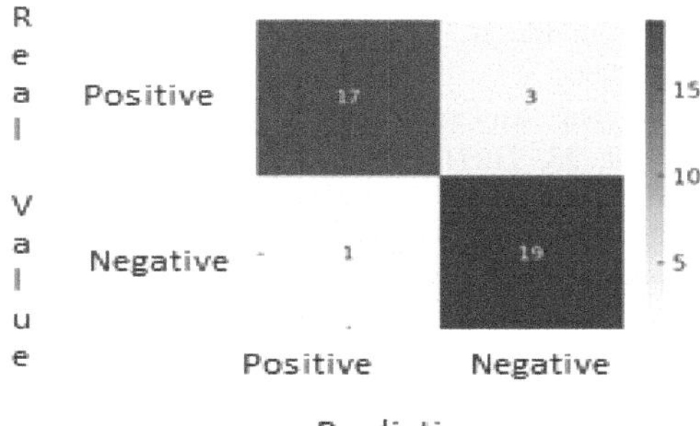

Fig. 9. Confusion matrix for RESNet

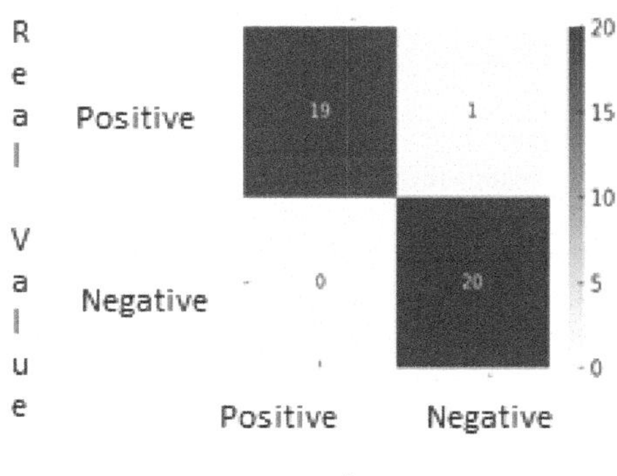

Fig.10. Confusion matrix for MobilNet

4 Conclusions

This project enabled the design, training, and deployment of an industrial image classification system using pre-trained convolutional neural networks, capable of running in a web browser using TensorFlow.js. Through experimentation, it was possible to demonstrate that models such as ResNet50 and MobileNetV2 can be effectively adapted to industrial environments with specific requirements, achieving high levels of accuracy, such as those demonstrated in this work. During the training phase, metrics such as accuracy and loss were monitored at each epoch, for both the training and validation sets. These metrics allow the evaluation of model learning and the detection of overfitting or undertraining. For the detection of good or defective cables, MobileNetV2 achieved 87% accuracy, while ResNet50 reached 94%, showing greater sensitivity to minor defects. These results are consistent with those reported in studies where ResNet has been preferred for tasks involving subtle signals.

References

Chen, T., Kornblith, S., Norouzi, M., Hinton, G.: A simple framework for contrastive learning of visual representations. International Conference on Machine Learning, pp. 1597–1607 (2020). https://doi.org/10.48550/arXiv.2002.05709

Goodfellow, I., Bengio, Y., Courville, A.: Deep Learning. MIT Press (2016). https://doi.org/10.7551/mitpress/11171.001.0001

Grill, J.-B., et al.: Bootstrap your own latent: a new approach to self-supervised learning. Adv. Neural. Inf. Process. Syst. **33**, 21271–21284 (2020). https://doi.org/10.48550/arXiv.2006.07733

García, D., Pérez, A., Torres, J.: Sistema de detección automática de defectos en líneas de producción mediante deep learning. Revista Latinoamericana de Ingeniería Industrial **19**(3), 101–112 (2022)

Haykin, S.: Neural Networks and Learning Machines (3rd ed.). Pearson Education (2009). https://doi.org/10.47051/RLII.2022.V19N3.ART07

He, K., Zhang, X., Ren, S., Sun, J.: Deep residual learning for image recognition. In: Proceedings of the IEEE Conference on Computer Vision and Pattern Recognition, pp. 770–778 (2016). https://doi.org/10.1109/CVPR.2016.90

Howard, A.G., et al.: Searching for mobilenetv3. In: Proceedings of the IEEE International Conference on Computer Vision, pp. 1314–1324 (2019). https://doi.org/10.1109/ICCV.2019.00140

Krizhevsky, A., Sutskever, I., Hinton, G.E.: ImageNet classification with deep convolutional neural networks. In: Advances in Neural Information Processing Systems, pp. 1097–1105 (2012). https://doi.org/10.1109/ICMLA.2012.133

LeCun, Y., Bengio, Y., Hinton, G.: Deep learning. Nature, **521**(7553), 436–444 (2015). https://doi.org/10.1038/nature14539

Mendoza, L., Reyes, C.: Clasificación automática del estado de maduración de espárragos mediante visión artificial y YOLOv8. Congreso Nacional de Tecnologías Agroindustriales (2024). https://doi.org/10.54808/CISCI2024.01.497

Pan, S.J., Yang, Q.: A survey on transfer learning. IEEE Trans. Knowl. Data Eng. **22**(10), 1345–1359 (2010). https://doi.org/10.1109/TKDE.2009.191

Powers, D.M.W.: Evaluation: from precision, recall and F-measure to ROC, informedness, markedness & correlation. J. Mach. Learn. Technol. **2**(1), 37–63 (2011). https://doi.org/10.13140/RG.2.2.29051.72489

Russell, S., Norvig, P.: Artificial Intelligence: A Modern Approach (4th ed.). Pearson. ISBN: 13: 978–0134610993 (2021)

Sandler, M., Howard, A., Zhu, M., Zhmoginov, A., Chen, L.C.: MobileNetV2: inverted residuals and linear bottlenecks. In: Proceedings of the IEEE Conference on Computer Vision and Pattern Recognition, pp. 4510–4520 (2018). https://doi.org/10.1109/CVPR.2018.00474

Smilkov, D., Carter, S., Sculley, D., Nicholson, C.: TensorFlow.js: Machine Learning for the Web and Beyond (2019). *arXiv preprint* arXiv:1901.05350. https://doi.org/10.48550/arXiv.1901.05350

Sokolova, M., Lapalme, G.: A systematic analysis of performance measures for classification tasks. Inf. Process. Manage. **45**(4), 427–437 (2009). https://doi.org/10.1016/j.ipm.2009.03.002

Zheng, Z., Zhou, Y., Sun, L., Cai, J.: A RNN-based multi-factors model for repeat consumption prediction. In: Kůrková, V., Manolopoulos, Y., Hammer, B., Iliadis, L., Maglogiannis, I. (eds.) ICANN 2018. LNCS, vol. 11141, pp. 105–115. Springer, Cham (2018). https://doi.org/10.1007/978-3-030-01424-7_11

Wang, Y., Liu, H., Zhang, X., Chen, Y.: Deep learning for visual inspection in industrial applications: transfer learning with limited data. J. Manuf. Syst. **58**, 317–327 (2021). https://doi.org/10.1016/j.jmsy.2020.12.016

Zhang, Q., Yang, L., & Zhang, Y. (2018). Interpreting CNNs via decision trees. In *Proceedings of theIEEE Conference on Computer Vision and Pattern Recognition* (pp. 6261–6270). https://doi.org/10.1109/CVPR.2018.00656

Zhao, Y., Lu, Y., Xu, X.: Smart factory implementation and process improvement based on deep learning in discrete manufacturing. J. Manuf. Syst. **59**, 304–315 (2021). https://doi.org/10.1016/j.jmsy.2021.03.003

Surinta, O., Enkvetchakul, P.: Effective Data Augmentation and Training Techniques for Improving Deep Learning in Plant Leaf Disease Recognition (2022)

Pan, G., Tian, Y., Alouini, M.-S.: Applying Deep-Learning-Based Computer Vision to Wireless Communications: Methodologies, Opportunities, and Challenges (2020)

Agent Cards: A Documentation Standard for Operational AI Agents

J. Carlos Urteaga-Reyesvera[1,2(✉)] and Juan Jose Lopez Murphy[1]

[1] Globant Inc., SW1E 6SQ London, United Kingdom
{carlos.urteaga,juanjose.lopez}@globant.com
[2] Universidad Americana de Europa, 77500 Cancún, Mexico
https://unade.edu.mx/ , https://globant.com/

Abstract. The rapid adoption of large language models (LLMs) into AI agents has created new challenges for transparency, reproducibility, and governance. While prior artifacts such as Model Cards and Data Sheets for Datasets support documentation of models and data, no analogous standard exists for describing the operational characteristics of AI agents. This paper introduces Agent Cards, a structured documentation artifact designed to capture the essential attributes of an agent, including its roles, memory taxonomy, tool integrations, communication protocols, monitoring hooks, governance scope, and evaluation metrics. By standardizing how agents are described, Agent Cards provide a lightweight yet powerful mechanism for enabling transparency, comparability, and auditability across deployments. A template is presented, accompanied by an illustrative example, followed by a discussion of the benefits of adopting Agent Cards within broader MLOps and LLMOps practices. Agent Cards are proposed as a potential foundation for future work on agent ledgers, audit bundles, and maturity frameworks, offering practitioners and researchers a common vocabulary for the responsible operationalization of agentic AI.

Keywords: AgentOps · LLMOps · Model Cards

1 Introduction

The advancement and deployment of AI agents systems that can plan, act, observe, and adapt are accelerating alongside unprecedented capital commitments. In September 2025, Oracle shares spiked after the company highlighted record AI bookings and a multi-year cloud partnership with OpenAI to expand data-center capacity [1], while Volkswagen announced plans to invest up to €1 billion in AI by 2030 to modernize development and operations, projecting up to €4 billion in efficiency gains by 2035 [17]. Yet scale without structure is risky. An MIT-covered report finds that 95% of enterprise generative-AI pilots are failing to deliver material value, highlighting gaps in governance, observability, and reproducibility [4]. When organizations embed agents without standardized

L. Martínez-Villaseñor et al. (Eds.): MICAI 2025, LNAI 16265, pp. 252–261, 2026.
https://doi.org/10.1007/978-3-032-17933-3_25

operational documentation, stakeholders struggle to trace what an agent does, how it makes decisions, how memory and tools affect outcomes, or where its failure modes lie raising compliance, safety, and cost risks precisely as investment ramps.

Recent work distinguishes between *AI agents* and *agentic AI* as related but separable paradigms [14]. In brief, AI agents are modular, task-focused entities (e.g., routing emails, calling tools, drafting replies) that plan act observe within bounded scopes. By contrast, agentic AI denotes distributed, collaborative assemblies that coordinate multiple specialized agents through joint planning, dynamic goal decomposition, shared and persistent memory, and explicit orchestration protocols. This split matters for documentation. Within a single AI agent, behavior shifts with memory design and tool permissions even under the same LLM. In agentic AI, these differences compound through coordination mechanisms (planner executor critic loops, message-passing protocols, shared context stores), making system behavior even more path-dependent. Clear and structured documentation that focuses on the operational surface, including agent roles, memory configuration, tool usage, and coordination protocols, can support meaningful comparison and long-term auditability.

Existing documentation artifacts have made important strides. Model Cards provide standardized summaries of machine learning models, including their training data, performance metrics, and known limitations [11]. Data Sheets for Datasets [6] offer transparency regarding the creation, collection, and intended use of data. System Cards and AI FactSheets [9] aim to describe deployment contexts and system-level behavior. However, none of these frameworks fully capture the operational dimension of AI agents. Agents function as dynamic systems. They retain short-term and long-term memory, integrate external tools and services, process diverse inputs and outputs, and often make decisions that require human oversight or governance. This evolving and layered architecture introduces multiple sources of risk and complexity, such as behavioral drift, unintended use of tools, opaque communication among agents, limited observability, and challenges in managing system versions.

In response to this gap, Agent Cards are introduced as a structured documentation artifact designed to capture the essential operational characteristics of agents in a lightweight yet standardized manner. An Agent Card records key dimensions such as agent roles (planner, executor, critic, orchestrator), inputs and outputs, memory taxonomy, communication protocols, tool and function integrations, monitoring hooks (logging and metrics), governance metadata (versioning and safety constraints), known limitations, and evaluation metrics. The aim is twofold: first, to assist those who develop, deploy, or audit agents in understanding and comparing them; and second, to promote higher levels of operational maturity, reproducibility, and accountability in agentic systems.

2 Related Work

Efforts to standardize documentation and transparency in machine learning have matured over the last decade. Model Cards [11] provide structured summaries of models (intended use, performance, limitations, ethical notes), while Data Sheets for Datasets [6] surface dataset provenance, collection process, intended uses, and known biases. Extending beyond a single artifact, IBM's AI Fact-Sheets [9] and public-facing System Cards from AI labs [12] broaden the lens to system-level disclosures, deployment context, safety measures, and compliance considerations. These artifacts demonstrate the value of lightweight, standardized documentation for responsible AI.

Beyond model and dataset artifacts, *AgentOps* work has emerged with a focus on observability, safety hooks, evaluation, and incident response for agentic systems positioned as a domain within the broader MLOps/LLMOps continuum. Whereas MLOps addresses general-purpose lifecycle management of models and data, and LLMOps extends this to the distinct runtime needs of foundation models (e.g., retrieval augmentation, prompt instrumentation, vector databases), AgentOps concentrates on the orchestration layer where those models are embedded as components of agents. Surveys and practice-oriented reports emphasize logging of tool calls and memories, failure taxonomies, human-in-the-loop gates, and fleet-level monitoring; yet, despite growing operational guidance, standardized *agent-level* documentation remains scarce. Agent Cards target this gap by specifying the operational surface of agents (roles, memory, tools, protocols, governance) in a compact, comparable schema. Moreover, emerging taxonomies distinguish *AI agents* from *Agentic AI* along axes such as autonomy, interaction style, memory strategy, reasoning mechanisms, and orchestration patterns [14]. Under this view, single agents with bounded tasks and lightweight memory differ materially from multi-agent collectives coordinating via planner executor critic roles, shared context stores, and standardized agent-to-agent protocols. Without clear classification and documentation, teams risk mis-specifying coordination requirements (e.g., deploying a single agent when orchestration is needed), undermining reproducibility, comparability, and governance.

Recent practice-oriented work remains overwhelmingly operational. Sinha et al. frame LLMOps as a subset of FMOps and propose an enterprise framework spanning chartering, architecture, data/ embedding infrastructure, evaluation/governance, serving, and monitoring [16]. Patel et al. curate a GenAI-specific release-readiness checklist from gray literature, highlighting challenges such as reliability, prompt-centric orchestration, embeddings management, and pre-deployment evaluation [13]. Complementing these, Burgueño-Romero et al. present a Kubernetes-based open-source MLOps architecture (MLflow, Seldon Core, Prefect, Prometheus/Grafana) and argue for a unified OSS approach [2]. Collectively, these works strengthen our observation that contemporary LLMOps advances prioritize pipelines, readiness gates, and platform architecture—leaving a gap in standardized *agent-level* documentation that Agent Cards aim to fill.

Alongside documentation artifacts, an important body of work has focused on the evaluation of *language models* and *related systems* including general-purpose LLMs, reasoning-focused Large Reasoning Models (LRMs), and retrieval-augmented generation (RAG) pipelines themselves. Chollet introduced the Abstraction and Reasoning Corpus (ARC) to measure general intelligence as skill acquisition efficiency, emphasizing generalization beyond task-specific benchmarks [3]. Hendrycks et al. proposed the MATH dataset to evaluate mathematical problem solving [8] and the Massive Multitask Language Understanding (MMLU) benchmark to assess broad academic and professional knowledge across 57 subjects [7], both highlighting persistent weaknesses in reasoning and transfer. More recently, researchers have targeted specific dimensions of model performance: Instruction-Following Eval (IFEval) focuses on verifiable compliance with natural language directives [19], Michelangelo evaluates long-context reasoning through latent structure queries [18], and RAGAS automates the assessment of retrieval -augmented generation pipelines [5]. Studies on LRMs have further questioned the limits of "thinking" traces, showing collapse in performance as problem complexity increases despite increased reasoning effort [15]. Complementing these, recent analyses argue that common benchmarking setups can *bias* models and metrics by discouraging calibrated uncertainty and underpenalizing overconfident guesses, thereby inflating apparent capability [10]. Collectively, these works underscore that while benchmarks are expanding beyond accuracy on narrow tasks, evaluation of reasoning, context synthesis, calibrated uncertainty, and operational robustness remains an open challenge.

Our work contributes to this emerging landscape by introducing Agent Cards, an artifact designed to capture the operational attributes of AI agents. In contrast to prior documentation standards. Our proposal of Agent Cards complements these efforts: rather than benchmarking capabilities alone, it introduces a documentation artifact to capture the operational properties of agents, bridging evaluation results with transparency and governance practices.

3 Agent Cards

The introduction of Agent Cards addresses a critical gap in current responsible AI practices: the absence of standardized documentation for AI agents. By explicitly capturing operational characteristics such as memory configuration, tool usage, communication protocols, monitoring hooks, and governance metadata, Agent Cards extend the logic of Model Cards and Data Sheets into the agentic era. Their primary value lies in enhancing transparency, auditability, and comparability across diverse deployments.

First, Agent Cards improve transparency by offering stakeholders developers, auditors, regulators, and end-users a clear view of what an agent does and how it is configured. Unlike models or datasets, which remain relatively static once trained or curated, agents evolve through tool integrations, orchestration schemas, and memory adaptations. A structured card allows these dimensions to be communicated concisely, reducing ambiguity about the system's scope and intended behavior.

Second, Agent Cards provide a foundation for auditability and governance. Regulatory bodies increasingly demand traceability of AI decision-making, particularly as agents are adopted in sensitive domains such as healthcare, finance, and education. Cards that record versioning, known limitations, and compliance metadata make it possible to reconstruct an agent's configuration at a given point in time recognizing that full behavioral reproduction requires versioned external dependencies (e.g., API/model/dataset snapshots, schema or interface hashes, and, when permitted, representative request/response traces) and may otherwise be approximate enabling post-hoc analysis of failures or misuses.. This aligns with ongoing conversations around "AI assurance" and "algorithmic accountability" in both policy and industry.

Third, Agent Cards facilitate comparability and reproducibility. Organizations frequently evaluate multiple agent systems for deployment, but without standardized descriptions, comparisons remain ad hoc. By documenting inputs, outputs, memory, and monitoring strategies, Agent Cards enable meaningful side-by-side evaluations of agents' capabilities and risks. Moreover, versioning and reproducibility hashes ensure that specific configurations can be replicated for experiments, audits, or incident investigations.

Beyond immediate benefits, Agent Cards open the door to future operational artifacts. Collections of cards could form Agent Ledgers, providing an organizational catalog of all deployed agents with their roles, limitations, and monitoring states. Such ledgers would support fleet-level governance, cost management, and compliance audits. Similarly, Agent Cards could be integrated into audit bundles that pair cards with execution logs, enabling continuous monitoring of agents in production. In the long term, these artifacts may become integral to AgentOps maturity frameworks, offering standardized checkpoints for organizations scaling from isolated prototypes to orchestrated multi-agent systems.

Agent Cards do not constitute a complete solution. They cannot eliminate the risks associated with emergent behavior or guarantee ethical alignment. Nevertheless, they represent a practical and actionable step toward achieving operational maturity. Just as Model Cards initiated widespread practices for model transparency, Agent Cards have the potential to seed a community standard for documenting agents, thereby enabling both innovation and accountability within the rapidly evolving landscape of agentic AI.

4 Concept and Proposal

To address the lack of standardized documentation for AI agents, the concept of Agent Cards is introduced. Inspired by artifacts such as Model Cards [11] and Data Sheets for Datasets [6], Agent Cards provide a structured format to capture the operational attributes of AI agents. In contrast to existing artifacts, which primarily describe static components such as models or datasets, Agent Cards emphasize the dynamic and operational dimensions of agents. These encompass core capabilities commonly identified in agentic AI frameworks perception, tool use, reasoning and planning, learning and adaptability, memory and knowledge management, and communication along with cross-cutting operational concerns such as monitoring hooks and governance metadata.

Table 1 presents the proposed schema. The template is lightweight, modular, and designed to be extensible as agent ecosystems evolve.

Table 1. Proposed Agent Card Template

Section	Description
Agent version	Semantic version of the agent release (e.g., 1.2)
Agent Name	Identifier of the agent (e.g., "TaxAdvisorBot")
Agent Role(s)	Planner, Executor, Critic, Orchestrator (list specific roles enabled in this release)
Inputs	Modalities accepted: text, files, APIs, structured data; input schemas with version or hash.
Outputs	Spreadsheets and API responses; output schema/version.
Memory	Short-term: current turn/context window profile, Long-term (Taxer Information), (logs).
Tools/Functions	Capabilities the agent can invoke beyond its core LLM, such as calculators, retrieval modules, external APIs, internal spreadsheets, or domain-specific tools. Document the type of tool, its intended purpose, and how it extends the agent's abilities.
Communication	Human interface (chat/UI); agent-to-agent protocols; message schemas/versions; handoff/approval policies
Monitoring	Logged metrics (latency, token usage, error rate); trace IDs; inference profile/feature flags; SLOs and alert routes
Governance	Safety filters/guardrails; PII/PHI handling; data retention and access control; approvals and audit checkpoints
Versioning	Release tag/date; prompt hash; toolchain/SBOM; external dependency versions; overall reproducibility hash
Known Limitations	Current scope boundaries; partial automation notes; known brittleness or non-determinism sources (e.g., upstream API variability)
Evaluation	Benchmarks/KPIs (e.g., RAG quality, long-context stress); calibration/abstention policy; evaluation datasets/snapshots; last run date and results

To illustrate the use of Agent Cards, a completed example is presented in Table 2, depicting a finance-oriented advisory agent, TaxAdvisorBot. This agent assists users in navigating Mexican tax regulations by retrieving relevant legal provisions and providing scenario-based guidance.

While Agent Cards are primarily a documentation artifact, they can also enable more systematic evaluation of agents. Each field in the card can be tied to metrics that support operational maturity:

- **Roles and Inputs/Outputs:** Compared across agents to assess functional coverage and overlap.
- **Memory:** Benchmarked with stress tests such as long-context reasoning tasks [18], highlighting limits of short-term and long-term retrieval.

Table 2. Example Agent Card: TaxAdvisorBot

Section	**Description**
Agent version	1.2
Agent Name	TaxAdvisorBot
Agent Role(s)	Executor (retrieves statutes and computes obligations); Critic (flags inconsistencies or missing evidence)
Inputs	User queries (ES/EN); structured SAT inputs (forms, JSON receipts); PDF/CSV uploads (limits: 20 MB/file) and CFDI (XML SAT format).
Outputs	Explanatory text; compliance checklists; summarized fiscal obligations; downloadable spreadsheet of calculations and SAT Response.
Memory	Short-term: 16k token context; Long-term: vector store of Mexican tax codes and SAT circulars (collection `mx_tax_v2025_08`); Episodic: per-session query/decision logs (30-day retention)
Tools/Functions	SAT API (taxpayer lookup, filings), currency converter, internal compliance rule engine, spreadsheet generator
Communication	Human-in-the-loop via chat UI; agent-to-agent handoffs to *AccountingBot* for bookkeeping tasks and accounting reconciliation queries.
Monitoring	Request logs; latency and token-usage metrics; error-rate alerts via Grafana; trace IDs for incident triage
Governance	Aligned to LISR/RESICO guidance; PII handling with masked logs; monthly audit-log export; role-based access controls
Versioning	Release tag: `v1.2` (Aug 2025); prompt hash `p_8f3c...`; dependency set `ds_2025_08`; reproducibility hash `sha256:7e4a...`
Known Limitations	Not a legal representative or tax preparer; scope limited to individual taxation; upstream SAT API variability; knowledge cutoff: 2025-06
Evaluation	50-case internal benchmark: 92% form-validation accuracy; RAG quality (faithfulness/answer relevancy) meets target; human review required for edge cases and appeals

- **Tools/Functions:** Evaluated for reliability and safety, e.g., by logging error rates, latency, and unintended tool invocations.
- **Communication:** Assessed through multi-agent or coordination tasks that reveal handoff quality, grounding, and interface robustness.
- **Monitoring and Governance:** Linked to compliance checks (auditability, safety tags) and incident response metrics (MTTD/MTTR).

- **Evaluation Field:** Provides a slot for reporting results on standardized benchmarks such as MATH [8], MMLU [7], or domain-specific stress tests [5].

By embedding these pointers, Agent Cards bridge documentation and evaluation: they not only describe what an agent *is*, but also provide a structured location to record how it *performs*. This dual role strengthens transparency, comparability, and reproducibility across deployments.

5 Conclusion

As AI agents transition from experimental prototypes to mission-critical systems, the need for transparent, standardized documentation becomes increasingly urgent. Existing artifacts such as Model Cards, Data Sheets for Datasets, and AI FactSheets have shown the value of lightweight reporting standards in fostering accountability, but they fall short of capturing the operational complexity of agentic systems.

This paper has introduced Agent Cards as a practical artifact for documenting AI agents in a structured and comparable manner. By capturing key attributes including agent roles, inputs and outputs, memory structures, tool integrations, communication protocols, monitoring hooks, governance metadata, and evaluation metrics Agent Cards offer stakeholders a concise yet comprehensive overview of an agent's configuration and limitations. Such documentation contributes to greater transparency, auditability, and reproducibility, while also establishing a foundation for organizational practices such as Agent Ledgers and audit bundles.

Agent Cards constitute an initial step toward standardized documentation and governance within the emerging field of AgentOps. Analogous to how Model Cards contributed to the normalization of model documentation, Agent Cards may serve as a foundation for the responsible operationalization of agentic systems. Future work should extend beyond community adoption and schema refinement to include the development of mechanisms that transform descriptive transparency into enforceable accountability.

Two complementary research directions are anticipated. First, Agent Contracts are envisioned as formal specifications that operationalize the metadata expressed in Agent Cards. These contracts would define type-safe interfaces, behavioral guarantees, and compliance boundaries, enabling agents to interact under verifiable and auditable conditions. Such a framework would move from static description toward dynamic governance, ensuring predictable behavior in multi-agent environments. Second, an Agent Ledger could provide a persistent infrastructure for recording the provenance, maturity, and lifecycle evolution of agents. By linking documentation, contracts, and evaluation records, the ledger would enable longitudinal traceability, facilitating reproducibility, benchmarking, and regulatory alignment across deployments.

In summary, Agent Cards offer a lightweight yet extensible contribution to the responsible deployment of AI agents. Their evolution toward contract-based and ledger-based mechanisms may ultimately support the establishment of mature, auditable, and governable ecosystems for agentic AI.

Disclosure of Interests. The paper is financially sponsored by Globant to support participation in the conference, but the research design, execution, and conclusions are solely those of the authors.

References

1. Oracle's shares surge as openai deal boosts outlook. https://moneyweek.com/investments/tech-stocks/oracle-shares (2025). Accessed: 17 Sept. 2025
2. Burgueño-Romero, A.M., Benítez-Hidalgo, A., Barba-González, C., Aldana-Montes, J.F.: Toward an open source MLOps architecture. IEEE Softw. **42**(1), 59–64 (2025). https://doi.org/10.1109/MS.2024.3421675
3. Chollet, F.: On the measure of intelligence. arXiv preprint arXiv:1911.01547 (2019)
4. Davos, L.e.: MIT report: 95% of generative AI pilots at companies are failing. Fortune (2025). https://fortune.com/2025/08/18/mit-report-95-percent-generative-ai-pilots-at-companies-failing-cfo/
5. Es, S., James, J., Espinosa-Anke, L., Schockaert, S.: Ragas: automated evaluation of retrieval augmented generation. In: Proceedings of the 18th Conference of the European Chapter of the Association for Computational Linguistics (EACL), System Demonstrations, pp. 150–158 (2024)
6. Gebru, T., Morgenstern, J., Vecchione, B., Vaughan, J.W., Wallach, H., III, H.D., Crawford, K.: Datasheets for datasets. Commun. ACM **64**(12), 86–92 (2021). https://doi.org/10.1145/3458723
7. Hendrycks, D., et al.: Measuring massive multitask language understanding. In: International Conference on Learning Representations (ICLR) (2021). https://arxiv.org/abs/2009.03300
8. Hendrycks, D., et al.: Measuring mathematical problem solving with the math dataset. In: Advances in Neural Information Processing Systems (NeurIPS) Datasets and Benchmarks. https://arxiv.org/abs/2103.03874 (2021)
9. IBM corporation: AI factsheets (2025). Version 5.1.2, part of IBM Cloud Pak for Data. https://www.ibm.com/docs/en/software-hub/5.1.x?topic=services-ai-factsheets
10. Kalai, A.T., Nachum, O., Vempala, S.S., Zhang, E.: Why language models hallucinate. arXiv preprint arXiv:2509.04664 (2025)
11. Mitchell, M., et al.: Model cards for model reporting. In: Proceedings of the Conference on Fairness, Accountability, and Transparency, pp. 220–229 (2019)
12. OpenAI: GPT-4o system card (2024). Published August 8, 2024. Includes Preparedness Framework evaluations and safety mitigations for GPT-4o. https://openai.com/index/gpt-4o-system-card/
13. Patel, H., Boucher, D., Fallahzadeh, E., Hassan, A.E., Adams, B.: A state-of-the-practice release-readiness checklist for generative ai-based software products: A gray literature survey. IEEE Softw. (2025). Date of publication: 8 August 2024; current version: 11 Dec. 2024. https://doi.org/10.1109/MS.2024.3440190

14. Sapkota, R., Roumeliotis, K.I., Karkee, M.: AI agents vs. agentic AI: a conceptual taxonomy, applications and challenges. arXiv preprint arXiv:2505.10468 (2025)
15. Shojaee, P., Mirzadeh, I., Alizadeh, K., Horton, M., Bengio, S., Farajtabar, M.: The illusion of thinking: understanding the strengths and limitations of reasoning models via the lens of problem complexity. arXiv preprint arXiv:2506.06941 (2025)
16. Sinha, M., Menon, S., Sagar, R.: LLMOps: definitions, framework and best practices. In: Proceedings of the 4th International Conference on Electrical, Computer and Energy Technologies (ICECET 2024). IEEE, Sydney, Australia , ISBN 979-8-3503-9591-4 (2024)
17. Staff, R.: Volkswagen to invest up to a billion euros in AI by end of decade. Reuters (2025). https://www.reuters.com/business/autos-transportation/volkswagen-invest-up-billion-euros-ai-by-end-decade-2025-09-09/
18. Vodrahalli, K., et al.: Michelangelo: long context evaluations beyond haystacks via latent structure queries. arXiv preprint arXiv:2409.12640 (2024)
19. Zhou, J., et al.: Instruction-following evaluation for large language models. arXiv preprint arXiv:2311.07911 (2023)

On the Interpretation of Clip Limit in Contrast-Limited Adaptive Histogram Equalization

Alejandra Díaz Barajas[1], José Manuel Salcedo Méndez[1], Dora E. Alvarado-Carrillo[2], and Emmanuel Ovalle-Magallanes[1](✉)

[1] Dirección de Investigación y Doctorado, Facultad de Ingenierías y Tecnologías, Universidad La Salle Bajío, Av. Universidad 602, Col. Lomas del Campestre, León 37150, Guanajuato, Mexico
adb76784@lasallebajio.edu.mx, jsm77250@lasallebajio.edu.mx, eovalle@lasallebajio.edu.mx

[2] Facultad de Ingenieria, Universidad Virtual del Estado de Guanajuato, Hermenegildo Bustos 129 A Sur Centro, Purísima del Rincón 36400, Guanajuato, Mexico
doalvarado@uveg.edu.mx

Abstract. Contrast - Limited Adaptive Histogram Equalization (CLAHE) is widely used to enhance local contrast in digital images, particularly in domains such as medical imaging, remote sensing, and low-light photography. Despite its broad adoption, the internal handling of key parameters in software libraries like OpenCV remains insufficiently documented. This work identifies that OpenCV internally rescales the user-defined contrast limit based on tile size, introducing a scaling effect not explicitly detailed in public documentation. As a result, the effective contrast-limiting behavior may diverge from both user expectations and the method's theoretical formulation. To address this, a mathematically consistent mapping is derived that ensures the contrast limit corresponds to the number of pixels per histogram bin before clipping. A wrapper function is proposed to implement this mapping, enabling predictable and reproducible behavior across different tile configurations. The analysis contributes to both the theoretical understanding and practical application of CLAHE in image processing pipelines.

Keywords: CLAHE · Clip limit · OpenCV · Parameter mapping · Contrast enhancement

1 Introduction

Contrast enhancement is a fundamental preprocessing step in many image processing and computer vision tasks. One of the most widely adopted techniques for this purpose is contrast-limited adaptive histogram equalization (CLAHE) [10], which improves local contrast while mitigating noise amplification a common

L. Martínez-Villaseñor et al. (Eds.): MICAI 2025, LNAI 16265, pp. 262–271, 2026.
https://doi.org/10.1007/978-3-032-17933-3_26

drawback of standard histogram equalization. Owing to its robustness and ease of integration, CLAHE has become the *de facto* choice in a wide range of applications, including medical imaging, remote sensing, and low-light image enhancement [2,4,5,15].

Despite its popularity, certain internal aspects of CLAHE, particularly as implemented in widely used libraries such as OpenCV, remain underdocumented or opaque. Among its parameters, the *clip limit* plays a central role: it governs the redistribution of histogram bins and helps prevent over-enhancement and visual artifacts. However, the exact influence of this parameter, especially in relation to tile size and the underlying histogram distribution, is not fully explained in existing documentation. As a result, practitioners often select clip-limit values empirically, without a precise understanding of how these values affect the algorithm's behavior.

This study investigates the internal handling of the clip-limit parameter in OpenCV's implementation of CLAHE. Through analytical examination and code-level inspection, the way OpenCV computes and applies the clip limit is uncovered, revealing an internal normalization that depends on tile size and intensity range. To make this transformation explicit, a mathematically consistent mapping is derived that aligns OpenCV's behavior with the theoretical definition of contrast limiting. The proposed mapping allows users to interpret and configure the clip limit in a predictable, tile-independent manner.

2 Related Work

CLAHE was initially introduced to enhance local contrast in images while limiting noise amplification by clipping histogram bins within local tiles and redistributing excess pixels. Since its introduction, various techniques have been proposed to optimize the selection of CLAHE parameters, particularly the clip limit and tile size, which strongly influence the trade-off between contrast enhancement and noise suppression.

Early methods used fixed or heuristic values for the clip limit. While effective in some cases, these approaches often resulted in suboptimal performance when applied to images with diverse or heterogeneous intensity distributions. To improve adaptability, several dynamic strategies have been proposed. For instance, Bhat and Patil [3] introduced an adaptive clip limit estimation method that combines a Least Mean Squares (LMS) algorithm with cumulative distribution function fitting to tune parameters based on local image statistics, improving contrast enhancement in medical images.

Joseph *et al.* [8] proposed an objective framework for determining optimal clip limits and histogram specifications through statistical and optimization techniques, allowing consistent performance across a variety of image types. In a similar direction, Sarker *et al.* [14] developed Selective Apex Adaptive Histogram Equalization (SLAAHE), which adjusts the clip limit dynamically by targeting histogram peak regions. This method reduces common CLAHE artifacts while enhancing image contrast.

More recently, Narla *et al.* [9] introduced a multimodal optimization framework for CLAHE. In this approach, both the clip limit and tile size are optimized using a firefly metaheuristic algorithm guided by quality metrics such as Peak Signal-to-Noise Ratio (PSNR) and Absolute Mean Brightness Error (AMBE), achieving robust results across different imaging modalities.

In deep learning pipelines, CLAHE is often employed as a preprocessing step to enhance visual quality prior to model training. Halloum and Ez-Zahraouy [6] studied the joint effect of CLAHE and transfer learning on brain image classification, reporting performance improvements. Similarly, Hayati *et al.* [7] used CLAHE for diabetic retinopathy classification with CNN architectures including ResNet34, VGG16, InceptionV3, and EfficientNetB4, observing notable gains for the latter models. Rifai *et al.* [13] combined CLAHE and white balance preprocessing for pneumonia detection in chest X-rays, enhancing the performance of a MobileNetV2 classifier.

Despite the extensive use of CLAHE in both classical and learning-based workflows, the internal treatment of its parameters (particularly the clip limit) remains underdocumented in widely used software libraries. As a result, practitioners frequently rely on empirical tuning without full visibility into how user-specified values are interpreted during execution.

To the best of current knowledge, no prior work has systematically examined how OpenCV internally handles the clip limit parameter in its CLAHE implementation. The present work addresses this gap by providing an analytical study of the parameter transformation and proposing a formulation that aligns OpenCV's internal behavior with the theoretical definition of contrast limiting.

3 Method

3.1 Mathematical Background

CLAHE is an advanced variant of histogram equalization designed to enhance local contrast by applying equalization within specific image regions, rather than globally as in standard histogram equalization. The method is parameterized by the tile grid size, denoted as $w \times h$, and the contrast limit, denoted as T_c.

The CLAHE process begins by dividing the input grayscale image $\mathbf{I}$ into non-overlapping rectangular tiles T of size $w \times h$ (e.g., 8×8). Each tile is processed independently to enhance local contrast. For each tile, a histogram of pixel intensities is computed as:

$$h_i = \sum_{(x,y)\in T_i} \delta(\mathbf{I}(x,y) = i), \quad i = 0, \dots, N-1 \tag{1}$$

where $\delta(\cdot)$ is the indicator function. A clip limit T_c is defined to cap the count of any histogram bin. If a bin exceeds this limit, it is clipped as:

$$h'_i = \min(h_i, T_c). \tag{2}$$

To preserve the total pixel count, excess pixels are redistributed uniformly across all bins:

$$h_i'' = h_i' + \frac{1}{N} \sum_{i=0}^{N-1} (h_i - h_i'). \tag{3}$$

From the adjusted histogram, the normalized cumulative distribution function (CDF) is computed:

$$\mathrm{CDF}_i = \frac{\sum_{j=0}^{i} h_j''}{\sum_{k=0}^{N-1} h_k''}. \tag{4}$$

This CDF serves as a lookup table to remap pixel intensities in the tile:

$$\mathbf{I}'(x, y) = \left\lfloor \mathrm{CDF}_{\mathbf{I}(x,y)} \times (N-1) \right\rfloor. \tag{5}$$

To avoid visible seams between tiles, CLAHE applies bilinear interpolation using the mappings of four neighboring tiles. The final interpolated intensity $\mathbf{I}_f(x, y)$ is computed as:

$$\begin{aligned} \mathbf{I}_f(x, y) = (1-\alpha)(1-\beta)\,\mathbf{I}'_{i,j}(x, y) & \\ + \ \alpha(1-\beta)\,\mathbf{I}'_{i+1,j}(x, y) & \\ + \ (1-\alpha)\beta\,\mathbf{I}'_{i,j+1}(x, y) & \\ + \ \alpha\beta\,\mathbf{I}'_{i+1,j+1}(x, y), & \end{aligned} \tag{6}$$

where α and β denote the relative distances of the pixel within the tile along the horizontal and vertical directions, respectively. After interpolation and recombination of all tiles, the enhanced image exhibits improved local contrast with reduced noise artifacts.

3.2 Observed Parameter Scaling in OpenCV

In OpenCV's CLAHE implementation, the contrast limit is internally rescaled based on the tile size and pixel intensity range. This transformation results in behavior where the user-specified contrast limit T_u does not directly correspond to the final value used by the algorithm. The effective contrast limit is computed as:

$$T_c = \max\left(\frac{T_u \times (h \times w)}{256}, 1\right), \tag{7}$$

where T_c is the internal clip limit, T_u is the user-defined contrast factor, $h \times w$ is the tile area, and 256 is the number of intensity levels in an 8-bit image.

For example, if $T_u = 0.5$ and the tile size is $(8, 8)$, the resulting T_c is 1. With $T_u = 10$ and the same tile size, the computed value is $T_c = 2.5$, which is lower than the original user input. Because histogram bin counts are integers, this scaling can produce outcomes that may not align with user expectations.

To better understand this relationship, the valid range of user input T_u can be bounded by solving the extremes of Equ. (7). The minimum occurs when $T_c = 1$:

$$1 = \frac{T_{\min} \times (h \times w)}{256} \quad \Rightarrow \quad T_{\min} = \frac{256}{h \times w}. \tag{8}$$

The maximum occurs when the entire tile area is used:

$$h \times w = \frac{T_{\max} \times (h \times w)}{256} \quad \Rightarrow \quad T_{\max} = 256. \tag{9}$$

Therefore, the user-defined contrast factor T_u should satisfy:

$$T_u \in \left[\frac{256}{h \times w}, \ 256\right].$$

3.3 Proposed Mapping for Contrast Limit

To provide a more interpretable way for users to specify the contrast limit, a mapping is proposed that inversely scales the user-defined value according to OpenCV's internal transformation. This allows T_u^* to directly represent the intended maximum number of pixels per histogram bin. The corrected clip limit to pass to OpenCV is defined as:

$$T_c^* = \min\left(\max\left(\frac{T_u^* \times 256}{h \times w}, \ T_{\min}\right), \ T_{\max}\right), \tag{10}$$

where T_u^* is the user-desired clip limit and T_c^* is the value passed to OpenCV. This mapping ensures consistent contrast-limiting behavior across tile sizes and aligns with the theoretical formulation of CLAHE.

By applying this transformation before calling `cv2.createCLAHE()`, users retain precise control over the clipping threshold. The following Python function implements this logic:

```
def clip_mapping(clip_limit, win_size):
    """ Compute the clip mapping for CLAHE. """
    area = win_size[0] * win_size[1]
    T_min = 256 / area
    T_max = 256
    mapped_clip = min(max((clip_limit * 256) / area, T_min), T_max)
    return mapped_clip
```

This formulation promotes interpretability and reproducibility when configuring CLAHE in practice. The default configuration in OpenCV's CLAHE implementation uses an 8×8 tile grid and a clip limit of 40. Larger grids, such as 32×32 or 64×64, are often used for high-resolution images (e.g., 1920×1080 or 3840×2160) or when broader contrast variation across the image is expected.

In this manner, this default configuration maps to $T_c^* = 160$ to apply a real clip limit of 40. On the other hand, without the mapping, the real clip limit became $T_c = 10$.

4 Results

4.1 Evaluation Metrics

To quantitatively analyze the effect of the proposed clip-mapping strategy on CLAHE-enhanced images, three no-reference image quality metrics were employed. These metrics capture different aspects of contrast enhancement, texture sharpness, and information content. All computations were performed on the enhanced images.

The Shannon entropy measures the distribution of gray levels and reflects the amount of information present in the image. Higher entropy values generally indicate greater intensity diversity:

$$H = -\sum_{i=0}^{255} p_i \log_2 p_i, \tag{11}$$

where p_i denotes the normalized histogram probability of intensity level i.

Root-Mean-Square (RMS) Contrast evaluates the global dispersion of pixel intensities around their mean:

$$C_{\text{RMS}} = \sqrt{\frac{1}{N}\sum_{n=1}^{N}(I_n - \bar{I})^2}, \tag{12}$$

where $\bar{I}$ is the mean intensity and N is the total number of pixels.

The Enhancement Measure Estimation (EME) [1] quantifies the local logarithmic contrast between bright and dark regions. In this work, it is computed per CLAHE tile to align with the adaptive histogram equalization grid. Let the image be divided into $w \times h$ tiles, and each tile Ω_{ij} have maximum and minimum intensities $I_{\text{max}}^{(ij)}$ and $I_{\text{min}}^{(ij)}$, respectively. The EME per tile is:

$$\text{EME}_{ij} = 20 \cdot \log\left(\frac{I_{\text{max}}^{(ij)} + \varepsilon}{I_{\text{min}}^{(ij)} + \varepsilon}\right), \tag{13}$$

and the overall image EME is obtained as the average over all tiles:

$$\text{EME}_{\text{mean}} = \frac{1}{h \cdot w}\sum_{i=1}^{h}\sum_{j=1}^{w} \text{EME}_{ij}, \tag{14}$$

where $\varepsilon = 10^{-6}$ avoids division by zero. This formulation ensures a direct correspondence between the local enhancement measurement and the CLAHE window configuration.

High entropy and RMS contrast indicate an image with richer tonal distribution, while high EME values represent stronger local contrast enhancement.

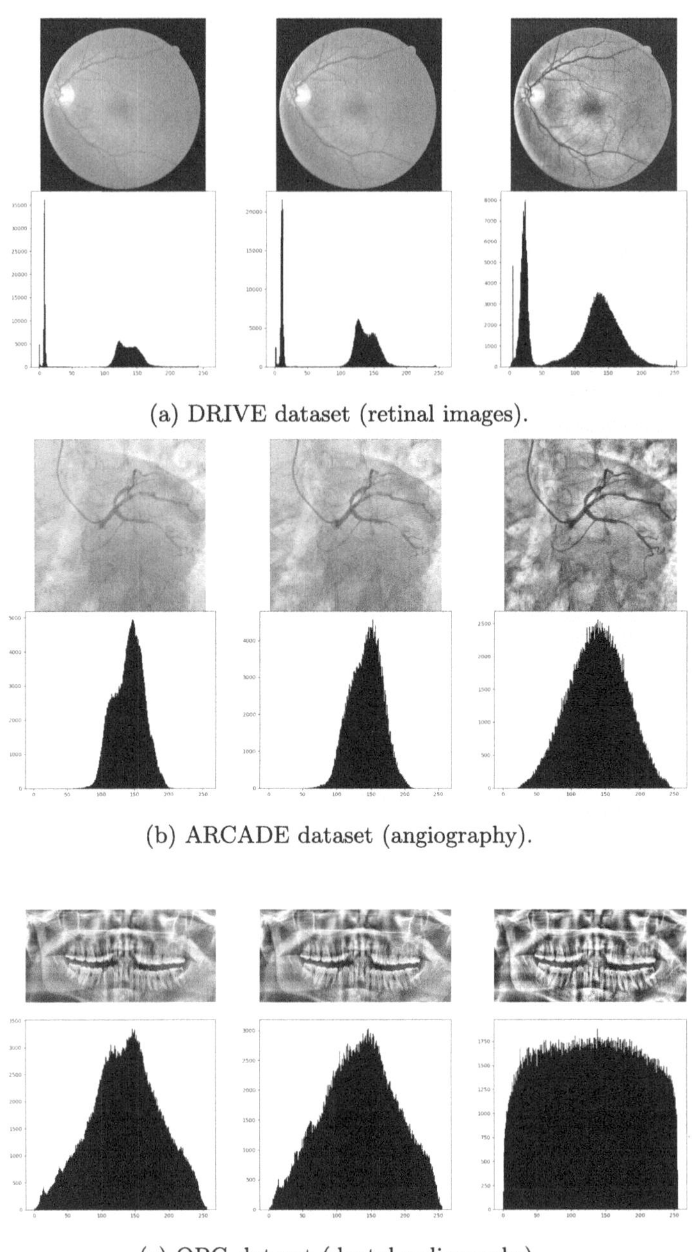

(a) DRIVE dataset (retinal images).

(b) ARCADE dataset (angiography).

(c) OPG dataset (dental radiographs).

Fig. 1. Visual comparison between the default OpenCV CLAHE formulation and the proposed mapped version across three representative medical datasets: (a) DRIVE, (b) ARCADE, and (c) OPG. For each dataset, images are arranged from left to right as: original image, default CLAHE result, and mapped CLAHE result; the corresponding histograms are displayed below each image.

4.2 Enhancement Comparison

To visually assess the proposed formulation, a representative example from three well-know medical dataset are employed: the DRIVE dataset [16], that has been created to enable studies on retinal vessel segmentation, the ARCADE dataset [11] for benchmarking AI models in coronary artery disease (CAD) diagnostics, and dental orthopantomogram (OPGs) X-rays for classification and object detection [12].

Figure 1 illustrates the visual differences between the default OpenCV implementation of CLAHE and the proposed mapped formulation. The comparison uses a typical configuration for medical imaging datasets, with a user-defined clip limit of $T_u = 0.5$ and a tile size of (8×8). For each dataset, the figure displays (from left to right) the original image, the result of the default CLAHE, and the result of the mapped CLAHE, with their respective histograms shown below. Visually, the mapped formulation produces a more balanced histogram distribution, avoiding oversaturation and excessive flattening of gray levels. This results in an improved contrast balance that highlights anatomical structures and fine textures more effectively, while preserving the natural appearance of soft tissues, emphasizing relevant structures without introducing visual artifacts.

Table 1 summarizes the quantitative performance of the proposed mapping across the DRIVE, ARCADE, and OPG datasets. In all cases, the mapped configuration achieves either comparable or superior entropy and markedly higher EME values compared to the default CLAHE, confirming a more effective redistribution of gray levels and stronger local contrast enhancement. For the DRIVE dataset, entropy increases from 6.09 to 7.11, indicating a richer tonal distribution, while EME rises moderately from 45.14 to 50.81. In the ARCADE dataset, the enhancement is more pronounced, with EME more than doubling (15.97 to 34.59) alongside a noticeable entropy gain (6.60 to 7.38). The OPG dataset exhibits the strongest response, where the proposed mapping significantly boosts EME from 54.95 to 228.01 and raises entropy from 7.75 to 7.98, showing that the normalization is especially effective in high-contrast radiographic images.

Table 1. Quantitative evaluation of CLAHE default configuration. Each dataset was evaluated under two configurations: Base (default CLAHE) and proposed mapped.

Dataset	Configuration	Entropy ↑	**RMS** ↑	EME ↑
DRIVE	CLAHE Base	6.0896	62.2303	45.1443
	CLAHE Mapped	7.1070	60.9450	50.8148
ARCADE	CLAHE Base	6.6019	23.7551	15.9745
	CLAHE Mapped	7.3782	24.0620	34.5881
OPGs	CLAHE Base	7.7514	53.7685	54.9518
	CLAHE Mapped	7.9819	69.8002	228.0143

5 Conclusion

This study analyzed the internal behavior of OpenCV's implementation of CLAHE, with particular attention to the interpretation and transformation of the contrast limit parameter. The analysis showed that OpenCV internally rescales the user-defined contrast limit based on the tile size and pixel intensity range, which may result in a mismatch between the user's intended configuration and the actual clipping behavior during histogram equalization. To clarify this behavior, the inverse of OpenCV's internal scaling was derived, yielding a corrected formula that maps the user-defined clip limit to the value expected by the library. This mapping ensures that the contrast factor accurately reflects the maximum number of pixels permitted per histogram bin prior to clipping.

Quantitative evaluations across multiple medical imaging datasets demonstrated that the proposed mapping yields improved entropy and EME values while maintaining comparable global contrast. Visually, it produces more balanced histograms and improved visibility of anatomical structures without over-enhancement or saturation artifacts.

By aligning the software behavior with the theoretical formulation of CLAHE, the proposed adjustment improves the interpretability and precision of contrast enhancement configuration. It also facilitates reproducible and consistent results across varying tile sizes, making CLAHE more predictable and mathematically grounded in practical applications.

References

1. Agaian, S.S., Panetta, K., Grigoryan, A.M.: Transform-based image enhancement algorithms with performance measure. IEEE Trans. Image Process. **10**(3), 367–382 (2001). https://doi.org/10.1109/83.908502
2. Almutiry, O., Iqbal, K., Hussain, S., Mahmood, A., Dhahri, H.: Underwater images contrast enhancement and its challenges: a survey. Multimedia Tools Appl. **83**(5), 15125–15150 (2024). https://doi.org/10.1007/s11042-021-10626-4
3. Bhat, M., Patil, T.: Adaptive clip limit for contrast limited adaptive histogram equalization (CLAHE) of medical images using least mean square algorithm. In: 2014 IEEE International Conference on Advanced Communications, Control and Computing Technologies, pp. 1259–1263. IEEE, Ramanathapuram, India (2014). https://doi.org/10.1109/ICACCCT.2014.7019300
4. Braik, M., Al-Betar, M.A., Mahdi, M.A., Al-Shalabi, M., Ahamad, S., Saad, S.A.: Enhancement of satellite images based on CLAHE and augmented elk herd optimizer. Artif. Intell. Rev. **58**(2), 38 (2024). https://doi.org/10.1007/s10462-024-11022-8
5. Haddadi, Y.R., Mansouri, B., Khodja, F.Z.I.: A novel medical image enhancement algorithm based on clahe and pelican optimization. Multimedia Tools Appl. **83**(42), 90069–90088 (2024). https://doi.org/10.1007/s11042-024-19070-6
6. Halloum, K., Ez-Zahraouy, H.: Enhancing medical image classification through transfer learning and CLAHE optimization. Curr. Med. Imaging **21**(1), e15734056342623 (2025). https://doi.org/10.2174/0115734056342623241119061744

7. Hayati, M., Muchtar, K., Maulina, N., Syamsuddin, I., Elwirehardja, G.N., Pardamean, B., et al.: Impact of CLAHE-based image enhancement for diabetic retinopathy classification through deep learning. Procedia Compu. Sci. **216**, 57–66 (2023). https://doi.org/10.1016/j.procs.2022.12.111
8. Joseph, J., Sivaraman, J., Periyasamy, R., Simi, V.: An objective method to identify optimum clip-limit and histogram specification of contrast limited adaptive histogram equalization for MR images. Biocybernetics Biomed. Eng. **37**(3), 489–497 (2017). https://doi.org/10.1016/j.bbe.2016.11.006
9. Narla, V.L., Suresh, G., Rao, C.S., Awadh, M.A., Hasan, N.: A multimodal approach with firefly based CLAHE and multiscale fusion for enhancing underwater images. Sci. Rep. **14**(1), 27588 (2024). https://doi.org/10.1038/s41598-024-76468-w
10. Pizer, S.M., et al.: Adaptive histogram equalization and its variations. Comput. Vis. Graph. Image Process. **39**(3), 355–368 (1987). https://doi.org/10.1016/S0734-189X(87)80186-X
11. Popov, M., et al.: Dataset for automatic region-based coronary artery disease diagnostics using X-ray angiography images. Sci. Data **11**(1), 20 (2024). https://doi.org/10.1038/s41597-023-02871-z
12. Rahman, R.B., Tanim, S.A., Alfaz, N., Shrestha, T.E., Miah, M.S.U., Mridha, F.: Dental OPG XRAY Dataset (2024). https://doi.org/10.17632/c4hhrkxytw.4
13. Rifai, A.M., Raharjo, S., Utami, E., Ariatmanto, D.: Analysis for diagnosis of pneumonia symptoms using chest X-ray based on MobileNetV2 models with image enhancement using white balance and contrast limited adaptive histogram equalization (CLAHE). Biomed. Signal Process. Control **90**, 105857 (2024). https://doi.org/10.1016/j.bspc.2023.105857
14. Sarkar, M., Mandal, A.: SLAAHE: selective apex adaptive histogram equalization. Franklin Open **3**, 100023 (2023). https://doi.org/10.1016/j.fraope.2023.100023
15. Sharma, R., Kamra, A.: A review on CLAHE based enhancement techniques. In: 2023 6th International Conference on Contemporary Computing and Informatics (IC3I), vol. 6, pp. 321–325. IEEE, Gautam Buddha Nagar, India (2023)
16. Staal, J., Abràmoff, M.D., Niemeijer, M., Viergever, M.A., Van Ginneken, B.: Ridge-based vessel segmentation in color images of the retina. IEEE Trans. Med. Imaging **23**(4), 501–509 (2004). https://doi.org/10.1109/TMI.2004.825627

Author Index

L. Martínez-Villaseñor et al. (Eds.): MICAI 2025, LNAI 16265, pp. 273–274, 2026.
https://doi.org/10.1007/978-3-032-17933-3